Studies of Development
and Change
in the Modern World

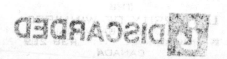

Studies of Development and Change in the Modern World

Michael T. Martin
Princeton University

Terry R. Kandal
California State University, Los Angeles

New York   Oxford
OXFORD UNIVERSITY PRESS
1989

Oxford University Press

Oxford   New York   Toronto
Delhi   Bombay   Calcutta   Madras   Karachi
Petaling Jaya   Singapore   Hong Kong   Tokyo
Nairobi   Dar es Salaam   Cape Town
Melbourne   Auckland
and associated companies in
Beirut   Berlin   Ibadan   Nicosia

Published by Oxford University Press, Inc.,
200 Madison Avenue, New York, New York 10016

Oxford is a registered trademark of Oxford University Press

Library of Congress Cataloging-in-Publication Data

Studies of development and change in the modern world.

Includes bibliographies and index.
1. Economic development.   2. Developing countries—
Economic policy.   3. Social change.   4. Developing
countries—Social conditions.   I. Martin, Michael T.
II. Kandal, Terry R.
HD75.S83   1989   303.4′4′091724   88-17909
ISBN 0-19-505646-9
ISBN 0-19-505647-7 (pbk.)

9 8 7 6 5 4 3 2 1
Printed in the United States of America

For our Fathers
Oliver Martin
and
Terry O. Kandal

Contents

III   Studies of the Semiperiphery and Core

IV   Toward a Reformulation of Models, Processes, and the Future Direction of the World Economy

Preface

This book is the continuation of a project begun when Terry Kandal, as editor of *California Sociologist*, invited Michael Martin to guest-edit a special issue on a topic and of a thematic scope that the journal had not as yet taken up. The call for papers purposely ignored formal disciplinary divisions and encouraged scholars to contribute original articles from across the range of the social sciences.

The issue was intended to advance the discussion about "uneven" and "dependent" development of societies within an internationally stratified world and increasingly interdependent global economy and to offer fresh critiques of traditional (and radical) models of social-economic development, political transformation, and revolutionary change in light of the ethnocentrism so often reflected by researchers in development studies. In short, it was our goal to frame the study of development and change in recognition of the world as a totality, characterized by the global divisions of capital and labor; and, considering the multiplicity of structural characteristics of societies, to view change not as a smooth evolutionary transformation but rather as a disruptive and conflict-laden historical process.

The thematic specificity and coherence of this call resulted in a collection of papers organized around some of the theoretical and practical-political issues posed by the world-system perspective. In fact, the papers fit so well with our intentions that we decided to pursue, with modifications and the addition of several new papers, their publication as a book to give them the wider distribution they merit.

Several points of clarification about the theoretical framework of the book: First, in the title the terms "development" and "social change" appear. We use the concept of development, given its place as part of our received intellectual heritage, to discuss certain kinds of changes in the contemporary world and, along with underdevelopment, as a classification of differences between and within nation-states. We simply wish to point out, first, that not all social change can be characterized as development: in addition to what economists refer to as (long-term) secular changes, there are shorter and longer cyclical patterns and those more rare but rapid and discontinuous ruptures in the histories of societies. Second, and more important, the theory of social-cultural development is fraught with implicit and debatable theoretical assumptions about societies and the causes and patterns of their changes (and persistence). Third, the impressiveness of Immanuel Wallerstein's contribution to the comprehension of the workings of the capitalist world economy has made it a necessary part of our discourse about the modern world. Our theoretical points of view are adumbrated in the introduction and in the editors' papers. As is evident from the papers, a range of perspectives about dependency, class struggle, and mode of production and world-system analyses is represented.

We might add that the book can be read and used both by those who want to learn about the recent history of several regions of the world and by those interested in the debates over theoretical and methodological approaches to the study of the contemporary world.

We want to thank the many colleagues who assisted us in the review process, especially the faculty of the Latin American Studies Program at California State University, Los Angeles—Donald Bray, Marjorie Bray, and Timothy Harding. We also thank the editorial board of *California Sociologist*, Steven Gordon, Marion Dearman, Nathan Horwitz, and Delos Kelly, Chair of the Department of Sociology, for their assistance and encouragement and for permission to reprint articles from the special issue of *California Sociologist*. Terry Kandal wishes to thank Anita A. Acosta for her assistance and support during the difficult process of producing the special issue.

Finally, we have dedicated this book to our fathers, for their life-long commitment to and participation in the progressive movement in the United States.

M.T.M.
T.R.K.

Contributors

Giovanni Arrighi is Professor of Sociology, State University of New York at Binghamton, and coauthor of *Dynamics of Global Crisis*.

George L. Beckford is Professor of Economics, University of West Indies, Mona, Kingston, Jamaica. A noted scholar on Caribbean plantation societies, he is the author of *Persistent Poverty*.

Henry Bienen is James S. McDonnell Distinguished University Professor of Politics and International Affairs at Princeton University, where he directs the Center of International Studies. His most recent book is *Political Conflict and Economic Change in Nigeria*.

Terry E. Boswell teaches sociology at Emory University and is co-editor of *America's Changing Role in the World-System* (forthcoming).

John Brohman is a doctoral candidate in geography at the University of California, Los Angeles. He teaches in the Department of Geography at Simon Fraser University.

Robert S. Browne is a development economist and staff director of the Subcommittee on International Development Institutions & Finance, U.S. House Subcommittee on Banking; and co-author of *The Lagos Plan of Action vs. The Berg Report*.

E. Bradford Burns is Professor of Latin American History, University of California, Los Angeles, and the author of numerous studies, including *A History of Brazil, Elites, Masses, and Modernization in Latin America*.

George K. Danns is Senior Lecturer of Sociology, University of Guyana, and the author of *Domination and Power in Guyana*.

Thomas D. Hall is Associate Professor of Sociology, University of Oklahoma, Norman, and author of *Social Change in the Southwest, 1350–1880*.

Peter T. Johnson is Bibliographer for Latin America, Spain, and Portugal and Lecturer, Program in Latin American Studies, at Princeton University.

Terry R. Kandal is Professor of Sociology at California State University, Los Angeles, and the author of _The Woman Question in Classical Sociological Theory_.

Çağlar Keyder teaches sociology at SUNY, Binghamton, and is the author of _The Definition of a Peripheral Economy: Turkey, 1923–1929_.

Perry Mars is Head of the Department of Political Science and Law, University of Guyana, Georgetown, and the author of numerous studies on Caribbean politics.

Michael T. Martin is Professor of Pan-African Studies, California State University, Los Angeles, and Visiting Professor of Afro-American Studies and Director of the Third World Center, Princeton University. He is the author of studies on development and Third World politics.

Lear K. Matthews is Lecturer of Sociology, University of Guyana.

Michael Moffitt is a New York investment adviser and the author of _The World's Money_.

Devon G. Peña is Assistant Professor of Sociology, Colorado College, and author of studies on industrial development and industrial relations in the Third World.

James F. Petras is Professor of Sociology, State University of New York, Binghamton. His many books include _Critical Perspectives on Imperialism and Social Class in the Third World_ and _Class, State and Power in the Third World_.

Immanuel Wallerstein is Director of the Fernand Braudel Center at SUNY, Binghamton. His many works include _The Capitalist World Economy_, _The African Liberation Reader_, and his seminal study, _The Modern World System_, Vols. 1–3.

Hilbourne A. Watson is Chair, Department of Political Science, Howard University, and author of numerous articles on Caribbean politics.

. . . if what we have in our country is civilization . . . , then we are better uncivilized because it is better to know where to go and not know how than it is to know how to go and not know where.

GILLO PONTECORVO, Queimada (1969)

Studies of Development
and Change.
in the Modern World

Introduction

Terry R. Kandal and Michael T. Martin

A variant of social change, "development," as it is referred to in the literature, is a product of history, and in the modern world is increasingly conditioned by the structures of the world capitalist economy. We have therefore intentionally organized this collection to reflect and parallel a structural approach to analyzing the world in terms of cores and peripheries. The substantive theoretical and methodological issues that this approach (in all its variations) raises have been the subject of considerable debate (see, e.g., Brewer, 1980; Chilcote, 1982, 1984). We are cognizant that recent Marxist theories about development and, especially, underdevelopment have become, as Peter Worsley contends, "bogged down in a seemingly endless multiplication of exercises in mode of productionism and world systematics in which the distinctive features of each country simply disappear and all become look-alikes, only distinguished from one another insofar as some are central, others peripheral or semi-peripheral" (1984:41). However, a model based on a structural dichotomy of core and periphery provides the conceptual framework to study the development experience in any country or region with regard to its position in the international division of labor. We are not suggesting that the international sphere necessarily, or even in the last instance, *determines* the outcome of specific processes of class formation and class struggle within all countries, in particular those in the periphery. Empirical evidence to support such a theory on a world scale has not amassed to date. We would argue that this model must be constructed to take into account the relative and varying autonomy of national and regional historical processes as they occur within and, in turn, affect the modern world-system.

According to Wallerstein (1974, 1979, 1980) and others, the modern world-system is constituted by the dominance of capitalist production relations, and especially the dominance of the world market (the sphere of exchange), by the most advanced capitalist economies. From its inception during the "long sixteenth century," capitalism has transformed classes within the core states into capitalists and wage workers and, in enveloping the world, has forcibly incorporated the peoples and states in the peripheries into its global system of production and exchange.

Somewhat less generally, systematic explanations of development and underdevelopment (as well as attempts to break out of the latter and overcome dependency along socialist lines) must be viewed in the context of the movements, and consequences thereof, of capital, determined by the rate of profit, the cyclic fluctuations and secular tendencies of world capitalism, and the competition among core states for control of the world political economy. While these factors are central to the development of countries and regions in the world economy, they are, in turn, shaped by the contradictory forces endemic to capitalism—principally the struggle of classes within states and on a global scale. It is within this context, characterized increasingly by constraints—what Otto Kirchheimer once conceived as the "confining conditions of revolutionary breakthroughs"—that the subject of this collection is addressed by many of the contributors.

At more concrete levels, beyond the class conflicts engendered by the relentless development of capitalism, explanations of the transformation of societies must take into account cultural factors, the overlapping of class, ethnicity, and gender in the struggles for (and resistance to) development, and the ways in which states and systems of states shape and are shaped by their position in the international division of labor. Development, underdevelopment, and attempts at revolutionary breakthroughs are, then, the results of the interrelationships of conditions both external and internal to a society.

The raison d'être of capitalism is unceasing and ever increasing accumulation. The postwar period (1945–1970), under U.S. hegemony of the Western anti-Communist alliances, was one of expansion, similar to the years 1815 to 1870, when Britain was the industrial sun around which the agricultural planets of the world economy revolved. An inherent feature of capitalist development is the recurrence of crises in the accumulation process. The first great crisis of advanced capitalism began in the

1870s, followed by a second major crisis beginning in the late 1920s and ending with World War II. During the early 1970s, another crisis of capital accumulation developed (Amin et al., 1982; Walton, 1986). Each successive crisis featured an intense rivalry and competition among core states for control of new markets. We are witnessing, during the current crisis, beginning about 1980, a similar competition among core states for markets, along with a relative decline of U.S. dominance in world production and trade.

Concomitantly, the last decade and a half, in the core states, have been distinguished by that anomaly of neoclassical economics, stagflation—inflation and persistently high unemployment—accompanied by antiinflationary state policies that have further lowered the living standards of the working class (organized and unorganized), attacks on social programs, and, especially in the United States, the feminization of poverty and the resultant increasing poverty of children. These conditions have been associated with the structural transformations occurring in core industrial economies (e.g., the decline of heavy industry and the increasing growth of the service sector, the employment of new high technology productive forces); the fractionation of the working class along income, ethnic, racial, and gender lines; the credit economy (private and public); and the commodification, privatization, and speed up of all aspects of social life (except for the unemployed)—all accompanied by a neo-liberal ideology of letting the market do its work (see Currie, Dunn, and Fogarty, 1985). The purpose of these structural and ideological changes has been to create the conditions to increase the rate of return on invested capital by cutting labor costs and the social wage.

As in previous "bottlenecks" of accumulation (e.g., the late 1870s), the current crisis is characterized by the increasing incorporation of the periphery into the world capitalist economy through the search for new markets and trade (Frank, 1982; Wallerstein, 1982) and the transnationalization of production ("runaway" shops as capital migrates to the low-wage periphery and to the low-wage areas of the core). The nations of the periphery have also been incorporated into the international financial system through loans and a debt of crisis proportions. These processes, along with military and economic aid, have resulted in further integrating the Third World periphery into the world market—the subsumption and replacement of precapitalist modes of production—with the consequence of the increasing transnationalization of commodities and labor on the assembly lines of the global sweatshops. The worldwide capitalist recession has meant for the Third World nations increasing misery of various kinds: they account for most of the one-quarter of the world's people living in poverty (in Wallerstein's judgment working harder for less than the rural producers of the sixteenth century), have stagnating national economies further debilitated by the enormous debt burdens to foreign commercial banks, and experience ethnic, national, and class conflicts as well as an increase of state repression. The deterioration and transformation of conditions in the Third World led in the 1970s to proposals for a new international economic order (NIEO) by the southern (underdeveloped) countries, which were resisted by the developed countries, and to the increased migration of labor to the North (with all its attendant xenophobic reactions in core countries). It has also led with variable successes to revolutionary struggles with the aim of national liberation (in some movements, with the goal of "de-linking" from the capitalist world economy).

In consideration of these trends, capitalist development in all its variations (dependent development and underdevelopment) and attempts at socialist construction are occurring in what appears, at this stage, as the (twi)light of the world capitalist economy and the international system of states. This is the case whether we are discussing the transformations in the core and peripheral regions of the United States, the blockages to socialist plans in France, Greece, and Portugal, the crises in Mexico and Brazil, the repressive capitalist regime in South Korea, the decolonization struggle in Namibia, the revolutionary struggles of Zimbabwe and counter-revolutionary intervention in Nicaragua, or the continuing struggle over which road to follow in the People's Republic of China.

Contrary to the dominant paradigm — modernization theory — of the 1950s and 1960s, fashionable in mainstream academic and policy circles, neither we nor any of the contributors subscribe to the proposition that development occurs through a succession of stages that are natural and inevitable, and results solely from conditions internal to society, and that all societies experience roughly uniform and continuous processes, resulting in one outcome or form of the modern nation-state. Variations of modernization theory notwithstanding, its theoretical and ideological foundations are rooted in the eighteenth- and nineteenth-century European idea of progress and its twentieth-century heir, the evolutionary functionalism of Talcott Parsons (Worsley, 1984; Smith, 1973). Ignored by most modernization theorists and policymakers, especially from the United States, were the multiplicity of historical differences and cultural characteristics of Third World societies (yet, ironically, some theorists emphasized and used cultural factors to explain the cause of underdevelopment) and especially the importance of international economic forces and the significance of power and opposed interests vested in the social classes of societies. The expectations and prescriptions of modernization theorists and development planners were dashed by the continued underdevelopment of the former colonial territories and the revolutionary paths to development taken by some newly independent Third World states. The historical, theoretical, and methodological weaknesses of modernization theory as an explanation of social change have been penetratingly discussed by Smith (1973) and Robertson (1984), among others. In general, it was a result of the efforts to address the empirical and concrete political issues emerging from the developmental problems of underdeveloped societies that new theoretical models emerged to gain ascendancy in the late 1960s.

To conceive of development (and therefore change) as a natural process is to ignore that it is fundamentally a historical process with cultural and political as well as economic components (a criticism that holds for evolutionist versions of Marxism). Marx, in a letter (November 1877) to the editorial board of a Russian journal concerning the application of his theory of capitalist development in Europe to Russia, addressed the issue succinctly. After noting that the expropriation of free peasants in Roman history did not make them wage laborers, but that alongside them was instituted a mode of production based on slavery, he stated,

> Thus events strikingly analogous but taking place in different historical surroundings led to totally different results. By studying each of these forms of evolution separately and then comparing them one can easily find the clue to this phenomenon, but one will never arrive there by use as one's master key a general historico-philosophical theory, the supreme virtue of which consists in being super-historical. (in Feuer, 1959:441)

It follows that what is required for an understanding of successful and unsuccessful attempts at development through revolutionary and nonrevolutionary means—what Barrington Moore, Jr., has referred to as routes to the modern world (Moore, 1966)—is a theoretically informed comparison of histories (see Bock, 1956; Teggart, 1939). A necessary step in this method is case studies, with all due respect for historical specificity. Comparisons must include studies within regions and nation-states as well as among them. Theories of social change stand or fall on the test of the widest range of historical-comparative evidence.

An appropriate comment on the papers in this collection, as well as on the moral and political issues they raise, can be found in Marx's ruminations in *Secret Diplomatic History of the Eighteenth Century:* "To understand a limited historical epoch, we must step beyond its limits, and compare it with other historical epochs. To judge Governments and their acts, we must measure them by their own times and conscience of their contemporaries" (Marx, 1969:85).

This collection of papers is bound by no formal disciplinary constraints as they are ensconced in the organization of knowledge by departments in modern universities. No comprehensive understanding of change, development, or underdevelopment can be obtained within the confines of any single social science discipline. We must draw on the best of the "bourgeois" disciplines and their radical offshoots—the historically informed tradition of classic social analysis advocated by C. Wright Mills (1959).

The papers have been grouped into four parts, the first of which covers broad theoretical and methodological approaches to revolutionary change and development in core and peripheral societies. In the opening paper, Terry R. Kandal examines the often neglected historical and journalistic writings and correspondence of Marx and Engels on revolution in the modern world. He argues, contrary to predominant views (e.g., Skocpol, 1979), that there is in these writings a systemic conception of the interrelations of the world capitalist economy, the international system of states, and class struggles in the causal pattern, courses, and outcomes of revolutions. What emerges from his reconstruction is a picture of Marx and Engels's views of nineteenth-century international relations as they conditioned and were altered by revolutions from the eighteenth century to Engels's death in 1895, a pattern they expected to be transformed by an impending Russian revolution occasioned by a world war. Kandal also contends that Marx and Engels possibly have better explanations of incomplete than complete revolutions, that their most successful theory is of revolutions in backward capitalist societies (or in the semiperiphery, as it might be termed today). It follows from his discussion that Marx's approach to revolution does not rely solely on long-term economic changes and class conflicts internal to societies or solely on world market considerations, to the exclusion of the international relations of states and the world-historical timing of a revolution. The implicit argument of Kandal's paper is that contemporary theoretical and political debate about the workings of the world-system and the role of revolutions within it might be advanced by going back to the source—the complete corpus of classical Marxism.

The world-system model associated with the work of Immanuel Wallerstein (around which the journal *Review* was established) has been the focus of fruitful research and controversy concerning the development of capitalism, underdevelopment, and the possibilities for socialist construction. In the second paper, Terry E. Boswell examines the utility of the world-system model for explaining social revolutions. He reviews the major criticisms of the model, that it neglects the relative autonomy of states and state relations (Skocpol, 1977) and that it focuses too much on (market) relations of exchange, to the exclusion of the relations of production and the conflict of classes (Brenner, 1984). In a laudatory break with academic taboo—even on the Left—Boswell looks to Lenin's analysis of imperialism, colonialism, war, and revolution in the aftermath of World War I to remedy the inadequacies of the world-system model. Lenin's notions of "weak links" and the contradiction between political and economic locations of a nation-state in the world capitalist system, Boswell argues, provide useful hypotheses for explaining social revolutions. While one might quibble with his examples, his concept of world formation contributes to the theoretical and political debate about underdevelopment and development that centers on the relative value of dependency and mode-of-production analyses (see Chilcote and Johnson, 1984). It must be noted that it does not follow that because capitalism dominates the modern world economy and subsumes all precapitalist production relations, then the latter are all capitalist, although there is a world-historical tendency for them to become so, except where authentic socialist revolutions succeed.

Henry Bienen's chapter focuses more on methodological and policy issues. He asserts that policy must be guided not by slogans but by careful, detailed historical case studies. The issue of whether Islam is a conservative or a revolutionary force, he contends, can be answered only by examining its uses in a variety of national and regional contexts. Similarly, he points to the absence of an automatic relationship between rapid urbanization and political unrest. We would suggest that the next step requires a comparison of these case studies to determine why revolutionary unrest occurs *when* and *where* it does—comparisons of, say, Paris in the 1790s and throughout the nineteenth century, Moscow and Petrograd in the early 1900s, Madrid and Barcelona in the 1930s, the rapid urbanization induced by bombing during national wars of liberation (e.g., Vietnam and contemporary El Salvador). As Bienen points out, policy makers want academics to devise simple theories to serve their purposes. He questions the wisdom of this approach. Thus Bienen's work can be connected with the wider literature discussed earlier, which calls for a historical-empirical approach to an understanding of stability and change.

In the lead article of Part II, which is devoted to the Caribbean and Latin American periphery, Michael T. Martin places the Reagan administration's Caribbean Basin Initiative (1982) in the context of the effects on the Third World of the global recession of the past decade. He returns to the classical theme of interimperialist rivalry for markets and points to the staggering proportions that Third World debt has reached. These processes have resulted in a deeper incorporation of the periphery into the world capitalist economy and the international financial system (possibly inaugurating a new stage of finance capitalism). The "conditionality" attached to IMF loans to Third World debtor countries entails reduced social spending and currency devaluation, with the consequences of increasing misery, protest, and revolutionary outbursts. On an international level, the nonpayment of debt, or the threat of it, appears to be the only leverage enjoyed by Third World countries. The inference from Martin's analysis is that the political-economic policies of the

Reagan administration run deeper and are more rational than the bizarre and dangerous nouveau riche anti-Communist rhetoric would lead us to believe. Right-wing populism masks a search for economic advantage in the Caribbean; where that fails, military intervention is the next step to prevent de-linking, as in El Salvador and Grenada. The Nicaraguan revolution is clearly a serious threat to the Reagan strategy, and has led to the administration's obsession with ridding the region of the Sandinista regime. Martin concludes that peripheral countries can change the balance of advantage between themselves and the core states by mobilizing bargaining power through the formation of counterhegemonies (e.g., cartels) for technology, raw materials, and the like. However, it can be argued that the basis for such economic alliances is being undercut by the process of incorporation that he has documented. Moreover, the contraction of world markets for minerals and basic foodstuffs will probably further inhibit this process as peripheral countries compete against one another for markets.

George L. Beckford, a scholar of plantation societies, points out that plantation capitalism was the first form of capitalism in areas of the New World (parts of the Caribbean, Brazil, and the U.S. South) and Africa, and that societies in which plantation capitalism has existed have been in the vanguard of the transition to socialism (e.g., Angola, Cuba). Not only are class and race fused in the plantation mode of production, but, as Beckford suggests, plantations were the first "factories in the field" and the first multinational corporations. It seems logical, in contrast to Marx's analysis in *The Eighteenth Brumaire of Louis Bonaparte*, of the isolated peasant mode of production, which, despite similar objective conditions, does not foster a common (i.e., class) consciousness, that plantation labor would create the potential revolutionary class consciousness (see Stinchcombe, 1966; Paige, 1975). The plantation mode of production illustrates the interplay of internal and external factors in historical processes.

The general argument of George K. Danns and Lear K. Matthews's chapter on Guyanan social history is that "a nation is as developed as the communities within it." The authors distinguish historical communities in Guyana: traditional and peripheral Amerindian; the dominant, exploitative, and repressive plantation community; slave and indenture; the reactive and survivalist black village; the sponsored and supportive Portuguese and Chinese communities; and the urban villages and mining-town communities. The focus of their analysis of Guyanan underdevelopment is not primarily on the external dependency relationships, but on the dependent underdevelopment created by the plantation system and the postcolonial state. The remainder of their study centers on intrasociety comparisons. What is clear from their exposition is that the effects of race and ethnicity are not the attributes of groups but are the outcome of social-historical processes. Their approach could be extended by bringing it into relation with Blauner's thesis on internal colonialism (1972), which encompasses race, class, culture, and resistance in the United States; with Hechter's work on internal colonialism, specifically the place of and impact on the Celtic fringe in the development of English capitalism (Coughlan and Zirker, 1985); and with classic Marxist writings on the "national question" (Davis, 1980). In short, the larger project is to explore comparatively the ways in which class, race and ethnicity, and gender are interrelated in systems of structured social inequality under the conditions of different modes of production, historical social formations, and phases of the world economy.

E. Bradford Burns, a historian of Latin America, presents a concise and elegant comparison of the histories of Central American countries, observing their similarities and differences as they were drawn into the world market through the development of capitalist export agriculture. Central to his analysis is the distinction between economic growth and social development: capitalist economic growth, as measured by statistical increases, in Central America did not mean (except for a time in Guatemala) social development for the masses, as measured by increases in the quality of life. Rather, it meant expropriation for the peasants, forced labor on the latifundia, the creation of an agricultural proletariat, and, to maintain these new class relations, a professional military class linked to the large landowners. One cannot help, when reading Burns's paper, but be reminded of Marx's depiction in *Das Kapital* of "primitive accumulation," which, of course, had a quite different world-historical outcome in England. Burns poses tough questions for mainstream social science, which fails to distinguish between economic growth and development—questions that must be addressed if we are concerned about the betterment of human life.

John Brohman presents a cogent historical treatment of the "Junker" road (by comparison with nineteenth-century Germany) taken by prerevolutionary Nicaraguan agricultural development—the transition from feudal estates to large capitalist farms (see Lenin, 1956). Instead of the formation of an independent peasantry—as in the "farmer" or capitalist road—the result was the progressive semiproletarianization of the peasantry in successive waves of expansion of large estates, forcing peasants off subsistence plots. Such relations of production involved the superexploitation of semiproletarian agricultural laborers who were paid less than the value of their labor power. The outcome was a "disarticulated" Third World economy, in which agricultural production is for export (not to feed an emerging urban working class), and there is no positive relationship between labor productivity and real wages or between economic growth and income distribution. Socially, the peasants became increasingly impoverished; politically, an increasing polarization and conflict of classes led to a potentially revolutionary situation. Brohman's paper can be linked with a larger literature about class conflicts in the Third World—for example, the work of Barrington Moore, Jr. (1966) on lord and peasant in the making of the modern world, Eric Wolf (1969) on peasant wars of the twentieth century, and Jeffrey Paige (1975) on export agriculture and agrarian revolution.

The present period is one of widespread migration of peoples. Hilbourne A. Watson's chapter provides the striking example that one-half (of the present number) of the Jamaican population migrated to the United States and the United Kingdom between World War II and the present. In a refreshing Marxist analysis based on "the logic of capital," Watson questions the capacity of neoclassical economic theory and unequal exchange and dependency models to explain migration in terms of population pressure, the relative (to capital) immobility of labor, or imperialism. He offers an alternative explanation: that migration is a state policy resulting from backward capitalism's inability to develop productive forces in both the domestic and the external (enclave) sectors because merchant capital still dominates productive capital in the Caribbean. (Once again, we are reminded of the centrality of the plantation mode of production to the social processes in that region.) It is these conditions, Watson argues, that create and "expel" the surplus population. The persuasiveness of his position notwithstanding, a wider range of data on international migration is required to test the merits of underdevelopment, world-system, and mode-of-production models. The role of state terror against revolutionary wars of national liberation cannot be overlooked in the patterns of migration in the periphery. In the larger context of the world economy, the migrations of labor follow the movements of capital as it envelopes the globe.

Peter T. Johnson's chapter concludes Part II. He presents an interesting analysis, based on an examination of primary documents, of an intriguing Peruvian revolutionary movement, Sendero Luminoso. Johnson contends that our knowledge of contemporary revolutionary movements is often limited by the manipulative rhetoric about terrorism reported in the bourgeois press. He traces the history of the Shining Path, noting the consistency of its strategy, the sectors to which it has appealed, and the roles of university students and, particularly, women in the movement. His study of Sendero Luminoso is of historical importance because following the death of Mao Zedong and subsequent changes in the foreign and domestic policies of the People's Republic of China, Maoist movements appear to have declined worldwide. Sendero Luminoso, however, with its imaginative use of popular culture and nationalist ideology in its propaganda, provides a fascinating exception, and clearly demonstrates that peasant and rural-based revolutionary movements have perceptions and traditions that are grounded in distinctly national histories.

In Part III, on social change and development in the semiperiphery and core, James F. Petras, a development scholar, provides an analytic and historical overview of the classes and the development of the political economy in the Mediterranean. He emphasizes the uneven development among and within the societies of the region. The "restructuring" of capital there has developed along with an underground economy of half-petty rentiers, the increasing employment of women, and the fractionation of the working class among farmers, older workers in traditional industries, youth in the new industries, and a separate state bureaucratic elite—all accompanied by a revivified ideology of market capitalism. In contrast to the popular movements of the 1960s and early 1970s, the late 1970s and the 1980s have seen the traditional Left put on the defensive. Issues raised in Petras's paper are a comparison of left-wing movements in the Mediterranean with radicalism in northern Europe and the conditions under which new working class movements might arise (see the chapter by Arrighi, Keyder, and Wallerstein). Most striking and interesting about this study is that if place names were removed, one could be reading about any core capitalist country.

Devon G. Peña's paper contains the major themes and issues considered by other authors in this collection: the shifting national and international division of labor, the movements of capital and restructuring of capitalist production relations, class struggles, and the changing ethnic composition of the working class. In a study, rich in detail and analysis, of the twin plants in Mexico and the enterprise zone proposals in the United States, Peña observes the movement of capital from the traditional Northeast to the lower social wage, nonunionized Southwest (e.g., the Texas boom, busted by the recent decline in oil prices), where the rate of exploitation is higher. Investment is in light industry and the service sector, which employ Mexican and other immigrant workers. Large monopolistic firms subcontract to small businesses, avoiding the costs of pensions and the provisions of safe working conditions. Tax concessions by states to attract industry are a further extension of the socialization of the costs of reproduction of capital–labor relations and, along with low wages, are a way to rekindle accumulation. Peña points out that capital has historically moved away from regions where the working class is organized, but that the current trend of unions to make concessions has not stopped the flight of capital. The critical questions posed in this study are whether organized labor can effectively respond to the new contradictions of its situation and whether in the course of time a new working-class militancy will arise in the twin plants and the enterprise zones. On theoretical grounds, we would anticipate these processes. As Peña notes, and as we suggested earlier, they must be seen as part of the transnationalization of commodities, capital, and labor. We are witnessing in these instances the coring of the semiperiphery (Mexico) and peripheralization in the core (the American Southwest). Such processes cry out for comparative analysis.

In Part IV, which might be characterized as the road ahead for method, theory, and practice, Thomas D. Hall places core–periphery relations in a wider historical context than do the other contributors to this book. His call is for a historical sociology that would examine the various outcomes of contacts between different core and peripheral societies—tribalization being a common outcome—taking into account economic as well as noneconomic factors (ecology, relations between tribes, the political-cultural division of labor) in the historical process of peripheralization. Like Wallerstein, Hall takes the position that "states create peoples," and not the reverse. More broadly, parallel to the work of Teggart (1918, 1925, 1939), Hall admonishes sociology for its ethnocentrism and its tendency to ignore the peripheries of various historical civilizations, without which their development cannot be totally grasped.

Next, Perry Mars presents a political sociology of knowledge analysis of competing models of underdevelopment: plural society, dependency, and Marxist. He observes the historical-intellectual conditions in which each has been predominant in academic and political circles and comes down on the side of Marxism (without giving their due to Marxist versions of the dependency model). While recognizing that theory is a political weapon, he poses the question of what is to be done without considering the role of the party in the formation of strategy, class consciousness, and mobilization. Moreover, his allusions to Kuhn, the claim to paradigmatic status of the several theories of development, suggest a historical comparison with debates about the correct Marxian theories of revolution in the nineteenth and twentieth centuries (see Kandal, 1973). Interestingly, like other Caribbean scholars represented in this book, Mars tends to downplay the role of imperialism in underdevelopment and to place more blame for it on the national bourgeoisie.

The last three chapters consider regional, continental, and national aspects of the world economy in the twentieth century.

Robert S. Browne's chapter follows with a critical assessment of the prospects for development on the African continent. In consideration of the historical underdevelopment and colonization of Africa and its repartition among colonial powers during the crisis of capitalism in the late nineteenth century, Browne resurrects the *Lagos Plan of Action* in the contemporary context of North–South relations and the economic and political obstacles to intra-African (South–South) trade and development. His criticism of the World Bank's export-driven development strategy for Africa (and the Third World in general), in light of the North's growing protectionism and Africa's severe debt-servicing problems and dependence on export markets, is contrasted with the development strategy proposed by Africans and endorsed by the fifty African heads of state in 1980.

Cognizant of the inherent weaknesses in the Lagos Plan and the economic and political barriers to its implementation, Browne nevertheless contends that the Lagos Plan represents a "new" approach that calls on Africans to develop the continent's resources for their own development and consumption. In anticipation of the twenty-first century, he asks some hard questions with no easy answers, as evidenced by the current economic and political crises on the continent. For example, the counterrevolutionary and economic pressures posed by the South African regime are impediments to attempts at development by progressive governments in the region.

Whether black Africa has the "will" and capacity to endure the social dislocations (especially for the African elite) that such a development strategy would invariably cause in the short run and form the transnational economic and political entities (African Economic Community) suggested by the author is the central question and organizing dilemma for the continent's leaders.

The penultimate chapter is appropriately, given the organization and themes of this volume, written by Giovanni Arrighi, Cağlar Keyder, and Immanuel Wallerstein. The authors focus on the development of southern Europe—Portugal, Spain, Italy, Greece, and Turkey—in the twentieth century, in the context of the modern world-system. This paper is also not without implications for the direction of the world political economy in the coming period. The authors observe that the beginning of the decline of British hegemony, Pax Britannica, coincided with the Great Depression of the last third of the nineteenth century and with rivalry among the imperialist powers for colonial markets and the markets of southern Europe, resulting, as Lenin made central to his theory of imperialism, in World War I. During the interwar years, with imperialist rivalry resumed, the specter of working-class revolution after October 1917 and the Great Depression of the 1930s led to the imposition of Fascist "solutions" to economic crises and class conflicts, culminating in Nazi Germany's attempt to create a new division of labor in the world political economy. After World War II, the United States supplanted Britain as the new world policeman. As Arrighi, Keyder, and Wallerstein suggest, the United States intervened in and undermined Communist movements in southern Europe and financed the rebuilding of capitalism throughout Europe, and economic chickens have since come home to roost. Moreover, postwar northern Europe has penetrated southern Europe, with the result that the latter has become increasingly integrated into a European political economy, leading to the "Europe versus America" equation. And as the authors point out, the deepening global crisis of the early 1980s intensified the rivalry "within and across national borders," resulting in the rise of "socialist" parties in southern Europe that have advanced labor-repressive policies and legitimated the demands of accumulation at the national and global levels. For example, in Italy, the *Scala Mobili* was abrogated under the "socialist" government of Craxi. Correspondingly, in the United States, where large impoverished Third World and working-class populations are concentrated in urban areas, liberal (and progressive) city administrations, some controlled by blacks, have made concessions (i.e., tax incentives) to corporations to encourage them to relocate to or remain in the city. The result has almost always led to the gentrification of inner cities (Detroit, Newark) and to the relocation of those displaced by urban redevelopment as they are dumped onto the scrap heaps of contemporary history.

What, then, are the implications of the experience of southern Europe in the 1960s and 1970s for the emerging period of world capitalism? Some of these changes are specified in the concluding chapter, by Michael Moffitt. What is similar to the interwar years is the decline of a hegemonic power, with the United States now challenged by the advanced capitalist economies of West Germany and Japan (and the emerging low-wage capitalist economies of east Asia). Unlike that of the pre–World War II period, the world capitalist economy of the late twentieth century has become dominated by multinational corporations, truly globalized, coincident with Reaganism, deregulated, and increasingly characterized by bizarre speculative financial activities. As Moffitt points out, given the multinationalization of production, to speak of "world trade" in conventional terms is little short of meaningless, since a significant portion of such trade involves intrafirm transfers. He argues that the United States and the world economy have fundamentally changed in recent years. One consequence of these changes is the loss of any pretenses of national economic autonomy:

> . . . we have the outlines of a true vicious circle: the world economy is dependent on growth in the U.S. economy, but the U.S. domestic economy is skewed more toward consumption than production and investment, and this consumption is in turn sustained by borrowing— at home and abroad. An economy sustained by debt, especially foreign debt, is always vulnerable to an interest rate shock, whether it is administered by the Fed or by the markets. Given foreign dependence on the U.S. market, a rate shock that is great enough to send the U.S. economy into a new recession thus virtually guarantees a world-wide economic collapse, with all that that implies for bankruptcies, defaults, and the widespread liquidation of debt. (Moffitt, 1987:572)

A further direct consequence, suggests Moffitt, is that the living standard will continue to decline in the United States. What this means for the working classes is the necessity to labor harder for less, in short, to suffer an increase in the rate of surplus value and in the reserve army of labor. But the struggle of classes regionally and on a world scale are topics he does not take up in his analysis of the United States and the world economy.

Whether and when and where the contradictions of capitalism create the conditions for social transformation to a society in which time is the room of human development rather than human beings existing as time's carcasses (Marx) depends not only on the state of the world economy, but also on the social forces affecting class consciousness and mobilization. This collection does not include all the geographical areas of the world economy, nor does it treat all aspects of the development process, in particular the increasing incorporation of women into production in the Third World and the low-wage industries and occupations of the First (see Peña and Petras). The emergence of informal economies worldwide, their impact on national economies, and more careful attention to the effects of neocolonialism on the politics of core societies are issues that require fuller consideration. Case studies of development in the core and peripheries of Asia or northern Europe; the class, national, and ethnic struggles in the Middle East; and the transformations in socialist societies are subjects for other studies.

We conclude with an observation: all the studies in this collection do not take up what seems to be a fundamental issue—that it is less difficult to overthrow an indecent society than to create a decent one.

References

Amin, Samir, Giovanni Arrighi, Andre Gunder Frank, and Immanuel Wallerstein (1982). *Dynamics of the Global Crisis*. New York: Monthly Review Press.

Blauner, Robert (1972). *Racial Oppression in America*. New York: Harper & Row.

Bock, Kenneth E. (1956). *The Acceptance of Histories: Toward a Perspective for Social Science*. Berkeley: University of California Press.

Brenner, Robert (1984). "The Origins of Capitalist Development: A Critique of NeoSmithian Marxism." *New Left Review* 104:25–92.

Brewer, Anthony (1980). *Marxist Theories of Imperialism: A Critical Survey*. London: Routledge & Kegan Paul.

Chilcote, Ronald H., ed. (1982). *Dependency and Marxism: Toward a Resolution of the Debate*. Boulder, Colo.: Westview Press.

——— (1984). *Theories of Development and Underdevelopment*. Boulder, Colo.: Westview Press.

Chilcote, Ronald H., and Dale L. Johnson, eds. (1984). *Theories of Development: Mode of Production or Dependency?* Beverly Hills, Calif.: Sage.

Chilcote, Ronald H., et al. (1981). "Dependency and Marxism." *Latin American Perspectives*, no. 8 (Summer and Fall).

Coughlan, Reed, and Daniel Zirker (1985). "The Dilemma of Internal Colonialism: Ethnicity, Class and the Hechter Compromise." *California Sociologist* 8:51–69.

Currie, Elliott, Robert Dunn, and David Fogarty (1985). "The Fading Dream: Economic Crisis and the New Inequality." In Jerome H. Skolnick and Elliot Currie, eds., *Crisis in American Institutions*, 6th ed. Boston: Little, Brown, pp. 94–113.

Davis, Horace B. (1980). *Toward a Marxist Theory of Nationalism*. New York: Monthly Review Press.

Feuer, Lewis S., ed. (1959). *Marx & Engels, Basic Writings on Politics and Philosophy*. New York: Doubleday, Anchor.

Kandal, Terry (1973). "The History of Marxian Theory of Revolution as a Series of Paradigm Shifts." Paper presented at the meeting of the American Sociological Association, New York (August).

Lenin, V. I. (1956) [1899]. *The Development of Capitalism in Russia: The Process of the Formation of a Home Market for Large-Scale Industry*. Moscow: Foreign Languages Publishing House.

Marx, Karl (1969). *Secret Diplomatic History of the Eighteenth Century* and *The Story of the Life of Lord Palmerston*. Lester Hutchinson, ed. New York: International Publishers.

Mills, C. Wright (1959). *The Sociological Imagination*. New York: Oxford University Press.

Moffitt, Michael (1987). "Shocks, Deadlocks, and Scorched Earth: Reaganomics and the Decline of U.S. Hegemony." *World Policy Journal* 4:553–82.

Moore, Barrington, Jr. (1966). *Social Origins of Dictatorship and Democracy: Lord and Peasant in the Making of the Modern World.* Boston: Beacon Press.

Paige, Jeffrey M. (1975). *Agrarian Revolution: Social Movements and Export Agriculture in the Underdeveloped World.* New York: Free Press.

Robertson, A. F. (1984). *People and the State: An Anthropology of Planned Development.* New York: Cambridge University Press.

Skocpol, Theda (1977). "Wallerstein's World Capitalist System: A Theoretical and Historical Critique." *American Journal of Sociology* 82: 1075–90.

——— (1979). *States and Social Revolutions.* New York: Cambridge University Press.

Smith, Anthony D. (1973). *The Concept of Social Change: A Critique of the Functionalist Theory of Social Change.* Boston: Routledge and Kegan Paul.

Stinchcombe, Arthur L. (1966). "Agricultural Enterprise and Rural Class Relations." In Reinhard Bendix and Seymour Martin Lipset, eds., *Class, Status, and Power: Social Stratification in Comparative Perspective.* 2d ed. New York: Free Press, pp. 182–90.

Teggart, Frederick J. (1918, 1925). *Theory and Processes of History.* Berkeley: University of California Press.

——— (1939). *Rome and China: A Study of Correlations in Historical Events.* Berkeley: University of California Press.

Wallerstein, Immanuel (1974). *The Modern World System.* Vol 1, *Capitalist Agriculture and the Origins of the European World-Economy in the Sixteenth Century.* New York: Academic Press.

——— (1979). *The Capitalist World-Economy.* Cambridge: Cambridge University Press.

——— (1980). *The Modern World-System. Vol. 2, Mercantilism and the Consolidation of the European World-Economy, 1600–1750.* New York: Academic Press.

Walton, John (1986). *Sociology and Critical Inquiry: The Work, Tradition, and Purpose.* Chicago: Dorsey Press.

Wolf, Eric (1969). *Peasant Wars of the Twentieth Century.* New York: Harper & Row.

Worsley, Peter (1984). *The Three Worlds: Culture and Development.* Chicago: University of Chicago Press.

PART I

Theoretical and Methodological Approaches to the Study of Development and Social Change in the Modern World

CHAPTER 1

Marx and Engels on International Relations, Revolution, and Counterrevolution

Terry R. Kandal

> [S]ocial revolutions cannot be explained without systematic reference to *inter*national structures and world-historical developments.
>
> THEDA SKOCPOL, *States and Social Revolutions*

Contemporary Marxists in the academy have continued the classical Marxist debate on the proper way to theoretically comprehend the workings of capitalism as a system. To borrow a formulation, "The substantive issue . . . concerns the appropriate unit of analysis for the purpose of comparison" (Wallerstein, 1974a:393). In its historical reach and influence, the most intellectually impressive attempt to advance our understanding is Immanuel Wallerstein's theory of the modern world-system (1974b, 1980). In it, the world capitalist system, which is dominated by "production for profit in a market," shapes and interacts with nation-states, and (already by 1640) is divided into cores, semiperipheries, and peripheries. The modes of surplus extraction and class relations are determined by this international and interregional division of labor. Explicitly in Wallerstein's view, states and social classes are subordinate to the capitalist world economy. In his model, there cannot be noncapitalist modes of production *within* the system (Wallerstein, 1979). Left-wing scholars who have wrested control of the academic terrain of Third World studies argue the primacy of dependency relationships or mode-of-production analysis as explanations of the underdevelopment of, and class struggles in, especially Latin America (see, e.g., *Latin American Perspectives*, 1981).[1] What might be termed the "Wallerstein thesis" is at the center of contemporary controversy over the direction of world history and the understanding of social revolutions within it.

By contrast, Theda Skocpol, in her powerful analysis of the French, Russian, and Chinese revolutions, employed "state/society as the basic unit of analysis" in explaining social revolutions, defined as "rapid basic transformations of a society's state and class structures; and they are accompanied and in part carried through by class-based [especially of peasants] revolts from below" (1979:22, 24). The skeleton of her argument is as follows: "revolutionary situations have developed due to the emergence of politico-military crises of state and class domination," and further "transnational relations have contributed to the emergence of all social-revolutionary crises and have invariably helped to shape revolutionary struggles and outcomes" (1979:17, 19).

However, against Wallerstein's world-economy approach to states, Skocpol takes the position "that nation-states are, more fundamentally, organizations geared to maintain control of home territories and populations and to undertake actual or potential military competition with other states in the international system." The international system "represents an analytically autonomous level of transnational reality—*interdependent* in its structure and dynamics with world capitalism, but not reducible to it" (1979:22). More concretely, Skocpol asserts:

> Modern social revolutions have happened only in countries situated in disadvantaged positions within international arenas. In particular, the realities of military backwardness or political dependency have crucially affected the occurrence and course of social revolutions. Although uneven economic development always lies in the background, developments within the international states system as such— especially defeats in wars or threats of invasion and struggles over colonial controls—have directly contributed to virtually all outbreaks of revolutionary crises. . . . International military balances and conflicts have, moreover, provided the "space" necessary for the completion and political consolidation of social revolutions. . . . In the final analysis, too, the outcomes of social revolutions have always been powerfully conditioned not only by international politics but also by the world-economic constraints and opportunities faced by emergent new regimes. (1979:23, and see 41–42)

While Skocpol faults Wallerstein for the economic reductionism of his approach to the system of international states, she also faults classical Marxism for its theoretical reductionism (in the last analysis) of state structures to class relations, arguing,

> We must also focus upon the points of intersection between international conditions and pressures, on the one hand, and class-structured economies and politically organized interests, on the other hand. State executives and their followers will be found to be maneuvering to extract resources and build administrative and coercive organizations precisely at this intersection. Here, consequently, is the place to look for the political contradictions that help launch social revolutions. Here, also, will be found the forces that shape the rebuilding of state organizations within social-revolutionary crises. (1979:32)

Finally, and most damaging, Skocpol maintains, "The fact remains . . . that classical Marxism failed to foresee or adequately explain the autonomous power, for good or ill, of states as administrative and coercive machineries embedded in a militarized international states system" (1979:292).

There is an important sense in which Skocpol's criticism of classical Marxism (in its theoretical imagery) is, of course, correct. Karl Marx, most notably in his famous preface *A Contribution to the Critique of Political Economy*, put forth a powerful but quite abstract and very general theory of those major changes in history that proceed by social revolutions in modes of production, with their attendant transformations of social relations, political and legal institutions, and structures of perception, culture, forms of consciousness, and ideologies. Presenting his theory as "the outcome of conscientious research carried on over many years," Marx stressed common processes and only hinted at factors that may lead to *variations* in the courses and outcomes of social revolutions (e.g., successful or incomplete political revolutions), leaving out altogether (except by inference) the trans- and international contexts of revolutions. One of the ways in which the problem can be treated with respect to the units that appear in classical Marxism, *and* as a way to flesh out its abstract and general theory of the workings of capitalism and working-class revolution, is to carefully examine Marx and Engels's historical and journalistic writings and correspondence on revolutions.[2] These writings have led an ambiguous existence in the corpus of classical Marxism, involving, as any general sociological perspective does, a tension between theory and history. What I propose to do is to make explicit their model of nineteenth-century international relations as the latter conditioned and were conditioned by wars, revolutions, and counterrevolutions. By so doing, we can examine Marx and Engels's more detailed specification of recurrent processes and varying outcomes in the class struggles of the nineteenth century. But before doing so, I will briefly consider their more general statements about capitalism as an emerging world economy and its relationship to states. Then I will switch to consider the international system of states as the focus, its relationship to the world economy, and its role in the varying courses and outcomes of revolutions.

Marx's Conception of the Trans- and International Dimensions of Capitalism

To paraphrase Engels, the causes, course, and outcome of a revolution cannot be fully understood without taking into account its "foreign relations" (1952:58). Before, after, and concurrent with their analysis of the foreign relations of revolutions, Marx and Engels set forth a general conception of the intrinsically "international character of capitalist system." In the late 1850s, when Marx resumed his economic studies, he planned to include the following subjects:

> (3) Concentration of bourgeois society in the form of the state. Viewed in relation to itself. The "unproductive" classes. Taxes. State debt. Public credit. The population. The colonies. Emigration. (4) The international relation of production. International division of labour. International exchange. Export and import. Rate of exchange. (5) The world market and crises. (1973:108; cf. Marx and Engels, 1965:104)

With this plan in mind, let us turn to a consideration of their approach to and characterization of the capitalist world economy.

Marx and Engels's unit of analysis was dependent on the problem they wished to analyze. I will briefly mention the different levels they treated in terms of scope. For certain problems, their focus was on the nation (or areas of a nation), which is used synonymously with society. A good part of their most theoretical work stays on this level. On another level, a historically developed "community" of nations and the relations between them was the focus of analysis.

Engels spoke of Europe as a "compact cultural area . . . a system of predominantly national states exerting mutual influence on each other . . . " This "closed area of civilization" was composed of Western Europe, with Poland, Hungary, and Scandinavia as "advance posts" (Engels, 1962:144; 1963:216–17). (He might have added parts of Russia.) Europe was, of course, the area with which they were most concerned. Finally, on the most general level, Marx and Engels took the whole historical world as their unit of analysis by constructing trans- and international models composed of nations and cultural areas and their relationship to other cultural areas (e.g., the impact of England and Europe on Eastern civilizations and the reciprocal effects of colonization). On all levels of analysis, the concept of a dominant "social formation" plays a major role (Tucker, 1969:223–24). The dominant social formation of concern here is bourgeois society, with its capitalist mode of production.

The Creation of a World Market and the Transnational Character of Bourgeois Society

According to Marx, "the specific task of bourgeois society is the establishment of a world market, at least in outline, and of production based on this world market" (Marx and Engels, 1965:111). Thus "the modern history of capital dates from the creation in the 16th century of a world-embracing commerce and a world-embracing market" (Marx, 1906:163).

In Volume 1 of *Capital*, Marx characterized the international and political aspects of the "primitive accumulation" as follows:

The different momenta of primitive accumulation distribute themselves now, more or less in chronological order, particularly over Spain, Portugal, Holland, France, and England. In England at the end of the 17th century, they arrive at a systematical combination, embracing the colonies, the national debt, the modern mode of taxation, and the protectionist system. These methods depend in part on brute force, *e.g.*, the colonial system. But they all employ the power of the State, the concentrated and organised force of society, to hasten, hothouse fashion, the process of transformation of the feudal mode of production into the capitalist mode, and to shorten the transition. Force is the midwife of every old society pregnant with a new one. It is itself an economic power. (1906:823–24).

A distinction was made by Marx between two periods in the history of Western European capitalism. "In the period of manufacture properly so-called . . . commercial supremacy . . . gives industrial predominance." Thus the importance of the colonial system at that time, whereas after the Industrial Revolution (ca. 1800) "industrial supremacy implies commercial supremacy" (1906:826). So while the world market "forms the basis for . . . [the capitalist] mode of production . . . the immanent necessity of this mode of production to produce on an ever-enlarged scale tends to extend the world-market continually so that it is not commerce in this case which revolutionizes industry but industry which revolutionizes commerce" (Marx and Engels, n.d.a:271). And with it went the creation of the means of transport and communication to carry on such commerce (see Marx, 1906:419–20).

Next, Marx and Engels characterized the trans- and international character of bourgeois society: civil society "embraces the whole material intercourse of individuals within a definite stage of the development of productive forces." To the extent that it does so, it "transcends the State and the nation, though, on the other hand again, it must assert itself towards foreign peoples as nationality, and inwardly must organize itself as State." This becomes completely the case only with bourgeois society (Marx and Engels, 1947:26–27). This is so—especially when industrial production became dominant—because "the need of a constantly expanding market for its products chases the bourgeoisie over the whole surface of the globe."[3]

The worldwide consequences of the expansion of bourgeois society were described by Marx and Engels in *The Communist Manifesto* as follows:

> The bourgeoisie has through its exploitation of the world market given a cosmopolitan character to production and consumption in every country. . . . All old-established national industries have been destroyed or are daily being destroyed . . . by industries that no longer work up indigenous raw material, but raw material drawn from the remotest zones; industries whose products are consumed not only at home, but in every quarter of the globe. . . . And as in material, so also in intellectual production. The intellectual creations of individual nations become common property. National one-sidedness and narrow-mindedness become more and more impossible, and from the numerous national and local literatures there arises a world literature.

Bourgeois society created "the universal intercourse founded upon the mutual dependency of mankind, and the means of that intercourse" (Marx and Engels, 1959:38). This meant the "transformation of history into world-history." That is, in contrast to the "local" existence of individuals there occurred "for the first time" the world-historical existence of individuals, i.e., existence of individuals which is directly linked up with world history" (Marx and Engels, 1947:39, 24–26). National and local isolation were broken down, and action came to have implications beyond the nation. It followed that individuals have potentially a world-historical consciousness, not only economically but also politically and culturally. As a result, as Marx and Engels observed, a material basis for the spread of revolutionary ideas was created. In summary, these phenomena result from "the entanglement of all peoples in the net of the world-market" and hence "the international [and transnational] character of the capitalistic regime" (Marx, 1906:836).

In the passage quoted above from the *Manifesto*, Marx and Engels stated that the introduction of new industries "becomes a life and death question for all civilized nations." They continued: the bourgeoisie "compels all nations, on pain of extinction, to adopt the bourgeois mode of production; it compels them to introduce what it calls civilization in their midst, i.e., to become bourgeois themselves. In one word, it creates a world after its own image." The nations that introduced the bourgeois mode of production, the advanced European ones, developed similar class structures. With the advances of the capitalist mode of production, social classes became transnational. Of big industry, Marx and Engels said, "Generally speaking, it created everywhere the same relation between the classes of society, and thus destroyed the peculiar individuality of the various nationalities" (1963:57). This meant that in each bourgeois nation there were similar classes with similar interests, similar class conflicts, and similar tendencies to action and ideas. For a nice example, Engels observed the existence of a "noble-bourgeois rationalist International—without fatherland" in the late eighteenth century (Marx and Engels, 1952:32). The transnational character of bourgeois society made possible the diffusion of revolutionary ideas and the phenomenon of simultaneous revolutions—the tendency for revolutions to cluster in time and space. Speaking of the basis for the communist revolution (but also with application to the bourgeois revolutions), Marx and Engels said that

> only with this universal development of productive forces is a *universal* intercourse between men established, which produces in all nations simultaneously the phenomenon of the "propertyless" mass (universal competition), makes each nation dependent on the revolutions of the others, and finally has put *world-historical*, empirically universal individuals in place of local ones. (1963:24–25)

For Marx and Engels, revolutions and the models of action they provide became world-historical events.

The World Economy, International Relations, and Revolution

Speaking of the last half of the fifteenth century, the age of the Renaissance, Engels said, "Royalty, with the support of the burghers of the towns, broke the power of the feudal nobility and established the great monarchies, based essentially on nationality, within which the modern nations and modern bourgeois society came to development" (1963:1). Despite the increasingly transnational character of bourgeois society, "the bourgeoisie of each nation still retained separate national interests" (Marx and Engels, 1963:57)—especially when confronting the bourgeoisie of other nations. This conflict of interests stemmed not only from the national frameworks within which bourgeois society developed and from traditional international rivalries of states, but also from the empirical fact of differences in the class structures of nations due to the "uneven" development of productive forces and diverse modes of production between them.

Briefly, I will note Marx and Engels's descriptions of the manifestations of international competition from about 1650 to 1800. The competition for colonial markets, and the world market in general, as a means to develop industry and thus secure economic and political leadership for the bourgeoisie of specific nations, stimulated efforts to establish colonial monopolies, the institution of protective tariffs, and trade wars. Here is Marx and Engels's characterization:

> Commerce and navigation had expanded more rapidly than manufacture, which played a secondary role; the colonies were becoming considerable consumers; and after long struggles the separate nations shared out the opening world-market among themselves. This period

begins with the Navigation Laws and colonial monopolies. The competition of the nations among themselves was excluded as far as possible by tariffs, prohibitions and treaties; and in the last resort the competitive struggle was carried on and decided by wars (especially naval wars). The mightiest maritime nation, the English, retained preponderance in trade and manufacture. Here, already, we find concentration on one country. Manufacture was all the time sheltered by protective duties in the home market, by monopolies in the colonial market, and abroad as much as possible by differential duties . . . . (1963:54)

As the quotation indicates, they were referring to the period of the beginning of England's domination of the world market.

More central here is Marx and Engels's analysis of the consequence of international competition for the development of the conditions of revolution. After commenting on the uneven development of capitalism within countries and how workers not employed in big industry are worse off than those who are, they pointed out, "The countries in which big industry is developed act in a similar manner [as they do on the backward districts in such countries] upon the more or less non-industrial countries, in so far as the latter are swept by universal commerce into the universal competitive struggle" (Marx and Engels, 1963:58). The concern here is first with the "less non-industrial countries," that is, the European ones. The international pressure of competition on backward countries—those late in establishing modern industry and then struggling to get a piece of the world market—caused (and causes) them to introduce such industry "hothouse fashion," disrupting traditional relations in such societies. Of their theory of revolution, centering on "the contradiction between the productive forces and the form of intercourse," Marx and Engels said:

> But also to lead to collisions in a country, this contradiction need not necessarily come to a head in this particular country. The competition with industrially more advanced countries, brought about by the expansion of international intercourse, is sufficent to produce a similar contradiction in countries with a backward industry (e.g. the latent proletariat in Germany brought into view by the competition of English industry. (1963:73–74)

And it followed that a contradiction between consciousness and social existence "can also occur in a particular national sphere of relations through the appearance of the contradiction, not within the national orbit, but between this national consciousness and the practice of other nations, i.e., between the national and the general consciousness of a nation" (Marx and Engels, 1963:20–21). As Marx had noted in the introduction to his "Contribution to the Critique of Hegel's *Philosophy of Right*," the advanced nations provide theoretical and practical models for action in backward nations in their attempt to catch up. (Of course, existing ruling classes and the intellectual representatives of potentially revolutionary classes will interpret such models differently, selecting various aspects of them.) What we can conclude, then, is that not only the transnational aspects of bourgeois society but also its international aspects have to be taken account of in the causal pattern of conditions for revolution.

War and Revolution: The Uneven Development of Societies

Of continental Europe, Marx wrote in the first preface to *Capital* that

> we . . . suffer not only from the development of capitalist production, but also from the incompleteness of that development. Alongside of modern evils, a whole series of inherited evils oppress us, arising from the passive survival of antiquated modes of production, with their inevitable train of social and political anachronisms. We suffer not only from the living, but from the dead . . . . (1906:13)

The conception of "uneven" development of societies in Marx and Engels's work can help us to account for the frequent association of war with revolution. Along with bourgeois societies, there have been nonbourgeois ones with more traditional modes of production, and thereby different classes, class interests, and consequently different domestic and foreign policies, which have been conditioned by these as well as by state interests of the more traditional variety. Not only do revolutions provide opportunities for such nation-states to advance and protect their interests, but bourgeois revolutions have been a threat to their legitimacy at home and in international politics. This is especially the case given the transnational character of bourgeois society, the consequent diffusion of revolutionary ideas, and the transnational character of new classes that develop within a "backward" nation-state when it introduces modern industry. Such classes have interests that transcend the nation-state and may put them in alliances with revolutionary classes elsewhere. This has been the basis for the intervention of states with the aim of stopping a revolution against a regime with which its legitimacy is tied up. The revolutionized nation may respond by revolutionary war to preserve its existence—thus the frequent association of war and revolution.

Turning the causal pattern around, Marx and Engels frequently observed that defeat in war plays a part in the causes of revolutions. War (whatever its cause) is a test for the legitimacy and political effectiveness of a backward nation-state. Defeat in war can be that event that changes the political situation, creating a revolutionary situation subjectively as well as objectively. In short, in the modern world, revolutions are international events.

International Stratification: The World Economy, Dependency, and Colonialism

In Marx and Engels's perspective there is another aspect of the expansion of bourgeois society in addition to its horizontal spread. It creates a pattern of international stratification through the advanced nations' domination of the world market and through colonialism. In *The Communist Manifesto*, Marx and Engels wrote:

> The bourgeoisie, by the rapid improvement of all instruments of production, by the immensely facilitated means of communication, draws all, even the most barbarian, nations into civilization . . . . Just as it has made the country dependent on the towns, so it has made barbarian and semi-barbarian countries dependent on the civilized ones, nations of peasants on nations of bourgeois, the East on the West.

In a more developed analysis in Volume 2 of *Capital*, Marx anticipated world-system theory when he said,

> Within its process of circulation, in which industrial capital functions either as money or as commodities, the circuit of industrial capital, whether as money-capital, or as commodity-capital, crosses the commodity circulation of the most diverse modes of social production, so far as they produce commodities. No matter whether commodities are the output of production based on slavery, of peasants (Chinese, Indian ryots), of communes (Dutch East Indies), of state enterprise

(such as existed in former epochs of Russian history on the basis of serfdom) or of half-savage hunting tribes, etc. —as commodities and money they come face to face with the money and commodities in which the industrial capital presents itself and enter as much into its circuit as into that of the surplus-value borne in the commodity-capital, provided the surplus-value is spent as revenue; hence they enter into both branches of circulation of commodity-capital. The character of the process of production from which they originate is immaterial . . . . It is therefore the universal character of the origin of the commodities, the existence of the market as world-market, which distinguishes the process of circulation of industrial capital. What is true of the commodities of others is also true of the money of others. Just as commodity-capital faces money only as commodities, so this money functions vis-à-vis commodity-capital only as money. Money here performs the functions of world-money. (1967:109–10)

In summary, the expansion of bourgeois society imposed social revolutions on traditional—that is, non-Western—societies by establishing colonies and disrupting their traditional modes of production (with its cheap commodities) and/or pushing them toward the production of commodities and thereby introducing the means of their "modernization." By so doing, it also "caused" anticolonial nationalism as a new form of consciousness.

To pull together the strands of the exposition at this point, Marx and Engels characterized the internal and external relations of a nation this way:

The relations of different nations among themselves depend upon the extent to which each has developed its productive forces, the division of labour and internal intercourse. This statement is generally recognized. But not only the relation of one nation to others, but also the whole internal structure of the nation itself depends on the stage of development reached by its production and its internal and external intercourse . . . . (1963:8)

Marx asserted in his lecture on free trade, in Brussels on January 9, 1948, "All the destructive phenomena which unlimited competition gives rise to within one country are reproduced in more gigantic proportions on the world market" (Marx, 1953:222). Further, on the impact of internal class conflicts on international competition, Marx stated in *The Poverty of Philosophy:* "If the monopolists restrict their mutual competition by means of partial associations, competition increases among the workers; and the more the mass of the proletarians grows as against the monopolists of one nation, the more desperate competition becomes between the monopolists of different nations . . ." (1953:152). Finally, on the impact of capitalism on the world, Marx observed, "The centralization of capital is essential to the existence of capital as an independent power. The destructive influence of that centralization upon the markets of the world does but reveal, in the most gigantic dimensions, the inherent organic laws of political economy now at work in every civilized town . . ." (Marx and Engels, 1959:38). It requires little imagination to see the workings of these organic laws of political economy in the contemporary First and Third Worlds and between them.

With this background of Marx and Engels's general *structural* conception of the world relations of capitalism, I will turn to their depiction of another dimension of social revolutions. As Skocpol has characterized it, "Another kind [other than the world capitalist economy] of transnational structure—an international system of competing states—has also shaped the dynamic and uneven course of modern world history" (1979:20, and see 21–22). This is precisely the dimension she has, incorrectly, accused classical Marxism of overlooking.

By way of clarification, a caveat is in order: the following reconstruction of Marx and Engels's conception of nineteenth-century international relations is *not* intended as an argument for the correctness of their views and their historical accuracy in all aspects. Marx and Engels can be criticized for their notions of the "great historic nations" and the ways it led them to underestimate, as examples, the force of Czech nationalism and the importance of the Italian *risorgimento* in reviving the democratic and workers' movements after the 1850s. And sharing the view of enlightened liberals (as did Max Weber) of the threat posed by Russia to European civilization, they overestimated the capacity of the czarist state to get its way in Europe (Fernbach, 1974a:49–52; 1974b:29, 33). The purpose is to call attention to and specify those neglected aspects of Marx and Engels's work that have a bearing on accounting for the variations in the outcomes of revolutionary upheavals.

Marx and Engels on Nineteenth-Century Patterns of International Relations and Revolutions

France: The Revolutionary Center

In the pattern of nineteenth-century international relations, France (and more particularly Paris) had played the role of the revolutionary initiator, specifically from 1789 to 1848 (and almost again in 1871).[4] For Marx and Engels, the great French Revolution of 1789 was *the* model of a (bourgeois) revolution. In addition, France was always a reference point in their writings on revolutionary tactics. This was so, according to Engels, because "France is the land where, more than anywhere else, the historical class struggles were each time fought out to a decision, and where, consequently, the changing political forms within which they move and in which their results are summarized have been stamped in the sharpest outlines" (in Marx, 1885:13–14). The French Revolution of 1789 had climaxed the bourgeois revolution of the eighteenth century and plunged Europe into a generation of wars and revolutions. Again, in 1830 the July Revolution in France set off a chain of upheavals. In 1844, Marx expected that the impending German revolution would be set off by a crowing of the Gallic cock—that is, by a revolution in France. And of the French revolution of 1848, Engels said in the year of his death that from France, which "had dominated the whole of European history since 1789," "now once again the signal had gone forth for general revolutionary change" (in Marx, 1935:12).

France's revolutionary mantle produced a whole ideological tradition and set of beliefs about the course of European revolution. Marx wrote in 1882:

> The little bit of republican internationalism between 1830 and 1848, was grouped around France, which was destined to free Europe. *Hence it increased French chauvinism* in such a way as to cause the world-liberating mission of France and with it France's native right to be in the lead to get in our way every day even now.

The Blanquists presented a caricature of this view, which could be dispelled only by historical events, as it was being dispelled in Engels's last view (Marx and Engels, 1952:117). The defeat of the June insurrection of 1848 in France and Bonaparte's parody of the Napoleonic Empire broke (temporarily) the revolutionary mission of France. During Bonaparte's Second Empire, France appeared to be the leading counterrevolutionary power on the Continent. The Franco-Prussian War of 1870 produced the downfall of the Second Empire, and the Paris commune for a brief moment appeared to Marx to have reestablished France's revolutionary role. The Germans showed the international historical respect for France's "glorious past" when they did not march on the Commune but only occupied a small section of the city, not even suggesting that the Parisians disarm (Engels, 1968:79). However, in Marx and Engels's revolutionary calculus, the defeat of France, and particularly the Commune, by the German and French governments definitely shifted the center of gravity of the working-class movement from France to Germany. Yet the historical position of France affected Engels's calculation of revolutionary probabilities up to the 1890s. Engels wrote to Friedrich A. Sorge on December 31, 1892, "this struggle will be fought out only in Germany, even if, as is possible, it first breaks out in France" (Marx and Engels, 1953:245). The historical experience in question and the ideology it produced were summarized by Engels's remark (1894) that "thanks to their century-long revolutionary activities, the French Republicans [and other European radicals] considered France to be the politically chosen nation" (Marx and Engels, 1952:230). In short, the Frenchmen were possessed of an "old tradition of revolutionary initiative."

Russian Czarism: The Counterrevolutionary State

On the other side of the coin, Russia—precisely, czarist Russia—was for Marx and Engels the leading counterrevolutionary state. In his brilliant essay "The Foreign Policy of Russian Czarism" (1890), Engels explained the twofold interest of the Western European labor parties in a victory for the Russian revolutionary party in this way:

> First, because the Russian Czarist empire forms the greatest fortress, reserve position and at the same time reserve army of European reaction, because its mere passive existence already constitutes a threat and a danger to us. Second, however—and this point has still not been sufficiently emphasized on our part—because it blocks and disturbs our normal development through its ceaseless intervention in Western affairs, intervention aimed moreover at conquering geographical positions which will secure it the mastery of

Europe, and thus make impossible the liberation of the European proletariat. (Marx and Engels, 1952:25)[5]

It is worthwhile to survey briefly Marx and Engels's analysis of the means by which Russian czarism achieved this putative position of dominance in European politics. The Russia of 1760 was a "homogeneous, unassailable country [that] had for neighbors only countries which either apparently or actually were falling into ruin, which were nearing dissolution and hence were pure raw material for conquest" (Marx and Engels, 1952:28–31, and see 63–64). So when Catherine came to the throne (1762), "never had the world situation been more favorable to Czarist plans for conquest." Europe was divided into two armed camps by the Seven Years' War. England had broken French sea power in America and India, and broke off its alliance with Frederick II of Prussia, who was forced to turn to Catherine for protection, with the hope of getting the part of Poland that kept East Prussia divided from the main part of his realm. In 1764, he and Catherine secretly agreed to defend with arms the Polish constitution against any attempt at reform. "Therewith the future partition of Poland was decided" (Marx and Engels, 1952:32–34).

Of central concern here is the relation of the French Revolution to Russian foreign policy. To quote Engels: "The outbreak of the French Revolution was a new stroke of luck for Catherine. Far from fearing the spread of revolutionary ideas toward Russia, she saw in it only a new opportunity to spread discord among the European states in order that Russia might thereby obtain a free hand." The revolution gave Catherine the opportunity of again chaining Austria and Prussia (which had been on Poland's side against Russia from 1787 to 1791) to an alliance with Russia and, while they were occupied at the French frontiers, of making new conquests in Poland (Marx and Engels, 1952:35).

In Marx and Engels's analysis, the outcome of the French Revolution and the defeat of Napoleon made Russia, through its leadership of the Holy Aliance, "the arbiter of Europe." Likewise in 1849, the Russians' assistance to Austria in defeating the Hungarian Revolution was a "decisive" moment in the success of the counterrevolution in central and eastern Europe. By virtue of its geographical position, diplomacy, and contribution to the counterrevolution, Russia was once again reaffirmed as the arbiter of Europe.

According to Marx and Engels, the Crimean War was the first weakening in the chain of Russian power. But due to the fear on the part of the Western governments and Russia of a general war turning into a European revolution, the war was not prosecuted seriously, and Russia came off better than could have been expected. The war was a turning point, however, in the internal development of Russia, a powerful stimulus to state-sponsored industrialization and consequent transformation of its traditional class structure. Even in 1875, after the Franco-Prussian War—which made Prussia strong enough to become a rival to Russia as the dominant power in Europe—when a war between Russia and Prussia seemed imminent, Russia could still appear as the arbiter of Europe (Marx and Engels, 1952:39–52, especially 46–47, 203). The czar again exploited the peace in Europe—as had traditionally been done—to move into the Near East. In Marx and Engels's view, the resulting Russo-Turkish War was as disastrous for the czar morally as materially. However, the major point that emerged from Marx and Engels's analysis was that Russian diplomacy had survived not only "undamaged, but with direct profit, so many European revolutions" (Marx and Engels, 1952:44). In short, Marx and Engels considered Russia to be the major brake on the European democratic and socialist movements. In fact, as Engels wrote in 1875, "the present Russian empire is the last great center of support for all reactionary forces in western Europe. . . . Therefore, no revolution in western Europe can be definitely and finally victorious as long as the present Russian state exists at its side" (Marx and Engels, 1952:203). Marx had written a year earlier, "And unless the internal development of Russia does not soon take a revolutionary course the German victory over France will as certainly bring about a war between Russia and Germany as the Prussian victory over Austria at Sadowa brought about the Franco-Prussian War . . . " (Marx and Engels, 1952:113–14).

The following is Marx's summary conclusion about the role of Russia in international relations and revolutions in the nineteenth century:

> . . . after the Napoleonic wars Russia took the lion's share of the former Prussian- and Austrian-Polish provinces, and now stepped

forward openly as the arbiter of Europe, a role which it continued to play without interruption until 1853. . . . During the revolutionary years the suppression of Hungary by Russia was a decisive factor in Central and Eastern Europe as the Paris June Days battle had been for the West; and when Czar Nicholas soon thereafter sat as judge in Warsaw over the King of Prussia and the Emperor of Austria, the supremacy of European reaction was assured jointly with the supremacy of Russia in Europe. . . . Only because in 1870 the Russian army prevented Austria from taking sides with France, could Prussia defeat France and achieve the Prussian-German military monarchy. In all these actions of vital national importance we see the Russian army in the background. . . . Yet, the Russian army will always be of service against an internal [revolutionary] movement in Prussia. Today official Russia is still the sanctuary and shield of the entire European reaction, its armies form the reserves of all the other armies which are charged with the suppression of the working classes of Europe. (Marx and Engels, 1952:113–14)

One more point in Marx and Engels's description of the international roles of France and Russia should be added: they were the two nations on the Continent that were surrounded by great historical ideologies. The belief in "the innate revolutionary initiative" of France, held by the French and other European radicals, has already been mentioned. As to the Russians (including radicals), they were "firmly convinced of the Panslavist mission of Russia," only a few being "free from Panslavist leaning or memories." In Marx and Engels's opinion, however, Pan-Slavism was "a smoke screen for world dominion, appearing in the cloak of a non-existent *Slavic* nationality, and therefore our, as well as the Russian people's worst enemy" (Marx and Engels, 1952:118).

Germany: Between Revolution and Counterrevolution

THE AUSTRO-HUNGARIAN EMPIRE

In the nineteenth century, Austria, despite its counterrevolutionary international policies, was, in Marx and Engels's view, an outpost against Russian advances in the Near East (Marx and Engels, 1952:56–90; see especially 57–58, 62, 65). However, with a revolution in Russia the Russian people would give up "the traditional policy of conquest of the czars," replacing the "phantasies of world conquest" with a concern for their vital interests at home, and "on the same day Austria will lose its single, historical justification for existence—that of a barrier against the Russian drive toward Constantinople." Further, not only would a world war usher in (or be prevented by) a Russian revolution, but it would "cause not only reactionary classes and dynasties but also entire reactionary peoples to disappear from the earth" (Marx and Engels, 1952:53–54, 67).

REACTIONARY PRUSSIA

According to Marx and Engels, the source of Russia's power in Europe was its control over Prussia. During the revolution of 1848, Marx and Engels had advocated that Germany carry out a revolutionary war against the Russians to keep the revolution on the Continent moving, shift the revolution in Germany to the left, and "call in question the entire European balance of power" by restoring Poland (Marx and Engels, 1952:93–94). But the Prussians put down the Polish movement and contributed to the counterrevolution in Europe and Germany.

> Up to now the Germans have always been called the mercenaries of despotism throughout all Europe. We are far from denying the shameful part of the Germans in the disgraceful Wars from 1792–1815 against the French Revolution, in the suppression of Italy since 1815 and of Poland since 1772. Who, however, stands behind the Germans, who uses them as its mercenaries or its advance guard? England and Russia. . . . (Marx and Engels, 1952:77–78)

In 1863, Bismarck helped Russia put down the Polish insurrection (and Russia supported Prussia's war for Schleswig-Holstein). Marx noted the reason for the suppression of the Poles: "The 'State' of Prussia (a very different creature from Germany) can exist neither *without* the present Russia nor *with* an independent Poland. The whole of Prussian history leads to this conclusion, at which the Herren Hohenzollerns (including Frederick II) arrived long ago" (Marx and Engels, n.d.b:41).

Louis Bonaparte supported Prussia in its war of 1866 against Austria, just as Russia supported Prussia in its war against France in 1870, and both had hoped for a long war that would exhaust the combatants. That did not happen. The war of 1870, as Marx and

Engels presciently observed, had serious consequences for the pattern of international relations. To quote Engels: "Russia's preponderant influence in Europe had as its necessary prerequisite its traditional power over Germany—a power which was now broken," that is, in 1870 to 1871 (Marx and Engels, 1952:49). The war had made Prussia the most powerful state in Europe—with Russian assistance. At the same time, this put Prussia into rivalry with Russia and drove France into Russia's arms, creating the situation for a world war that would pit Germany and its allies against France, Russia, and their allies. (Engels also pointedly noted that "there are no greater Francophobes in the world than the Prussian Junkers" because of the material damage to their interests done by the French, as well as the worse "fact that the godless French by their outrageous revolution had so turned people's heads that the old Junker domination was more or less finished with even in Prussia" [Engels, 1968:771.] Engels suggested that German "militarism," namely the Prussian army and state, "will go to smash—most likely in a war with Russia, which can last four years and where the only thing you can get is sickness and shattered bones" (Marx and Engels, n.d.b: 49–50).

In conclusion, I have noted Marx and Engels's view that Russia was the bastion of European reaction and that this was especially important to Germany: "Germany is the nearest neighbor. Germany must sustain the first shock from the armies of Russian reaction. The overthrow of the Russian tsarist state and the dissolution of the Russian empire is therefore one of the first conditions for the final victory of the German proletariat" (Marx and Engels, 1952:203). A war, one that might usher in a Russian revolution, or set back the socialist movement, especially in Germany, might be provoked by some Poles, *"which is to liberate them with German aid"* (Marx and Engels, 1953:248).

Poland: The Key Revolutionary Nation

For Marx and Engels, Poland was, from an *international* point of view, the key revolutionary linch pin in Europe—more important than France, after the latter had exhausted its revolutionary mission. Poland was the link between the reactionary Holy Alliance and the Revolution. After 1848—despite the failure of the revolutions—

except for Ireland and Poland, the major European nations achieved independence. As Marx put it in 1882,

> We may leave Ireland out of consideration here, since it affects the situation on the European continent only very indirectly. But Poland is situated in the center of the continent, and the maintenance of its partition is the very tie which binds the Holy Alliance together again and again. We have, therefore, great interest in Poland. (Marx and Engels, 1952:116)

The Polish defense of its constitution of 1791, which incorporated the principles of the French Revolution, saved the latter from the First Coalition (Marx and Engels, 1952:111). Also, as Marx and Engels saw it, the Warsaw insurrection in 1830 saved the French from a second anti-Jacobin war. An additional reason for Marx and Engels's considering Poland so important in the occurrence and course of European revolutions is expressed in Marx's letter to Engels of December 2, 1856:

> . . . what has decided me definitely for Poland, on the basis of my latest studies of Polish history, is the historical fact that the intensity and vitality of all revolutions since 1789 can be gauged pretty accurately by their attitude to Poland. Poland is their "external" thermometer. This can be demonstrated in detail by French history. It is obvious in our short German revolutionary epoch, and equally so in the Hungarian.

This held for all revolutionary governments, *"including that of Napoleon I,"* with the excepton of the Committee of Public Safety, which refused to intervene in Poland because of its mistrust of Kosciusko's ideology and policy (Marx and Engels, 1965:95). Marx and Engels argued that the European bourgeoisie had constantly betrayed Poland in its struggle for independence against the Holy Alliance, especially after socialist tendencies occurred in the Polish movement of 1846 (Marx and Engels, 1952:118). Most important, the restoration of Poland was a necessity for two peoples, the Germans and the Russians. Why?

> A people which oppresses another cannot emancipate itself. The power which it uses to suppress the other finally always turns against itself. As long as Russian soldiers remain in Poland, the Russian people cannot free itself either politically or socially. But, at the

present state of Russian development it is certain that on the day on which Russia loses Poland the [revolutionary] movement in Russia itself will be powerful enough to overthrow the existing order of things. Independence of Poland and revolution in Russia mutually determine each other. And the independence of Poland and revolution in Russia—which is much nearer than appears on the surface due to the boundless social, political and financial disorder and to the corruption penetrating all official Russia—these events mean for the German workers: the limiting of the bourgeoisie, of the governments in short, of the reaction in Germany to their own resources—forces with which we will be able to deal in time ourselves. (Marx and Engels, 1952:115)

It followed for Marx and Engels that a revolution in Russia would be followed by revolutions in Poland, Prussia, and Austrian Germany.

Poland was interesting to Marx and Engels because of the connection of its nationalism with the international components of European revolutions. As Engels put it:

From the day of their repression on, the Poles came forward as revolutionaries and thereby bound their oppressors the more tightly to the counterrevolution. They forced their oppressors to uphold the patriarchal feudal system not only in Poland but also in their other domains. And particularly since the Cracow uprising of 1846, the struggle for the independence of Poland has also been a struggle for agrarian democracy—the only kind possible in Eastern Europe—against patriarchal-feudal absolutism. (Marx and Engels, 1952:92–93)

And Marx concluded,

I hold the view that there are *two* nations in Europe which do not only have the right but the duty to be nationalistic before they become internationalists: The Irish and Poles. They are internationalists of the best kind if they are very nationalistic. The Poles have understood this in all crises and have proved it on the battlefields of all revolutions. (Marx and Engels, 1952:118)

The mention of Ireland brings us to Marx and Engels's assessment of the place of England in world affairs.

England: Despot of the World Market

England was for Marx the classic case of the historical development of capitalism, showing the nations of Europe their future selves, and provided him with the empirical material for his theoretical analysis in *Capital*. As Marx and Engels made central to their depiction of global relations, after its bourgeois revolution of the seventeenth century, England became the dominant manufacturing and maritime nation in the eighteenth century, engaging in trade wars with its great rival, France. England was the first country to experience the Industrial Revolution, which not only changed class relations in England, but also put every other European nation in a state of economic backwardness. The resulting pressure caused other nations to adopt machinery. England's position in the world was close to hegemony at the outbreak of the French Revolution. And as Marx and Engels remind us, England joined the coalition of European states against the French Revolution, taking the opportunity to completely dominate France as a rival for control of the world market. England in 1815 had become without question the dominant industrial power in the world, its "workshop" and, as Marx labeled it in 1849, "the despot of the world market."

After the crisis of 1847, England's economic advance was even more astounding. As Engels characterized it:

> The revival of trade, after the crisis of 1847, was the dawn of a new industrial epoch. The repeal of the Corn Laws and the financial reforms subsequent thereon gave to English industry and commerce all the elbow-room they had asked for. The discovery of the Californian and Australian gold-fields followed in rapid succession. The colonial markets developed at an increasing rate their capacity for absorbing English manufactured goods. In India millions of hand-weavers were finally crushed out by the Lancashire powerloom. China was more and more being opened up. Above all, the United States—then, commercially speaking, a mere colonial market, but by far the biggest of them all—underwent an economic development astounding even for that rapidly progressive country. And, finally, the new means of communication introduced at the close of the preceding period—railways and ocean steamers—were now worked out on an international scale; they realised actually what had hitherto existed only potentially, a *world-market*. This world-market, at first, was composed of a number of chiefly or entirely agricultural countries grouped around one manufacturing centre—England—which consumed the greater part of their surplus raw produce, and supplied them in return with the greater part of their requirements in manufactured articles. No wonder Eng-

land's industrial progress was colossal and unparalleled, and such that the status of 1844 now appears to us as comparatively primitive and insignificant. . . . [emphasis added]

The assumption of the contemporary Free Trade Theory of Manchester was, as Engels noted, a vision of "England, the great manufacturing centre of an agricultural world, with an ever-increasing number of corn and cotton-growing Irelands revolving around her, the industrial sun . . . " (Marx and Engels, 1962:18–19, 25–26). This assumption turned out (as it is for the United States at present) to be untenable—but of this more below.

This economic dominance of England had several consequences in addition to the pressure it put on other European nations to industrialize. In Marx and Engels's conception, England's economic strength made it the material ingredient of the hub of European politics through the effect of the commercial crises, originating in England, on the Continent—they caused political revolutions. Further, English dominance of the world market linked Europe with Asia, so that crises and rebellions in Asia had an effect not only on England but, in their wake, on Europe also (see below).

Politically, in Marx's view, England had sided with the European reaction. (Marx even suspected England of a pro-Russian policy, despite the fact that its objective interests conflicted with those of Russia in Asia and the Near East. This Marx attempted to demonstrate in his *Secret Diplomatic History of the Eighteenth Century* and *The Story of the Life of Lord Palmerston* [1969].) In relation to European revolutions one might argue, by inference from Marx and Engels, that England was saved from revolutions by the American Revolution and the French revolutions of 1789 and 1848—or, more precisely, that reaction in England was most intense on the occasion of European (French) revolutions. This was due to the fact that the Irish, like the Poles, took the occasion of European revolutions to free themselves, in this instance from English domination. In summary, for Marx and Engels, England, by its economic superiority over Europe and domination of the world market, was able to finance European reaction against the radical bourgeois and proletarian movements, and saw as its mission propagating English constitutionalism there.

The long and the short of England's strategic role in world politics was, as Marx put it in a letter in 1870:

> England, being the metropolis of capital, the power which has hitherto ruled the world market, is for the present the most important country for the workers' revolution, and moreover the *only* country in which the material conditions for this revolution have developed up to a certain degree of maturity. Therefore to hasten the social revolution in England is the most important object of the International Working-men's Association. The sole means of hastening it is to make Ireland independent. . . . (Marx and Engels, 1962:552)

But there was only one circumstance that would allow for a successful Irish revolution: a world war. "The Old England can only be overthrown by a world war," and "the first result of a victorious working-class revolution in France will be European war," which by England's participation would be fought in Canada, Italy, India, Prussia, and Africa, and on the Danube. Such a war would create the conditions for a successful working-class uprising in England (see Marx and Engels, n.d.a:231). And, as Marx had it, once this "demiurge of the bourgeois cosmos" was in the hands of the working class, the Continent would follow.

The Sixth Power in Europe

What I have presented is a review of Marx and Engels's model of nineteenth-century international relations, including the "five so-called 'great' Powers": England, Russia, France, Prussia and Austria. But there was a "sixth power in Europe": "That is the power of the Revolution," in Marx's phrase, "which at given moments asserts its supremacy" over the reactionary states and "makes them tremble, every one of them," threatening and disrupting their legitimacy—that is, religion, property, and order—and shaking the "balance of power." Against Russia, "the great movement of 1789 called into potent activity an antagonist of formidable nature. We mean the European Revolution. . . . Since that epoch there have been in reality but two powers on the continent of Europe— Russia and Absolutism, the Revolution and Democracy" (Marx and Engels, 1952:183, 132–33, 169). The conflict of these two "powers" was the form of the major contradiction of the historical system of European trans- and international relations in the nineteenth century, first between the bourgeoisie and the nobility, and after 1848 between the bourgeoisie and the proletariat. Their revolutionary perspective makes clear Marx and Engels's grasp of worldwide forces stemming from the *transnational* character of bourgeois society and its classes. The set of "secondary" contradictions was the rivalries and wars between European states stemming from political and national as well as economic factors. This was the international aspect of the system. The two played together in the association of wars with revolutions and the clustering of revolutions.

The Clustering of Revolutions

The obvious conclusion one can arrive at from this presentation of Marx and Engels's approach to modern European revolutions is that in their view, major social revolutions are international events (see Tucker, 1969:223–24). In the most general sense, some of them represent major historical turning points—for example, the English Revolution of the seventeenth century, especially the French Revolution of 1789, the insurrection in Paris in June 1848, the Civil War in the United States, the Paris Commune—in short, they are "world historical." What Marx meant by this is that such revolutions bring into being and result from a new type of dominant social formation and hence bring new classes into power and/or new stages of class conflict to the fore.

Moreover, the revolution of one nation has an impact on the revolutions of others. First, in the least direct sense: nations that have advanced economically and politically through revolution cause pressure for nations in their cultural areas to imitate their advance and catch up, leading to hothouse change and disruptions of traditional class relations in "backward" societies. More specifically, a revolutionized society provides ideas and models for action for those in a less advanced society who are interested in revolutionizing it. The instances taken from Marx and Engels's historical writings that exemplify these phenomena are the influence of the Dutch Revolution on the English, the English (and American) on the French Revolution of 1789, and the last on nineteenth-century revolutions.

A somewhat different connection between revolutions, closer in time (and space), as Marx and Engels note, is the occurrence of revolutions simultaneously—that is, when the occurrence of a revolution in one place is the occasion for revolutions elsewhere. Some examples recognized and discussed by Marx and Engels were the clustering of peasant revolts during the pre-Reformation and Reformation periods in Europe; the spread of the Calvinist Reformation around the time of the revolt of Holland from Spain; the revolutions attending the English Civil War in Naples, Messina, and Lisbon (and Ireland), patterned on that of Holland; the revolutions during the great French Revolution; and the French revolution of July 1830. This occurs most clearly in the signal given for European revolutions by the French revolution of February 1848. Going beyond the mere empirical facts, such events indicate the pressure of the same causes across a whole cultural area or areas stemming from the diffusion of ideas and models of political and economic action and class forces rooted in the trans- and international character of bourgeois society.

A slightly different cause of the occurrences of simultaneous revolutions, made clear in Marx and Engels's writings about revolutions and their prescriptions for revolutionary action, is that revolutionary movements in nations under foreign domination take revolutions as opportunities for independence—for example, the Irish and Polish revolutions following the French ones in 1789 and 1830. Further, the course of the class conflicts of one revolution has effects on those of another revolution—for example, the French on the German revolution(s) of 1848. Finally, evidence that Marx and Engels employed such historical regularities in their expectation of proletarian revolution is their assertion that such a revolution could succeed only by the combined action of the proletariat of the most advanced European nations, England, France, and Germany (although the argument is usually developed theoretically). As a historical example, Marx argued that one reason for the defeat of the Paris Commune was the absence of simultaneous revolutions in the capitals of Europe.

War and Revolution: Some Relationships

The relationships between the events of these two broad categories are various. First, the general connection: in the middle of 1853, Marx, as noted above, wrote that the timid attitude of the Western governments to Russian advances in the Near East stemmed "from fear of a general war giving rise to a general revolution." The reactionary Western governments thus suffered "humiliation" in the face of their peoples, and "the approaching industrial crisis, also, is affected, and accelerated quite as much by this semi-Eastern complication as by the completely Eastern complication of China." A half year later, Marx incorrectly saw the commercial crisis and scarcity of food as reawakening agitation and disquietude among the proletariat. For a revolution to occur, "a signal only is wanted. . . . This signal the impending European war will give," and he said that such a war would look like that of 1792 to 1800. Russia was "more afraid of the revolution that must follow any general war on the Continent than the Sultan is afraid of the aggression of the Czar" (Marx and Engels, 1952:164, 182–83, 139). But war, or the threat of it, can prevent revolution—acting as a lightning rod.

Preparation for or playing at war, as Marx and Engels often noted, is one tactic of ruling classes and their governments to divert class conflict and restore prestige at home (see, e.g., Marx, 1940:32–33). Louis Bonaparte provided for Marx and Engels the type of this policy of how the necessity "of divesting revolutionary currents outwards produced wars," using the pretext of "the principle of nationality" (Engels in Marx, 1935:77). Of the possibility of a war in Italy in 1859, Marx wrote to LaSalle (February 6, 1859) that in addition to Bonaparte's needing a war to restore his prestige and solve his government's financial problems, "Russia is horrified by the prospect of an internal agrarian revolution and war abroad would perhaps be welcomed by the government as a diversion, not to mention all kinds of diplomatic purposes." He concluded,

> The war would naturally have serious consequences, and in the long run revolutionary ones for sure. But at the start it will bolster up Bonapartism in France, drive back the internal movement in England and Russia, arouse anew the pettiest passions in regard to the nationality issue in Germany, and will therefore, in my opinion, have first and foremost a counter-revolutionary effect in every respect. . . . (Marx and Engels, 1965:115–16)

To be clear about the mechanisms at work in the relationship between preparation for war and counterrevolutionary policy, Marx and Engels suggested that the power of reaction in Europe from the 1860s on, and especially after 1870, was buttressed by standing armies. The positive side to this, as Engels saw it, was that universal conscription and standing armies gave the working class military training and practice in arms, which skills they might one day put to use—against their own governments (Engels, 1962:235–36). But more important than standing armies in *preventing* revolution are wars, in that they promote nationalism. Engels wrote to Bebel in the 1880s that he regarded "a European war as a misfortune" that would "produce a conflagration of chauvinism for years to come, as every people would be fighting for its existence." All the work of the Russian revolutionaries "who are on the threshold of victory" would be destroyed by such a war. The German and French socialist parties would be overwhelmed by a wave of national hatred and chauvinism. At the height of the Bulgarian crisis in 1886, Engels wrote again to Bebel: "Among all the uncertainties, one thing only is certain—that after the war we should have to start again from the beginning, though on a more favourable basis than we have even today." Engels seemed to consider the unleashing of a general war as the only hope for stopping the growing revolutionary movement: for the ruling classes "a peace worse than war the result—at best; or a world war" (Engels, 1968:26–27).

Another, and equally obvious, relationship of war and revolution is that defeat in war or unsuccessful war can further erode the legitimacy and effectiveness of or produce a revolution against a state that is already weak in fact and in the opinion of its supporters.[6] Defeat in war was the occasion for the declaration of a republic following Bonaparte's defeat by the Germans in 1870. Also, Marx and Engels saw the Crimean and the Russo-Turkish wars as hastening the upheaval approaching in Russia. In September 1870, Marx wrote,

> What the Prussian jackasses do not see is that the present war is leading just as inevitably to a war between Germany and Russia as the War of 1866 led to the war between Prussia and France. . . . And such a war No. 2 will act as the midwife of the inevitable social revolution in Russia. (Marx and Engels, 1953:80–81)

Revolutions, being international events that threaten the international "balance of power" and, given the tendency of revolutions to spread, threaten the regimes whose legitimacy is tied up with the one(s) overthrown, serve to provoke intervention to affect their course and restore the old regime. In short, *major* social revolutions tend, in general, to divide the international world into revolutionary and counterrevolutionary states, and the affected societies into revolutionary and counterrevolutionary political tendencies. Writing of the social crises caused by the struggle between workers and capitalists (1867), Marx said that "it will also, like every internal conflict, call for aggression from without. Once more this conflict will clothe Russia anew with the role it had during the anti-Jacobine war and since the Holy Alliance, that of the pre-destined savior of order. It will enlist in Russia's ranks all the privileged classes of Europe" (Marx and Engels, 1952:108)—a prophetic remark.

As Marx and Engels noted, one response of a revolutionary state to such intervention may be war in defense of the revolution—revolutionary war (of various degrees). The most important instances of the phenomena mentioned above are the Wars of the Coalition during the radical phase of the French Revolution. Speaking of "the *critical period of the French Revolution*, namely from 10 August to 9 Thermidor," Engels said:

> The whole French Revolution is dominated by the War of the Coalition, all its pulsations depend upon it. If the allied army penetrates into France—predominant activity of the vagus nerve, violent heart-beat, revolutionary crisis. If it is driven back—predominance of the sympathetic nerve, the heart-beat becomes slower, the reactionary elements again push themselves into the foreground; the plebians, the origins of the later proletariat, whose energy alone has saved the revolution, are brought to reason and order.
>
> The tragedy is that the party supporting war *à outrance* [to the death], war for the emancipation of the nations, is proved in the right and that the Republic gets the better of all Europe, but only after that party itself has long been beheaded; while in place of the propagandist war comes the Peace of Basle and the bourgeois orgy of the Directory. (Marx and Engels, 1965:406)

Thus Marx and Engels believed that when revolutionary states are faced with counterrevolutionary intervention and carry out successful revolutionary wars, revolutionary power is consolidated and accelerated ideologically and organizationally (at least in the short run).

But, the absence of international counterrevolutionary challenge to the February Government in France in 1848 was the missing element for pushing the revolutionary government forward or throwing it overboard. In 1892, Engels was still governed by the model of the French Revolution when he wrote to Sorge in the United States of the danger of war becoming greater, and added that

> if the Russians start war against us, the German Socialists must fight the Russians and their allies, whoever they may be, *à outrance*. If Germany is crushed then we shall be too, while in the most favorable case the struggle will be such a violent one that Germany will be able to maintain itself only by revolutionary means, so that very possibly we shall be forced to come into power and play the part of 1793. . . . But although I think it would be a very great misfortune if it came to war and if the latter brought us to power prematurely, still one must be armed for this eventuality . . . (Marx and Engels, 1953:128)

Further, there is another consequence of intervention, with contemporary relevance. Speaking of the Chinese "revolution" of the 1850s, Marx said, "an interference on the part of the Western governments at this time can only serve to render the revolution more violent . . . " (Marx and Engels, n.d.a:21). Last, defeat in revolutionary war can result in defeat of a revolution, as was the case in Hungary in 1849 (or with the defeat of Napoleon, according to Engels).

Let us consider briefly the relationship of war, social change, and economic advance: the crisis of war, by breaking down traditional social patterns, can release social energies (see Marx and Engels, 1952:108, 183). On the connection of war and economic development, Marx said, "Economic expansion is greatly influenced by the army 'especially in times of war.' " (Yet Marx once remarked that a war is like dropping all the productive forces of a nation into the ocean.) In fact, "The whole history of the structure of middle-class society is clearly summarized in the history of armies" (see Marx and Engels, 1965:97, 180). War, as we have seen, can lead to social revolution, as in the Crimean War's effect on Russia. More precisely, it seems that the effects of war on social development depend on the "stage of development" of a society: war tends to consolidate social power in a society on the ascendant and contribute to the breakdown of a society on the decline. In a more prosaic way, success in war can contribute to economic advance through the medium of reparations.

Nineteenth-Century European International Relations and Revolution: A Summary

At this point, I will conclude by summarizing Marx and Engels's model of the pattern of nineteenth-century European international relations as they were conditioned by and, in turn, conditioned European revolutions. Europe in the nineteenth century was a victim of "double slavery," that is, *"English-Russian* slavery" (Marx, 1933:15). On the Continent, Russian czarism was the bulwark and reserve army of feudal and bourgeois reaction, deriving its influence in Europe from its traditional control over Prussia. The Franco-Prussian War altered this historical pattern. In the first place, according to Marx and Engels, the revolutionary center of gravity had shifted to Germany, which had the most advanced working-class movement, from France, which had played the role of revolutionary nation giving the signal for European revolutions and wars from 1789 to 1848. In the second place, the wars of 1866 against Austria and 1870 against France had made Prussia the most powerful state in Europe, making it the major rival to Russia, dividing Europe into two armed camps, and forcing France into alliance with Russia. Thus the situation was created for world war, which could be prevented only by a Russian revolution or a European revolution that would be a midwife to the impending Russian revolution.

At any rate, for Marx and Engels such a revolution would decisively alter the previous historical structure, for it would remove the international reserve fortress of European bourgeois and feudal regimes, putting them on their own—no longer protected by the Russian reactionary umbrella from the storm of revolution—and thus prepare for the settlement of the major transnational conflict in Europe, that between the bourgeoisie and the proletariat. Specifically, a Russian revolution would occur in conjunction with a revolution in Poland—whose partition had bound together the Holy Alliance and thus made Poland the catalyst in a Russian revolution—that would remove Austria's historical justification for existence as a barrier to Russian expansion into the Near East and, in turn, would have revolutionary implications for Germany.

However, for Marx and Engels, England held the balance of power in Europe, historically choosing to side with the "restoration" against European revolutions. England was able to finance European reaction against the radical democratic and proletarian movements by virtue of its economic control over Europe and the world market, which made a working-class revolution in England crucial. Such a revolution in England was possible only following a victorious proletarian revolution in France, England's historic rival, resulting in a world war that would make possible a successful Irish revolution and/or crises involving England's Asian markets, anticolonial revolts, and competition from other advanced capitalist countries—all of which would create the conditions for working-class revolution in England. Finally, the United Staes emerged on the horizon of European international relations, destined to become the leading capitalist society and the first true world power, through its control of the world market. Nevertheless, the class struggle in Europe after 1848 could be fought out only by altering the nineteenth-century form of Russian and English imperialism versus the proletarian revolution, and this would occur only when the secondary contradictions between states resulted in a "*world-wide war*" between "the proletarian revolution and the feudalistic counter-revolution" (Marx, 1933:15).

It is rather obvious from the foregoing that—contrary to popular academic opinion—Marx and Engels held a systematic conception of the international system of states in the nineteenth century. The relations within that system, in Marx and Engels's theoretical conception, are conditioned by, but not reduced to, the uneven development of capitalism and the class conflicts within nation-states, as well as the political-military capacities of states (themselves functions of economic strength and popular support) and the historical memories resulting from wars and revolutions. The extension of this analysis to the present is a rather straightforward exercise—only the names of the states have changed—and the proletarian revolution has succeeded (at great cost) here and there, with the consequence of altering the balance of forces for the major contemporary counterrevolutionary power, the United States, which on a world scale has inherited the counterrevolutionary roles that both Russia and England played in the nineteenth century.

The Emergence of the United States as a World Power

As early as 1844, Engels noted that America was the country capable of withstanding English competition—even after the abolition of the Corn Laws—and gaining a monopoly of world manufacturing:

America has in less than ten years created a manufacture which already competes with England in the coarser cotton goods, has excluded the English from the markets of North and South America, and holds its own in China, side by side with England. If any country is adapted to holding a monopoly of manufacture, it is America. . . . (Marx and Engels, 1962:332)

And at the beginning of the Crimean War, Marx believed that "America is the youngest and most vigorous representative of the West" (Marx and Engels, 1952:168).

Fifty years later, Engels was even more emphatic about the effects of American competition on England. Engels wrote to Sorge (March 21, 1894):

After the tariff business is put in order somewhat over there and the import duty on raw materials is abolished, the crisis will probably subside and the superiority of American over European industry will have a telling effect. Only then will things [the working-class movement] grow serious here in England; but then they'll do so rapidly . . . (Marx and Engels, 1953:261)

Yet Engels on one occasion (far ahead of his time) suggested that the three rivals on the world market, England, America, and Germany, would create a situation of chronic stagnation that would affect America too, for it would not be able to get hold of the monopoly of the world market:

America will smash up England's industrial monopoly—whatever there is left of it—but America cannot herself succeed to that monopoly. And unless *one* country has the monopoly of the markets of the world, at least in the decisive branches of the trade, the conditions—relatively favorable—which existed here in England from 1848 to 1870 cannot anywhere be reproduced, and even in America the condition of the working class must gradually sink lower and lower. For if there are three countries (say England, America, and Germany) competing on comparatively equal terms for the possession of the *Weltmarkt* [world market], there is no chance but chronic overproduction, one of the three being capable of supplying the whole quantity required. . . . (Marx and Engels, 1953:149–50)

In Engels's opinion, the Americans "simply cannot discount their future"—class conflict.[7] In a nice comparative description, Engels wrote to Sorge, who was in New Jersey:

The class struggles here in England, too, were more turbulent during the *period of development* of large-scale industry and died down just in the period of England's undisputed industrial domination of the world. In Germany, too, the development of large-scale industry since 1850 coincides with the rise of the Socialist movement, and it will be no different, probably, in America. It is the revolutionising of all traditional relations by industry *as it develops* that also revolutionises people's minds. (Marx and Engels, 1965:451–52)

Such events would have serious consequences on the level of international class ideology. To quote Engels: "What the downbreak of Russian Czarism would be for the great military monarchies of Europe—the snapping of their mainstay—that is for the bourgeois of the whole world the breaking out of class war in America. For America after all was the ideal of all bourgeois . . . " (Marx and Engels, 1965:451, 393). Extending the net to its widest, I will briefly present Marx and Engels's assessment of proletarian revolution and nationalist rebellions in Asia—their model of the relations of the parts of the emerging world-system.

Capitalism, Proletarian Revolution, Imperialism

To restate the thrust of my argument: an examination of the full range of Marx's and Engels's writings makes evident that their approach to revolutions does not rest exclusively on factors internal to societies. From at least *The German Ideology* and Engels's draft in catechismal form of *Principles of Communism*, their position is that to be successful the proletarian revolution would have to occur "all at once" in the most advanced capitalist societies (Marx and Engels, 1968:78). The point is that for Marx and Engels, the production of working-class revolution rests on forces operating both *within* and *across* societies *and*, as has been demonstrated above, is conditioned by (and often contingent on) relations *between* states as they are patterned in an international system.

What has not, however, been stressed here is the increasing entanglement of all peoples in the net of the developing world capitalist economy through the search by advanced capitalist countries, especially England, for markets, raw materials, and cheap goods, carried out through colonial intrusions (see Avineri, 1969). The global reach of Marx and Engels's perspective can be illustrated by their 1853 and 1857 analyses of the import of the Opium Wars and the Taiping Rebellion for China, and the potential return in kind to Europe. Speaking of the consequences of the opium trade forced by the British on the Chinese, Marx wrote,

> All these dissolving agencies acting together on the finances, the morals, the industry, and political structure of China, received their full development under the English cannon in 1840, which broke down the authority of the Emperor, and forced the Celestial Empire into contact with the terrestrial world. . . . Now, England having brought about the revolution of China, the question is how that revolution will in time react on England, and through England on Europe. This question is not difficult of solution. (Marx and Engels, n.d.a:17)

He observed:

> Since the commencement of the 18th century there has been no serious revolution in Europe which had not been preceded by a commercial and financial crisis. This applies no less to the revolution of 1789 than to that of 1848. . . . (Marx and Engels, n.d.a:22)

It followed that

> Under these circumstances, as the greater part of the regular commercial circle has already been run through by British trade, it may safely be argued that the Chinese revolution will throw the spark into the overloaded mine of the present industrial system and cause the explosion of the long-prepared general crisis, which, spreading abroad, will be closely followed by political revolutions on the Continent. It would be a curious spectacle, that of China sending disorder into the Western World while the Western powers, by English, French and American war-steamers, are conveying "order" to Shanghai, Nanking, and the mouths of the Great Canal. . . . (Marx and Engels, n.d.a:20)

Engels concluded his analysis of events in China with a world-historical judgment:

> Civil war has already divided the South from the North of the Empire, and the Rebel King seems to be as secure from the Imperialists (if not from the intrigues of his own followers) at Nanking, as the Heavenly Emperor from the rebels at Peking. Canton carries on, so far, a sort of independent war with the English, and all foreigners in general; and while British and French fleets and troops flock to

Hongkong, slowly but steadily the Siberian-line Cossacks advance their stanitzas [village or administrative district] from the Daurian mountains to the banks of the Amur, and the Russian marines close in by fortifications the splendid harbours of Manchuria. The very fanaticism of the southern Chinese in their struggle against foreigners seems to mark a consciousness of the supreme danger in which old China is placed; and before many years pass away, we shall have to witness the death-struggle of the oldest empire in the world, and the opening day of a new era for all Asia. (Marx and Engels, n.d.a:116)

But a year later (1858) Marx, employing a historical comparison, reflected in a letter to Engels on the consequences of the modernization of the now fashionable "Pacific Rim" for the possibility and fate of socialist revolution in Europe.

We cannot deny that bourgeois society has experienced its sixteenth century a second time—a sixteenth century which will, I hope, sound the death-knell of bourgeois society just as the first one thrust it into existence. The specific task of bourgeois society is the establishment of a world market, at least in outline, and of production based upon this world market. As the world is round, this seems to have been completed by the colonisation of California and Australia and the opening up of China and Japan. The difficult question for us is this: on the continent the revolution is imminent and will immediately assume a socialist character. Is it not bound to be crushed in this little corner, considering that in a far greater territory the movement of bourgeois society is still in the ascendant? (Marx and Engels, 1965:111)

In conclusion, suffice it to note here that in Marx's view the discovery of gold in California had caused the third major shift in world trade: "the center of gravity of world trade—in Italy in the Middle Ages and in England in Modern times—is now on the southern half of the North American hemisphere. . . ." What historical ironies in Marx's letter to Sorge when he said, "California is very important to me, because nowhere else has the upheaval caused so shamelessly by capital centralization taken place—with such speed" (see the wonderful discussion in Lyman, 1978:255–59). To complete the theoretical circle of the classical Marxist analysis of revolutions—complete and incomplete—the relationships of the variables—"internal" and "external" to societies—it comprises will be briefly stated.

A Schematic of Marx and Engels's Analysis of Social Revolutions

A close examination of all of Marx's and Engels's writings—but especially their more empirical-historical, journalistic writings and correspondence—makes evident that they took into account, generally speaking, the following classes of "variables" in their analysis of the causes, courses, and outcomes of revolutions: (1) changes in the mode of production and economic development and their effects on class relations; (2) the structure and context of trans- and international relations; (3) the character of state/political institutions; and (4) cultural traditions and forms of consciousness (Table 1.1).

The first class of variables requires little comment because changes in the mode of production constitute for Marx and Engels the coal of social revolutions firing the locomotives of history. Changes in modes of production are associated with economic development and transformation and, most important theoretically, with the formation and struggles of classes. Marx and Engels usually began their analyses of historical revolutions with a description of the economic changes of the preceding period, and especially the classes and fractions of classes that constitute from their point of view the major players in the drama of revolution. A wonderful and classic example is Engels's *Revolution and Counter-Revolution of Germany in 1848*.

What does require comment—as is evident from the preceding sections—is that Marx and Engels connect national and regional social-economic change with relations to the capitalist world economy. This brings us to the second class of variables, the international setting, which includes (1) the just-mentioned transnational world economy, including its state (crisis or advance), the relations of its parts, and their uneven development as they condition and are conditioned by the "internal" changes in economies and class conflicts, and (2) though often neglected in the literature, as clearly demonstrated above, the fact that Marx and Engels made central to their analysis of revolutions the relations between states, the international system of states conditioned by the two previously mentioned factors, national and regional changes in the forces and relations of production, and the state of the world market. Major revolutions, when they occur, *and* their effects on the international arena can

Table 1.1 A Schematic of Marx and Engels's Analysis of Revolutions

Country Providing Paradigm or Expectation of Revolutions (by time)	Revolutionary History	International Setting: Relation to World Market (Timing); Role in International Politics
France 1840s (1870–1871)	1789 1830 Bourgeois 1848 Revolution 1871 "Proletarian" (May 1968)	Economic backwardness in relation to England; international rivalry; Napoleonic Wars Revolutionary nation; political model
England 1844, Engels After 1850	Bourgeois revolution in seventeenth century after Holland	Early ("first") advance; Industrial Revolution "Despot of World Market" Colonialism, imperialism Held balance of power Competition from Germany and U.S. after 1870
Germany 1844 After 1870	1525, 1848 Incomplete bourgeois revolutions; "revolutions from above" after 1850s (1919, 1933)	Backwardness; "late" on world market Battleground of Europe Reactionary Prussianism
Russia After mid-1850s; 1870s, 1880s– 1895	Expectation (1905, 1917)	Backwardness *The* reactionary state in Europe; expansionist
U.S. (to 1895)	1776 and Civil War (bourgeois revolutions)	Late on world market but achieving dominance in economic competition; model bourgeois state

	Economic Development, Its Character, Consequences for Class Relations	State Organization Institutions/Traditions
France	Less developed capitalism Rapid in eighteenth century but agricultural crisis Peasants get land; modernization on their backs; nobility seen as repressive class; economically backward but class-conscious bourgeoisie	Centralization but weak support (statism) Revolutionary tradition
England	Long, rapid bursts (followed by class conflict), deep, "bourgeois aristocracy," strong industrial bourgeoisie, large, organized (but partly "bourgeois") working class; "no" peasants	Strong, gradualist institutions Personal freedom (feudal law)

Table 1.1   A Schematic of Marx and Engels's Analysis of Revolutions (*continued*)

	Economic Development, Its Character, Consequences for Class Relations	State Organization Institutions/Traditions
Germany	After 1850 rapid and widespread; Junker class (continues to exist) allied with economically strong bourgeoisie; big proletariat, politically organized; petty bourgeoisie large Large agricultural proletariat	Counterrevolutionary tradition Decentralization, strong paternalistic institutions, "Bonapartist" state after 1850
Russia	State instigated capitalism on backs of peasants Rapid in cities; rapidly developed big bourgeoisie Ruined nobility/disrupted large peasantry/kulaks/ Rapidly formed proletariat	Statism; weak institutions Peasant commune basis for transition to socialism?
U.S.	Rapid after 1865 (financial speculation) Big bourgeoisie; large immigrant proletariat Prosperous native workers	No feudalism, pure bourgeois society (with "feudal" institution) "Racism"

	Social and Political Theory; Consciousness of Masses	Comment
France	Critical social theory (philosophes); "utopian" and revolutionary socialism; enlightened public: all classes politically conscious	Relation of "backward" economy and advanced politics
England	Empiricism; bourgeois hegemony; respectability (status consciousness)	Why Marx's theory of proletarian revolution under advanced capitalism wrong
Germany	Most theoretical people, but petty-bourgeois mentality (abortive revolutionary tradition)	"Bonapartist" state as normal form in capitalist societies (nationalism)
Russia	Proliferation of ideologies: populism, anarchism, Pan-Slavism, constitutionalism, Marxism Change in masses	Like eighteenth-century France
U.S.	Liberalism, pragmatism. No challenge to bourgeois hegemony	Comparison with England

be taken as the markers in the major shifts in what Skocpol refers
to as "world time" (1979:23–24). Such considerations are central
to all of Marx and Engels's analyses of revolutions.

The third broad class of factors Marx and Engels considered
is the structure and forms of state (democratic or authoritarian)
and government (degree of centralization in particular) and the
character of legal institutions and traditions (their strength). The
last class of factors, the one downplayed by structuralists (Marxists)
and the most elusive, is the forms of consciousness—that is, the
structures of perception.[8] These include a number of levels—broad
cultural traditions, everyday consciousness, and the more elaborated
theoretical consciousness of professional thinkers (ideologists). The
phenomena that compose this category are shaped by the character
of and developments in modes of production, and by class conflicts,
nation-state histories, cultural contacts, the rivalries of states, wars,
revolutions, and the dynamics of intellectual life. They, in turn,
in Marx and Engels's view, are part of the causal pattern, and
influence the varying courses and outcomes of revolutions. With
this general discussion in mind, I will turn to a very brief illustration
of the relationship of "external" and "internal" factors in Engels's
comparative analysis of the course of Germany's late-nineteenth-
century history.

Germany's History of Incomplete Revolutions

The history of German revolutions might be summed up by stating that the Germans attempted their first revolution, in the sixteenth century, too early and their second, in the nineteenth century (and third, 1918–19), too late. Following Engels, both
Germany's economic backwardness and its advances and revolutions
in the sixteenth and nineteenth centuries can be attributed (in part)
to its being drawn into (and then in the first case excluded from)
the world market, and to the "religious" wars fought on German
soil. At the turn of the nineteenth century, Germany was under
pressure from France politically, from the spread of the ideas of
the French Revolution, the anti-Jacobin wars, and the resistance
to Napoleon. It was at the same time under pressure economically
from England. Writing of the period, Marx said, "As for the European nations, they were driven to adopt machinery owing to English
competition both in their home markets and in the world market"

(Marx and Engels, 1965:38). As a consequence of these international pressures, there began in Germany a limited development of capitalism and with it the emergence of an industrial and commercial bourgeoisie. Yet the majority of the classes and their strata in Germany remained petty bourgeois, which, as Engels made central to his analysis, were destined to affect decisively the course and outcome of the German revolution of 1848. When that sufficient condition of revolution was present—all classes united against the government, as Engels formulated it—the German revolutions broke out in response to the French revolution in February 1848. The conflicts between the classes opposed to the old regime, the decentralization of Germany, its involvement in the ethnonational conflicts in East Europe, and the course of the counterrevolution in France led to the success of the counterrevolution in Germany (Engels, 1952). As Marx had pointed out in 1844, Germany was about to make its democratic revolution when social developments elsewhere in Europe and the progress of political theory had already called the middle-class viewpoint into question.

After 1848, the capitalist modernization and unification of Germany by wars with Denmark (1864), Austria (1866), and France (1870) were completed "from above" under the leadership of the "Iron Chancellor," Otto von Bismarck. The political economy of Germany came to be composed of an economically powerful but feudalized bourgeoisie allied with the politically powerful Junker class against a relatively well organized and socialist-led working-class movement. In an interesting comparative analysis titled *The Housing Question* (1872), Engels also described the effects on class developments of Germany's having arrived late on the world market.

> Germany appeared late on the world market. Our large-scale industry dates from the 'forties; it received its first impetus from the Revolution of 1848, and was able to develop fully only after *the Revolutions of 1866 and 1870* had cleared at least the worst political obstacles out of its way. But to a large extent it found the world market already occupied. . . . we finally came to possess a large-scale industry and to play a role on the world market. But our *large-scale* industry works almost exclusively for the home market (with the exception of the iron industry which produces far beyond the limits of home demand), and our mass export consists of a tremendous number of small articles, for which large-scale industry provides at most the half-finished

manufactures, which small articles, however, are supplied chiefly by rural domestic industry.

He continued, pointing comparatively (with relevance to the present) to the potential consequences for revolution in Germany:

> However, with the expansion of domestic industry, one peasant area after the other is being drawn into the present day industrial movement. It is the revolutionisation of the rural areas by domestic industry which spreads the industrial revolution in Germany over a far wider territory than is the case in England and France; it is the comparatively low level of our industry which makes its extension in area all the more necessary. This explains why in Germany, in contrast to England and France, the revolutionary working class movement has spread so tremendously over the greater part of the country instead of being confined exclusively to the urban centres. . . . In France, the movement always originated in the capital; in Germany, it originated in the areas of big industry, of manufacture and of domestic industry; the capital was conquered only later. Therefore, perhaps, in the future also the initiative will continue to rest with the French, but the decision can be fought out only in Germany.

Engels concluded,

> But in Germany the destruction of rural domestic industry and manufacture by machinery and factory production means the destruction of the livelihood of millions of rural producers, the expropriation of almost half the German small peasantry; the transformation not only of domestic industry into factory production, but also of peasant agriculture into large-scale capitalist agriculture, of small landed property into big estates—an industrial and agricultural revolution in favour of capital and big landownership at the cost of the peasants. Should it be Germany's fate also to undergo this transformation while still under the old social conditions then it will unquestionably be the turning point. If the working class of no other country has taken the initiative by that time, then Germany will certainly strike first, and the peasant sons of the "glorious army" will bravely assist. (Engels, 1872:14, 16–17)

It should be noted in passing that Marx already had written to Engels, on April 16, 1856, that the outcome of events "in Germany will depend on the possibility of backing the proletarian revolution by some second edition of the peasant war" (Marx and Engels, 1965:41).

Finally, let us consider Marx and Engels's description of the state structures, cultural traditions, and consciousness that were products of German history. First, there was the militarized, bureaucratic, and paternalistic state structure of Prussia that dominated Germany—a "Bonapartist" state that Engels came to see as the normal form of class rule under advanced capitalism (Engels, 1966:22–24). (This was a structure that, as it turned out, could withstand almost any revolutionary quakes.) The development of German capitalism and its external relations and state structures had resulted in a history of unsuccessful revolutions and the prevalence of a petty-bourgeois mentality. The Germans may have been, in Engels's description, "the most theoretical people of Europe," but, as Marx wrote as a young man, they only thought what other nations did, never getting beyond being the latter's *"theoretical conscience."*

This skeleton of Marx and Engels's analysis of the incompleteness of Germany's revolutions suggests, however, a direction Engels did not consider; it points to some of the conditions that Barrington Moore, Jr., specified as leading to fascism as a "solution" to twentieth-century class conflicts (1966:chap. 8).

Put in terms of contemporary theoretical discourse, it can be said that Engels described Germany's shift from a semiperipheral to a core status in the nineteenth-century capitalist world economy—an analysis weakened by the Achilles' heels of Marxism, consciousness, and the resilience of modern state structures. Also, one might think of Marx and Engels's analysis of the development of capitalism and the prospects for revolution in Russia as a description of its move from the periphery to the semiperiphery of the world capitalist economy. Indeed, there is much in Marx and Engels's conception of capitalism as a world economy that anticipates the world-system perspective (see Wallerstein, 1974a, 1974b; Chase-Dunn, 1984:75–104, especially 76–80). However, Christopher Chase-Dunn argues that there is one important difference:

> Marx's analysis of capitalism does not posit the existence of "peripheral capitalism" in which commodity production employs politically coerced labor. For Marx, the extra-economic coercion occurring in the perphery is merely part of primitive accumulation, the use of force to create the institutional basis of a capitalist mode of production that, once created, will sustain itself. World-system theory has claimed that *peripheral* capitalism is a normal and necessary part of the capitalist mode of production, and that the reproduction of

expanded accumulation in the core requires the existence of primary accumulation in the periphery. (1984:98)

I would suggest that the matter of the extent of Marx's recognition of the world relation of capitalism is more complex. It is true that it was left to twentieth-century theorists of imperialism—especially Lenin—to explore more fully the exploitative relations of cores and peripheries (see Boswell, 1985). Nevertheless, it is not difficult to argue that classical Marxism grasped the totality of the world system and the relations of its parts and its operative mechanisms more thoroughly than any previous or contemporary social theorists (the social evolutionism of Comte, Spencer, or Tylor, for example)— and most subsequent ones also.

Discussion

Skocpol has called for an approach to social revolutions that combines theory and history through the method of comparative historical analysis (1979:5–6, 33–40). My argument, most generally restated, is, first, that Marx and Engels have already combined history with theory (historical materialism, that is) in their analyses of historical revolutions[10] and, further, that these writings have been overlooked as sources of insight into the causes, courses, and outcomes of revolutions. The foregoing exposition was not intended to offer a critique of Skocpol's analysis of states and social revolution, but to criticize her judgment of the perspective of classical Marxism—one that she is not alone in making. Second, and substantively, there is in these writings a rather systematic depiction of trans- and international relations, particularly in the nineteenth century, as they were transformed by and made up the contextual constraints on revolutionary upheavals. What has not been attempted here is to state Marx and Engels's conception of international relations as such, nor to discuss whether they have a theory of the autonomy and capacities of the military and administrative apparatuses of states. There may be more on these issues in their writings than is usually granted—for example, on the expansionary character of the czarist state and the history of the French state's relative autonomy (see Sayer and Corrigan, in Shanin, 1983:77–94). Also, their explanation of nationalism and national alliances has not been addressed directly. It is clear from the foregoing that nationalism was not a phenomenon about which Marx and Engels had nothing to say. It is also not the case historically that segments of working classes were never internationalist in outlook or, obversely, were always unrepentantly nationalist in outlook. In their analysis of revolutions, Marx and Engels stressed the capitalist world-economic and class context of international relations (and vice versa). Of course, theory does not clearly see that for which it is not looking. But bringing the state and international relations to center stage should not be at the cost of leaving the mode of production, the struggles of classes and the world economy in the wings.

Critical also of the Marxist stress on long-run economic development in class-divided societies, Skocpol contends that

> the interaction between Marxist theory and history is incomplete because historical cases have not been used to test and modify the explanations offered by the theory. . . . They have not devised ways to test whether these factors really distinguish between revolutions and other kinds of transformations or between successful and abortive revolutionary outbreaks. . . .

This is due to their failure to pay attention to "the often much more striking and immediate transformations that occur in the structure and function of state organizations such as armies and administrations, and in the relations between the state and social classes"— leading them to miss what is distinctive about revolutions as patterns of social change (1979:34–35). It can be argued that, contra to Skocpol, Marx and Engels had a more powerful (and successful) theory of revolutions in backward capitalist societies than in advanced ones. This fact stands to reason, for the revolutions they studied (as opposed to predicted) were mostly unsuccessful—or rather, incomplete—by the criteria of total transformation. Further, the main cases on which Marx and Engels based their generalizations (theory) were not limited to their expectation of revolution in Russia as Shanin's (1983) treatment implies, but included those in sixteenth- and nineteenth-century Germany, nineteenth-century Spain (Marx and Engels, 1939) and France, and Russia. Finally, their specification of the causes of the occurrence and failure of these revoltuions took into account the strengths and weaknesses of state structures, as well as the contradictory forms of consciousness of the classes and parties participating in these revolutions.[11] Yet it remains the case that revolutionaries taking power in backward countries face the problems of transforming societies in the face of remaining class interests and traditional conflicts and prejudices and of educating the oppressed classes as well as intimidating, cajoling, and repressing the privileged classes. There are opportunities created by revolutionary situations — opportunities seized and opportunities lost. As Skocpol points out, and Marx and Engels knew, the difference in the outcome may be contingent, in the last analysis, on the international system of state powers extant at the time.

It follows from this presentation that Skocpol is incorrect in her assessment of the literature of classical Marxism on the international aspects of revolution. While it does not have the theoretical integrity of the logic of capital, it is rich in inter- and transnational analysis, and in fact may anticipate more Wallerstein's analysis of the modern world-system than Skocpol's more "Tocquevillian — Weberian" analysis.[12]

To end on a political note: structural perspectives would seem either to make problematic or to overemphasize the moral bases of socialist revolution. For Wallerstein, there are no true socialist societies today, only states ruled by Communist parties in a world capitalist economy. For Skocpol, however, socialist transformation would have to be based on long-term and gradual "nonreformist reforms" occurring simultaneously in the advanced countries (1979:293). It seems to me that Wallerstein captures the limits to socialist transformation in the contemporary world (*vide* Mitterrand and Papandreou) and that Skocpol's work suggests the apparent indestructibility of the most modern states (although the "anomaly" that inspired her work, South Africa, may end up contradicting her). But it also seems that the crisis of capital accumulation and the international and national repressiveness of imperialist state structures will not, in the short and long runs, allow the class struggles to rest.

Notes

I want to thank Edward S. Malecki, my friend and colleague, for his substantive and editorial suggestions for clarifying the presentation of my argument. Also, my friend and coeditor, Michael T. Martin, for his suggestions for the core of the paper, and above all, for his patience. I want to thank Immanuel Wallerstein for the encouragement he gave me some years back to pursue my work on Marx and Engels's vision of revolution in the modern world. Additionally, I want to thank Anita A. Acosta for her support, advice, assistance, and tolerance in the completion of this study. Finally, I want to thank David Fogarty, my friend and comrade, for his critique of the entire manuscript. He helped me to understand it all in the first place.

1. The assumption of this chapter is that readers are familiar with the recent literature on the international aspects of capitalism, the controversies over dependency and mode-of-production approaches to development and underdevelopment, theories of imperialism and world-system analyses, and the role of states, classes, ethnic and gender relations, nationality, and culture in social changes in the contemporary world. For a representative sample, see the literature cited in the introduction to this volume. Of the later Marxists, the most important theorists of trans- and international relations are the Austrian Marxist Otto Bauer on nationalism, Rosa Luxemburg on capital accumulation on a world scale, Leon Trotsky on the uneven and combined development of capitalism, Mao Zedong on war and national liberation and, of course, V. I. Lenin on imperialism, colonialism, and revolution. During the 1960s and early 1970s, I often had the impression that younger radicals had more familiarity with Mao, Trotsky, and Lenin than with the writings of Marx and Engels from which the whole Marxist intellectual-political tradition derives. Given these considerations, my intention is to present in a systematic fashion the less well known writings of Marx and Engels on nineteenth-century international relations and revolutions. This task is undertaken with the purpose of contributing to the clarification of critical issues concerning the historical-comparative analyses of twentieth-century developments. In fact, it could be argued that some of what Marx and Engels wrote about the inherent tendencies of capitalism is more true of the late twentieth century than it was of the capitalism of their own day.

2. This chapter draws on research begun twenty years ago and interrupted by other writing commitments. The only other research to consider the full range of the writings of classical Marxism is Hal Draper's three volumes, *Karl Marx's Theory of Revolution, State and Bureaucracy* (New York: Monthly Review Press, 1977), *The Politics of Social Classes* (New York: Monthly Review Press, 1978), and (with the assistance of Stephen F. Diamond) *The "Dictatorship of the Proletariat"* (New York: Monthly Review Press, 1986).

3. To somewhat minimize citations, I do not cite by page numbers such familiar and readily available texts as the *Manifesto of the Communist Party* and Marx's Introduction to "Contribution to the Critique of Hegel's *Philosophy of Right.*"

4. Once again, the text is to be read as an exposition of the full range of the insufficiently examined writings of Marx and Engels, including their

correspondence. To avoid grammatical awkwardness and some repetition, I have often put the materials as if I am stating my position.

5. Of course, there is no book by Marx and Engels titled *The Russian Menace to Europe*. Nevertheless, this cold war–inspired collection, selected and edited by Paul Blackstock and Bert F. Hoselitz, is extremely useful.

6. One of the best descriptions of the impact of war on a decrepit regime is to be found in Leon Trotsky's *History of the Russian Revolution*.

7. I have purposely excluded a full exposition of Marx and Engels's writings on the United States because of the knotty problems of American "exceptionalism," theoretical digestion, and so on. See the Moscow volume *Marx and Engels on the United States* (1979). See also the refreshing treatments in Ira Katznelson and Aristide Zolberg, eds., *Working Class Formation: Nineteenth-Century Patterns in Western Europe and the United States* (Princeton, N.J.: Princeton University Press, 1986), especially the Introduction and the Conclusion.

8. I have taken this conceptualization from my teacher and friend Philip Selznick.

9. I realize that Marx and Engels's analyses over time of each of the countries are debatable and merit a book. I have tried to use their various remarks to complete my argument—particularly their rather thorough consideration of international factors in revolutions and how these relate to "internal" changes in societies.

10. See Engels's discussion of the epistemological constraints and limitations of the data on "Marx's first attempt, with the aid of his materialist conception, to explain a section of contemporary history from the given economic situation" in *The Class Struggles in France* (1935:9–11). In his preface to the third edition of *The Eighteenth Brumaire of Louis Bonaparte*, Engels said that Marx applied "the great law of motion of history," that historical struggles are at bottom the result of class struggles conditioned by their position in changing modes of production. This was to be Marx's "key to an understanding of the history of the Second French Republic. He put his law to the test on these historical events, and even after thirty-three years we must still say that it has stood the test brilliantly" (1885:14). Contemporary commentators have also viewed these writings favorably; see, for example, Christopher Hill, "The English Civil War Interpreted by Marx and Engels," *Science and Society* 12 (Winter 1948): 130–56. Leonard Krieger attempted (problematically) to deal with Marx's writings on French revolutions in relation to his theory by viewing them as operating on different levels of reality, the empirical-historical and the theoretical. See his "Marx and Engels as Historians," *Journal of the History of Ideas* 14 (June 1953). See also Irving Zeitlin, *Marxism: A Re-Examination* (Princeton, N.J.: Nostrand, 1967), 129–55, wherein the major writings on historical revolutions are used to generate a

list of twenty questions Marx asked, including variables going beyond his general theory of capitalism and the working class. As to Marx's own testimony, he wrote that as a result of the necessity of earning a living writing for the *New York Tribune*, he "was compelled to become conversant with practical detail which, strictly speaking, lie outside the sphere of political economy" (preface to *A Contribution to the Critique of Political Economy*).

11. The evidence for these assertions would require another paper at least.

12. For the sake of clarity, I am not making the anachronistic argument that Marx and Engels were *world-system* theorists. Rather, the scope (unit) and theoretical underpinnings of their analyses resemble Wallerstein's more than Skocpol's. However, it is clear that her consideration of states and social revolutions is not without its prefigurations in Marx and Engels's approach to revolutions.

References

Aron, Raymond (1968). *Main Currents in Sociological Thought I*. New York: Doubleday.

Avineri, Shlomo, ed. (1969). *Karl Marx on Colonialism and Modernization*. New York: Doubleday.

Bottomore, T. B., and Maximillien Rubel, eds. (1964). *Karl Marx: Selected Writings in Sociology and Social Philosophy*. New York: McGraw-Hill.

Bottomore, Tom, and Patrick Goode, eds. (1978). *Austro-Marxism*. Oxford: Oxford University Press.

Engels, Friedrich (1872). *The Housing Question*. New York: International Publishers.

——— (1962). *Anti-Duhring*. Moscow: Foreign Languages Publishing House.

——— (1963). *Dialectics of Nature*. Clemens Dutt, trans. and ed. New York: International Publishers.

——— (1968). *The Role of Force in History*. Jack Cohen, trans. New York: International Publishers.

Feuer, Lewis S., ed. (1959). *Karl Marx and Frederick Engels: Basic Writings on Politics and Philosophy*. New York: Doubleday.

Hill, Christopher (1948). "The English Civil War Interpreted by Marx and Engels." *Science and Society* 12 (Winter):130–56.

Lenin, V. I. (1916). *Imperialism, the Highest Stage of Capitalism*. Moscow: Foreign Languages Publishing House.

Lichtheim, George (1965). *Marxism: An Historical and Critical Study*. New York: Praeger.

Lyman, Stanford M. (1978). *The Seven Deadly Sins: Society and Evil.* New York: St. Martin's Press.

Marx, Karl (1885). *The Eighteenth Brumaire of Louis Bonaparte.* Moscow: Foreign Languages Publishing House.

——— (1906). *Capital.* New York: Random House.

——— (1933). *Wage-Labour and Capital.* New York: International Publishers.

——— (1934). *Letters to Dr. Kugelmann.* New York: International Publishers.

——— (1935). *The Class Struggles in France.* E. P. Dutt, ed. New York: International Publishers.

——— (1940). *The Civil War in France.* New York: International Publishers.

——— (1963). *The Poverty of Philosophy.* New York: International Publishers.

——— (1969). *Secret Diplomatic History of the Eighteenth Century* and *The Story of the Life of Lord Palmerston.* Lester Hutchinson, ed. New York: International Publishers.

Marx, Karl, and Friedrich Engels (n.d.a). *On Colonialism.* Moscow: Foreign Languages Publishing House.

——— (n.d.b) *Reactionary Prussianism.* New York: International Publishers.

——— (1939). *Revolution in Spain.* New York: International Publishers.

Marx, Karl [Friedrich Engels] (1952). *Revolution and Counter Revolution or Germany in 1848.* Eleanor Marx Aveling, ed. London: George Allen and Unwin.

Marx, Karl, and Friedrich Engels (1952). *The Russian Menace to Europe.* Paul W. Blackstock and Bert F. Hoselitz, eds. Glencoe, Ill.: Free Press.

——— (1953). *Letters to Americans, 1848–1895.* New York: International Publishers.

——— (1961). *The Civil War in the United States.* New York: Citadel Press.

——— (1962). *On Britain.* 2d ed. Moscow: Foreign Languages Publishing House.

——— (1963). *The German Ideology.* R. Pascal, ed. New York: International Publishers.

——— (1965). *Selected Correspondence.* Moscow: Progress Publishers.

——— (1959). *The First Indian War of Independence, 1857–1859.* Moscow: Foreign Languages Publishing House.

——— (1968). *The Communist Manifesto. Including Principles of Communism.* Paul M. Sweezy, trans. New York: Monthly Review Press.

Moore, Barrington, Jr. (1966). *Social Origins of Dictatorship and Democ-*

racy: Lord and Peasant in the Making of the Modern World. Boston: Beacon Press.

———— (1972). *Reflections on the Causes of Human Misery and Upon Certain Proposals to Eliminate Them.* Boston: Beacon Press.

Moore, Stanley (1963). *Three Tactics: The Background in Marx.* New York: Monthly Review Press.

Rejai, M., ed. (1970). *Mao Tse-Tung on Revolution and War.* Garden City, N.Y.: Doubleday, Anchor.

Shanin, Teodor (1983). *Late Marx and the Russian Road.* New York: Monthly Review Press.

Skocpol, Theda (1979). *States and Social Revolutions.* New York: Cambridge University Press.

Tilly, Charles (1970). "The Analysis of a Counter-Revolution." In *Protest, Reform, and Revolution: A Reader in Social Movements,* ed. Joseph R. Gusfield. New York: John Wiley, pp. 47–67.

Tocqueville, Alexis de (1955). *The Old Regime and the French Revolution.* Stuart Gilbert, trans. Garden City, N.Y.: Doubleday, Anchor.

Trotsky, Leon (1959). *The Russian Revolution.* New York: Doubleday, Anchor.

Tucker, Robert C. (1969). *The Marxian Revolutionary Idea.* New York: Norton.

———— (1978). *The Marx-Engels Reader.* 2d ed. New York: Norton.

Wallerstein, Immanuel (1974a). "The Rise and Future Demise of the World Capitalist System: Concepts for Comparative Analysis." *Comparative Studies in Society and History* 16 (September): 387–415.

———— (1974b). *The Modern World-System I: Capitalist Agriculture and the Origins of the European World-Economy in the Sixteenth Century.* New York: Academic Press.

———— (1979). *The Capitalist World-Economy.* Cambridge: Cambridge University Press.

———— (1980). *The Modern World-System II: Mercantilism and the Consolidation of the European World-Economy: 1600–1750.* New York: Academic Press.

CHAPTER 2

The Utility of World-System Theory for Explaining Social Revolutions: A Comparison of Skocpol and Lenin

Terry E. Boswell

Social revolutions have until recently been primarily analyzed from an internal-conflict point of view, with international relations serving largely as a backdrop. In her landmark study of social revolutions, Skocpol (1979) directly challenges this approach, successfully arguing for the inclusion of world economic and political relations in the analysis of revolution (see also Skocpol and Trimberger, 1977–78). Skocpol (1979:6–33) outlines four prominent theoretical perspectives on social revolution: Marxist class theories; aggregate-psychological theories; systems/value-consensus theories; and political-conflict theories. Each of these is found wanting due to an insufficient consideration of social structural relations, international relations, and autonomous state relations (1979:5, 14–31). When applied in practice, even Marxist theory, from which Skocpol derives her theory of social structure, is found to emphasize voluntarist notions of a vanguard rallying the masses to revolution (1979:15–17). Skocpol argues that theories of revolution must recognize that "revolutionary situations have developed due to the emergence of politico-military crises of state and class domination," and in "no sense did such vanguards . . . ever create the revolutionary crises they exploited" (1979:17). The source of the crises, particularly the military crises, is directly tied to the country's international power relations.

Skocpol defines social revolutions as "rapid, basic transformations of a society's state and class structures; and they are accompanied and in part carried through by class-based revolts from below" (1979:4). Basically, the sufficient conditions of a revolutionary situation are sociopolitical structures which facilitate widespread revolt of the lower classes and state organizations susceptible to administrative and military collapse under intense pressure from more developed countries (Skocpol, 1979:154). In her comparative analysis of social revolutions in France, Russia, and China, Skocpol convincingly demonstrates the fruitfulness of her structural theory of the causes of social revolutions and how they are consolidated.

It would appear that inclusion of world dynamics in theories of revolution would easily lend itself to utilization of the world-system perspective. A social revolution depends on the conjuncture of a variety of national and international factors. But a world-system analysis alone cannot explain why that conjuncture came about. However, a world-system analysis should be able to tell us what features of the world-system make revolutionary situations more or less likely. Yet Skocpol explicitly avoids using world-system theory because of two important criticisms. First, she criticizes its emphasis on the world market and questions whether "national economic developments are actually determined by the overall structure and market dynamics of a 'world capitalist system'" (1979:20). (Brenner's criticism of the overreliance on exchange relations found in Wallerstein [1974] is cited by Skocpol [1979:299, n.50] as evidence of the weakness of the world-system theory.) The second criticism Skocpol makes is that the world-system theory is economically reductionist (1979:22; 1977). In particular, she points out that the world economic system and the international states system are "analytically autonomous" (1979:22). While the two are interdependent, the international states system existed prior to world capitalism and cannot be reduced to it. National and world class relations strongly affect the state, but Skocpol argues that the fundamental dynamics of the state, interstate military competition, and the maintenance of coercive and administrative apparatuses are not reducible to or directly determined by socioeconomic dynamics (1979:22, 29). While I prefer Poulantzas's (1973) theory of relative autonomy of the state over Skocpol's (1979) potential autonomy, her criticism of economic reductionism in world-system theory is well taken.

Are these insurmountable criticisms? If they are, then world-system theory would seem to have little to offer to the study of social revolutions, as Skocpol claims. Skocpol does note that "transnational economic relations have always strongly (and differentially) influenced national economic developments" (1979:20). However, this recognition is not the same as analyzing social revolutions from a world perspective. A world perspective on social relations is the fundamental insight of world-system theory (Bergesen, 1980). I basically agree with Skocpol's criticisms. The incorporation of production dynamics and an autonomous position for political relations are the two most pressing problems in world-system theory. However, I think the criticisms are something of a red herring in regard to jettisoning the world-system perspective as a whole. In the next section, I want to first briefly review Brenner's (1976) criticism of world-system theory, for I find this critique to be especially important, although not insurmountable. In particular, I think the work of Laclau (1971) and Amin (1977, 1980) avoids the stress on exchange relations which plagues other theories of the world-system.

Once the production-versus-exchange debate is put to rest, the problem of economic reductionism will be dealt with. I will review Lenin's (1939) theory of imperialism as an example of a theory of world relations which explicity avoids economic reductionism. The last section will explore ways to update Lenin's theory to the postcolonial world. I will present an exploratory theory of the stratification of nations in the world-system which distinguishes the autonomy of political dependence from economic dependency. It will be argued that nations which are in contradictory locations[1] in the world-system have the conditions which make a revolutionary situation more likely. These conditions include: (1) state apparatuses which are susceptible to collapse under pressure from core countries; (2) dominant class power-blocs which are internally divided between the national and comprador bourgeoisie; and (3) the existence of a sizable industrial working class.

Production Dynamics and the World-System

The central weakness of world-system theory as explained by Brenner is

> that the method of an entire line of writers in the Marxist tradition has led them to displace class relations from the center of their analysis of

economic development and underdevelopment . . . they conceive of (changing) class relations as emerging more or less directly from the (changing) requirements for the generation of surplus and development of production under the pressures and opportunities engendered by a growing world market. . . . As a result, they fail to take into account either the way in which class structures, once established, will in fact determine the course of economic development or underdevelopment over an entire epoch, or the way in which these class structures themselves emerge: as the outcome of class struggles whose results are incomprehensible in terms merely of market forces. (1977:27)

Capitalism as a distinct mode of production is generally described as having the essential characteristics of contradictory classes of free labor and free capital in the relations of production, and increasing relative surplus value expropriation in the forces of production. This results in an expanding sphere of commodity exchange which is separate from but determined by production. It also results in the necessity of firms to adopt the most productive level of technology. Brenner (1977) argues that Wallerstein (1974) considers only free capital (that is, relatively unfettered profit determination of accumulation and investment) and commodity exchange expanded to a world level as the key characteristics of capitalism. Since Wallerstein includes as capitalist all forms of labor which have as their result production for the world market, free labor is not an essential feature of capitalism in his theory. Serfdom, slavery, and wage labor are all simply different forms of labor control for Wallerstein.

According to Brenner, Wallerstein's position results in four crucial deficiencies in his world-system theory: (1) it ignores the role of class struggle in producing free labor and free capital; (2) it fails to recognize the necessity of free labor in order for free capital to be put to the most profitable use; (3) it has no mechanism for requiring technical innovation and increasing relative surplus value expropriation (as opposed to absolute surplus value expropriation); and, therefore, (4) class structure and differential productivity are seen not as determining unequal exchange but as being determined by it. Without an organization of the mode of production which enforced both the productive use of wealth (thus producing capital out of wealth) and a continuous process of accumulation via innovation, nothing more would have resulted from the "primitive accumulation" than "the creation of cathedrals in the core and starvation on the periphery" (Brenner, 1977:67).

Productivity and Unequal Exchange

Brenner's (1977) critique questions significantly a world-system method of analysis. In order for the world-system perspective to be viable, these methodological deficiencies must be overcome (Bergesen, 1982, 1983; Boswell, 1984). Laclau (1971:37–38) argues that the central cause of the problems of world-system theory are a result of the confusion of two concepts: the capitalist mode of production and participation in a world capitalist economic system. A capitalist economy consists of separate spheres of production and exchange. This is the distinction that Marx made between the sphere of capital and the sphere of money (Marx, 1973; 1967:167–68; see also Urry, 1982). It is precisely the acknowledgment of this distinction in Marxist theory which separates it from classical Smithian economics. In the sphere of exchange, the only one Smithian economics recognizes, commodities are exchanged at their value under competitive conditions. The social relationships in this sphere are relations of "Freedom, Equality, Property and Bentham" (Marx, 1967:176). It is ruled by the laws of supply and demand. In the sphere of production, on the other hand, the social relations are characterized by domination, inequality, and exploitation. The central dynamic here is class struggle; it is here that surplus value is expropriated. But it is in the sphere of exchange that surplus value is realized.

The differential rates of exploitation in production create the unequal consequences of the exchange of equal values. Amin (1977) has spelled out this point in extensive detail. For our purposes, consider two countries exchanging commodities in the world market. The countries have equal exchanges of reinvestment of profit realized from the equal exchanges of value. This will result in *unequal* rates of industrial development to the degree that the productivity rates in the dominant industries of the two countries are different (for example, investment in electronics versus an equal investment in sugar plantations).

Even though production relations determine the inequalities of development resulting from otherwise equal exchange, it does not follow that production always dominates exchange in every instance. Highly productive synthetic fiber plants may fold and anti-quated textile mills may flourish if fashion demand switches from polyester to corduroy suits. But the reign of consumer sovereignty is ephemeral. The systematic processes of uneven and unequal world development occur over decades and last for centuries. The essential dynamics of these processes over the long term are production dynamics.

By maintaining the distinction between the sphere of production and the sphere of exchange, it is quite possible for there to be more than one mode of producing for a single world market. Commodities produced by slaves, serfs, peasants, or petty commodity producers may be exchanged in the capitalist world market without our having to consider these (as Wallerstein does) capitalist labor relations. The same is not true of a world-system theory which posits the determination of production by exchange, as Brenner points out. This is critically important for the study of world relations, as most of the world economy is occupied by peasants producing for a capitalist market. The economic determinants of peasants' social behavior in the market are capitalistic, but the determinants of their behavior in production are not. Nevertheless, the multiple modes are not symmetrical. Noncapitalist modes are dependent on capitalist production and can exist only in "niches" of the capitalist world-system (unless they are isolated from it). As Marx pointed out in reference to the slave system of the old South, "slavery is possible at individual points . . . only because it does not exist at other points; and appears as an anomaly opposite the bourgeois system itself" (1979:464). The recognition of multiple modes of production and the differential effects of unequal productivity on equal exchange in no way negates the existence of the capitalist world-system. Instead, these are the central dynamics of its operation.

In summary, the capitalist world-system can be considered the world sphere of exchange. A variety of capitalist and noncapitalist modes of production enter into the world-system, but it is dominated by capitalist production. With this conception of the world-system, the confusion between the capitalist mode of production and the capitalist world market can be avoided (Laclau, 1971:33–38; see also Amin, 1980, and Boswell, 1984, for more elaborated expositions). This conception resolves the problems that Brenner

(1977) illuminated, and thereby Skocpol's first major criticism of world-system theory. So constructed, the world-system perspective has a viable method of analysis, and the debate over production versus exchange determination can be put aside.

Economism and the State

The preceding discussion suggests that while Brenner's critique of world-system theory is substantial, it is not insurmountable. A world perspective cannot simply be dismissed in the analysis of revolutionary situations. But before revolutions can be studied from a world perspective, it is necessary to deal with Skocpol's (1979:22; 1977) criticism of economic reductionism in world-system theory. Her criticism is definitely correct, and economism stands in the way of any analysis of the revolutionary overthrow of states. However, there is no reason the relative autonomy of the state (Poulantzas, 1973; Skocpol's "potential autonomy," 1979:24–32) cannot be acknowledged in world-system theory.

The state is relatively autonomous from the economy and capitalist class, for organizational and structural reasons. The organization of modern states is bureaucratic, with a set of rules and procedures that are designed to be impervious to the will of the rulers. The economic pressures on state actors, even those with capitalist backgrounds, are determined by bureaucratic instead of market principles (the same is true of the managers of huge corporations). The vicissitudes of the capitalist market have only indirect effects on state actors. While the state must maintain the economic vitality of the nation, and thus the general vitality of capitalists in a capitalist economy, it is structurally autonomous from particular capitalists. Their individual vitality is consequential to the state to the degree that the economy as a whole is dependent on their capital (monopoly capital and oligarchic families are always consequential). The state is relatively autonomous from the collective interests of capital to the degree that the state faces internal pressure from the lower classes or internal support from the dominant classes of non-capitalist modes of production (such as landlords or the petty bourgeoisie).

Most important, the state faces external pressure, particularly military pressure, from other states to act in ways which may be contrary to the interests of internal actors. For instance, in the above discussion of production and exchange, two obvious but important points should be made. The economic dynamics of unequal exchange and unequal development in the world-system were initiated by the interstate system through colonialism and constantly reinforced by military means. Second, the domination of capitalism over other modes of production and of monopoly capitalism over other forms of capitalist production is tied to the domination of one state over another.

If the relative autonomy of the state is included in world-system theory, then the conception of world relations is analogous to the concept of a social formation. A social formation may contain within it a variety of modes of production, but usually one is dominant. The dominant mode structures the overall character of the ensemble of economic, political, and ideological relations, but the economy, state, and ideology are relatively autonomous from the dominant mode of production and the dominant class (Althusser, 1971; Poulantzas, 1973, 1978). If the analogy from a social formation to a world perspective is carried through, then the object of analysis is what I would call a "world formation" and not the world market, dominant mode of production, or interstate system (Boswell, 1984). The perspective of a world formation is intended to incorporate the concrete manifestations of modes of production, the world market, and interstate relations as components of a single world unit of analysis.

Certainly, states and state actions are an important part of Wallerstein's (1974, 1980a) theory of the origin of the world-system. Yet his theory contains no analysis of the state or relative autonomy of state action, and is vague on the connection between the conceptual components of the theory in general (Stinchcombe, 1982). One could reconstruct Wallerstein's historical analysis allowing for the relative autonomy of political-military domination. I am not about to do this. It suffices to say that the analysis would be enriched by knowing which states could act more autonomously and which states were confined to act in the interests of the dominant classes.

The concepts of core, semiperiphery, and periphery can be reconceptualized to take into account the relative autonomy of the state. To be sure, political power and economic power are causally interrelated, but one cannot be reduced to the other. The extraordinary military power of semiperipheral states such as Israel and Taiwan and the military weakness of core states such as Germany and Japan belie any unilateral typology of the world-system. I will propose a reconceptualization of core, semiperiphery, and periphery in the next section. For now, rather than continue to extrapolate the concept of relative autonomy of the interstate system in a world formation, I want to review a theory of world relations and of social revolutions which explicitly includes that concept. I am referring to Lenin's (1939) theory of imperialism.

Lenin's Theory of Imperialism

Skocpol (1977) generally ignores Lenin's theory of imperialism (even when examining the Russian Revolution) and claims that he only followed Marx's class theory (1979:284). When discussing the inadequacies of Marxist analysis of revolution, Skocpol and Trimberger explicitly avoid "the changing emphases to be found in writings on revolution by Marxists since Marx" (1977–78:103, n.5). Wallerstein (1980b) criticized Lenin's theory of imperialism for reifying cyclical processes of capital export into a stage of capitalist development (supposedly the last stage). But he did not consider the political components of Lenin's theory or the relation between his political and economic ideas. It seems to me that Lenin's theory of imperialism addresses the analysis of social structural relations, world relations, and autonomous state relations which Skocpol (1979:5, 14–31) found wanting in other theories of revolution.

Lenin (1939, 1943, 1970) developed a typology of the hierarchy of nations in the world formation similar in form to the concepts of core, semiperiphery, and periphery. However, Lenin characterized the relations between nations according to their political as well as economic dependency. His typology consisted of great powers, semicolonies, and colonies. He measured political dependence primarily on the basis of colonial status. Military power was also a consideration, especially in defining great-power status. For economic independence, he mainly considered foreign debt and foreign ownership of industry.

Hierarchy in Lenin's typology was based on the degree of independence. Great powers are both politically and economically independent. All other nations are economically dependent on the great powers to greater or lesser degrees. Colonies are politically dependent on the great powers as well. States in colonies are, by definition, administered by an imperial nation. The states in semicolonies are controlled by the great powers, but not directly administered by them. For semicolonies, Lenin had in mind such situations as prerevolutionary China, which had a separate state administration but was thoroughly dominated by the great powers. There is a strong association between political and economic independence in Lenin's categorization. However, Lenin specifically referred to countries such as Argentina and Portugal as examples of how politically independent nations are nonetheless dependent economically (1939:81, 85–86).

In Figure 2.1, I present a rough approximation of relative location of the categories of great powers, semicolonies, and colonies in Lenin's theory. I have also attempted to hypothetically locate a variety of countries as examples in the diagram which Lenin (1939, 1943, 1970a) used (with the exception of colonies, which are obvious). Imperial Russia, for instance, is located on the border of the great-power category. In relation to the other great powers, Imperial Russia had an extensive (land-based) military apparatus and was not directly administered by any other great power, yet it had a high level of economic dependence. In relation to the semi-colonial and colonial countries, Russia maintained a colonial relationship over most of the rest of its empire and exerted military-administrative pressure over the Slavic regions of the Balkans.

As an indicator of potential revolutionary situations, the position of a nation in the "imperialist chain" can tell us something about the susceptibility of a state to collapse under pressure from other states, as well as the likelihood of widespread class conflict. Revolutionary situations are most likely to occur in nations located in the interstices of the system. Nations in these situations are the "weak links" in the maintenance of the existing international structure of domination. Each great power faces military pressure both from the other great powers seeking to strip away its colonies and from the resistance of its colonial peoples. At the same time, all the great powers have an interest in maintaining the system of colonialism (except, to some degree, the United States, which has had few external colonies). An economically dependent power is generally constrained to ally itself

Figure 2.1 The Imperialist Chain of the Pre–World War I World Formation*

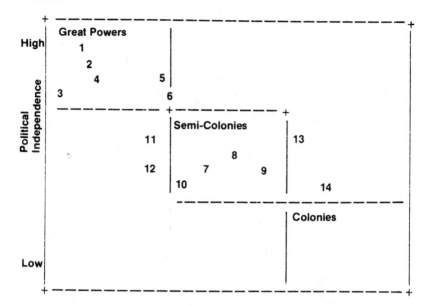

Great Powers	Semicolonies	Mixed Positions[†]
1. Great Britain	7. China	11. Belgium
2. Germany	8. Turkey	12. Holland
3. United States	9. Persia	13. Portugal
4. France	10. Ireland	14. Argentina
5. Japan		
6. Russia		

*The hypothetical locations of nations on the diagram are based upon classifications and descriptions of these countries made by Lenin (1939, 1943, 1970). They are placed on the diagram for heuristic purposes only.

[†]These are nations that Lenin used to contrast with the countries in the semicolonial list. These "mixed positions" indicate countries which are dependent on the great powers but have not made legal-administrative concessions to them as semicolonies have.

with its financiers, increasing its military obligations and decreasing its options for colonial expansion.

Lenin was, of course, most interested in the revolutionary prospects for Imperial Russia. Russia's military strength and domination of colonial areas compensated to a limited extent for its lack of industrial development and finance capital (Lenin, 1943:758). Yet it was highy dependent on foreign capital from the other great powers. It was especially dependent in precisely those areas — heavy industry, armaments, technology, and so on — in which it lagged behind the other great powers. This placed the Russian state in a precarious position in relation to pressure from the other great powers. Having to participate in the world war was a type of blackmail imposed on Russia as a price for being *able* to participate in the war for its own limited objectives (see Trotsky, 1959:14–15). Continuing this participation long after its own objectives were no longer realizable certainly contributed to the collapse of the czar's and, especially, Kerensky's governments.

Discussion

The previous description of the effects of Imperial Russia's position in the world formation on the likelihood of its being in a revolutionary situation does not differ in historical substance from Skocpol's (1979) description of the international pressures on the Russian state. Mine is not a quibble of historical facts. The question is whether there are theoretical concepts about position in the world formation which can be used to study revolutions in general. Lenin's theory suggests that there are. However, the post-World War II decolonization has made Lenin's terminology archaic. Most of the nations in the current world formation would now have to be considered semicolonies according to Lenin's typology. Also, Lenin's theory does not tell us much about the nations which do not fall into his three main categories. Finally, the concept of "weak links" is limited in applicability to economically dependent great powers. Revolutionary situations in great powers are relatively rare, the last one occurring in Germany in 1918, or perhaps France in 1968. A theory of revolutions should tell us about the situations where revolutions most frequently occur. This is a major limitation of Lenin's theory, and of Skocpol's as well.

Lenin's insights on revolution can be incorporated into a reconceptualization of the concepts of core, semiperiphery, and periphery in world-system theory. This would be an expansion of the theory in order to take economic and political dependency as intercausal but relatively autonomous variables in the world formation. These two factors should be treated as continuous variables which are

Figure 2.2 Contradictory Locations in the Post–World War II World Formation*

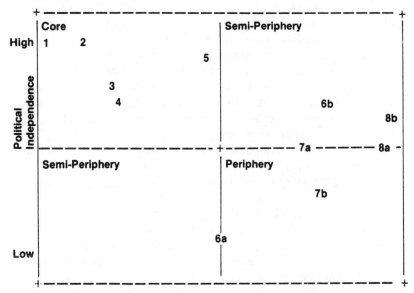

*The location of nations on the diagram is entirely hypothetical, intended for heuristic purposes only. Emptiness would occupy a large space between the core and the rest of the world if this were drawn to scale. The same is true of a somewhat smaller space between the superpowers and the rest of the core. The structure of the diagram allows comparison of country locations along only one of the independence variables at a time, holding the other variable constant. In order to indicate simultaneous movement along both the economic and political dimensions of independence, turn the diagram sideways until it forms a diamond shape. In each case, the prior instance would be the period of multiple sovereignty immediately prior to the revolution (or, in the case of Poland, the imposition of martial law).

sufficiently bimodal to form meaningful categories. Nonetheless, the distinctions between categories should not be reified, especially between the semiperiphery and the periphery. A very tentative outline of the reconceptualized categories is presented in Figure 2.2. I have located a variety of countries on the table for purely illustrative purposes. These are also intended as heuristic examples. As pictured, I doubt if the United States or even the Soviet Union would fit on the page, and most of the middle of the table would be blank if this were drawn to scale. Therefore, the categories have been stretched out for exemplary purposes, somewhat as Greenland is on a flat map.

The core category of the world formation is defined by high levels of both economic and political independence. This allows us to distinguish countries in the core which have an immense political-military power but are economically weak (such as China), as well as countries which are economically powerful but have a relatively small military force (Japan and West Germany). All countries outside the core are dependent on it to a large degree. The periphery of the world formation is the converse of the core. Countries in the periphery are both economically and politically dependent. The remaining colonies would be located in the periphery, as would those nations which Lenin would have considered semicolonial.

The semiperiphery has been split in two. This category represents nations which are in contradictory locations in the world formation. They have a converse relationship between economic and political dependency. The advantage of this reconceptualization of the semiperiphery is that nations which may have a dependent economy yet are politically very independent from the core powers (such as Nicaragua) do not have to be given a peripheral status, as an economic reductionist conception would have it. Likewise, countries which have a much more independent economy relative to the periphery yet are politically or militarily dependent on a core nation (such as South Korea) can also be located in a nonreductionist manner. The degree of economic and political independence of semiperipheral nations is in relation to the periphery. All of the semiperipheral countries are dependent on the core both politically and economically, but to a significantly lesser degree than the peripheral countries.

The contradiction between political and economic dependence facilitates revolutionary situations in the semiperiphery. The contradictory status of semiperipheral countries limits the ability of the state to act in the long-term interests of the internal power bloc. The term "power bloc" refers to the coalition of dominant classes and class fractions which have organized their economic interests into political interests in such a way that the country as a whole benefits or suffers depending on whether those interests are served (see Poulantzas, 1974, 1978).[2] Failure of the state to respond to the interests of the power bloc can place the nation in economic crises and possibly lead to the formation of opposing power blocs. The opposing power blocs would then contend for sovereignty (Tilly, 1978; see also Trotsky's [1959] description of "dual power").

Economic and political dependency on the core results in constraints on both peripheral and semiperipheral state actions which might engender widespread disaffection with the state (the dictation of severe economic restraints in the state policy of indebted nations by the International Monetary Fund is a recent example). But in the redefined semiperiphery this is more likely to lead to a revolutionary situation than in the periphery, because the disjunction between the polity and the economy is greater. In particular, those countries located in the interstices between a semiperipheral and a core or a peripheral status, or those otherwise moving along one dimension but not the other, are in the most intensely contradictory positions in the world formation.

Also critically important are the internal factors involved in Tilly's (1978) analysis of the development of multiple sovereignty. As his central thesis points out, disaffection alone is insufficient to create a revolution unless the opposing parties have the resources and organization to contest for sovereignty. Examples of such resources more readily available in the politically dependent but economically less dependent semiperiphery are the funds, organizations, and leadership provided by a national bourgeoisie, an industrial working class, and an intellectual stratum (often the offspring of the national bourgeoisie). These key resource groups are likely to be disaffected because the state is constrained to serve the interests of some great power (and the comprador bourgeoisie). Semiperipheral nations with high levels of economic independence (relative to the periphery) but low political independence usually pursue a proimperialist state policy of repressing the labor force in order to attract and keep foreign capital. The interests of workers, intellectuals, and national capitalists (in that order) consequently tend to be excluded from the dominant power bloc.

To be sure, revolts by the peasantry and agricultural labor force without support of the national bourgeoisie and even without the industrial workers can bring on revolutions in the periphery and semiperiphery. The converse, a proletarian revolution in agrarian countries without the support of the peasantry, has not happened and is not likely to happen. However, the participation in the political process of the national bourgeoisie and/or industrial working class found in the semiperiphery can provide the organizing resources which make the formation of a contending power bloc more likely and more formidable. In the case of the more politically independent but economically dependent category, countries tend to have leftist governments which provide resources and mobilize the disaffected but otherwise unorganized peasantry (either unintentionally or in order to retain power). Relevant to my argument, Paige (1975) demonstrates the increased likelihood of revolutions in countries with social democratic governments.

The importance of disaffection among key resource groups can be found in some of Skocpol's recent work. For example, Skocpol's (1981:8–16) analysis of prerevolutionary Iran describes the state as seemingly more attuned to "cues from the United States, than to the indigenous demands of the Iranian people" (1981:16). She also points out how the state policy of imperialist development split the interests of the bazaar merchants away from those of the rest of the dominant classes. The merchants and their religiously educated offspring were central in forming an opposition power bloc with other disaffected parties, particularly the industrial workers in the oil fields. Skocpol's analysis of the Iranian revolution is a good example of the effects of a contradictory status in the world-system between political dependence and relative economic independence (see also Zeitlin's [1973] analysis of the Cuban revolution).

Conclusion

I have attempted three projects in this essay. The first was to deal with Skocpol's (1979) rejection of world-system theory due to its overreliance on the world market as the explanatory dynamic of world relations. I reviewed Brenner's (1977) important criticisms of world-system theory, and offered solutions from Laclau (1971) and Amin (1977, 1980) to the problems he raised. Second, I have taken Skocpol's criticism of economic reductionism in world-system theory as a serious challenge to its explanatory power. As a result, I have attempted to reconceptualize the categories of core, semiperiphery, and periphery in order to take into account Lenin's insight on the intercausal but relatively autonomous relations between political and economic dependency. This creates a view of world dynamics analogous to the view of social dynamics in a social formation.

Consequently, I have labeled this a world-formation perspective. The concept of a world formation is intended to incorporate the determinacy of multiple and differential modes of production on world exchange, unequal exchange and unequal development in the world-system, and the relatively autonomous system of interstate relations.

The third project was to explore ways in which world-system theory could provide general concepts about world formations which could be useful in the analysis of social revolutions and their consolidation. I have, tentatively, suggested that the concept of contradictory locations in the world formation serves such a purpose. Contradictory locations exist in the semiperiphery where political dependency and economic dependency do not coincide or are moving in opposite directions. This situation creates disjunctures between the state and civil society which facilitate the emergence of contending power blocs and revolutions.

The concept of contradictory locations in the world formation lends itself to further research, which could go in the direction of deep comparative studies of a few revolutions or quantitative studies of many. However, I do not think that analyses of revolutions throughout the history of the capitalist world-system should be done as if the same conditions applied throughout. While the system has always been capitalist by definition, the structure of world political and economic relations has varied tremendously.

World-system theory cannot tell us much about the intense struggles which bring about social revolutions. What it should be able to tell us is what world political and economic relations facilitate the conditions necessary for a revolutionary situation to exist. It should also be able to tell us about those conditions in the areas of the world where social revolutions are actually taking place, and not rely solely on expecting the pattern of great revolutions of the past to repeat themselves. While this is only an exploratory analysis, it charts a theoretical course for the analysis of social revolutions within the world-system perspective.

Notes

I would like to thank Edgar Kiser, Bill Lockwood, Al Bergesen, and the anonymous reviewers for comments. An ealier version of this paper was presented at the annual meetings of the Pacific Sociological Association in Seattle, 1984. Support for this work was provided by a grant from the Emory University Research Fund.

1. Wright (1979) uses the concept of contradictory locations to signify occupations with a mixed position relative to the major classes. I am using the term in a similar manner to describe the position of "semiperipheral" countries relative to the core and periphery. However, this does not mean that I consider core and periphery to be class-type relations (see Boswell [1984] for a criticism of Bergesen's [1982, 1983] theory of world classes).

2. The power bloc is usually dominated by the most economically powerful fraction of the dominant classes, such as monopoly capital in the United States. It may also form alliances with subordinate classes or class fractions (such as the so-called aristocracy of labor). An especially obvious example of the power bloc's translating its economic interests into political ones which affect the entire nation is the Chrysler bailout.

References

Althusser, Louis (1971). *Lenin and Philosophy*. London: New Left Books.

Amin, Samir (1977). *Unequal Development*. New York: Monthly Review Press.

——— (1980). *Class and Nation, Historically and in the Current Crises*. New York: Monthly Review Press.

Bergesen, Albert (1980). "From Utilitarianism to Globology: The Shift from the Individual to the World as a Whole as the Primordial Unit of Analysis." In *Studies of the Modern World System,* ed. A. Bergesen. New York: Academic Press.

——— (1982). "Is There a World Mode of Production? A Comment," *Contemporary Crises* 6:91–96.

——— (1983). "The Class Structure of the World System." In *Contending Approaches to World System Analysis,* ed. W. Thompson, Beverly Hills, Calif.: Sage.

Boswell, Terry E. (1984). "World Formation or World Mode of Production? Alternative Approaches to World System Analysis." *Contemporary Crises* 8:378–84.

Brenner, Robert (1984). "The Origins of Capitalist Development: A Critique of Neo-Smithian Marxism." *New Left Review* 104 (July–August):25–92.

Laclau, Ernesto (1971). "Feudalism and Capitalism in Latin America." *New Left Review* 67 (May–June):13–38.

Lenin, Vladimir I. (1939). *Imperialism the Highest Stage of Capitalism*. New York: International Publishers.

———— (1943). "Imperialism and the Split in Socialism." In *The Theoretical Principles of Marxism, Selected Works*, vol. 11:748–63, New York: International Publishers.

———— (1970). "The Right of Nations to Self-Determination." In *Selected Works in Three Volumes*. Moscow: Progress Publishers.

Marx, Karl (1967). *Capital*, vol. 1. New York: International Publishers.

———— (1979). *The Grundrisse*. New York: International Publishers.

Poulantzas, Nicos (1973). *Political Power and Social Classes*. London: New Left Books.

———— (1978). *Classes in Contemporary Society*. London: Verso.

Skocpol, Theda (1977). "Wallerstein's World Capitalist System: A Theoretical and Historical Critique." *American Journal of Sociology* 82:5 (March):1075–90.

———— (1979). *States and Social Revolutions*. Cambridge: Cambridge University Press.

———— (1981). "Rentier State and Shi'a Islam in the Iranian Revolution." In *Theory and Society* 11:3 (May):265–83.

Skocpol, Theda, and Ellen Kay Trimberger (1977–78). "Revolutions and World-Historical Development of Capitalism." *Berkeley Journal of Sociology*, 22:101–13.

Stinchcombe, Arthur L. (1982). "The Growth of the World System." Review essay, *American Journal of Sociology* 87:6 (May):1389–95.

Tilly, Charles (1978). *From Mobilization to Revolution*. Reading, Mass.: Addison-Wesley.

Trotsky, Leon (1959). *The Russian Revolution*. F.W. Dupee, ed. New York: Doubleday.

Urry, John (1982). *The Anatomy of Capitalist Societies*. London: Macmillan.

Wallerstein, Immanuel (1974). *The Modern World-System*. New York: Academic Press.

———— (1980a). *The Modern World-System II*. New York: Academic Press.

———— (1980b). "Imperialism and Development." In *Studies of the Modern World System*, ed. A. Bergesen. New York: Academic Press, pp. 13–23.

Wright, Erik Olin (1979). *Class Structure and Income Determination*. New York: Academic Press.

Zeitlin, Maurice (1973). "The Cuban Revolution." In *Revolutions: A Comparative Study*, ed., L. Kaplan. New York: Random house, pp. 419–430.

CHAPTER 3

Change, Stability, and Slogans

Henry Bienen

Dwight Eisenhower and John Foster Dulles proclaimed a fear of "falling dominoes" in Southeast Asia. John F. Kennedy told us that there was a "missile gap." Richard M. Nixon and Henry A. Kissinger promulgated the idea of "the new influentials"—Brazil, Nigeria, Saudi Arabia, Iran—and hoped they might act as America's regional surrogates. Jimmy Carter and Zbigniew Brzezinski, surveying the Persian Gulf, the Middle East, and Southwest Asia, were concerned about "arcs of crisis." And since the Iranian Revolution, policy makers have been proclaiming the "Islamic resurgence." Ronald Reagan and Caspar W. Weinberger want to close "the window of vulnerability." And "détente" and "linkage" remain undefined terms to describe United States–Soviet relations or to invoke a desired state of those relations.

Officials long have tried to capture complicated events and to dominate public discussion of foreign policy by using simple phrases and slogans. They engage in phrase making in order to reach wide audiences. The news media, too, promulgate slogans and labels—shorthand that makes simple summaries possible.

But, perhaps more fundamental, the use of labels, metaphors, and phrase making, whether in foreign policy or in analysis of modernization, is a result of a globalism which is itself a desire to simplify events and forces. Inside and outside, what government "globalists" in modernization and foreign policy analysis have in common is a desire to be sweeping, unequivocal, popularized, and able to deduce definite policy stances from their positions. Those who want to differentiate within regions and countries (and they are frequently area experts inside and outside government) must complicate life, must take account of many variables and be ready to admit more uncertainty, especially as they move from analysis of one country to comparisons with another.

High-level policy makers cannot be expected to master the details of particular settings. The desire to capture complicated events and forces through sweeping generalizations stems in part from an impatience with the particular and an inability to master it. Generalists do not want to be at a disadvantage vis-à-vis specialists. Furthermore, it is difficult to frame regionwide policies based on "many particulars." The general thrust of policy, its contours, gets hedged with too many qualifications in an attempt to come to grips with the particulars. Thus slogans, catch phrases, and "theories" are used to structure debate. Regional and country specialists can be said to be parochial in their concerns, to operate at a low level of generality, and to miss the big picture. Invariably, the generalists capture attention and dominate the terms of the discussion until the specificity of place forces itself upon a sweeping perspective. The semantic symbols cannot dictate what the real world is. They become terms in search of a policy, but the policy cannot be hammered out on the basis of slogans and phrases.

There is a tendency to want to label countries and processes, because we hope to create order out of a seeming chaos. But there are significant costs to sloganeering and labeling. The first danger is that of mislabeling. But even if, taxonomically speaking, we lump countries in similar categories (e.g., military regimes, Communist party systems, one-party states), what have we learned? Not much. We should know by now that it is fallacious to make easy deductions from the fact that a country is ruled by military officers or calls itself Marxist-Leninist. We learn little about economic policy or state intervention from those labels. Is state intervention larger in Zaire or Congo-Brazzaville? Who bargained harder with multinational corporations, conservative Brazil or Velasco's Peru?

Take the related catch phrases "Islamic resurgence" and "arcs of crisis." They are intended to suggest that there has been a revival of fundamentalist Islamic appeals to mass audiences in Africa, the Middle East, Southwest Asia, and Indonesia. Islam, it is true, continues to provide the symbols and vehicles for understanding of power and justice in Egypt, Syria, Iran, Turkey, and other countries. Organizations such as the Moslem Brotherhood in Egypt, the National Salvation Party in Turkey, and the Moslem Brethren in

Syria have waxed and waned, depending on government repression, the quality of their own leaders, and the success or failure of secularly based elites. But these groups are not similar from country to country. The appeals of Iran's clerical regime are not identical to those of Islamic movements in Sunni Moslem countries; the claims of Colonel Muammar el-Qaddafi of Libya are different from those of Egyptian and Syrian religious fundamentalists.

Americans' perspectives on change—the ways we define issues and problems–are all consequential for our national interests. Of course, it is extremely difficult to come to grips with the subjects of unrest, instability, and rapid change. These terms can be defined in many ways. It is not easy to establish criteria for knowing when something has changed in society, much less to specify causal factors making for change. When we also consider time factors, our perspectives on change and stability frequently shift. Was Mexico (or Iran) stable until the Mexican (or Iranian) Revolution? Or should we consider the period leading to the revolution one of incipient instability? Or is that period better described as one setting the conditions for more radical change because critical issues were not solved and there was a deepening of social conflict, albeit conflict that was not openly expressed? What of the perspective of more than fifty years after the Mexican Revolution? How much change or stability has there been? What of situations of persistent violence, strikes, coups, which are themselves patterned, endemic, but do not lead to structural change, for example, in Bolivia? In order to usefully deal with change, levels of generality must be specified and time frames made clear. The behaviors, institutions, personnel to which change refers must be made very clear also.[1]

Our perspectives on change, the ways that we define issues and problems, the ways that we operationalize concepts, are all consequential for whether or not we see U.S. interests as threatened by developments in the Third World. Of course, specifying those interests, making them concrete, is itself a process with its own difficulties. Whether we believe that our society as a whole has a set of interests, or that different social, ethnic, and economic groups have interests which they try to impose, is a matter of no small difference.

Too often as analysts explore relationships, they define away the subject under investigation. For example, the literature on modernization has defined so much into "modernization" as a dependent and/or independent variable that cause-and-effect relationships have disappeared as problems to be understood. We can *define* what we mean by a modern society, but it is not very helpful to do so. If we treat modernization as a process, rather than as an end state, as most of the literature came to do in the 1960s, modernization turns out to be a highly complex process indeed. Thus analysts came to try to break up aspects of what they meant by modernization and to use concepts for which they could find empirical indicators: social change (literacy, urbanization, secularization, years of education), economic development (growth in per capita GNP, structural change from agriculture to industry; more recently, income shares and equity across a population), political change and stability (institutionalization, levels of political participation, sometimes democracy, centralization of authority, rationalization of authority). Obviously, operationalizing these concepts—that is, being able empirically to measure them, more or less—is easier to do both in theory and in practice for some than for others. Analysts would disagree less among themselves about what literacy should mean (although there are differences of opinion) than they would about how we should understand and thus measure equity in a society.

Arguments over definitions, meanings, and ways of measuring are important, because setting the definition or operationalizing a concept is half the battle in getting people to understand processes the way one does. This is especially true in fields where prediction is difficult. When we ask how modernization disrupts traditional patterns, just what is the modernization that is doing the disruption? What is being disrupted? "Tradition"? Which traditions? We can find many indicators in societies for various social changes—for example, the ending of some set of traditions associated with specific beliefs or patterns of cultivation or landowning. But the import of these changes is another matter. A process may occur in many different countries, but its meaning and significance will be contextually determined.

We know that internal stability is affected by both forces external to a society—for example, new power blocs or sweeping religious movements—and forces intrinsic to a society's own dynamics, such as population growth or generational change. In the real world, it may be hard to separate interstate instabilities and changes in the international system from the internal dynamics of a given society. More attention is given here to the latter than the former, admitting the interconnectedness of internal and external relationships.

In order to explore the difficulties in coming to grips with modernization and unrest, I want to give some examples from the subject of rapid urbanization and unrest. There does appear to be more agreement on definitions of and measures for urbanization than modernization. When we ask, Is rapid urbanization creating the potential for widespread unrest? Does Third World urbanization create or go hand in hand with the expansion of revolutionary forces in society? the answers seem less hedged than most social science answers.[2]

Urbanization almost everywhere in the Third World is creating large populations in the so-called informal sector. Most migrants are being absorbed not in unionized labor, not in high-productivity, large-scale industries, but in small-scale production, trade, and services and in illegal or quasi-legal activities. Informal-sector workers change jobs frequently and often have no permanent place of abode.

Many analysts have compared cities by the age, sex ratios, functions, and income levels of their work forces. Striking variations appear. For example, the proportion of the work force in the informal sector will vary between and within countries. It is very large in a big city like Ibadan in Nigeria, which has almost no industry. A more mixed picture exists in a highly industrial city like Mexico City or São Paulo.

Analysts have used survey data from many cities to argue persuasively that high rates of rural to urban migration are not necessarily associated with rising discontent and that cities are not revolutionary hotbeds because of their large semiemployed populations, even when unemployment rates are very high.[3] Indeed, migrants respond frequently that they are better off than they were in rural areas, that they look forward to a better life for themselves and their children. Also, case studies have shown that it is hard to organize people in the informal sector and that insofar as most low-income urban residents participate in politics they do so through local patron-client networks and not through working-class parties, trade unions, or urban revolutionary groups. We can conclude that rapid urbanization by itself is not creating the potential for widespread unrest.

However, current studies give us a complicated picture, not a simple one. The ways that people get drawn into politics and either co-opted or intimidated by governments are important factors in the equation of social and political unrest. The process of massive urbanization in Third World countries is not yet played out. How long will it go on at current rates of increase, from 6 to 12 percent? Can the informal sector continue to grow? What happens when one generation of migrants settles down only to be pressed by a new wave of people needing jobs, services, and housing? No study that shows migrant satisfaction and low levels of organized political participation has concluded that there is no potential for widespread unrest. Views range from Barbara Ward's (1976) apocalyptic scenarios of huge urban conglomerations of more than 20 million people in Jakarta and Mexico City, seething with rebellion and/or sunk in apathy, to studies which show that most urban demands, whether in Lagos or Rio or Manila, have been for clean water, better housing and title to housing, and access to jobs through improved transportation, rather than demands for massive redistribution of economic goods and political power. These studies suggest that Third World governments have policy space to play off groups, to deal with demands incrementally and through reformist policies. Whether they will be successful is another matter. Obviously, they are not always: time runs out. Policies can be counterproductive.

Many British farmers went to the cities in the nineteenth century, or earlier, bringing their own grievances over land issues and rural injustice. Some joined working-class parties, but no radical working-class party turned the political system upside down. In nineteenth- and early-twentieth-century Russia, peasants were organized by factory workers and party organizers and powerfully added to revolutionary impulses in the towns and in the army, as well as on the land. The answers to why revolution occurred in Russia but not in England range from explanations that stress individual leadership, to the response of an autocratic government in Russia driving its opposition underground, to collapse in war, to different landholding patterns and relationships between landed elites and peasants and between landed elites and urban ones, to the role of ethnicity and religion, to timing and phasing of political, social, and economic changes.

Social scientists and historians spend a great deal of effort trying to understand the possibilities for reform or revolution and abstracting the conditions which produce one outcome or another. Political leaders and would-be leaders, too, go back to history to understand or misunderstand their changes; leaders have underestimated their chances to seize power or, more commonly, overestimated their chances to seize power or stay in power. Among the hardest things for academic analysts and policy makers to do are to state time frames within which action is likely to take place and to be very specific about the scope of unrest and its forms, intensities, and duration.

Again, we can take the relationship between urbanization and unrest to illustrate difficulties of analysis, for a good deal is known about the nature of demands of groups and their attitudes, and yet we have a hard time making accurate predictions about "unrest." Part of the problem is that there are too many intervening variables between urbanization and unrest for us to easily specify cause and effect. Part of the difficulty is that all societies receive exogenous shocks. But this does not mean that we have no useful indicators to predict change. It does not mean that we have no generalizations or theories with which to understand the processes of change.

We know, for example, that high rates of urbanization and increasing size of the industrial sector do not lead ipso facto to diminution of communal feelings in any society. What differs in urban contexts are the amounts and kinds of resources available for competition, and the structures through which people compete. It is the form of the struggle and the relative weight of the factors which lead us to describe conflict as class or communal. Naked opposition of cultures—that is, dislikes of some people for the habits, smells, foods of others—may be rather rare as a dominant motive for conflict, but more likely to occur in urban than in rural societies, if for no other reason than the proximity of groups in urban contexts. The answer to why some political leaders are able or unable to use communal appeals in Nigeria or Kenya or India cannot be determined by finding out the level of industrialization or urbanization. We must look at how rates of change affect different groups, the groups' internal values and organization, the specific issues that are salient at given times.

The importance of communal feelings depends on the content of the value systems attached to ethnic or religious groups and on the specific contexts in which ethnic communities coexist. Ethnicity can create solidarity across functional divisions, but it can also create divisions within classes, hampering political organization among workers. The salience of class and ethnic demands is not constant within a society or within one city. Thus Islam in northern Nigeria binds formal-sector and informal-sector workers together, but it also creates a wider community within which workers, foremen, and even managers act. Yet when Islamic norms are violated, feelings of injustice fuel economic grievances of workers and give these grievances wider political meaning. Islam can be both a radicalizing and a conservative force in Nigeria.

We come now full circle back to Islam, slogans, and U.S. foreign policy. "The return of Islam" is meant to connote a phenomenon in international relations: the increased power, importance, and activity of Islamic states. It also refers to a phenomenon within societies: the presumed revival of fundamentalist Islamic appeals to mass audiences and the demonstrable increase in the power of elites whose base rests on Islamic institutions and/or appeals (Iran) or who aspire to power by using such appeals and institutions (Indonesia), or leaders who now try to co-opt the appeals and institutions (Pakistan), have done so for a long time (Saudia Arabia), or walk a line between co-opting the appeals and suppressing certain Islamic organizations (Egypt, Iraq, Syria, Turkey). There is also the actual spread of Islam as a belief system, a phenomenon hard to measure accurately but one which many observers believe is occurring (not necessarily at the expense of Christianity) in East Africa, moving from the coast inland, and in West Africa, moving toward the coast and growing in cities, as new migrants take up Islam in Nigerian or Senegalese towns.

The spread of Islam; the salience of Islamic rhetoric, symbols, and appeals; the coming to power of a clergy-based regime in Iran; and the renewed activity of fundamentalist groups elsewhere may or may not be related. The connections have to be shown, not assumed. "The return of Islam" cannot explain important geopolitical events in the Gulf, the Horn of Africa, or the Middle East, any more than that phrase can capture the crises and instabilities in Islamic countries. Did Islam ever go away in Iran, or in Egypt? How secular has Turkey been? These are questions demanding answers. It is possible that large numbers of people turned away from Islam and then came back to it in these countries. But it is more likely that Islam has remained an important part of life for the majority of people in Egypt, Turkey, and Iran; it has continued to provide the norms, symbols, and vehicles for people's understanding of justice and power.

There has been a widely shared perception that what Manfred Halpern (1964) called the new middle class in the Middle East has failed in development, in eliminating corruption, and in handling equity issues. Civilian and military-based leaderships in the Middle East, and also in Southwest Asia, from Bourguiba to the Shah and the Pakistani generals, have lost mass support. The failure of regimes to deal successfully with Israel has been an important element too. Sadat's 1973 war is a major exception to a record of defeat. Given the domestic and foreign policy failures, Islamic groups have provided an alternative by default. But they are not the same groups everywhere. The Brethren in Egypt and Syria have not made the same appeals as Khomeini or Qaddafi. The latter two make sweeping radical appeals that do carry them beyond their borders. But it is not clear that within their countries their appeal to professional middle classes is on Islamic grounds rather than on nationalistic grounds. Middle-class and professional people will act on complex matters from several interests. When the Shah's regime abused middle-class children, he lost the support of those whose class interests might have led them to stay with him.

Like the leaders themselves, the middle classes may reach out to Islam as a defensive measure. That is, Islam is a binding force for the community and insulates classes from demands for redistribution and radical change. The Egyptian middle classes embrace Islam as a defense mechanism, and so do traditional authorities, businessmen, and civil servants in northern Nigeria. At the same time, groups like the People's Redemption Party in Nigeria, led by the late Aminu Kan, and radical Islamic groups in Iran make revolutionary appeals in the Islamic idiom.

To try to understand the political upheavals in North Africa, the

Middle East, Southwest Asia, and the Gulf through recourse to ideas about Islamic revival cannot take us very far and will mislead us. There can be no substitute for specific and contextual analysis. Indeed, there is a parallel between sloganizing, the dangerous tendency to try to capture complex events with semantic symbols, and the hope of modernization theorists that with their frameworks and "theories" they can capture the relationships between complex variables and express them in catch phrases such as "takeoff" or "continuous transformation." Most of so-called theorizing about modernization has been the creation of metaphors. Cause-and-effect relationships have not been shown that could enable us to predict events.

Can policy be formulated on the basis of general theories or what have come to be called middle-level theories? We cannot do without generalizations and theories. The trick is to make them testable, operational, and relevant—real theories. Two decades of work on modernization shows that it is difficult to take propositions and make them policy-relevant. But it can be done. Demography provides an example of a field in which extensive data collection, sophisticated analytical techniques, and testable theories allow us to draw important policy conclusions.

The relationship between economic development and population growth has long been debated. Demographers can now specify how population growth affects savings and investment, social services, and the structure of economies.[4] This entails coming to grips with many variables, not just a few. If we want to understand the political implications of high rates of population growth, we can build on excellent demographic work. But to the specification of current population size and per capita income, fertility structure, and resource base, we would have to add the ability of a political elite to affect consumption and investment ratios, to impose population policies down the line. It will be hard to examine the relationship between population growth and unrest, for all the reasons given in the discussion on urbanization and unrest. Without necessarily attributing to excess fertility every impediment to social and economic development, we can say that for a large number of countries high rates of population growth narrow political and economic options and make policy trade-offs much sharper. High rates of population growth are a starting point for looking at land-pressure problems, inadequate agricultural productivity, massive rural-to-urban migration, and pressure on resources and environmental quality. The impact of increasing population affects the so-called modernization variables and, in turn, affects the ways that they interact. To capture the political consequences of high population growth is not beyond our ability.

Nor, to end up where I started, is it beyond our ability to understand the relationships between urbanization and unrest, or the impact of Islam in specific societies. To generalize is not the same thing as to overgeneralize. Knowing the limits of our general statements and propositions is a first step. A next step involves providing contextual analyses so that theories are not devoid of meaning, propositions can be tested in the real world, and policy implications can be drawn from them. It is difficult, at best, to understand the policy implications of complicated and long-term social, economic, and political forces. If we overgeneralize and sloganize, we will not be able to discuss U.S. interests meaningfully, even presuming that we can state those interests with some degree of specificity.

The interests of the United States are usually put forward, at least for public consumption, in such a general way that they are frequently hard to relate to developmental and political trends. To say that the United States is interested in peaceful change, growth with equity, the promotion of human rights, is to state meaningful goals. But they are goals that sometimes conflict with one another, and they do not give much policy guidance for our positions concerning the social and political changes we see around us. Our policy stances tend to be guided by short-run interests that are understood conventionally in terms of access to critical resources, balance-of-power politics, and maintaining regimes that will do economic and political business with us. These interests can contend with a desire for peaceful political change, for growth and equity, and for human rights. But they tend to dominate, in part because they are immediate and concrete, and because policy makers think they understand them and their implications better than the implications of trying to maximize more diffuse interests and trying to react to complicated social forces, undertakings which are perceived as riskier because there are more unknowns.

Neglecting complicated social and political forces may be the highest-risk policy stance of all. Thus, it is necessary for those who want U.S. policies to reflect an awareness of important changes within and between countries to be able to specify the impact of those changes both on concrete interests and on more general and broader goals. The very elaboration of U.S. interests ought to involve asking, under what conditions is stability or instability congenial to us? Whose growth threatens and whose development will be a positive force for us? The less-developed countries cannot be discussed as a group, and an understanding of the large-scale processes which we call modernization or sociocultural change rarely will be able to provide us with policy guidance, because most statements that we make about them will, if true, be too often trivial. There will be no shortcuts to doing the hard country-by-country analyses and making them relevant for our understanding of international economic and political change.

Notes

1. For a review of attempts to deal with these questions in studies of revolution and internal war see Bienen (1968).

2. I have dealt with these themes at length in Bienen (1974:661–91).

3. Nelson (1979) has cogently presented and analyzed a large amount of data. To cite just two major studies of individual cities and countries, see Cornelius (1975) and Karpat (1976).

4. For a study which accomplishes a great deal along these lines in a short space, see Coale (1978:415–29).

References

Bienen, Henry (1968). *Violence and Social Change*. Chicago: University of Chicago Press.

———— (1974). "Urbanizational Political Stability." *World Development* 7:661–91.

Coale, Ansley J. (1978). "Population Growth and Economic Development: The Case of Mexico." *Foreign Affairs* (January):415–29.

Cornelius, Wayne (1975). *Politics and the Migrant Poor in Mexico City*. Stanford, Calif.: Stanford University Press.

Halpern, Manfred (1964). *The Politics of North Africa and the Middle East*. Princeton, N.J.: Princeton University Press.

Karpat, Kemal (1976). *The Gecekondu: Rural Migration and Urbanization*. Cambridge: Cambridge University Press.

Nelson, Joan (1979). *Access to Power: Politics and the Urban Poor in Developing Nations*. Princeton, N.J.: Princeton University Press.

Ward, Barbara (1976). *The Home of Man*. New York: Norton.

PART II

Studies of the Caribbean/ Latin American Periphery

CHAPTER 4

The Current Economic Crisis and the Caribbean/Central American Periphery: U.S. International Economic Policy During the Republican Administration of 1981 to 1984

Michael T. Martin

> In the international capitalist economy accumulation on a world scale can no longer proceed as it did in the postwar era of expansion, until and unless unequal development and dependent accumulation are put on a new footing.
>
> ANDRE GUNDER FRANK

During the first two years of the Republican administration, in two significant and related addresses before international forums, President Reagan enunciated the central principles that would govern U.S. international economic policy toward the Third World in general and the Caribbean periphery in particular. (For this discussion, Central America is included in the Caribbean periphery.)

First, at the Cancún Summit Conference in 1981, Reagan outlined his administration's approach to North–South economic relations (Reagan, 1981). And second, before the assembly of the Organization of American States (OAS), Reagan proposed the Caribbean Economic Recovery Act or Caribbean Basin Initiative (CBI), which signaled the beginning of the latest stage in U.S. relations with the region (Reagan, 1982).[1] Significantly, during his address to the OAS, Reagan proclaimed that the U.S. "will do whatever is prudent and necessary to insure the peace and security of the Caribbean area" (1982:5). Recent U.S. military and covert paramilitary activites in the region demonstrate the Reagan administration's determination to pursue U.S. national security and economic interests within a foreign policy framework of a narrow bilateralism that rewards friends, destabilizes opposition, and benignly ignores the rest of the world.[2]

Thus any consideration and analysis of the current U.S. international economic policy toward the Third World, and especially the Caribbean periphery, must be assessed in the context of the global security requirements and orientation of the Reagan administration. Within this framework, the CBI constitutes one component of an articulated economic and military strategy for the 1980s to maintain the United States' predominance in the Carbbean periphery.

In this essay, then, I will examine the issues most relevant to U.S. national security concerns and economic interests in the Caribbean region during the first term of the Reagan administration, 1981 to 1984. I will discuss the "free market" approach to Third World economic development proposed by Reagan at Cancún and embodied in the CBI in the framework of a strategic plan designed (1) to support a dual economic-military program of intervention to contain revolutionary movements in the region; (2) to maintain the region's economic dependence on the U.S.; (3) to mitigate the impact of the current economic crisis on the U.S. economy by expanding production, trade, and investment to sites in the Caribbean periphery, and by transforming domestic economies in the region to the requirements of the U.S. market; (4) to consolidate, in a period of intense core-country rivalry and struggle for markets, the U.S. predominance in both the hemisphere and the world economy; and (5) to interdict the growing tendency since the 1960s of countries in the region to pursue independent foreign policies that link them to the nonaligned countries in Asia and Africa and/or to the socialist bloc.

In consideration of the above, I will conclude this essay with a discussion of alternative development strategies for the Caribbean periphery which have direct relevance to the practice of development in the Third World in general.

The Current Crisis in the World Economy

The Core in Relation to the Global System

Capitalist development, on a world scale, is distinguished by two phases since the post–World War II era: rapid growth (punctuated by cyclical downturns) for a period of twenty-five years (to 1970), followed by a relative decline in growth (including one major recession) in the 1970s, leading to a second major recession and stagnation in the early 1980s. Within the second phase, two major recessions have greatly strained the international trade and financial systems and severely affected the economies of most countries in the world. In the core countries, the recession of 1974 and 1975 caused a relative decline in growth in gross domestic product (GDP) to 0.8 percent in 1974 and 0.4 percent in 1975 compared with 6.1 percent rate of growth in 1973 (World Bank, 1984). While the second or most recent recession of 1980 to 1983 was not as sharp as the 1974 to 1975 recession, it lasted longer. GDP gain for the core countries fell from 3.3 percent in 1979 to 1.3 percent in 1980 and 1981, and dropped further to 0.5 percent in 1982; estimates for 1983 indicate that GDP increased to about 2.3 percent (World Bank, 1984).

The longest since the Great Depression of the 1930s, the severity of the 1980 to 1983 recession featured a relative decline of production, profits, and investment; increased unemployment; undermined financing of social programs in most countries of the world; and renewed the struggle over markets between the core capitalist countries. Explanations for the causes of the two recessions and the current crisis in the world economy vary. The World Bank contends that while the 1980 to 1983 recession was triggered by the rise in oil prices in 1979 and the disinflationary policies adopted by governments in the major industrial countries after 1980, it was rooted in "the rigidities that were steadily being built into economies from the mid-1960s onward. The rising trends in unemployment and inflation were the manifestation of increasingly inflexible arrangements for setting wages and prices and for managing public finances" (World Bank, 1984:1). In assessing the financial crisis resulting in the recession of 1974 and 1975, Frank (1981) asserts that it was "motivated by a struggle over markets, developing through changes in exchange rates and currencies, with the goal being to win and hold onto more markets than one's rivals" (1981:8).[3]

Figure 4.1 Growth, Inflation, and Unemployment in Seven Major Industrial Countries, 1966–83

The countries are Canada, France, Germany, Italy, Japan, the United Kingdom, and the United States.

*Estimated.

Source: OECD, 1983.

A review of the economic performance of the major capitalist countries since 1965 indicates the presence of cyclical patterns in GDP growth accompanied by increases in unemployment and inflation. According to Organization for Economic Co-operation and Development (OECD) analyses of GDP growth in seven major industrial countries, three downturns occurred since 1968 (Figure 4.1). The progressive deterioration from cycle to cycle is also evident and has become sharper in the past decade. Explanations for the slow growth and the recent sharp cyclical disturbances experienced in the core countries include (1) the increase of nominal wages and decline of bond prices and exchange rates when countries were perceived to be headed on an inflationary path; (2) the development of

Japanese and Western European technological competition with the United States, resulting in a decline in significance of one source (technology) of enormous growth; (3) the shift of workers from the agricultural to the manufacturing sector was largely expended; (4) the increase of the service industries' share of GDP reflected in lower growth of productivity than in manufacturing; and (5) the economic policies the core countries had pursued resulted in real wage increases and the growth of public spending, taxation, and budget deficits. These last two factors, argue World Bank analysts, "contributed to four major problems (in the core countries) since the late 1960s: inflation, unemployment, declining profitability, and a broadly defined protectionism" (World Bank, 1984:16).

The disinflationary policies pursued by the core countries in the early 1980s are the direct consequence of the accumulation process of the previous decade and are responsible especially for the increase in real interest rates. Concomitantly, the enormous budget deficits of the United States (currently in excess of $170 billion) and the decline in surplus of the oil-exporting countries after 1980 decreased the supply of real savings and contributed also to the rise of real interest rates. Though disinflation reduced consumer price increases sharply, especially in the United States (from 13.5 percent in 1980 to 3.7 percent in 1985), Japan (from 8 percent in 1980 to 1.4 percent in 1985), and Britain (from 18 percent in 1980 to 6.1 percent in 1985), it conversely, along with the 1980 to 1983 recession, adversely affected world trade. According to the World Bank, "world trade grew by 1.5 percent in 1980, stagnated in 1981, and then declined by 3.6 percent in 1982" (1984:22), compared with an average growth rate of 5.7 percent a year in the 1970s (World Bank, 1981).

Deflationary policies in the core countries in the early 1980s also severely strained the international financial system through a combination of two factors: U.S. domestic economic policy and the overvalued dollar, and the growing tendency of some industrial and, particularly, developing countries toward indebtedness.

The first [factor] was the mix of fiscal and monetary policies pursued by the United States. Because of a growing budget deficit financed by borrowing in a country with a relatively low savings rate, interest rates rose. They attracted a substantial capital inflow and helped produce a large real appreciation in the dollar's exchange rate. Since the bulk of international indebtedness is denominated in dollars, the appreciation of the dollar greatly increased the debt servicing cost for all, including the developing countries. (World Bank, 1984:22)

The second factor concerns the relationship between real interest rates and indebtedness.

> During 1960–73 the real interest rate in Eurocurrency markets . . . averaged only 2.5 percent; during 1973–79 it averaged only 0.7 percent and at various times was negative . . . The tendency toward increased indebtedness was a general feature of economic life, and in no way unique to developing countries . . . When real interest rates jumped to almost 7 percent in 1981 and 1982, serious difficulties were bound to follow. The difficulties were most conspicuous in the case of developing countries, particularly those which had borrowed heavily from commercial banks in the previous ten years. (World Bank, 1984:22)

Beset by large exchange rate fluctuations and high unemployment, especially in most Western European countries (Paye, 1985), the international financial system was further strained as world trade declined from 1980 to 1982 and commercial debt increased while real interest rates rose to about 7 percent (Figure 4.2) in 1981 and 1982. By the end of 1982, both core and periphery of the international economy were inextricably enveloped in the crisis.

The Periphery in Relation to the Core

Since 1973, economic conditions in most developing countries have progressively deteriorated (except for limited expansion between 1976 and 1979) as the relative growth in the core countries declined (Figure 4.3). Peripheral countries that neither exported oil nor manufactured commodities were harmed most. The oil exporters, on the other hand, were able to mitigate the effects of slow growth in the core and other industrialized countries by the rise in petroleum prices in 1973 and 1974 and 1979 and 1980; they too, however, ran into deficit problems and reduced imports by 1981 as oil prices declined. In general, the sharp rise in real interest rates after 1979 and the increase of consumer prices and exchange rates (e.g., the dollar appreciated by 33 percent against the German mark between 1979 and 1982) hurt most developing countries, especially

Figure 4.2 Interest Rates, Real and Nominal, 1970–82

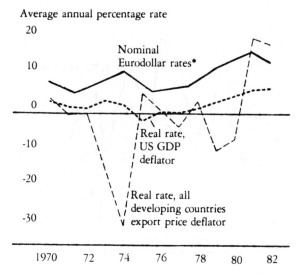

*Eurodollar rate is the average daily quotation on three-month deposits.
Source: World Bank, 1983.

the large borrowers in Latin America. An international monetary
system besieged by volatile exchange-rate fluctuations and the subsequent recession of 1980 to 1983 severely compromised and further weakened the economies of the periphery and raised the specter
of a global financial collapse.

In foreign trade, 65 percent of the Third World's exports enter
the markets of industrial countries (World Bank, 1984). All the
developing countries (except for the oil exporters) experienced a
relative decline in the terms of trade in the 1970s, and between
1980 and 1982 their position further deteriorated with the decline
in world prices for primary commodities (Table 4.1). As foreign
exchange earnings of most developing countries decreased in the
mid-1970s to the early 1980s because of the moderate and then high
real interest rates, the oil price increase of 1973 and 1974, and the
relative decline in growth and demand for imports in the industrial
countries, their aggregate accumulated foreign debt jumped from

Figure 4.3 Growth Rates of GDP for Developing and Industrial Countries, 1961–83

*Estimated.

Sources: For developed countries, OECD, 1983; for developing countries, World Bank data.

$68 billion in 1970 (World Bank, 1983) to $715 billion in 1982 (World Bank, 1984) to $895 billion in 1984; and was estimated at $970 billion for 1985 (Kristof, 1985a). However, by 1979 it was already evident that the ability of some developing countries to service their external debt obligations was questionable.

Moreover, because two-thirds of developing countries' debt is denominated in dollars and a large amount at *variable* interest rates, the costs of borrowing increased substantially as, correspondingly, the dollar appreciated from 1979 onward. It is important to note that prior to the 1970s, capital flows to developing countries were primarily channeled through official transfers and direct foreign investment, while in the 1970s to the mid-1980s the major mode was through commercial bank lending. Consequently, as the share

Table 4.1 Change in Export Prices and in Terms of Trade, 1965–83 (average annual percentage change)

Country Group	1965–73	1973–80	1981	1982	1983*
Change in Export Prices					
Developing countries					
Food	6.6	7.8	−16.6	−14.1	5.2
Nonfood	3.7	10.1	−14.6	−9.4	10.3
Metals and Minerals	1.6	5.6	−12.0	−8.0	−2.2
Fuels	6.7	24.7	−10.5	−2.6	−14.5
Industrial countries					
Manufacturers	4.7	10.9	−4.2	−1.8	−3.2
Change in Terms of Trade					
Low-income Asia	−0.5	−1.4	−0.1	−1.6	−0.6
Low-income Africa	−0.1	−1.5	−9.9	−0.9	4.6
Middle-income oil importers	−0.6	−2.2	−5.5	−1.9	3.0
Middle-income oil exporters	1.1	8.1	9.0	−0.4	−7.0
Developing countries	0.4	1.6	−0.5	−1.2	−0.6

Note: Calculations are based on a sample of ninety developing countries.

*Estimated.

Source: World Bank, 1985.

of direct foreign investment (non–debt creating) decreased relative to commercial bank lending and to the aggregate of capital transfers (Table 4.2), the debt-carrying burden on developing countries increased (Barsony, 1984).

In 1980, in order to meet their external debt-servicing obligations, many developing countries reduced the volume of imports. Between 1979 and 1982, the ratios of debt to GDP and debt service to exports of developing countries rose to critical levels. For example, in 1981, 21 percent of developing countries' export earnings covered external debt-service payments (Cooper, 1981), and in 1982, the interest payments on the external debt were about $66 billion (World Bank, 1984). The buildup of debt in some developing countries (e.g., Brazil, Argentina, and Mexico) compounded and deepened the global crisis that led Mexico in August 1982 to announce that it would be unable to service its debt obligations. Moreover, in the following year debtor countries required thirty-six reschedulings, amounting to $67 billion. In the same period, 1979

Table 4.2 Components in the Increase of Financial Resource Flows, 1970 and 1982.

Grants, direct investment, and other official and private financial flows with maturities of more than one year. Real terms: 1981 prices and exchange rates.

	1970		1982	
	$ billion	% of total	$ billion	% of total
I. Official Development Assistance (ODA)	21	41	35	36
II. Private grants	2	2	2	2
III. Non-concessional				
(a) Private commercial direct investment*	10	20	61	62
Capital market finance (bank sector + bonds)	8	16	23	23
(b) Official or officially supported export credits (DAC countries)	7	14	12	12
Other	1	2	5	5
Multilateral	2	4	7	7
Total	51	100	98	100
Memo Items:				
Official sector + private grants [I + II + III(b) + III(c)]	33	64	61	62
Private commercial III(a)	18	36	37	38

*For direct investment, the 1982 figure is in fact an average of 1981 and 1982. Direct investment flows have fluctuated considerably in the last few years, and the 1981–82 average seems a reasonable representation of the trend level in the recent period.

Source: Development Co-operation. Report by the Chairman of the Development Assistance Committee. OECD, 1983.

to 1982, concern for the creditworthiness of other debtor developing countries increased. Commercial bank loans declined from $50 billion in 1981 to $34 billion in 1982, and most commercial lending was coordinated under the aegis of the International Monetary Fund (IMF).

The "conditionality" associated with new loans by commercial and multilateral banks and the IMF have contributed further to undermining the stability of governments and to the deterioration of the economies of an increasing number of countries in the periphery. IMF-conditioned new loans and rescheduling agreements require borrower countries to implement a combination of austerity measures that (1) reduce public spending through the elimination of subsidies for food, education, infrastructural development, and health, (2) devaluate national currencies, (3) increase taxes, and (4) alter the development schemes pursued by national governments to the requirements of the core countries and international capital. Evidence of the IMF's affect on the economic and political stability of developing countries is apparent in the 1984 riots in the Dominican Republic and the 1985 military coup in the Sudan (Farnsworth, 1985a).

In his analysis of the relationship between the core countries and the loan policies of the IMF and commercial banks in Latin America, MacEwan asserts:

> Yet the "conditionality" which accompanies new loans from the center includes much more than austerity. Latin American governments are being pressed to ease regulations on the inflow of foreign investment (e.g., to ease joint venture and export requirements), to reduce currency controls that might be used to insulate and protect their national development, and to abandon stimulatory fiscal policies. Moreover, they are pushed to rededicate themselves to export promotion as to the route to economic growth. The programs being imposed on the periphery by central powers in their efforts to resolve the debt crisis thus amounts to a counter-offensive against national development. (1985:11)

MacEwan's (1985) position is clear: the "debt crisis" is an integral part of the current global crisis, and the core countries, in their efforts to resolve the crisis in the center, are forcibly reimposing (unilaterally and collectively) in the periphery, a form of dependent development associated with imperialistic penetration against which nationalist development had made some headway.

Also Frank's (1981) analysis of the crisis in the early 1970s (leading to the 1974 to 1975 recession) is relevant to the discussion of the current global crisis because both crises feature as a central dynamic the intense rivalry and struggle between core countries for markets. Moreover, Frank contends that "the greatest qualitative changes in the international division of labor occur during a period of crisis in capital accumulation, and that these changes are then quantitatively extended during a following period of expansion, which has been facilitated by these changes" (1981:8). This latter aspect of Frank's analysis is especially important because he identifies the critical period when changes occur (during the moment of the crisis) in the relative position of economic powers in the world economy. If his thesis is correct, the outcome of the subsequent period of expansion is the consolidation of core (and perhaps peripheral) countries' relative position in the international division of labor that changed during the crisis. Evidence to support Frank's (1981) position in the context of the current crisis is difficult to discern at this time because the upswing occurring in several core countries since the 1980 to 1983 recession is problematic.[4] We can assert, however, that the United States' predominant position in the world economy (albeit in decline) appears not to have changed as a consequence of the 1980 to 1983 recession; in fact, the U.S. position may have been tenuously strengthened in relation to that of its principal rivals (e.g., Japan and the European Economic Community [EEC] bloc) because the growth of the world-economy still largely depends on the U.S. economy.

The current international debate—centered on global trade policy (whether to have an open or a restrictive trading system), the volatility of exchange rates and the overvalued dollar, the high real interest rates, the enormous U.S. budget deficits, and, especially, the deflationary policies of the United States—clearly demonstrates the extent and intensity of the struggle between the core economic powers. Because the outcome of this struggle is unclear, we cannot predict the configuration of the realignments that are developing in the international division of labor as economic blocs (e.g., the United States and Latin America or Japan and East Asia) are strengthened or altered into new arrangements.

Several conclusions, though, can be drawn from the varied analyses of the current crisis and from concrete events: (1) like the global crisis of the early to mid-1970s, the current one was created by and manifested itself initially in the *core* and then spread to the *periphery* (World Bank, 1984); (2) more than a major cyclical crisis, it is rather an outgrowth of a long-term structural crisis in the accumulation process (MacEwan, 1985); (3) because it encompasses the world economy, socialist countries are affected as well (specifically Hungary and Yugoslavia, the only two European socialist countries to have received loans from the World Bank); (4) it has renewed and heightened the struggle between the core countries for markets in the periphery; (5) the current international economic policies of core countries, especially the United States, are the direct consequence of and response to the crisis; (6) the core countries are trying to resolve the crisis in the center, as they have in preceding crises (e.g., the crisis of 1873), at the cost of the growing exploitation of the periphery; and (7) the outcome of the current crisis, in terms of the accumulation process on a world scale, is unclear.

No doubt, new forms of dependent capitalist development have already evolved in the periphery since the 1970s, as evidenced in Latin America (Evans, 1979; Cardoso and Faletto, 1979). The combination of and interaction between foreign and domestic capital, the lineup of class forces, the crucial role of the state, and the international context (state system and the global economy) will largely determine the future course of development in the periphery through the second half of the 1980s and beyond.

The remainder of this essay is largely devoted to a discussion of the relationship of the United States and international capital to the Caribbean periphery during the first term of the Reagan administration (1981–84) and in the context of the current crisis and struggle between core countries for markets.

U.S. International Economic Policy and the Periphery: 1981–84

Three significant factors conditioned the Reagan administration's international economic policy in the first term: (1) the disastrous state of the world economy in 1980, which threatened the international financial system, (2) the rapidly deteriorating condition of the U.S. economy, and (3) the increasing dependence of the U.S. economy on world trade and, especially, on the periphery for markets and investments. The first factor was discussed at length in the preceding section.

The second factor concerns the state of the U.S. economy in 1980, having deteriorated to an unprecedentedly low level since the post–World War II expansion. Distinguished by chronically high unemployment, high real interest rates, an enormous debt,[5] huge trade deficits, an overvalued dollar,[6] and a decline in industrial productivity and competitiveness in domestic as well as world markets traditionally dominated by American-based multinational corportations (MNCs), especially in the Latin American periphery, the United States staggered into the longest recession (1980–83) since the Great Depression of the 1930s.

The third factor is the growing export dependence of the U.S. economy on the periphery. During a period when the U.S. economy is rapidly becoming even more internationalized, current (and past) U.S. trade policy supporting an "open" world trading system underscores its reliance on world markets. In 1980, 20 percent of U.S. output was exported, compared with 9 percent in 1970 (Schotta, 1984–85). As the U.S. economy increasingly specializes, new and expanded world markets are required for its two principal exports, agricultural goods and high-technology products (including arms-related exports). For example, according to a statement by the administration concerning the agricultural sector of the U.S. economy, "two of every five acres of harvested U.S. cropland now produce for the export market" (Department of State [DOS], 1985a:1), and "40 percent of agricultural production goes to exports" (Schotta, 1984–85:60). Moreover, agricultural exports accounted for about 20 percent of U.S. exports in 1984 and since the mid-1970s have been a positive factor in improving the U.S. balance of payments. It is clearly imperative for the United States, as a major supplier in the world trade of wheat (35 percent), soybeans (75 percent), and cotton (30 percent), to have export markets for its agricultural goods.

The importance of the periphery to the U.S. economy and to the administration's security concerns is evident from the following facts gleaned from a statement issued by the Department of State (1985b):

1. Between 1974 and 1984, the proportion of U.S.–manufactured exports to less-developed countries (LDCs) increased by 33 percent. For example, in 1983 LDCs purchased $75 billion (38 percent) of U.S. merchandise exports, notwithstanding an $8 billion decrease from a year earlier.
2. In 1983, about 43 percent ($15 billion) of U.S. export agricultural products was sent to LDCs.
3. In 1983, 22 percent ($51 billion) of U.S. private direct investment abroad was concentrated in the periphery.
4. Over 50 percent of the strategic minerals (e.g., bauxite, tin, cobalt, and tungsten) and 100 percent of the natural rubber, cocoa, and hard fibers required by the U.S. economy were supplied by countries in the periphery.

5. Approximately 70 percent of bilateral U.S. assistance and 50 percent of the U.S. contributions to multilateral development banks are spent by LDCs to purchase U.S. goods and services.

These figures clearly indicate the importance of the periphery (or at least some sectors of it) to the U.S. economy and help to explain the security concerns of the Reagan administration. It is within the context of these three factors that the administration formulated and then modified its international economic policy as the relative importance of each factor changed during the period of the first term.

However, on the subjective or ideological level, three basic principles shaped the administration's international economic policy and response to international economic issues. The first and foremost principle was "security" and the reaffirmation of U.S. interests and leadership in international affairs (Haig, 1981a). Driven by the concern for security and convinced that the United States' dominant position in the world was seriously compromised by the economic failures, political errors, and lack of resolve and credibility of the preceding Democratic administration, the new Republican administration adopted a confrontationist position and style, especially with regard to U.S. relations with the Soviet Union and the socialist bloc. Former secretary of state Alexander Haig succinctly articulated the Reagan administration's foreign policy criteria and stance in 1981: "the need to promote and protect our security will be the prime determining factor in formulating economic policy, in allocating our resources and in deciding on international economic issues" (1981b:2).

Along with reaffirming U.S. leadership among its allies and in international affairs, the Reagan administration emphasized bilateral rather than multilateral approaches to promote U.S. international security interests. This bilateral approach of the administration often conflicted with the interests of other core countries, especially in Western Europe. The administration's action to restrict the transfer of U.S.–manufactured technology for construction of the Siberian pipeline and its effort to change the criteria, levels, and flow of foreign aid to some developing countries (e.g., Nicaragua and Grenada) indicate the extent to which the East–West conflict and the concern for security is factored into (and continues to influence) the Reagan administration's foreign and international economic policies.

The second principle that shaped both the domestic and the international economic policies of the United States was the central role assigned to market mechanisms by the administration (Reagan, 1981a, 1981b; Shultz, 1983, 1984). The view of administration policy makers was that the less the market (domestic and international) was interfered with, the greater would be the prospects for global economic growth. This position was consistently underscored in international economic and foreign policy statements by administration officals (Reagan, 1981a; Shultz, 1983).

Similarly, the administration emphasized the role of the private sector in promoting international (and domestic) economic growth. Reaffirming the administration's international investment policy, Reagan stated in September 1983 that "the United States believes that international direct private investment plays a vital and expanding role in the U.S. and world economies" (1984–85:141) and that "an open international investment system responding to market forces provides the best and most efficient mechanism to promote global economic development" (1984–85:141). Removing, then, the obstacles that inhibit the "free" operation of the market and promoting the expansion of the private sector's participation in international investment constitute two major precepts of the new administration's international economic policy.

The third principle concerns the importance the Reagan administration assigned — as the basis for restoring global economic growth — to the reorganization of domestic economic policy of countries determined to be vital to the maintenance of the international financial system and to U.S. security and economic interests (Reagan, 1981a; Shultz, 1983). The measures the administration prescribed for economic recovery and growth, especially to countries in the periphery, were largely derived from the Economic Recovery Program (ERP) Reagan proposed to the Congress in February 1981. These measures included a combination of fiscal and monetary actions that, according to the economic orientation of administration policymakers, would substantially reduce government expenditures and subsidies, decrease inflation, and improve the domestic environment of countries for foreign investment and international trade.

The opposite, however, occurred, as the evidence indicates, for many countries in the periphery that were affected by and/or adopted the austerity measures prescribed by the Reagan administration and IMF. Rather than improve the prospects for global economic recovery and expansion, the deflationary policies of core countries, particularly those of the United States, have contributed, as we discussed in the preceding section of this essay, to the deepening of the crisis in the periphery (World Bank, 1984). This is apparent in the mounting debt crisis, despite official announcements to the contrary (Cooper, 1981; Kristof, 1985b), the growing incidence of social disorders associated with domestic economic austerity in some developing countries, the significant decline in relative growth in most developing countries, and the economic stagnation manifest in some subregions of the periphery (e.g., sub-Saharan Africa).

The three principles summarized above that shaped the administration's international economic policy, during the first term, were applied to the formulation of U.S. trade policy in particular. Favoring a liberalized or "open" trading system, the administration has consistently articulated major U.S. requirements: (1) the restoration of noninflationary domestic growth in national economies in order to improve the environment for foreign investment and for U.S.–based MNCs in the international market, and (2) the reduction of trade (and investment) barriers that inhibit both exports and imports in the world trading system (Reagan, 1981a).

The administration's adherence to the principles that informed its trade policy, however, was not followed consistently in practice because of the economic disorder in the global economy, the rivalry between core countries for markets, and the deterioration of the domestic economic environment (e.g., high unemployment, high real interest rates, and the decline of productivity in significant sectors of the economy) in the United States. For example, the progressive decline in U.S. industrial superiority since the 1960s and, consequently, in international competitiveness, compounded by the enormous growth of the U.S. trade deficits, reported by the Department of Commerce (New York Times, 1985a) for 1982 ($42.7 billion), 1983 ($69.4 billion), and 1984 ($123.3 billion), have caused both the Reagan administration and Congress to adopt tougher protectionist measures to mitigate the impact of foreign imports on the U.S. textile,[7] automobile, and steel industries. These protectionist measures aggravated tensions between the United States and other core countries (e.g., Japan and the EEC).

With regard to the impact of U.S. trade policy in the periphery, in 1981 the administration effected a revision of the Multifiber Agreement that lowered import growth levels of textiles and garments below 6 percent per annum, reducing the export earning (from the U.S. market) of the major exporters in Asia and Latin America (Sistema Económica Latinoamericano [SELA], 1984). Moreover, in 1984, a further deterioration in some developing countries' trade relations with the United States occurred when the administration renegotiated and renewed the Generalized System of Preferences program (see DOS, 1985a; Pease and Goold, 1985).

Concomitantly, U.S. financial policy affected the periphery through multilateral organizations and bilateral aid programs. The administration, in the early stages of the first term, preferred a bilateral rather than multilateral approach to foreign aid to the developing countries because it was a more effective and direct means to promote U.S. security and economic interests. While "development aid" to countries in the periphery contracted in real terms, aid related to the promotion of U.S. security interest (administered by the Agency for International Development [AID]) substantially increased from 1981 to 1984, along with large increases in military assistance grants and loan guarantees for the sale of military equipment abroad (SELA, 1984).

The Reagan administration's relationship to the IMF is also relevant to this discussion. Prior to 1983, the administration argued that the IMF should reduce its lending role to developing countries by increasing commercial bank loans. The administration also pressured the IMF to impose stricter conditionality and to require borrowers to adopt the deflationary policies of the United States.[8] By the end of 1982, however, the debt burdens of some developing countries had reached a magnitude that threatened the international economic system and the financial stability of several major U.S.–based banks. Consequently, by the end of 1982, the administration had reversed its position and supported additional funding for the IMF in 1983. Furthermore, as a consequence of the global recession and the sharp decline in commercial bank lending to debt-burdened developing countries in 1981 and 1982, the administration supported the IMF's decision "to subject their own credit packages to the maintenance of credit flows by private banks to economies in difficulty" (SELA, 1984:58). This decision cast the IMF in a new role in relation to the commercial banks and the debt crisis (Bello and Kinley, 1983; Payer, 1985).

Significantly, the Department of State recently announced that the IMF "has figured prominently in the U.S. strategy for managing international debt problems. Much of the recent success of that strategy can be attributed to the willingness of countries experiencing severe debt-servicing problems to act in concert with the IMF to address their balance-of-payments" (1985d:2). With support from the United States, then, and other core countries, the IMF was assigned the task of insulating the international financial system (and in doing so, protecting especially the United States) from the adverse effects of the debt crisis by coordinating the loan programs in the periphery on behalf of finance capital.

A central feature of this stage of advanced capitalism is the rapidly accelerating unification of the world's capital markets. This feature of the accumulation process was described by a senior official in the U.S. Department of the Treasury:

> Financial trade—movement of capital between nations—is by far the dominant economic activity in world markets. There now really exists one worldwide market for the spectrum of borrowing, lending and investment activities. Twenty-four hours a day, banks around the world make foreign loans with other funds they borrow in New York, London, Frankfurt, Singapore or other places. (Schotta, 1984–85:60–61)

In summary, the periphery is an integral part of the world economy (Grabendorff, 1984; Barsony, 1984; Paye, 1985). The resolution of the current global crisis, in order to allow for a new phase of expansion, lies in the superexploitation of the periphery at this stage of finance capitalism's development.

As competition between core countries sharpened during the 1980 to 1983 recession, markets traditionally dominated by the United States were further penetrated by, especially, the EEC countries and Japan. The administration's response has been to reassert the U.S. presence in regions of the periphery through a combination of economic measures, political pressure, and/or direct military or covert intervention under the guise of the East–West conflict. This suggests that a concomitant feature of the current global crisis, during this stage of capitalist development, is the resurgence of militarism resulting in the militarization of the regions in the periphery determined vital to U.S. security and economic interests. This development is most apparent in the Caribbean periphery. The following section is devoted to a discussion of the Caribbean Basin Initiative (CBI), because it embodies the three principles of the Reagan administration's international economic policy, and because it may very well constitute a test case, at the regional level, of an emerging U.S. global strategy to reshape and control vital areas in the periphery.

The Caribbean Basin Initiative: A Case Study of U.S. International Economic Policy in the Periphery

The position taken by the Reagan administration at the Cancún summit in October 1981 is important because it established the ground rules for U.S. economic relations with the Third World in the context of the changes in the international financial system and the global crisis. The Cancún summit was ostensibly intended, in view of the North–South "debate," to address the major problems and obstacles to the economic development of the Third World and to take the first step toward implementation of the Brandt Commission's recommendations, most notably a reorganization and change of the IMF and World Bank's financing procedures and policies (Brandt, 1980). Of special concern to the leaders of the fourteen developing countries represented at Cancún were the world monetary system, trade, energy, food, and the role of the Multilateral Development Banks (MDBs) in the development process.

Notwithstanding the objections from most of the leaders of the developing countries who attended the summit, Reagan, supported by Margaret Thatcher of Great Britain, proposed a "free-market" approach to Third World development. The administration, moreover, conditioned U.S. participation in future North–South negotiations on the bases that (1) the IMF, World Bank, and General Agreement on Tariffs and Trade (GATT) maintain their present functions and powers in the international financial system; (2) the developing countries improve the climate for private-sector capital flows and investment and create markets that would stimulate international trade; and (3) the developing countries achieve political stability and create policies that remove obstacles to or restraints on the international marketplace (Reagan, 1981b).

The framework and "principles" established for future U.S. participation in global negotiations and the "free-market" approach to development prescribed by the Reagan administration (and supported by Great Britain and West Germany) at Cancún are of fundamental importance to the practice of development in the periphery. Significantly, the administration's international economic policy for development is of immediate relevance to the peoples, countries, and colonial possessions in the Caribbean periphery because of the economic and political and military dilemmas posed by the CBI.

The CBI is both an economic and a military assistance program in that it provides a combination of official aid, investment incentives, trade concessions, and technical and military assistance to select countries and territories in the Caribbean periphery. Under the guise of improving internal stability in developing countries, facilitating the economic development of the region, and thereby helping solve the causes of illegal immigration to the United States, the CBI is promoted by the administration to appeal to both U.S. and local capital and governments in the region.

The major elements of the CBI are (DOS, 1982a):

- Free (one-way) trade for Caribbean products exported to the American market for twelve years.
- Tax incentives and investment insurance for direct U.S. investment to encourage the location of new production sites in the region.
- For fiscal year 1982, supplemental military and economic assistance of $410 million to select countries in the region.
- Technical assistance and training (e.g., export marketing and investment promotions) to private investors in the region.
- Coordination of U.S. development programs with those of other donor nations (initially Canada, Venezuela, and Mexico) and the multilateral financial institutions providing "aid" and assistance to the region.
- Establishment of Puerto Rico and the Virgin Islands as the "transportation hub for the Caribbean region" by developing research facilities, technical assistance training centers, and the islands' infrastructures.

- Increase of "security" (military) assistance to "friendly" nations in the region in order to contain the spread of alleged foreign-backed "Cuban-style" revolutions (Bosworth, 1982; DOS, 1982b).

Furthermore, the administration stipulated that assistance "will be focused increasingly on private sector support. Both capital and technical assistance will be provided to ameliorate infrastructure, credit, institutional, and training constraints to trade and investment expansion throughout the area" (DOS, 1982a:6). These elements constitute the basic provisions of the CBI. They embody the principles and security concerns of the administration, and they are designed to promote direct private U.S. investment in the region and to facilitate the penetration and transformation of local economies to conform to the requirements of the U.S. economy.

The IMF, the World Bank, and the Inter-American Development Bank (ADB) and their regional affiliates (the Caribbean Group for Cooperation in Economic Development and the Central America Group) were also assigned roles in the CBI by the administration. These institutions are ostensibly supposed to coordinate their lending programs for the region with that of the bilateral programs in the CBI. Since the United States maintains a dominant position in the IMF especially, the administration in conjunction with U.S. bank capital presumably will be able to influence or indirectly control the multilateral assistance programs in the region. In the case of bilateral assistance, aid is conditioned by the following requirements (DOS, 1982):

The administration will designate the Caribbean nations as beneficiaries of the free-trade zone. Selection will, in part, be conditioned by "the attitude of the beneficiaries toward private enterprise and the policies recipient countries are pursuing to promote their own development" (1982:4). Specifically:

- Bilateral investment treaties will be established with Caribbean nations to ensure that U.S. capital is protected and compensated for (e.g., unrestricted transfer of assets) in the event of nationalization.
- "Concessional aid" programs (e.g., development assistance, ESF, and PL 480 food aid programs) will be conditioned by the "macroeconomic policy" reform measures taken by recip-

ient countries in agricultural production. The administration's concern for the modernization of the agricultural sector to meet "the food needs of the region's growing populace and to enhance export earnings," will also faciliate U.S. agroindustries' penetration of the region.

- Finally, the Agency for International Development (AID) will coordinate all U.S.–sponsored assistance programs for the development of the private sector in the region. Funding will depend essentially on "the current condition of the private sector; the business climate; government policies affecting the private sector; public and private institutions serving the private sector; and bottlenecks to significant expansion of investment, production, exports, and particularly jobs" (DOS, 1982:8).

The assistance programs in the CBI and the conditions required of beneficiary countries clearly support the basic position and approach to development the Reagan administration adamantly defended at Cancún. The administration's economic development policy for the Caribbean periphery (and for the Third World in general) is twofold. First, it is designed to organize the myriad assistance programs to support the trade and investment requirements of the U.S. economy and American-based capital. And second, through an alliance with local capital and the Right (in both their authoritarian and bourgeois-democratic forms), its purpose is to contain and roll back progressive movements and governments in the region.

The CBI: Who Benefits from Dependent Capitalist Development?

The framework for and approach to development promoted by the Reagan administration at Cancún established the parameters for the CBI. The CBI is the first significant assertion and test, with the Caribbean periphery as the laboratory, of the administration's international economic policy for the Third World. Moreover, the CBI heralds an emerging global strategy of the United States to consolidate its hegemony against rivals in regions of the periphery during a period of crisis, sharp relative decline of U.S. industrial superiority (Bergesen and Sahoo, 1985), and intense competition for markets (Grabendorff, 1984; Islam, 1984).

The CBI is not a novel program for the economic development of the region or hemisphere. Puerto Rico's development experience during the late 1940s (Operation Bootstrap) did little more than concentrate U.S. capital on the island, cause severe social dislocations in society, and increase its economic dependence on the United States (Lewis, 1981). Similarly, John F. Kennedy's Alliance for Progress, launched in 1961 and modified under Lyndon Johnson, worsened the national economies affected by the program by causing further underdevelopment and deeper dependency on U.S. capital and the American market. Because of its emphasis on counterrevolutionary "security" programs, this policy was responsible, in large part, for the proliferation of military dictatorships in the hemisphere.

What follows is a critique of several important aspects of the CBI as they relate to the development of the Caribbean periphery.

1. The total dollar amount of economic and military assistance allocated by the admininstration for the region in 1982 was $996.74 million, including $410 million supplemental assistance under the CBI (DOS, 1982). This amount represents about 17 percent of the external financing needs of the region, estimated to exceed $4 billion net in 1982 (Feinberg and Newfarmer, 1984). When compared with other countries receiving U.S. aid, this amount was substantially less than the assistance the United States gave to Israel in the same year (about $3.5 billion). Similarly, when we compare the administration's economic and military assistance requests for fiscal year 1986 for the region ($1.797 billion [Motley, 1985]) and for Israel ($3.7 billion, [New York Times, 1985b]), Israel's share of U.S. assistance is still about twice as high as that of the region's.

Moreover, the conditionality of the economic assistance programs in the CBI underscores the administration's intention to provide support for only the sectors of the region's economies vital to the U.S. economy, while the development needs of the region as a whole are ignored. When compared with the nearly $10 billion spent on the Alliance for Progress, the economic assistance portion of the CBI amounts to a callous disregard for the needs of the populations in the region.

2. Despite the administration's assurances that Puerto Rico and the U.S. Virgin Islands will be developed as the "transportation

hub for the Caribbean region" and that their industries will be "safe-guarded" against imports from the countries participating in the free-trade zone, the CBI will adversely affect the islands' economies. For example, by eliminating tariffs for most of the Caribbean's exports to the U.S. market and by granting tax credits to the region, the CBI extends the economic benefits of investing in Puerto Rico to the rest of the region (Madera, 1981; Pastor, 1982).

The CBI enables U.S. capital more readily to relocate its overseas subsidiaries and investments and concentrate in sites offering greater advantages for the accumulation of capital. Such transfers of capital from the island (U.S. companies have actually been pulling out since 1980) to other sites in the region will further contribute to the severe social dislocations already manifest on the island.[9] The former governor of Puerto Rico, Rafael Hernández Colón, expressed his concern in 1982 regarding the CBI's impact on the island's deteriorating economy:

> The attraction of new industries is being outpaced by the departure of old ones, thereby creating a new loss of jobs and a 5% decline in real investment per year. Unemployment figures have reached depression levels. Our construction sector is virtually paralyzed. The government, facing a budget deficit, has had to resort to higher taxes. As a result, all local economists are predicting negative growth over the next few years. As we entered the 1980s, regression replaced stagnation. In the light of this adversity, Puerto Rico must restructure its economy to overcome the loss of federal aid, and to provide new jobs. The Caribbean Basin Initiative makes this task virtually impossible. (Gonzalez, 1982:54)

3. In order to ensure that the aid programs sponsored by the IMF and World Bank and its regional affiliates are channeled to finance private-sector imports, the administration proposed in the CBI that the ESF funds be coordinated with the IMF and World Bank group's assistance programs (DOS, 1982). Beneficiary countries will be further constrained to adopt IMF-imposed domestic economic measures, including the establishment of aid-financed projects that require the purchase of U.S. exports.

In this context, the IMF and the MDBs operate essentially as conduits for the transfer of capital from the Caribbean periphery to the U.S. mainland in order to prop up the U.S. export market. If this process is successful and the local economies are integrated into the U.S. market, they will be transformed into an extension of the U.S. economy and become thereby more dependent and unequal. Of course, this process of regional integration into the U.S. economy predates the CBI; it would, however, be accelerated under the program.[10]

The IMF's relationship to some Caribbean countries has been particularly harmful, especially to the socialist countries in the region. A case in point is the IMF's role in the downfall of the Manley government in Jamaica.[11]

> Stabilization and recovery programs undertaken by the government between 1977 and 1979 to meet the requirements of IMF loans completely undermined its popularity and alienated its most important sources of political support. The programs also drew the government into a series of acute contradictions between stated political and social philosophy and actual economic policies. This destroyed its credibility and made it impossible for the leadership, even after the break with the IMF, in 1980, to convince the public that it had a feasible economic alternative. The IMF therefore was a critical instrument in the process of demonstrating to the people of Jamaica that passive participation in the international capitalist system and acceptance of its rules is the only way for a small dependent country to survive. (Girvan and Bernal, 1982:35)

Referring to both the IMF and the World Bank, Franklin (1982) asserts that:

> these international lending agencies have several crucial functions. They can help topple recalcitrant governments (Chile, Jamaica), they can rush in to support right-wing military governments immediately after a coup (Argentina, Turkey), they can reward governments that become more hospitable to imperialism (Yugoslavia, China), and they can in general impose conditions on each borrower to make it safe for the later investment of private capital. (1982:26-27)

In view of the preponderant position of the United States in the IMF, and the proposed coordination among it, the MDBs, and the U.S. bilateral assistance programs in the CBI, the governments in the region will be increasingly pressured to acquiesce to foreign capital's control of their economies. If successful, the United States will exert an unprecedented influence and control of the development (and underdevelopment) of the Caribbean periphery through the mid-1980s and beyond.

4. While the administration contends that the CBI will promote sustainable economic growth in the region, and therefore help solve the problems causing widespread unemployment, balance-of-payment deficits, rampant inflation, and so on, the CBI will in fact deepen the crisis in the region. No doubt, the offer of "one-way free trade" for Caribbean products for twelve years and the investment incentives for the private sector have drawn support for the CBI from some governments (most notably the Seaga administration in Jamaica) in the region. However, while some sectors of the region's national elites will benefit in the short run from the CBI, their countries' dependence on the U.S. market will significantly increase over time as local economies are further integrated into both the international financial system and the U.S. economy. For example, the CBI included a 10 percent domestic tax credit for new investments in the region. The 10 percent tax credit would have stimulated capital-intensive rather than labor-intensive investment, precisely because the tax credit applies to new outlays in plant and equipment (Pastor, 1982). Many development economists, however, acknowledge that what is needed in most developing countries are labor-intensive agricultural and manufacturing schemes, rather than production schemes that require sophisticated farm and manufacturing technology (Johnson and Clark, 1982). The 10 percent tax credit investment incentive would have stimulated agricultural and manufacturing enterprises that are not suited for the region's economies and that, more important, increase the region's dependence on foreign technology and technical assistance (Feinberg and Newfarmer, 1984).

The status of the CBI is problematic. The economic assistance program of the bill was passed by Congress in August 1983. Economic aid, like military aid, is disproportionately assigned to El Salvador. The twelve-year program of preferential duty-free treatment was implemented in January 1984 for imports from twenty countries and territories in the region. Results of the Free Trade Area (FTA), according to administration officials, are "hard to interpret, but nonetheless, promising" (DOS, 1985e). The FTA's impact will probably not be significant, because only about 5 percent of the region's exports to the United States are affected by the free-trade provision of the CBI; 87 percent of the region's exports to the United States entered duty-free independent of the CBI. And efforts to develop supportive environments for private investment in the region have not been realized to date. Evidence of the failure of the administration's international economic policy (including the CBI) is apparent in the eastern Caribbean (Black, 1984) and especially in Jamaica (Massing, 1983). Moreover, the region's economic deterioration has far exceeded the administration's predictions.

Despite the passage of the bill, domestic opposition to some sections of the CBI was evident in Congress and in organized labor's effort to block the FTA provision because it would adversely affect employment in the United States. International opposition to the CBI was also carefully articulated by Canada and France. Their opposition, however, is for their ideological and political gain in the Third World. The strongest opposition to the CBI has come from several leaders in the region, principally, and expectedly, from the late prime minister Maurice Bishop of Grenada. Bishop argued that the CBI constitutes "a prostitution of the original ideas discussed by Mexico, Canada, Venezuela and the U.S." at a meeting held in 1981 in the Bahamas (1982:264) and that the CBI is designed to destroy regional unity and facilitate the recolonization of the region (Bishop, 1982). Bishop's concerns were not unfounded, especially as they apply to Grenada. The Reagan administration terminated aid to Grenada in 1982 and attempted to block any portion of the U.S. contribution to the Caribbean Development Bank that was directed to Grenada. The administration also tried, unsuccessfully, to persuade European capital not to finance an airport-extension project on the island. Ironically, the administration used this project—which is now being completed—to justify the U.S. invasion of Grenada in 1983.

To conclude, the Reagan administration is convinced that the security (and economic) interests of the United States are threatened in the region (as well as in the Middle East and southern Africa). The CBI embodies the three basic principles that inform the international economic policy of the United States: it emphasizes private investment, a free-market approach, and anticommunism. The program politicizes trade and investment, contrary to the rhetoric of the administration, and it is marked by a distinct preferential regionalism, despite the administration's stated objective of establishing an "open" and unrestrained world trading system. In addition, the CBI inhibits rather than enhances the prospects for the infrastructural development of and economic integration between countries in the region. This is most evident in the conditionality of the assistance programs and the private-sector investment provisions of the CBI.

Backed by the financial and industrial/agricultural transnational sectors of U.S. capital, and supported by the IMF, the CBI (along with the recommendations of the Kissinger Bipartisan Commision Report) is promoted to facilitate the transformation of countries in the Caribbean periphery into client states and extensions of the U.S. economy. This process is occurring during a period of crisis in the world economy marked by an intense struggle between core countries for markets.

The efficacy, however, of U.S. capital's long-term global economic strategy for the region, and the periphery in general, depends on whether the Reagan administration and successive U.S. governments can pressure (economically and politically) and/or coerce (economically and militarily) governments in the region to abandon their programs for national development and adopt the austerity measures and policies prescribed by the administration. In this regard, the IMF has been assigned the role of a debt-collection agency for transnational commercial banks and a major instrument for achieving U.S. foreign and international economic policy objectives.

While the CBI is intended to consolidate the Right in the region, this goal will become increasingly difficult to accomplish and, if initially successful, sustain, as economic and social conditions worsen in most countries of the region. As the first significant test of the administration's international economic policy in the periphery, the CBI has obvious implications for other peripheral areas of the world economy.

While the administration's strategy to expand accumulation, with U.S. capital at the helm, will temporarily block some governments from pursuing independent foreign policies that economically and politically link them to other peripheries and the socialist bloc (Payne, 1981; Singham and Hune, 1982), it will no doubt further contribute to the instability in the region and, in doing so, heighten the contradiction between core and periphery, and increase rather than contain the revolutionary tendencies manifest in the region.

On the Concept and Formation
of Counterhegemonies

Two significant forecasts for the 1980s were announced by World Bank analysts in 1981. First, the relative and absolute gaps between the richest and the poorest countries will widen, including the gap between middle- and low-income developing countries, and the 750 million people living in absolute poverty in 1981 will increase by at least 100 million people (World Bank, 1981). Second, the primary force and impetus for world growth are located in the advanced industrial centers of the world economy (World Bank, 1981). Two corollaries necessarily follow from the World Bank's forecasts: (1) the immense gap between the national elites and the poor in developing countries will further widen, and (2) the core economies and international capital will continue to direct and dominate the development of the periphery for the remainder of this decade and beyond.

The approach to and framework for the development of the periphery in the CBI contain many of the prescriptions promoted by the World Bank. Not surprisingly, the World Bank and the CBI assign financial institutions "a key role to play in becoming more prominent in facilitating international flows of commercial capital" (World Bank, 1981:3). The result will be to draw developing countries deeper into the orbits of the MNCs and world markets dominated by the core countries, resulting in greater technological and economic dependence for the LDCs.

As dismal as the scenario may appear, real social change is possible because core–periphery relations, as they are presently constituted, are not a permanent or fixed feature of capitalist development. That is, the core creates counterhegemonies in the periphery that challenge its hegemony.

While we cannot predict the collapse of the capitalist world-system in the near future, we can argue that the formation of counterhegemonies in the periphery is both possible and a necessary requirement for the economic and human development of the Third World. By counterhegemonies, I mean the creation of regional and global institutions, production schemes, trade agreements, and such *between* developing countries that promote intraregional and interregional development rather than vertically dependent development.

These counterhegemonies would challenge the hegemonic control of the periphery by the core countries by gaining control of markets and organizing production within and between peripheries that benefit first and foremost the peoples of the developing countries. The concept of a counterhegemony is not novel. It is both the subject of debate on development and essential to the practice of development.[12] For example, nothwithstanding how problematic and divisive OPEC may be, it constitutes a counterhegemony (albeit one subject to fluctuations in the price of oil on the world market).

What I propose to do is identify and outline several key elements of what would in theory and in practice form a counterhegemony for the Caribbean periphery. Most, if not all, of the elements have been better articulated by others than myself. It is, however, the concept of and framework for a counterhegemony within which these elements would coalesce that merit further discussion.

1. The formation of a counterhegemony in the Caribbean periphery should herald a significant shift in both the conceptualization of development and in the strategies for promoting development. The underlying principles that would inform the project are: (a) the development plan must meet the basic material needs of all the people in the region rather than the needs of primarily indigenous elites and foreign capital; (b) while the goal of development will be to increase GDP, a shift in its composition favoring the production of basic goods for internal or regional consumption is imperative (Divan and Livingston, 1979); (c) ideological differences between regional governments should not constitute a barrier to participation in programs of economic cooperation and integration (Bishop, 1983); and (d) each country must be ensured the right to permanent sovereignty over its natural resources.

2. The development plan should promote collective reliance and cooperation at the regional, subregional, and interregional levels of the periphery in order to (a) stimulate the region's infrastructural development and economic integration;[13] (b) defend the prices of the region's exportable commodities and improve Caribbean basin countries' access to new markets within and between peripheries; (c) increase the region's imports (South–South trade) from other peripheries in Asia and Africa, extend these regions' preferential treatment of their exports, and remove more favorable treatment of

imports from the core countries (Mazrui, 1980); (d) stimulate efforts to organize, diversify, and improve the region's agricultural production to achieve self-sufficiency in basic grains; (e) strengthen efforts to utilize regional institutions, indigenous resources, and traditional technology in development projects; and (f) encourage cooperation and institutional links between peripheries in the areas of energy, agriculture, science and technology, industry, transportation, and communications.

3. In order to finance national and regional development programs, countries in the region should increasingly solicit the support from the few remaining capital-surplus (oil-exporting) developing countries and the socialist bloc countries.

4. Concomitantly, as the development plan would proceed in the Caribbean periphery and extend to other peripheries, regional governments as a collective body and in concert with other peripheries could move to challenge and counterpenetrate the core economies. To cite an example, capital-surplus developing countries, suggest Girvan and Bernal (1982), are in a position to influence the loan policies of international bankers and to manipulate capital markets in the United States and Western Europe by investing in industry and by purchasing banks and shares in transnational corportations (Mazrui, 1980).

The elements of a development plan described above would collectively constitute a counterhegemony in the Caribbean periphery. This development strategy would not eliminate the dependent relationship between the core and the periphery, but it could erect economic structures that opposed in the practice of development the hegemony of the core countries and of international capital. Moreover, the proposed plan would improve the quality of material life for the majority of people in the region and, in the long run, contribute to the transformation (and possibly the collapse) of the world-system.

Notes

The latter two parts of this essay were presented at the Ninth Annual SIETAR conference in San Gimignano, Italy, 1983. Support for this research was provided by California State University, Los Angeles.

1. Two aspects are to be distinguished: the Reagan administration's articulated approach to development at Cancún is both the ideology and the rationale for U.S. international economic policy in the Third World, while the CBI constitutes the program.

2. The Reagan administration has mounted an intense media campaign against the Soviet Union, Cuba, and, most recently, Nicaragua (see, for example DOS, 1981a, 1981b, 1982b; Enders, 1982a, 1982b, 1983; Haig, 1982). The United States supplies arms and military advisers to El Salvador, Guatemala, and Honduras; trains Salvadoran officers and troops in Panama; and approved the use of U.S. military advisers to train the Costa Rican police (Brinkley, 1985). Covert actions have been coordinated by the CIA to destabilize the government of Nicaragua, including the mining of a Nicaraguan harbor, and manuals have been provided by the CIA to the contras instructing them on assassination and terrorism. The United States has conducted joint military maneuvers with Honduras (Holloran, 1985). Moreover, with congressional approval (until April 1985), the United States supplied the contras with military aid. The most serious U.S. military intervention in the region, however, was in the 1983 invasion of Grenada. Most recently, the Reagan administration invoked a U.S. trade embargo against Nicaragua in May 1985.

3. MacEwan (1985) also contends that the "general" or international crisis is an outgrowth of the problems spawned in the advanced capitalist countries since the early 1970s. He writes that a feature of the international crisis in the 1970s was the rapid expansion of liquidity in the international economy, which, because of the decline in investment in the core countries, could not be absorbed in the core and consequently was pushed out through commercial banks into the periphery, where dependence on and demand for credit was especially high in the 1970s.

4. For example, the U.S. economy expanded after the 1980 to 1983 recession, but its recent growth rates have been sluggish. The Commerce Department reported 0.7 percent in growth for the first three months of 1985 (Kilborn, 1985).

5. The U.S. government debt as of June 30, 1984, was $1,512.7 billion (Sweezy and Magdoff, 1985). The United States was borrowing about $15 to $20 billion a quarter to finance both government deficits and private-sector investment (see Westlake, 1984).

6. The Business Council, representing the nation's sixty-five largest corporations, warned that unless the dollar was devalued and foreign competition contained, the current economic expansion in the United States would be curtailed (see Farnsworth, 1985b).

7. Congress was debating the Textile and Apparel Trade Enforcement Act of 1985. The bill, promoted by the domestic textile and apparel indus-

tries, would limit foreign producers to about 40 percent of the U.S. market (see Chaikin, 1985). In 1984, the United States unilaterally introduced new "country-of-origin rules" in order to reduce imports of textiles from Third World exporters. The administration argued that the measures were designed to prevent exporters from exceeding existing quota agreements (Manning and Raghavan, 1984).

8. These two concerns with regard to the IMF were also evident in the administration's efforts to reduce the U.S. contribution to the Multilateral Development Banks, and to pressure especially the World Bank to apply stricter "graduation" criteria and to require borrowers to adopt disinflationary policies based on the U.S. model (SELA, 1984). Moreover, the United States was criticized in 1984 for not providing adequate financial support for the World Bank and the IDA (see *Third World Quarterly*, 1985).

9. For an overview of Puerto Rico's development experience, see Heine (1983); for its relationship to MNCs, Gonzalez (1982) and Heine (1983); for a comparative analysis of development on the island and mainland, Campos and Bonilla (1982); and for an assessment of proposed tax reform before Congress that affects the island's economy, *New York Times* (1985c).

10. The U.S. contribution to the MDBs has also yielded significant dividends for the U.S. economy and for U.S. capital. It is estimated that by 1982 the cumulative U.S. contribution of $850 million to the World Bank generated a return of nearly $15 billion to the United States (Kuczynski, 1982).

11. See also Bolles (1983). Note that less than five months after the Manley government was voted out of office, eight major international banks agreed to give Seaga's government $70 million in new credit and to refinance another $103 million of existing debt (Bennett, 1981). For an analysis of the Reagan administration's relations to the Seaga government, see Massing (1983).

12. See two studies by Diwan and Livingston (1979) and Mazrui (1980). Although the concept of a counterhegemony is not discussed in the two studies, the programs and framework proposed for the development of the Third World constitute it in theory and practice.

13. Earlier efforts at economic integration (e.g., the Latin America Free Trade Area and the Central American Common Market) in the region and hemisphere have largely failed. The causes for the failures must be studied in order to strengthen ongoing and future efforts at regional economic integration. Note that despite the administration's rhetoric, U.S. capital is adamantly opposed to any plan that would foster the region's infrastructural development and economic unity.

References

Barsony, André (1984). "The Dialogue Between Developed and Developing Countries: In Search of a New Consensus." *OECD Observer*, No. 130:24–28.

Bello, Walden, and David Kinley (1983). "The IMF." *Multinational Monitor* 4:11–14.

Bennett, Robert A. (1984). "8 Major Banks Agree on Jamaica Credit Plan." *New York Times*, March 3.

Bergesen, Albert, and Chintamani Sahoo (1984). "Evidence of the Decline of American Hegemony in World Production." *Review* 8:595–611.

Black, George (1984). "Dominica: Where Magic of the Marketplace Is Failing." *Multinational Monitor* 5:16–19.

Bishop, Maurice (1983). "Three Years of the Grenada Revolution." In Bruce Marcus and Michael Taber, eds., *Maurice Bishop Speaks: The Grenada Revolution, 1979–83.* New York: Pathfinder, pp. 255–72.

Bolles, A. Lynn (1983). "IMF Destabilization: The Impact on Working Class Jamaican Women." *TransAfrica Forum* 2:63–75.

Bosworth, Stephen W. (1982). *Caribbean Basin Initiative in Perspective.* Current Policy, No. 381. Washington, D.C.: Department of State.

Brandt, Willy (1980). *North–South: A Program For Survival.* Cambridge, Mass.: MIT Press.

Brinkley, Joel (1985). "U.S. Military to Train Costa Rican Police." *New York Times*, May 7.

Campos, Ricardo, and Frank Bonilla (1982). "Bootstraps and Enterprise Zones: The Underside of Late Capitalism in Puerto Rico and the United States." *Review* 5:556–90.

Cardoso, Fernando, and Enzo Faletto (1979). *Dependency and Development in Latin America.* Berkeley: University of California Press.

Chaikin, Sol. C. (1985). "Sewn into a Corner." *New York Times*, May 22.

Cooper, Wendy (1981). "Bankers Claim the Danger of Global Collapse Is Receding." *Multinational Monitor* 2:19–20.

Department of State (DOS) (1981a). *Communist Interference in El Salvador.* Special Report No. 80. Washington, D.C.

———— (1981b). *Cuba's Renewed Support for Violence in Latin America.* Special Report No. 90. Washington, D.C.

———— (1982a). *Background on the Carribean Basin Initiative.* Special Report No. 97. Washington, D.C.

———— (1982b). *Cuban Armed Forces and the Soviet Military Presence.* Special Report No. 103. Washington, D.C.

——— (1985a). "Agriculture in U.S. Foreign Economic Policy." *Gist*, May. Washington, D.C.

——— (1985b). "U.S. Prosperity and the Developing Countries." *Gist*, January. Washington, D.C.

——— (1985c). "Generalized System of Preferences." *Gist*, February. Washington, D.C.

——— (1985d). "International Monetary Fund." *Gist*, January. Washington, D.C.

——— (1985e). *Sustaining a Consistent Policy in Central America: One Year After the National Bipartisan Commission Report*. Special Report No. 124. Washington, D.C.

Diwan, Romesh K., and Dennis Livingston (1979). *Alternative Development Strategies and Appropriate Technology*. New York: Pergamon.

Enders, Thomas O. (1982a). *Cuban Support for Terrorism and Insurgency in the Western Hemisphere*. Current Policy, No. 376. Washington, D.C.: Department of State.

——— (1982b). *Dealing with the Reality of Cuba*. Current Policy, No. 443. Washington, D.C.: Department of State.

——— (1983). *Nicaragua: Threat to Peace in Central America.* Current Policy, No. 476. Washington, D.C.: Department of State.

Evans, Peter (1979). *Dependent Development: The Alliance of Multinational, State, and Local Capital in Brazil*. Princeton, N.J.: Princeton University Press.

Farnsworth, Clyde H. (1985a). "The I.M.F.'s Help Can Sometimes Hurt." *New York Times*, April 14.

——— (1985b). "Business Fear: Strong Dollar." *New York Times*, May 11.

Feinberg, Richard E., and Richard Newfarmer (1984). "The Caribbean Basin Initiative: Bold Plan or Empty Promise?" In Richard Newfarmer, ed., *From Gunboats to Diplomacy: New U.S. Policies for Latin America*. Baltimore: Johns Hopkins University Press, pp. 210–27.

Frank, Andre G. (1984). *Reflections on the World Economic Crisis*. New York: Monthly Review Press.

Franklin, Bruce (1982). "Debt Peonage: The Highest Form of Imperialism." *Monthly Review* 33:15–31.

Garcia, Emilio P. (1984). "Puerto Rico: The Making of a Corporate Satellite." *Multinational Monitor* 5:12–15.

Girvan, Norman, and Richard Bernal (1982). "The IMF and the Foreclosure of Development Options: The Case of Jamaica." *Monthly Review* 33:34–48.

Gonzalez, Heliodoro (1982). "The Caribbean Basin Initiative: Toward a Permanent Dole." *Inter-American Economic Affairs* 36:23–59.

Grabendorff, Wolf (1984). "The Role of Western Europe in the Caribbean Basin." In Alan Adelman and Reid Reding, eds., *Confrontation in the Caribbean Basin*. Pittsburg: Center for Latin American Studies, pp. 276–95.

Haig, Alexander (1981a). *Opening Statement at Confirmation Hearings*. Current Policy, No. 257. Washington, D.C.: Department of State.

———— (1981b). "Statement Before the Senate Committee on Foreign Relations." *Department of State Bulletin*, April. Washington, D.C.: Department of State.

———— (1982). *Update of International Developments*. Current Policy, No. 373. Washington, D.C.: Department of State.

Halloran, Richard (1985). "Army Plans for 'What if' Latin War." *New York Times*, May 4.

Heine, Jorge (1983). "Beyond Bootstrap: Puerto Rico's Development Experience and the Third World in the 1980s." *TransAfrica Forum* 1:65–80.

Islam, Shada (1984). "Cold Hands, Warm Heart." *South*, No. 50:24.

Johnston, Bruce, and William C. Clark (1982). *Redesigning Rural Development: A Strategic Perspective*. Baltimore: Johns Hopkins University Press.

Kilborn, Peter T. (1985). "Growth of Economy Falls to 0.7% Rate; Strong Dollar Cited." *New York Times*, May 22.

Kristof, Nicholas (1985a). "That International 'Debt Bomb' Hasn't Stopped Ticking." *New York Times*, March 31.

———— (1985b). "Debt Crisis Seen as Ending." *New York Times*, February 4.

Kuczynski, Pedro Pablo (1982). "Action Steps After Cancún." *Foreign Affairs* 60:1022–37.

Lewis, Gordon K. (1981). "The Failings of Operation Bootstrap." In R. M. Delson, ed., *Readings in Caribbean History and Economics*. New York: Gordon and Breach, pp. 262–70.

MacEwan, Arthur (1984). "The Current Crisis in Latin America and the International Economy." *Monthly Review* 36:1–18.

Madera, José R. (1981). "Interview with José Madera." *U.S. News & World Report*, March 22, pp. 93–94.

Massing, Michael (1983). "The Jamaica Experiment." *Atlantic Monthly*, September, pp. 37–56.

Mazrui, Ali A. (1980). "Beyond Dependency in the Black World: Five Strategies for Decolonization." In Aguibou Y. Yansane, ed., *Decolonization and Dependency*. Westport, Conn.: Greenwood Press, pp. 84–97.

Motley, Langhorne A. (1985). *Aid and U.S. Interests in Latin America and the Caribbean*. Current Policy, No. 666. Washington, D.C.: Department of State.

Multinational Monitor (1980). "Puerto Rico: The Multinational Presence." *Multinational Monitor* 1:16–18.

New York Times (1985a). "Out of Balance: America's Trade Deficit." May 19.

———— (1985b). "Israel to Get Additional U.S. Aid, Officials Report." May 1.

———— (1985c). "A Bad Idea Worries Puerto Rico." May 13.

Pastor, Robert (1982). "Sinking in the Caribbean Basin." *Foreign Affairs* 60:1038–58.

Paye, Jean-Claude (1985). "Agenda for the Second Half of the Eighties." *OECD Observer*, No. 133:3–5.

Payer, Cheryl (1985). "The IMF in the 1980s: What Has It Learned; What Have We Learned About It?" In Altaf Gauhar, ed., *Third World Affairs 1985*. London: Third World Foundation, pp. 1–9.

Payne, Richard J. (1981). "U.S. Policy Towards Caribbean Economic Problems." *The Round Table*, No. 285:360–372.

Pease, Don J., and William Goold (1985). "The New GSP: Fair Trade with the Third World?" *World Policy Journal* 2:351–66.

Reagan, Ronald (1981a). "Cooperative Strategy for Global Growth." In *Realism, Strength, Negotiation: Key Foreign Policy Statements of the Reagan Administration*. Washington, D.C.: Department of State, pp. 138–42.

———— (1981b). *Opening Statement at Cancún Summit*. Current Policy, No. 335. Washington, D.C.: Department of State.

———— (1982). *Caribbean Basin Initiative*. Current Policy, No. 370. Washington, D.C.: Department of State.

———— (1984). *Promoting Global Economic Growth*. Current Policy, No. 616. Washington, D.C.: Department of State.

———— (1984–85). "Statement by President Reagan on the International Investment Policy of the United States, September 9, 1983." *American-Arab Affairs*, No. 11:138–44.

Schotta, Charles (1984–85). "U.S. Foreign Investment Policy and the U.S.–Arab Experience." *American-Arab Affairs*, No. 11:56–62.

Shultz, George P. (1983). "The U.S. and the Developing World: Our Joint Stake in the World Economy." In *Realism, Strength, Negotiation: Key Foreign Policy Statements of the Reagan Adminstration*. Washington, D.C.: Department of State, pp. 146–50.

———— (1984). *Democracy and the Path to Economic Growth*. Current Policy, No. 641. Washington, D.C: Department of State.

Singham, A. W., and Shirley Hune (1982). "The Caribbean Basin Initiative: The U.S. Response to Caribbean Non-Alignment." *TransAfrica Forum* 1:11–24.

Sistema Económica Latinoamericano (SELA) (1984). *Latin American– U.S. Economic Relations*, 1982–1983. Boulder, Colo.: Westview.

Sweezy, Paul M., and Harry Magdoff (1985). "The Deficit, the Debt, and the Real World." *Monthly Review* 37:1–11.

Third World Quarterly (1984). "The International Monetary Fund (IMF) and World Bank." *Third World Quarterly* 7:412–13.

Westlake, Melvyn (1984). "Where Will the Buck Stop?" *South*, No. 50:76.

World Bank (1981). *World Development Report 1981*. New York: Oxford University Press.

———— (1983). *World Development Report 1983*. New York: Oxford University Press.

———— (1984). *World Development Report 1984*. New York: Oxford University Press.

CHAPTER 5

Plantation Capitalism, Underdevelopment, and Transformation: With Special Reference to the Caribbean

George L. Beckford

Capitalism first emerged in Western Europe after the collapse of feudalism. The establishment of the plantation system in the New World during the sixteenth century was critical for the consolidation of capitalism within Europe. Furthermore, the plantation variant of capitalism was always antecedent to the major transition phases of capitalism on a world scale. Multinational corporations (MNCs) may be said to have appeared first in plantation production and trade. And we hypothesize the societies characterized by plantation capitalism are in the vanguard of the transition to socialism in the Third World today.[1]

Human society has a history of different social formations dominating in particular places and times. These social formations are identified as: (1) primitive communal, (2) feudal and other tribute-paying systems, (3) slave (plantation), (4) capitalist, and (5) socialist. Different societies have experienced different sequences of those dominant formations. Thus, for example, Caribbean societies passed historically from (1) to (3) to (4).[2] Meanwhile, Europe, Asia, and parts of Africa passed from (1) to (2) to (4).[3] Such differences in historical transitions indicate that there is no mechanistic and linear change from one given social formation to another. As in all historical processes, it is the material conditions of life within each society, and the concurrent impact of contact with other societies, that ultimately shape patterns of social change and transformation.

Our interest here is the specific case of the development of plantation capitalism, from its beginnings with the slave plantation mode of production and exchange[4] to its contemporary articulation within the international capitalist system. The plantation mode of production and exchange was significant, if not dominant, in many of those Third World nation-states pushed by revolutionary struggle onto the road to socialism. A reexamination of that system of plantation capitalism seems appropriate in light of this observation.[5] And theoretical advances made by other scholars such as Amin (1978) and Emmanuel (1974) provide some basic ingredients for making this reexamination.

Evolution of World Capitalism and Plantation Societies

We begin with the simple observation that the presence of all black people in the New World today is directly attributable to the plantation system. African people were forcibly removed from their homeland and brought to the New World to provide labor power for the production of plantation commodities like sugar, cotton, and tobacco. Under conditions of slavery, this black labor power generated huge surpluses for the economic advancement of Europe (and later the U.S. Northeast and the Brazilian Center-South). As a result, black plantation societies became dominant in the "colonies of exploitation."

Having overcome the indigenous Indian populations in the Caribbean, the Guianas, the U.S. South, and the Brazilian Northeast, European merchant capitalists established plantations on land captured from the Indians and with capital and labor extracted from the Africans. And so slave plantation societies emerged in the New World. (It was the Portuguese who first developed the system in São Tomé and Principe on the other side of the Atlantic and introduced it into Brazil early in the sixteenth century. The Portuguese later established the system in their African colonies—Guinea, Angola, and Mozambique.) From its initial establishment in Brazil, the plantation system spread rapidly into the Guianas, throughout the Caribbean islands, and into the U.S. South as other European nations expanded on the base and experience set by the Portuguese. The Spanish, French, Dutch, and British merchant capitalists promoted this expansion in various parts of the New World.

Modern plantation society has its roots in the slave plantation system that began in the sixteenth century and lasted to the mid to late nineteenth century, enjoying a veritable economic golden age under the mercantile capitalism of the seventeenth and early eighteenth centuries. It is important to note that the character of the slave society was significantly different from that of slavery in ancient times (e.g., the slave societies of Greece and Rome). New World slave plantation societies produced commodities for sale in international capitalist markets. And the surpluses generated from the exploitation of slave labor power fueled the process of accumulation that gave rise to the development of industrial capitalism in Europe. Thus slave plantation society was an integral part of the international capitalist system.

To return to the concern stated at the outset, only Cuba (and Grenada briefly) in the New World has made the transition from capitalism to socialism. In Africa itself, Guinea-Bissau, Angola, and Mozambique, along with the oldest plantation societies, São Tomé and Principe offshore, have also transformed to socialist societies.

Historically, this struggle for national independence and socialism displays two discernible forms at the level of nation-states: the revolutionary and the evolutionary. Only the revolutionary path has led to socialist transformation to date. Some plantation societies on the evolutionary path are said to be in the process of "transition." Guyana and Jamaica during the Manley era (1974–80) were said to be somewhere in this transition stage. Walter Rodney (1978:1) points out that "transition must necessarily have mixed features of capitalist relics and embryonic socialism, but the latter would exist in a position of dominance." He makes the further point, "Transition is movement in a given direction—it is not a shuttle service" (1978:6). So plantation societies, like Indonesia and Sri Lanka, where nationalization of foreign plantations was subsequently reversed were obviously not on the transition *belt*. Nor was Jamaica, for the Manley government was swept from office in 1980 in a manner that clearly indicated failure to lay the foundation for transition.[6]

From our discussion so far, we can conclude that the future of plantation societies is extricably bound up with the future of international capitalism. That future, in turn, will be determined by the interaction of two opposing forces: (1) the continuing imperialist expansion of capitalism in new shapes and forms as it makes accommodation to (2) the strengthening of popular forces worldwide for national liberation, involving the repatriation of land and other means of production in a general pursuit of "non-capitalist" paths to development. The operations of multinational corporations (MNCs) have adjusted in several ways, and there is an increasing control of them by the multinational banks (MNBs), which, as well, lubricate the financial transactions of Third World countries through loans to nation-states. Supported by the International Monetary Fund (IMF), MNBs' hegemony over resources in the capitalist Third World is increasing rapidly.[7]

Thus at one level we can say that the future of plantation societies is no different from the future faced by all Third World countries locked within the international capitalist system. That is to say, either they continue to underdevelop under capitalism, or they make the transition to socialism as a precondition for development. But we can go a step further, to analyze the contours and likelihood of that choice in the particular case of plantation societies. To make the analysis, however, we need a clear understanding of the distinctive character of plantation society.

Race and Class in the Plantation Mode of Production[8]

In a typology of Third World societies by their modes of production and exchange, the plantation mode distinguishes itself. Racial domination and oppression characterize the plantation mode of production, which also involves the systemic generation of a surplus of labor. That process always brings in a new race of people to provide labor power where an existing race of people is reluctant to sell its labor power (or resist overt coercion) for "bare-subsistence" wages. Surpluses from plantation production and trade are maximized by this mechanism. First slavery, then indenture with land monopoly, then machine capital and intensified land monopoly have been the instrumental devices used by plantation capitalists.

We already stated that slave plantation society was the creation of mercantile capitalism. The society was formed by planting African people on land that had been captured from other people, the indigenous Indians of the Americas. The economic base was established by the coercive application of the labor power of these transplanted Africans in the cultivation of crops for which commercial markets existed in Europe. White Europeans owned the means of production, and a hierarchical chain of command from the *white* "backra" to the *mulatto* (half-caste) "busha" mobilized the *black* African slaves to produce commodities for export, and for slave and estate consumption, as well as capital goods that could be produced with slave labor (houses, factory buildings, fence posts, etc.).

This particular hierarchical occupational structure served to institute race in the process of production from the outset and set up a class society of a particular kind. Plantations were, in a real sense, the first factories in the field. The slaves were machines driven by paid managers (attorneys) and foremen and unpaid (in money) "drivers." The associated factories for processing raw sugar, cotton, and other products were industrial concerns. The plantation was, in a real sense, a precursor to industrial capitalism. (The economic inefficiency of the slave mode of production became obvious as industrial capitalism replaced mercantile capitalism in Europe, as well as in the U.S. Northeast and the Brazilian Center-South.) It was a rudimentary form, but this essence of it has escaped the notice of most students of the development of capitalism.

Emancipation came in the mid- to late nineteenth century[9] and led to the transformation of slave plantation society to minimum (bare) subsistence-wage plantation society and sharecropping tenancy systems. The latter was designed to tie the African ex-slave to the plantation and was circumscribed by legislation, like the Black Codes in the U.S. South, to ensure that the labor power of black people would continue to be available to the capitalist plantations in a system of semislavery. "Half slave, half free" is an appropriate description of the economic condition of black people in all plantation societies after emancipation. For even where wage labor substituted for slave labor, wages paid never rose beyond minimum subsistence, as the governors of plantation societies systematically created a "reserve army of labor." In order to counter the efforts of the Africans to secure an independent economic base, governments in plantation societies imported indentured Asiatic labor, mainly East Indians, whose role in plantation production was hardly different from that which existed under slavery.[10]

Thus the capitalists who continued to monopolize the means

of production were able to maintain intact the general economic substructure of the society. The African freedmen had one of two choices, depending on the availability of land. Wherever some land of whatever quality existed, they managed to establish themselves as a semi-independent peasantry. But whenever plantations had already engrossed all arable land, they were forced to continue working on plantations for subsistence wages or migrate. Migration was, and remains, an important outlet for dispossessed black people in all New World plantation societies.

The forced movement of labor *into* the plantation economy during its foundation period and *out of* it during its period of maturity and decline is one feature of plantation society that gives it a certain uniqueness among the general class of capitalist societies. The economic raison d'être of plantation society is the production of commodities for export. And that trade has been marked by what is now called "unequal exchange." This unequal exchange, which keeps plantation society backward relative to the industrial capitalist societies, arises from the existence of a reserve army of labor in plantation society.[11] However, migration has had a dampening effect on the inherent contradictions of inequality of plantation society. For one thing, migration reduces the size of the reserve army of labor. For another, remittances sent by migrants to relatives improve the survival chances of those still in the grip of plantation society.

But migration has important negative effects. First, migrants disposed of what little land and other means of production they came to own as a result of their economic struggle within the constraints imposed by the plantation system. Invariably, such land was bought up by MNCs in mining and tourism in the Caribbean and by capitalist corporations in the U.S. South and the Brazilian Northeast.[12] Second, migration acts as a safety valve that reduces economic frustration, thereby postponing revolutionary change of a kind that could bring socialist transformation à la Cuba. The dispersal of black people outside of their ancestral home base robs plantation societies of skilled human resources that could provide the organization and wherewithal for making the transition. We shall have to return to these matters when we consider the dynamics of change and transformation in the next section.

What emerges so far in our analysis is that the economic substructure of plantation society remained virtually unaltered in the period after emancipation. To be sure, peasant producers emerged in some places, but the peasantry was (and is) dominated by the plantation. Nonagricultural activities came into being—in the Caribbean, mining, tourism, and light manufacturing, and in the U.S. South and Brazil mainly light manufacturing and mining in some places. These new activities diversified the mix of commodity production and complicated the class structure. The simple social stratification of white merchant/planter bourgeoisie, brown petty bourgeoisie, black agroproletariat, and black peasants of plantation society became more diversified. With "industrialization" there is the growth of an urban proletariat and an urban lumpen proletariat (from the reserve army of displaced peasants). White, Levantine, and Chinese comprador capitalists expanded the bourgeois class, at the other end of the scale. The ranks of the petty bourgeoisie opened up to the black professionals and peasants, but the major class formation here comes from the growth of the state bureaucracy.

With the economic substructure modified only slightly, the institutionalization of race and class remained within the mode of production. (In the Caribbean, color assumes importance as a proxy for race. Workers and small peasants are unmistakenly black, e.g., African and East Indian; the bourgeoisie are unmistakenly "white," i.e., nonblack; and the petty bourgeois class is predominantly brown, e.g., Afro-Saxon. The dominant culture is European, and the nativized African and Indian cultures are suppressed.) The superstructure of plantation capitalist society reflects these facts. Thus in the independent countries, the state represents the interests of the capitalist class and provides meager welfare and material dispensations for workers and small peasants. An "ideology of dependence" becomes entrenched among the ruling class. Thus the political directorate views the economic possibilities for national advancement from the point of view of external assistance for markets, capital, technology, and management; "industrialization by invitation" becomes the order of the day. Cheap labor is the drawing card for these foreign capital inflows, while in the U.S. South and northeastern Brazil, it is domestic capital from the more industrialized regions of these countries. But the effects are the same so far as the plantation regions are concerned. The process serves to entrench plantation society further in the international capitalist system, and makes a future break with that system seemingly more difficult to achieve.

The Dynamics of Change and Transformation of Plantation Society

Plantation society is a society in constant crisis. That crisis stems from the inherent contradiction between white capital and black labor. The capital–labor antagonism is central to all capitalist economies, but in plantation society the antagonism is heightened by the element of race. The constant situation of conflict places a special responsibility on the state to invest in instruments of violence in order to contain the conflict ("maintain law and order").

The limited capacity of the state to redress the economic inequalities between white capitalists and black workers and peasants (who because of the poor quality and small size of the land are unable to support their families and must become half-agroproletarians) leads to recurrent social upheaval. And here the second function of the state is brought to the fore—the institutions of state repression, the army and the police, virtually take charge when things get out of line. It is important to note that in plantation society, the army is less concerned with dealing with external aggression than it is in maintaining internal social peace. The army, in effect, is a military police force.

There are two patterns of adjustment in the fact of the class inequalities and conflicts. One is a "reformism" that brings change by making significant adjustments on the margin within the capitalist framework. But because this is never sufficient, massive out-migration of labor is the critical factor of adjustment. The other pattern is "revolution," which sets the stage for transformation of the capitalist plantation society to socialism.

The limits of reformism can be gauged by the rate of outmigration of labor from the plantation societies. For the Anglophone Caribbean as a whole, between the intercensal years 1960 and 1970, the estimated loss of 1.12 million people "is equivalent to nearly one-third of its population at 1960."[13] As for the labor force itself, net emigration represents 80 percent of the increase of the male working force over the decade. Given the fact that emigration from the region has been significant since the late nineteenth century, it would hardly be surprising to find that more West Indians live outside of the West Indies today than within the region. Puerto Rico presents a similar picture. In the U.S. South, the outmigration of black people escalated during the first imperialist war. During the 1910s, over 350,000 black people departed from six plantation states. By the 1920s, this had doubled to nearly 700,000. The Depression of the 1930s slowed down the rate; but by the 1950s, 1.1 million were making their way north and west (Mandle, 1979: 72–74).

Reformism achieved certain qualitative changes in plantation society. In the U.S. South, official response to the civil rights movement of the 1950s and 1960s enfranchised the black voter, desegregated schools and public places, increased the number of black elected officials, opened opportunities for black capitalism to develop, and enhanced tolerable race relations elsewhere in the United States. These positive achievements in the political realm have not been matched by significant improvements in the material (economic) welfare of black people relative to the white population. A similar situation developed in the Caribbean. In response to the rebellions of the late 1930s, Crown Colony government was abandoned for fully representative government through the introduction of universal adult suffrage, and led eventually to internal self-government and constitutional independence. But with the economic substructure unchanged, this independence turned out to be more symbolic than real.[14]

Among the Anglophone Caribbean states, reformism reached a relatively high level in Guyana and in Jamaica under Manley, where efforts to change the economic substructure have been attempted. Under the ideological rubric of "cooperative socialism," the Guyana government since 1971 nationalized the foreign-owned bauxite and sugar companies. And today about 80 percent of that economy is within the state sector. But race and class remain embedded in the social production fabric in a manner that makes it difficult to accept the notion that the society is in any way on a path of transition to socialism. State capitalism seems a more appropriate description of that society. Jamaica is even further removed from the stage[15] of transition to socialism. The Manley regime introduced the ideology of "democratic socialism" beginning in 1974 but did little to change the economic substructure. State participation in production was rehabilitative—government purchase of capitalist enterprises facing financial difficulties in sugar, tourism, and utilities. Only in the bauxite sector was there a positive state participation, with the repatriation of bauxite lands to the state amounting to a 51 percent share of bauxite mining. But that left the lion's share from alumina production untouched; for the bauxite-alumina companies, the state share was a mere 6 to 7 percent. For plantation society, land and agrarian reform is the single most important policy instrument for initiating a transition. But neither Guyana nor Jamaica made any move in this direction.

Revolution is the alternative path to reformism. By "revolution" we mean an abrupt change in the social-economic parameters of the society: specifically, the capture of state power by a worker–peasant alliance and the socialization of the means of production—in particular, land (including plantations) and facilitating institutions that govern capital formation (e.g., banks and other financial intermediaries, external trading institutions, and utilities). Such revolutionary change—more likely than not—must involve the violent overthrow of the ruling class. Plantation society was created by violence and is maintained by violence, and the logic suggests that it can be transformed only by violence. We need only to recall the brutal and direct military interventions by the United Kingdom in Jagan's Guyana in 1953, by the United States in Arbenz's Guatemala in 1954, Cuba's "Bay of Pigs" in 1961, Juan Bosch's Dominican Republic in 1965, and Bishop's Grenada in 1983. (Let us not allow the stress on plantation societies to exclude mention of Mossadegh in Iran in 1953, Allende's Chile in 1973, etc.). In the New World, Cuba is the only plantation society that has transformed from underdeveloped capitalism to rapidly *developing* socialism. In Africa, Guinea-Bissau, São Tomé-Principe, Angola, and Mozambique are firmly on the transition belt. In all these cases, violent revolution set the stage for the transformation.

The economic social and political achievements of socialist Cuba are already well known. The struggle to make the transformation has been long, torturous, and violent as the overthrown bourgeoisie and the U.S. government joined forces in numerous attempts to subvert the revolution since the revolutionary government came to power in January 1959. The success of the government of what is today socialist Cuba can be attributed to the speedy manner in which it began to redress the economic and social imbalances deriving from the race and class contradictions of plantation society. Within a few months after the overthrow of the Batista regime, the preconditions for transition were laid with the launching of a massive land reform program accompanied by urban reform that reduced the rent burden of the urban poor. The dynamic of change led inevitably to confrontation with foreign powers, and this, in turn, stimulated nationalization of all foreign-owned (mainly U.S.) property.

The transition to socialism was formalized in 1965 with the formation of the Cuban Socialist party, and within a decade the internal organizational changes resulted in real popular participation in matters of state decision making with the introduction of the organs of people's power. Institutionalized racism was eliminated from the productive and social orders, and class receded in importance. All these transformations released the creative energies of the people and led to a rapid development of the productive forces. And today, in addition to providing basic needs for its entire population Cuba is in a position to extend technical assistance to other Third World countries—especially in education, health, housing, agriculture (particularly in livestock), and fishing—while providing strategic military assistance to the liberation struggles of black people in southern Africa. Its achievements have been made possible also by assistance provided by other socialist states (especially the Soviet Union) in the early critical years of the revolution. And Cuba's present membership in the Socialist Council for Economic Assistance contributes to its continuing economic development.[16]

Grenada made history in the Anglophone Caribbean when, on March 13, 1979, Maurice Bishop led a successful coup d'état that overthrew the eccentric dictator Eric Gairy. Bishop's People's Revolutionary Government (PRG) made rapid progress in improving the material, social, and spiritual welfare of the Grenadian people. The PRG inherited from the Gairy regime a state sector consisting of nationalized plantations and Gairy's personal estate. There was, thus, limited internal resistance to the redistributive policies and programs of the PRG. But external resistance from the U.S. government started immediately, and culminated in the brutal U.S. invasion of the tiny *dominion* in October 1983.[17]

The PRG was a populist social democratic regime with "Marxist-Leninist" pretensions sufficient to attract external assistance from friendly socialist governments in Cuba, Eastern Europe, and, to a lesser extent, the Soviet Union, and from nonaligned oil-rich "socialist" countries in the Middle East and Africa. With this assistance, and tight internal budget management, the PRG succeeded in a program of economic transformation that reduced unemployment from 50 percent of the labor force in 1979 to 14 percent in 1982 to 1983; achieved a growth rate of 5.5 percent when other West Indian economies were experiencing negative growth; expanded mass consumption in areas of basic needs such as food, health, and education (thus increasing the social wage);[18] and created institutions of popular democracy at the community, parish, and national levels. These achievements were nothing short of remarkable during the period, when export prices of the country's major exports — bananas, cocoa, and nutmeg — were on the decline.

It was this performance that, more than anything else, threatened the United States. For if Grenada could achieve such results, it would encourage other neighboring West Indian islands to opt for the socialist/"communist" path of development. This is what really constituted the "threat to the national security of the U.S.A.," as Mr. Reagan described it. This perceived threat was covered by the obvious pretense that a military design was the raison d'être of the Point Salinas international airport, which was being constructed with assistance from Cuba and other friendly (including non-socialist) states. In fact, the airport was designed and constructed to provide a major thrust in the development of tourism. The geopolitical algebra seems to dictate that the United States will not stand by and allow the emergence of "another Cuba" in the Western Hemisphere — least of all in its "back yard," the plantation capitalist Caribbean and its somewhat associated "banana republics" in Central America.

The Future as History

What the future holds for the capitalist plantation societies of the New World is clear if we apply the lessons of history. That future depends on two sets of factors: one internal to the particular plantation society and the other external to it. The future of capitalist plantation societies rests both on the internal resolution of contradictions inherent in those societies and on the repercussions that such resolutions are likely to have on the international balance of

·power between the major world-systems, capitalist and socialist. Such repercussions will affect the reaction of these external forces to change and transformation in particular plantation societies.

The reaction of the United States, to even the advanced reformist changes effected in Guyana and in Jamaica under Manley provides some lessons. There is sufficient evidence to substantiate official claims that the CIA sought to "destabilize" the economy of Jamaica over the period 1976 to 1980 (Manley, 1982). And the IMF and the bauxite-alumina multinationals (BAMs) reinforced the CIA's efforts. The BAMs cut back production that accounted for 75 percent of (visible) export earnings. The IMF imposed the hardest "austerity measures," including massive devaluations that put pressure on workers, peasants, and the poor in general. Meanwhile, there was little tangible support from the international socialist system, perhaps because no internal efforts were made to set the preconditions for a transition to socialism, but also because the Soviet Union accepts that the region is outside its "sphere of influence" according to the Kennedy–Khrushchev settlement of the 1962 "October crisis" over deployment of missiles in Cuba.

On a world scale, the forces struggling for national liberation and socialism are gaining increasing ascendancy. And the international capitalist system is being weakened by a prolonged economic crisis that appears to be a conjuncture of crises of accumulation and of realization, accentuated by competitive rivalry for markets among the core nations in that system. In these circumstances of changing balances of power, Caribbean plantation societies face an external environment that could favor some measure of transformation. But geopolitics will pose formidable constraints on that process. Much depends on the course of change within the U.S. "plantation" society and its migrant offshoots in the black urban ghettos of the Northeast, industrial Midwest, and West Coast. The struggles of black people within the United States will strengthen and reinforce the struggles of black people in the Caribbean and in Africa, and the rest of the Third World as well.

Notes

This is a revised and roughly updated version of a paper originally written in May 1979 for a symposium on the "Political Economy of the Black World," held at the University of California at Los Angeles (UCLA).

It was presented in this form at the First World Plantation Conference, held at Louisiana State University, Baton Rouge, October 1984.

1. The usage of Third World here follows the conceptual outline provided by Abdalla (1978:18–20). It consists of all countries of the modern world that have been exploited by direct colonization. That is all of Africa and Asia (excluding Japan and China), Latin America, and the Caribbean.

2. And now from (4) to (5) in Cuba.

3. And now from (4) to (5) in Eastern Europe and China.

4. The slave plantation system established by the Europeans in the New World is a specific social formation of modern times. It is distinctly different from ancient slavery in that it was linked directly to international capitalist markets. It is not simply a "mode of production," as indicated by Mandle (1979:3–15). The slave mode of production has a raison d'être in a capitalist mode of exchange that is international (eventually global).

5. My original exploration of this system of capitalist organization was made in Beckford (1972), albeit within a structuralist paradigm.

6. The significance of making a distinction between "stage" and "belt" in the discussion of transition will become obvious later. (See n. 15.) The reasons for Manley's defeat are clearly set out by Levitt (1983).

7. For further discussion on the increasingly critical role of the MNBs, see Sweezy (1978). On the role of the IMF and its effects on borrowing by Third World nations, see Payer (1974).

8. My earlier analysis of plantation society (Beckford, 1972) has several weaknesses that I attempt to correct (or elaborate) in what follows. Specifically, its handling of the class question was overshadowed by the emphasis on race, whereas what is needed is a synthesis of how race and class makes plantation society a "special case" in the history of social formations. See also Beckford (1976).

9. The revolutionary struggle of the slaves under the leadership of Toussaint L'Overture overthrew French rule, and Haiti eventually, in 1804, became the first black nation-state. This was a clear signal to the European merchant/planter class that slavery would no longer be a viable proposition. The cost of containing revolt everywhere became increasingly prohibitive.

10. This movement of Asiatic labor set the stage for the acceleration of unequal exchange that lasts to the present day. Lewis (1977) points out that between 1870 and 1944, the period marking the birth of imperialism, about 50 million Europeans migrated to North America, Australia, New Zealand, and South Africa, while about the same numbers of Asiatic people were indentured to work on tropical plantations, in mines, on the infrastructure of rail transport, and the like. This explains the low labor productivity that prevails in the periphery today, relative to that of the core states.

11. Lewis (1954, 1955) was the first to articulate this, but recently Marxist scholars have elaborated the concept of unequal exchange. See Emmanuel (1974) and Amin (1976).

12. See Browne (1973) for the U.S. case and Girvan (1972) for the Caribbean example. More intensive studies of this land displacement are urgently needed, for the alienation from the means of production constitutes the single most important factor in the persistence of poverty among the masses of black people in New World plantation societies.

13. G.W. Roberts, as quoted in Beckford (1977).

14. The term "flag independence" describes this quite appropriately.

15. The distinction between "transition *stage*" and "transition *belt*" used earlier in this essay is important. "Belt" is meant to connote a dynamic unidirectional movement (à la Rodney, "transition is a movement in a given direction"). "Stage" implies a static situation; the society can move in either direction, forward to socialism or backward to fascism.

16. The Sino-Soviet split beginning in the 1960s creates a dual international socialist system. The People's Republic of China acts independently, in fact in direct opposition to the socialist system of Eastern Europe (centering on the Soviet Union as *primum inter pares*). Third World socialist states are associated with one or the other or both.

17. For an analysis and chronicle of the United States' consistent campaign of destabilization and the PRG–led Grenadian people's resistance, see Searle (1983).

18. These economic achievements are recorded in the World Bank Report on Grenada (1983).

References

Abdalla, K. (1978). "Heterogeneity and Differentiation: The End for the Third World?" *Development Dialogue* 2:18–20.

Amin, Samir (1976). *Unequal Development: An Essay on the Social Formations of Peripheral Capitalism*. New York: Monthly Review Press.

Beckford, George L. (1972). *Persistent Poverty*. New York: Oxford University Press.

——— (1976). "Plantation Society: Towards a General Theory of Caribbean Society." In P. Figueroa and G. Persaud, eds., *Sociology of Education: A Caribbean Reader*. London: Oxford University Press, pp. 33–46.

——— (1977). *Race, Class and the Plantation: Dependent Capitalism and Alienation in the Caribbean*. Mimeograph presented to the Joint Meeting of LASA and ASA. Houston: November 2–5.

Browne, Robert (1973). *Only Six Million Acres: A Decline of Black-Owned Land*. New York: Monthly Review Press.

Emmanuel, Arghiri (1974). *Unequal Exchange*. New York: Monthly Review Press.

Girvan, Norman (1972). *Foreign Capital and Economic Underdevelopment in Jamaica*. Kingston: New World Group.

Levitt, Kari (1983). *Banking on Poverty*. Toronto: Macmillan.

Lewis, William A. (1954). *Economic Development with Unlimited Supplies of Labor*. Manchester: School of Economic Research.

———— (1955). *Theory of Economic Growth*. London: Allen and Unwin.

———— (1977). *Evolution of the International Economic Order*. Princeton, N.J.: Princeton University Press.

Mandle, Jay R. (1979). *The Roots of Black Poverty*. Durham, N.C.: Duke University Press.

Manley, Michael (1982). *Jamaica: Struggle in the Periphery*. London: Oxford University Press.

Payer, Cheryl (1974). *The Debt Trap*. New York: Monthly Review Press.

Rodney, Walter (1978). "Transition." *Transition* (University of Guyana) 1:1–12.

Searle, Chris (1983). *Grenada: The Struggle Against Destabilization*. London: Writers and Readers Publishing.

Sweezy, Paul (1978). "Multinational Corporations and Banks. " *Monthly Review,* January, pp. 1–9.

World Bank (1983). "Report on Grenada." *World Bank Report*. Washington, D.C.: Government Printing Office.

CHAPTER 6

Perspectives on the Development and Underdevelopment of Communities in Guyana: A Sociohistorical Analysis

George K. Danns and Lear K. Matthews

Dependency theorists in the Caribbean (Thomas, 1976; Frank, 1969; Beckford, 1972; Girvan, 1971; Best, 1968; Brewster, 1973) point to the underdevelopment in the region stemming from its dependent incorporation into the world capitalist system. These theorists advocate strategies of national self-determination and self-reliance, while others (Demas, 1965; McIntyre, 1971) suggest the necessity of regional integration in order that these nations can break out of the syndrome of underdevelopment. In this article, we revisit the issues of dependence and underdevelopment. The focus, however, is not on international dependency relationships that are resulting in the "persistent poverty" and continuing lack of development of countries in the region. Instead, the thrust of our analysis is on the dependency relationships created by a dominant economic plantation sector and the state system with the various communities and therefore the society as a whole. Our contention is that the transformation of dependency at the level of the nation must be preceded by a marked reduction of dependency at the level of the community.

Pablo Gonzales Casanova (1970) applied center–periphery analysis to what he describes as a pattern of internal colonization and dependency between the urban–rural polarization in Mexico that has resulted in the dependent underdevelopment of rural communities. A similar pattern exists in Guyana, not so much between rural and urban communities but rather between the state system, its control of the dominant economic sector, and the communities (both urban and rural) within the nation. The relation of dependency between the state system and the communities in postcolonial Guyana is not, however, one of direct exploitation, but rather one of policy direction and misdirection, resource allocation and misallocation, as well as resource deprivation. The relation of dependence in colonial Guyana was, however, one of exploitation by the dominant plantation sector and the state of the communities in the society.

A community may refer to a plantation, a village, or an urban locale. Also, there are communities not defined by geographical boundaries, that is, functional communities. In this paper, however, we focus largely, though not exclusively, on communities that are geographically defined. By definition, a community consists of some measure of autonomy that sets the parameters of its boundaries and influences its relations with other communities. For our purposes, communities are distinct and differentiable from a society (or nation) and are considered as its basic units.

The social structure of Guyana consists of plural and heterogeneous ethnic and cultural groupings historically rooted in distinct communities. Our concern is to examine both historical and contemporary manifestations of such communities and their role in development and underdevelopment. From this examination, new perspectives of the historical form and development of communities in light of the peculiar relationship of such communities to the ruling class and the state are derived.

The Plantation Community

The plantation community was:

1. A geographically defined social and economic unit in which people were organized primarily for the purpose of producing invariably a single agricultural crop for export.
2. A feudal-type organization in which the master of the plantation or his managerial representatives held largely unquestioned power over the lives and activities of the labor force.
3. A color/caste and color/class system of stratification in which ascendant status within the stratification hierarchy depended on "whiteness" or nearness to "whiteness."

The plantation, particularly during slavery, was a restricted community in which interactions with the environment (mainly other plantation communities) were carefully regulated. Subordinate members of the community, who composed the majority, were prohibited from associating with non-community members. They were also very restricted in their relationships with the superordinate members of the plantation and largely denuded of any sense of personal and human worth. The custodial nature of the plantation leads to adoption of Goffman's (1968) notion of the "total institution" to typify the plantation community. Total institutions are institutions like prisons, mental asylums, and military camps, in which relations with the environment are carefully circumscribed; there is rigid separation between staff and inmates, rules and set procedures define the daily round of activities, and inmates are made to undergo a process of "self mortification." The plantation community was what could be termed an exploitative custodial community, which defined the form and function of social organization in the colony of British Guiana.

During the periods of slavery and indenture, the colonial society in what is now Guyana consisted of these semi-isolated social units in which social life was plantation community life; social existence was plantation community existence; social production was plantation community production; and societal development was plantation community development. Plantation communities were the basic units of the colonial society, and relations within and among the plantation communities defined relations within the society. It was this conglomeration of plantation communities that linked the colony into a status of dependency and underdevelopment *within* the international capitalist system. It was also the stratification system of the plantation community that structured the stratification system of the society at large. In short, the plantation community was the microcosm of the colonial society.

Scholars in the region attribute the persistence of dependency to the continuity of a plantation economy. It seems, however, that in order to transform the plantation economy, attention must be given to the community within which plantation production takes place. Economic activity is always carried on within some form of social organization. The social cocoon around economic relations of production and distribution forms a protective fabric that must be penetrated for effective transformation to occur. Economic activity must be understood in terms of the social organization that engenders it.

The colonial state functioned to provide a halo of protection and support for the plantation system. The state maintained a legal and coercive framework legitimizing the productive relations of the plantations. Plantation production relied on a large supply of unskilled labor power. The colonial state both sanctioned and subsidized the supply of slave and, later, indentured labor. Providing further supportive services was an emergent urban commercial sector consisting of merchants who imported stocks and equipment and some food supplies that were not produced in the colony and to which plantation owners and managers were accustomed. The plantation community was, however, considerably autonomous and exhibited a great degree of self-sufficiency and self-reliance. It is recognized that the social institutions of slavery and indenture—within which this autonomy and self-sufficiency existed— were oppressive and exploitative. In terms of economic production, however, it must be borne in mind that such a community (other things being equal) generated tremendous wealth and profits.

An argument can be made that some measure of autonomy is essential for the development of communities. Of course, the colony was not a nation, and during the days when the plantation communities existed there was no concept of a nation or national development. The plantation owners were outward-looking, and profits generated by the plantations were channeled toward the development of the metropolitan country rather than the colony of British Guiana. Insofar as development occurred within the colony through the instrumentality of the plantation community, such development was largely incidental. The plantation was as much an instrument of community underdevelopment as it was an instrument of colonial underdevelopment and dependency.

The plantation community can be seen as passing through two major phases. The first is the era of plantation slavery, followed by the era of plantation indenture. What is common to these two phases is that the plantation community was a closed social system exhibiting the characteristics of a total institution.

The importation of captive peoples from Africa signaled the coming into being of the plantation slavery community. Blacks were enslaved and provided the cheap and abundant labor force necessary for plantation production. The Dutch were the first colonizers of Guyana and began to lay the foundations of the plantation system in the early seventeenth century. By the middle of the eighteenth century, hegemony of the plantation was entrenched. Battles between the Dutch, French, and British culminated in the colony's being eventually ceded to the British by the Dutch through a treaty in 1803. Previous Dutch attempts to enslave the sparse population of indigenous Amerindians had failed, and efforts to recruit white labor to work in harsh tropical conditions had met with a similar lack of success (Menzes, 1977). It seemed, then, that if plantations were to be established, a large labor force, willing or unwilling, had to be acquired. The large number of imported Africans provided an unwilling labor force.

The abolition of slavery in 1833 witnessed a period of compulsory apprenticeship for the slaves, who were anxious to flee the plantation community and the savage memories it held for them. This era of "manumission" lasted until 1838. For the recalcitrant ex-slaves it was a preparatory phase to introduce them as indentured laborers on the plantation. The abolition of slavery signaled the coming into being of the era of the plantation indenture community. The ex-slaves fled the plantations and set up communities of their own in villages. These communities were "reactive communities" in the sense of being bold attempts by the blacks to organize communities that were separate from or independent of the plantation — communities that would contain elements that had been absent in their previous deprived existence.

The plantation indenture community was a "contractual community." Table 6.1 shows the arrival of immigrants from different countries during the era of indenture. The population in the colony increased from 98,154 in 1841 to 288,541 in 1921, mainly as a consequence of immigration (Mandle, 1973). Portuguese, Chinese, and later East Indians were imported as laborers on a five-year contractual system. Africans and black West Indians were also imported as indentured labor. For reasons that will become clear later on, both the Chinese and the Portuguese did not stay for any length of time on the plantations, and indentured East Indians replaced the black labor force. The contracts that bound them to the land of the plantation guaranteed payment and return passage to

Table 6.1 Gross Immigration by Area of Origin, 1835–1920

Year	India	Madeira	West Indies	Africa	Other	Total
1835–40	396	429	8,092	91	278	9,286
1841–50	14,100	16,744	4,806	9,893	—	45,543
1851–60	23,381	9,587	—	1,968	3,288	28,224
1861–70	387,151	1,533	10,180	1,403	9,343	61,174
1871–1880/81	53,273	2,170	12,887	—	903	69,233
1881/82–1890/91	38,851	—	4,161	—	—	43,012
1891/92–1900/01	39,464	—	707	—	—	40,171
1901/02–1910/11	23,769	—	—	—	455	24,224
1911/12–1920	9,216	—	923	—	200	10,339

Source: Dwarka Nath, *History of Indians in British Guiana* (London: Nelson, 1950), Table 1.

the land of their origin. The "indentures" were allowed, in part, to maintain their cultural practices, which reinforced a sense of community among them. But the total institutional nature of the plantation system, too, was maintained. The indentured laborers were powerless to change harsh and inhumane working conditions. Theirs was a slavelike existence insofar as work relations were concerned. They were, however, "free" and could look forward to a less harsh existence after indentureship. The slave could have looked forward only to death as an emancipating force. The slaves were property, while the indentured immigrants were workers (Rodney, 1981). Although the conditions of indenture are often equated with the conditions of slavery, they were in fact qualitatively very different. The coercion of indentures was based on contractual obligations, while the coercion of slaves was based on absolute ownership and control. Further, a missing ingredient in the slave community that was to be found in indenture is the maintenance of a sense of identity and cultural beliefs and practices.

Like the plantation slavery community, the plantation indenture community was essentially concerned with monocrop production for an export market. An important derivative of this economic organizational imperative is the fact that both communities were owned not by their residents but by the minority white dominant group. These communities, then, were as much economic concerns and private property of their owners as they were total communities of the conglomeration of participants.

Table 6.2 Distribution of Population by Place of Residence, Guyana, 1851–1970

Year	Urban and Suburban	Estates	Villages, Farms, Settlements
1851	23.6%	30.8%	45.6%
1861	22.8	37.2	40.0
1871	21.7	35.1	43.2
1881	21.0	34.5	44.6
1891	22.9	33.2	43.9
1911	22.4	24.0	53.7
1921	22.8	22.2	54.9
1932	26.0	21.7b	50.5
1970	26.0	—	—

Source: Census Reports, 1851–1970. S. D. Singh, "The Demography of Social Change in Guyana" (Ph.D. diss., University of California, Berkeley, 1977), p. 50.

The ending of the contracts of indenture and the eventual curtailment of the indentureship practice in 1917 witnessed a withdrawal of the East Indians and other immigrants from the confinement of the plantations and the dissolution of the plantation communities. Faced with the problem of having to maintain plantation production, the white planters were forced to offer added inducements to the predominantly East Indian labor force. In some cases, East Indian immigrants were reindentured for another five years. Grants of land and other resources were given to them in lieu of return passage to India. East Indian village communities were mainly established close to the sugar plantation production. Later we will treat the East Indian village communities in more detail. It will suffice to say here that the abolition of slavery and later the curtailment of indentureship resulted in a dissolution of the plantation community that culminated in the establishment of pockets of plural ethnic communities within the society. Table 6.2 shows the distribution of population by place of residence between 1851 and 1970. The estate population declined steadily as the proportion of the village and urban and suburban population increased.

The dissolution of the plantation as a total institution not only resulted in the setting up of new communities distinct and separate from the plantation, but also transformed the nature of the plantation itself. What effectively occurred was structural and functional differentiation, whereby the plantation changed from its diffuse functioning and all-inclusive structural character to a complex organization concerned exclusively with specific functions of production and maintaining structures directly related to such production. Shorn from the plantation was the community that it encapsulated. The plantation was now a business firm—a formal organization. Such a development was indicative of a tide of modernization and revolution in capitalist production, where free labor was preferable and more efficient and profitable than either enslaved and indentured labor. The capitalist was no longer to be responsible for the total welfare of the workers. Instead, the worker was to be responsible for himself and his family, and the imperative of earning a living necessitated the sale of his labor to the capitalist. The plantation owners' main concern as capitalists was to ensure the maintenance of an adequate and cheap supply of willing labor. The plantation had changed from a feudal-type institution to a quasi-modern capitalist business enterprise.

Scholars have a tendency to ignore this revolution or transformation in the plantation itself as a community and to argue that the total institutional and systemic character of the plantation still remains. The position taken here is that the plantation ceased being a total institution and a community and became a business firm, a formal organization concerned exclusively with production. The plantation economy, however, persisted, and social relations within the society tended to be inexorably influenced by this organization for the production of material life. Just as dominant business enterprises (e.g., as in mining towns) form the nucleus and generator for social activities and communal life around them, so the plantation as a business enterprise influences social relations in adjoining and adjacent communities.

The forces of modernization affecting the colony were tied to the emergence of monopoly capitalism. Separately owned and unconnected plantation firms became merged and integrated into organized arms of two multinationals: Bookers Brothers, John McConnell Limited and Jessels Limited. The one-to-one relatedness of particular plantation firms to adjoining and adjacent communities was soon transformed into generalized business-policy practices throughout the society and among communities. This change involved the plantation firms being transformed into plantation corporations. Plantation corporations then confronted communities, and the society as a whole, as giant economic forces. Plantation corporations largely defined economic activities in the colony and were the primary employers of the working population. This dominant influence of sugar companies remains to the present day. What is important is that these business concerns became separate and distinct entities from the rest of the community. Protests against them took the form not of rebellion, but of industrial strike action and other forms of worker agitation. Such industrial protest is indicative of the institutional separateness of the economic form of the social and political, and of the community, from business.

A climate of continuous industrial protest, vagaries in the supply of labor, and fluctuating world market prices for sugar had combined to bankrupt some plantations and constrain the owners of several others to sell to the multinational corporations. Mandle (1973) chronicled the role of the British firm of Bookers Brothers, John McConnell Limited, which had totally dominated the local sugar industry by World War II. (This firm was the product of a merger between Bookers Brothers and John McConnell and Company in 1900.) Mandle pointed out that in 1921, Bookers was listed as owning only six of the country's estates, but by 1938 to 1940 Bookers or its subsidiaries were named as owners of eighteen of the twenty-eight estates in the country and in addition dominated the export of sugar from the colony. By 1960, it was reported by R.T. Smith that Bookers owned fourteen out of the nineteen estates in the colony. The narrowing of the ownership structure of the sugar industry was accompanied by increases in production through the application of improved technology, as opposed to the traditional exclusive reliance on "brawn power." The Bookers monopoly had transnational connections in Britain and other countries, but had none with the local village communities from which it purchased labor power.

The granting of political independence in 1966 and the advancement to republican status in 1970 witnessed a qualitative change in the relationship of the sugar multinationals to the local communities and the society at large. In the first place, the demand for Guyanization of these enterprises gradually resulted in Guyanese nationals managing the sugar estates. Soon, however, cries for an increased share in profits and 51 percent ownership by the state saw the eventual nationalization of Bookers's enterprises in 1976. The nationalization of Jessels's holdings in Guyana soon followed. Nationalization demanded that ethnic, partisan, and area loyalties be transformed into loyalty to the nation. Such nationalist sentiment can sometimes result in the actual blurring of community lines. The sugar estates no longer belonged to foreign multinationals but to "the people," the nation as a whole. Production and profits from estates were production and profits for Guyanese society as a whole; no longer were profits to be exported, but they were to be used for the benefit of the Guyanese "community." This type of nationalist outlook and policy as advocated by the state sacrificed local communities in Guyana for the nation. The nation was now one big "community," and sugar estates must contribute to the welfare of this "community" as a whole. Under both foreign and state ownership, the sugar estates were not oriented to the development of the communities in which they were located.

Village Communities, Class, and Ethnicity

With the Amerindians as a notable exception, village communities are either reactions to or derivatives from the plantation community experience. Village communities epitomize the ethnic plurality and separateness of Guyanese society. Village settlements are geographical enclaves in which the population tends to be dominantly and sometimes almost exclusively characterized by members of one particular ethnic group. These ethnic settlements are historical manifestations that owe their origins to peculiar association with, or dissociation from, the plantation system. Essentially, village communities in Guyana are historically the product of three dominant factors:

1. Nomadic and communal settlement of the indigenous Amerindians.
2. The abolition of slavery and the withdrawal of the freed blacks from the plantations. Blacks either purchased abandoned plantations or squatted in clusters on Crown lands, particularly in the interior.
3. Colonial state and plantation policies of settling indentured laborers in areas adjoining plantations or on other Crown lands and granting, leasing, or selling such lands to the settlers.

The emergence of villages represented not only a withdrawal of labor from the sugar estates over time, but also the gradual and then ultimate breakdown of the plantation community and the concomitant emergence of the plantation firm. The local villages were, however, still strangled by the dominance and organizational power of the sugar estates, which were well supported by colonial state policies. In 1851, about 46 percent of the population lived in villages separate from the plantations. By 1911, 55 percent inhabited the villages (Mandle, 1973). After 1911, the village population began to decrease as villagers migrated to urban centers for employment and education. In 1921, 50 percent of the population lived in villages.

There are several varieties of village communities in Guyana: Amerindian village communities, black village communities, East Indian village communities, urban village communities, and mining towns. Urban centers are treated in this study as a conglomeration of villages because, like the rural and hinterland village settlements, they manifest pockets of ethnic clustering. Moreover, the underdeveloped and relatively unsophisticated nature of these urban centers probably warrants their typification as urban villages. Indeed, some of these urban centers were previously village settlements.

Amerindian Village Communities

The Amerindians are the indigenous peoples of Guyana. They live largely in the forested regions of the country and were originally a nomadic people who lived in small communal clusters, often numbering fewer than five hundred people. There are several distinct tribes of Amerindians in Guyana: Arawaks, Macusi, Wapishianas, Caribs, Akawaio, and Arecunas.

As tribal communities, they maintained traditional cultural patterns and, with the intrusion of European civilization, retreated even farther into the interior of the forested regions. For the Amerindians, their particular tribal community was their world. Their concept of community and society was synonymous with that of the tribe, since for the most part they lived in self-contained units "in their own territories." They were marginal to the colonial plantation system and colonial society as a whole. Some of them were, for an abortive period, a functional part of the plantation community in the capacity of slaves. Subsequently, they were utilized by the planters as "interior police" to capture runaway African slaves in exchange for gift payments (Menzes, 1977).

As a community, the Amerindians maintained *Gemeinschaften* relationships and gave mutual support to one another and worked together in sustaining their own communities. Here we find, as with the plantation community, the Amerindian village communities being autonomous, self-reliant, and self-sufficient. Unlike the plantation community, however, they pursued a system of altruistic and cooperative rather than coerced productive activity. Decision making about community affairs took place within the community. Community or tribal development, therefore, was a result of self-designed plans and self-imposed implementation of such plans. Unlike the plantation community, which was integrated by force and the continuous threat thereof, the Amerindian village community was integrated by the normative and regulative bonds of a traditional culture. Further, the individual was bound to the tribe by affinal and consanguinal ties as well as by ties of loyalty, rather than by shackles of restraint. The Amerindian's community, then, was a free society, with threat to its members stemming not from internal but from external factors (e.g., hostile encounters with other tribes).

While these Amerindian communities were not, because of their nomadic nature, conquered and dominated by the plantation system, they succumbed to the proselytizing and Christianizing efforts of white missionaries. The missionaries functioned as the main link between colonial society and the marginality of the Amerindian tribal system. Schools and churches were established and initially run by missionaries in Amerindian villages, which because of this association soon became known as Amerindian missions. The remoteness of these tribal communities, however, kept them from being completely overrun and co-opted by the colonial society. The Amerindians, then, remained during the colonial era the only real traditional community within Guyana. Colonial state policy toward Amerindian communities soon became one of protection and for the most part noninterference.

With the granting of political independence in 1966, the national government sought to actively integrate the Amerindian settlements within the mainstream of activity in the Guyanese society. By this time, Amerindians were leaving their tribal communities and were obtaining low-status jobs with mining concerns and other business activities being developed by the larger society in the remote and forested regions. Others were migrating to urban centers and becoming assimilated in the rest of the society. The Christianizing pursuits of the Catholic, Anglican, and Seventh-Day Adventist churches had enabled the Amerindians to speak English, as well as forgo much of their indigenous traditional culture. Amerindian chiefs were invited to a conference held in the early 1970s in the capital city, where for the first time they met with state leaders in the nation's legislative assembly. The state co-opted the Amerindians by appointing them rural constables in charge of keeping the peace in their villages. The state also formally recognized their chieftainship and awarded them a monthly salary, thus transforming, in great measure, their traditional authority and relations with their tribe to rational–legal authority and an official position with the central government.

The necessity of co-opting Amerindian communities into the mainstream of Guyanese life became all the more imperative in the light of border disputes with Brazil, Venezuela, and Surinam. Since the Amerindians were a nomadic people, they wandered back and forth across borders, and to this day largely pay no national allegiance to any of these societies. Insofar, however, as they do have permanent settlements in Guyana, the government was concerned with soliciting their national loyalties to the state of Guyana. More, in the Rupununi Savannah region, Amerindians formed the vanguard of a secessionist movement. Government officials in the area were either shot or held prisoner. Prompt action by the Guyana Defense Force (GDF) and the police put down the secessionists, most of whom fled across the border to Venezuela along with the white ranchers who led the rebellion. It would appear that the Amerindians involved, most of whom worked for ranchers of European descent, may have been instigated to pursue that course of action. Nevertheless, the state viewed the Amerindian involvement with great concern and sought to strengthen the co-optation policies toward the Amerindians. Increasing numbers of scholarships were awarded, and Amerindians were recruited into the armed forces, the nursing profession, and other occupations in which they displayed interest.

Along with the integrative efforts of the state, increased attention was given to providing adequate educational and health facilities within or near Amerindian villages. Many Amerindians who became teachers and nurses assisted this integrative and modernizing process. The state prohibited "outsiders" from paying visits to village settlements except with the express approval of the Ministry of Regional Development and of the Amerindian chieftains. The GDF also assisted in the modernizing and integrative efforts of the state by providing medical assistance and other services, thus strengthening the linkages between the state and such communities.

The exposure of the Amerindians to modernizing influences is resulting not only in the rapid breakdown of their traditional culture, but also in mass withdrawal from traditional communities. Perhaps the majority of the Amerindian population of Guyana now resides in areas peopled by other Guyanese. Many others have emigrated to neighboring Brazil and Venezuela. Amerindians, though still maintaining traditional village settlements, have developed a relatively large functional community outside of village communal life.

The villages' main form of economic activity is subsistence farming using simple methods of slash-and-burn agriculture. Some Amerindian communities engage in some kind of handicraft production, but not to any significant extent. Thus there are no forms of significant economically rewarding activities developed or being carried on in Amerindian villages that could serve to develop the village communities. Government provides services, but the "modernized" Amerindians must seek employment elsewhere. It seems, then, that modernizing forces, while successfully co-opting formerly traditional and peripheral communities into the mainstream of Guyanese societal life, have failed to improve the backward economic conditions of such village communities.

The Amerindian communities, however, possess a larger measure of community autonomy than most of the other village communities. Despite such autonomy, these communities are not self-reliant but now heavily dependent on the rest of the society for their survival. Amerindians, too, are still fighting to remove the stigma of the label "buckman," reflecting the condescending attitude of the rest of the Guyanese society toward these formerly traditional peoples.

Black Village Communities

Black settlements emerged as reactive communities, formed in response to the harsh experience of plantation slavery. Paul Singh observed:

> The abolition of slavery transformed human beings from "the category of property" to "the category of citizenship." Most of the liberated Negroes, wishing to improve their standard of living, to establish homes and to preserve their newly won freedom, trekked away from the sugar estates and settled elsewhere. The rise of the village settlements was symbolic of the continuation of the revolt against the plantation system by freed labor, reinforced by the advantages denied them under slavery. (1972:9–10)

The ex-slaves' purpose was to establish village communities and to strive for self-sufficiency and development. For them, their freedom would be meaningful only when they would have demonstrated that by working together in cooperation they could attain the standard and levels of living of their former masters. To this end, "between 1839 and 1954 they spent $332,900 in purchasing seventeen estates, prices ranging from $2,000 to $80,000 each . . ." (Singh, 1972:10).

This revolutionary effort by the blacks occurred in the face of mounting opposition and hostilities by the white plantocracy, who saw the rise of the black village movement not only as a serious threat to their economic dominance, if not their very existence, but also as depriving white-owned plantations of a large supply of cheap labor. The village movement was facilitated by the availability of large tracts of vacant lands. Singh noted that there were three categories of land theoretically available to the blacks:

> the forfeited lands which might be purchased from the Crown and which attracted many of the most independent and ambitious of the freed slaves; the marginal lands which might be purchased or leased from the estate owners by wage earners on the property and the mountainous forest reserves which might be squatted on. (1972:10)

The blacks who largely opted for the first alternative accumulated money for the purchase of land during the five-year period of compulsory apprenticeship between 1833 and 1838.

Despite their determined attempts at establishing self-sufficient cooperative villages, opposition from the plantocracy and the colonial government negated and frustrated black efforts in the following ways:

1. In 1839, a Crown Land Policy was introduced that stipulated that the minimum size of a lot should be 100 acres and the statutory price $10 an acre. These requirements inhibited purchases by individuals and prevented the emergence of independent peasant proprietors (Mandle, 1973:36).

2. The plantocracy, the colonial government, and the white merchant group refused to lend money to black communities for the purpose of capital investment. The blacks had exhausted their savings in purchasing settlements and had no money left to build and invest.

3. The plantation owners controlled most of the irrigation outlets and used them to flood the black village settlements.

4. The police harassed black villagers. The police kept vigilant in black villages, refusing to allow any assembly of blacks numbering more than five persons without the express written permission of the authorities. The result was the shattering of any constructive efforts at building communities on a cooperative basis. The rationale for refusing such assembly was that the blacks would return to their primitive tribal and religious practices, which were deemed unlawful. The fear was that the free and unhindered assembling of black villagers could result in uprisings against the white ruling class. *It is of interest to note that the police force was established in 1839, immediately upon the release of the blacks from the slave plantations.* Police stations and outposts in Guyana are with few exceptions located in black communities. Such location is historically indicative of the efforts at surveillance of the freed slaves (Danns, 1982).

As a consequence of these major structural barriers facing the development of black village communities, the attempt at independent settlement was greatly weakened. The village residents migrated to the urban centers, forming to this day the majority of the urban industrial proletariat. Others migrated to the interior regions as "porknockers" in search of gold and diamonds. It was largely the men, however, who migrated to the interior regions of the country after failing to build an economic base of support for their families within the village settlements. This economic failure, coupled with the tendency of the black male to migrate in search of employment, contributed to the breakup of many homes. The result is the significant matrifocality so salient among black families. In the absence of the fathers, grandmothers tend to be the titular head of the black family. Of those who remained in the villages, subsistence farming of ground provisions like plantain, cassava, and sweet potatoes represented the dominant mode of existence. They also continued to sell their labor power to the sugar plantations, particularly in the more skilled jobs in the sugar factories.

The upshot of this thwarting of the black village movement was that the sugar plantation remained supreme. Efforts by the white ruling class at preserving plantation dominance frustrated and ultimately underdeveloped black village communities. Black village communities were kept in a state of dependent underdevelopment by the plantation system. The aim of the plantocracy and the colonial government was to force the "upstart" blacks to return to their low status as laborers on the plantations. Both Singh (1972) and Sukdeo (1979) pointed to the political and legal maneuvers that resulted in the failure of black village communities and their subsequent reduced interest in agriculture and farming. Singh (1972) noted that the rates and taxes imposed on black villages by the colonial government were severe and discouraging. Further, he pointed to some other barriers in the path of black villagers in noting:

> the difficulty of maintaining an effective and expensive drainage system, the difficulty of securing titles to their lands are attendant on their having bought in common estates which they desired to hold in severalty, and the difficulty of fulfilling the obligation which rested on owners of plantations to repair the public roads which ran through their properties. They made gallant attempts to sustain their plantation cooperatives but lack of capital militated against them. (1972:11)

In sum, not only did the plantation dominance underdevelop black communities, but the colonial government itself was instrumental in the failure of the black village movements.

The blockage by the plantocracy and the colonial government of any viable economic activity within black communities also underdeveloped the society as a whole, since both produce and profits from sugar plantations were exported. Had the plantation owners used their profits to diversify the economy, Guyana as a society would have been far more developed. The resident planter class in the United States plowed its profits into the development of that society. In Guyana and the Caribbean region as a whole, the plantation owners were invariably absentee proprietors, with Britain (or France, Spain, or Holland) being considered their real home. The ruling class in the colonial era was outward-looking, immigrant, and transient. This analysis highlights the obvious necessity of locating economically viable activities within the communities if development is to be realized.

The colonial government, having frustrated black community developments, was faced with the necessity of defusing and redirecting the energies of the blacks who demonstrated recalcitrance insofar as working on the plantations was concerned. Further, cultural assimilation of blacks into a cosmology in which whiteness was seen as superior and blackness as inferior, depraved, and primitive became necessary. Christianization by priests and missionaries functioned to socialize black communities into accepting other worldly values. Heaven was for the black man his true home, while his life on earth was hell. Money and riches were to be seen as vile and productive of evil.

The introduction of formal education also functioned to socialize the blacks into acceptance of a "British" way of life. Blacks were soon equipped to take up jobs as clerks, junior civil servants, teachers, and the like. Education was styled as the highest good a black person could aspire to and acquire. Both education and Christianization redirected black efforts away from community development and prepared them instead to occupy inferior status in a stratification system legitimized by the myth of white superiority (Hintzen, 1977).

Efforts, then, by the freed blacks to develop their communities largely failed. The failure was due to the plantation dominance and the inability of the blacks to set up and maintain economically viable activities within their village communities. To this day, in comparison with other ethnic communities, black village communities remain conspicuously undeveloped and blatantly devoid of any economically viable and vibrant activity. One result is a higher rate of rural–urban migration among blacks than among the East Indians. As Sukdeo succinctly stated, "Although historically

Negroes predominated in the village population, they are presently an insignificant minority" (1979:8). Moving away from the villages also highlights black disillusionment with agriculture as a basis for economic development. It is not that blacks are not or cannot become efficient farmers. It is rather that historical forces relating to the plantations had frustrated attempts at community survival and development and have left a bitter memory. It was the blacks who during slavery made plantation farming viable; it was Christianization and colonial education that cultivated a "trained incapacity" and a seeming "ethnic aversion" to agriculture.

In short, the effective colonization and underdevelopment of the people of Guyana were first and most harshly experienced by its black population. For them community development was community survival. Blacks have survived, but their communities remain underdeveloped.

East Indian Village Communities

Like the black village communities, the East Indian villages were a direct outgrowth of the plantation system. The East Indians came to Guyana as indentured laborers and largely constituted the population of the plantation indentured communities. Between 1851 and 1917, a total of 228,743 Indian immigrants were brought in and indentured (Rodney, 1981). Sukdeo explains:

> The terms of indenture required each person to serve for a five year period after which the immigrant could have been reindentured. After a period of indentureship of five years and continuous residence in the country for 10 years, every immigrant was entitled to a return passage to India. In 1894, a special committee was appointed to allocate grants of land to the East Indians in lieu of their passage rights. As early as 1870, over 30,000 immigrants, by fulfilling their period of indentureship and residing for ten years in the colony, had earned the legal right to be returned to India at Government's expense. Plantations still required a large labor force and the feeling was that the Indians were themselves interested in land and the Government felt that their offer would be widely accepted. Concomitant with this policy was the practice of encouraging settlements near the sugar estates in order to maintain surplus labor nearby. The general idea was that the Indians could be induced to utilize wage labour to augment their somewhat meager farming income. (1979:27–28)

Thus East Indian village communities were induced settlements brought about by the imperative of maintaining a large supply of cheap labor to work on the plantations. The colonial government and the plantocracy resorted to a policy of purchasing land and leasing it or giving it to the East Indian indentured laborers. The handing out of land for East Indian settlement was necessary if a large labor supply was to be maintained and if the East Indians were not to leave the society.

Jay Mandle noted that the incentives to Indian immigrants took two forms: an easing of the terms of purchase of government-owned lands and the establishment of government-owned and -managed land-settlement schemes on three former sugar estates. In the first place, the Crown Land Policy established in 1834 to deny the access of land to the emancipated slaves underwent drastic changes in the 1890s. The purchase per acre price was reduced from $10 to $1, and the 100-acre minimum was changed to 25-acre lots of homesteads. In the latter instance, the colonial government bought plantations, Helena, Whim, and Bush Lot, in order to distribute parcels of land with the hope of enticing the Indian immigrants to remain. Repatriation meant not only the loss of labor from the sugar plantations but also a strain on the economy of the colony because of the transportation costs for large numbers of repatriates and the savings they took with them (Mandle, 1973:34–35). Between 1841 and 1920, the number of East Indians who were repatriated to India totaled 51,488. About 88 percent of all East Indian immigrants remained in the colony.

East Indian settlements were not only induced communities, but also associative communities. Such communities have direct links with and are dependent on the plantation. These communities were often located within a three-mile radius of the sugar plantations. The Indians were encouraged to farm rice and vegetables to supplement their meager earnings on the plantations. The geographic location of their village communities was further strategic in that the village settlements were dependent on the sugar plantations for irrigation. The general idea was for the Indians to engage in economic activities outside the plantation on a limited and controlled scale. Such economic activity was viable enough to encourage them to remain, yet not productive enough to facilitate self-sufficiency and self-reliance. The economic activities that East Indian villagers engaged in were meant to supplement plantation earnings and not challenge plantation dominance. Land was leased to individuals and families but not to the entire community, with the intention of discouraging community-organized productive activity. The upshot of all these arrangements was that the associative village communities of the East Indians were effectively kept in a state of dependent underdevelopment by the plantation system.

The economic underdevelopment of East Indian communities was further affected by the restrictions imposed on East Indians toward the acquisition of education. East Indians were dissuaded by both law and practice from acquiring formal education. It was not until the early 1930s that a law was passed making it compulsory for East Indians to acquire formal education. Further, it was a common practice to deny East Indians employment in the urban centers, thus constraining them to remain on or near the plantation that demanded their labor.

It is not that the East Indian immigrant had any "unique agricultural qualities" or natural affinities for farming; it is rather that structural constraints bound them to the land, from which they were forced to earn a living. The cultural features of East Indian village settlements are: (1) the bonds within the East Indian communities were those of common cultural orientation and a common ethnic background; (2) the bulk of East Indians at that time saw their communities as temporary, hoping one day to end their sojourn in the colony and return home with their acquired wealth to "mother India," so, like the white planter class, the majority of Indian immigrants were "outward looking"; and (3) the communities were kept as far as possible separate from black village settlements and often encouraged to conflict with black communities.

Whereas the blacks had struggled, saved, and acquired their communities by purchase, East Indian communities were acquired in lieu of payment by the colonial government and the plantocracy. The period of indenture and after was known for frequent industrial unrest, strikes, and rioting by East Indians insisting on better payment and treatment by the plantocracy. Indenture was thus a somewhat less infernal condition than slavery.

But the indentured laborers in less than a decade obtained payment and grants of land denied the blacks. This is not to say that East Indians were not punished under the plantation system, but that their lot was less harsh and less unrewarding than the blacks'.

Whereas the blacks in attempting to develop their villages were discouraged, the East Indians were permitted a very limited measure of autonomous economic enterprise. However, the denial of education to East Indians induced a false sense of "social superiority" on the part of the blacks who had open access to formal education. The realities were, and are, that even in their underdeveloped state, East Indians as an ethnic group and East Indian communities are economically less underprivileged than blacks and black communities.

Together with the black village communities, East Indian village communities highlight the dependency and underdeveloped nature of the society as a whole. The historically contrived geographic separateness of the blacks and the East Indians operated to facilitate the strategy of divide and rule by the British. The ethnic and geographic separateness of village communities in Guyana have contributed in no small measure to the heightening and exploiting of ethnic tensions that are solidified by the historically differential occupational pursuits.

Finally, East Indian village communities were the recipients of a number of welfare and recreational facilities denied blacks as a direct consequence of their association with the sugar estates. Community centers and medical dispensaries as well as other welfare benefits were passed down by the plantocracy in a further effort to induce East Indian labor to remain loyal to the plantations. East Indian villages are invariably less underdeveloped and better organized and contain more amenities than black villages. Consequently, there has been a much lower rate of migration to urban centers by East Indian villagers than by blacks. It was found that unemployed East Indians are much more likely to remain in their villages than unemployed blacks (Sukdeo, 1979). The unemployed or underemployed East Indian can always eke out a living from his attachment to a still prevalent extended-kinship system and from ownership of land. The unemployed black youth must migrate if he or she is to survive.

Chinese Communities

Both the Portuguese and the Chinese arrived in Guyana as immigrant indentured labor. In comparison to the blacks and the East Indians, Portuguese and Chinese indentures represented a mere trickle. Weber (1931) noted that 647 Chinese immigrants arrived in Guyana in 1852 and 1853. He observed:

> What is the most reckless and immoral part of the venture was that of these 647 immigrants, there was not a single female among them, and that for eight years after their departure from China, they never saw a female of their race. Not even in slave days was such a crime against the country perpetrated; whatever may be said on behalf of the men themselves. But canes were growing. (1931:42)

In similar fashion, Moore (1975) noted the paucity in numbers of the Portuguese immigrants: "Between 1835 and 1850, only 17,008 Portuguese from Madeira went to the colony, while between 1851 and 1881, when the last group arrived, only 13,535 Maderians and 164 persons from the Azores emigrated to Guiana."

The Chinese immigrants failed to stand up to the harsh tropical environment, novel pestilences, and rigors of plantation labor. Their inability to survive as plantation indentured laborers led to their resettlement by the colonial government, mainly at Hopetown in the Camourie creek, which was settled by about 200 Chinese immigrants (see C.O. 111/353 of September 19, 1865; C.O. 111/353, December 18, 1865, on Chinese immigration and Chinese settlements). The Chinese settlements were led by an ingenious and charismatic figure called O. Tye Kim, whose oratorical qualities and interpersonal skills seem to have endeared him not only to the Chinese immigrants, but also to the white ruling class. Some of the Chinese who arrived in the colony never went on the plantations, due to the intervention of O. Tye Kim, who immediately settled them at Hopetown.

The Chinese settlements engaged in the manufacture of charcoal and shingles. These represented the dominant form of economic activity within the Chinese community. Because of their "nearness to whiteness," coupled with the paucity of their numbers, the Chinese were not forced by the white ruling class into subservience to the plantation. Indeed, the whites even encouraged and assisted them fully in setting up their community. The charcoal and shingles manufactured were marketed at two central outlets in Georgetown, organized and run by the Chinese immigrants under the leadership of O. Tye Kim. Chinese industry and dedication soon saw them monopolizing the production of charcoal and shingles, and their business prospered.

Their settlements were, however, short-lived. This is because as much as their leader and ambassador, O. Tye Kim, had a magnetic personality, so too was he unscrupulous. Much of the charcoal and shingles was not arriving at the outlets, but was being sidetracked and sold elsewhere by O. Tye Kim. Kim swindled the community out of its profits and earnings and fled the country secretly before the colonial authorities could bring him to justice. Soon the majority of the Chinese settlers emigrated to the urban centers and villages and joined the Portuguese in retail trade, particularly the sale of "salt goods." A few diehard Chinese remained in the settlements for a short while and carried on the charcoal business.

The Chinese communities, then, were supportive and sponsored communities. They were supportive communities in that they formed a "light-skinned" buffer between the freed blacks and the dominent white ruling class. The were sponsored communities in that their settlement was made possible by the colonial government, which aided and fostered their enterprises. It is of interest to note, however, that the Chinese immigrants had to work together on a communal basis to repay the cost of their import to the colonial government. What is also noteworthy about the Chinese communities is that they were tightly integrated. The activities of the individual supported the activities of the whole community, and the activities of the whole community benefited the individual. This close interdependence among the Chinese was in no small measure due to their common allegiance to the charismatic leader O. Tye Kim. After the disbanding of the settlements, the Chinese changed from a geographically and ethnically distinct community to a functional community. Yet they maintained a Chinese association and supported one another in their enterprises.

Portuguese Communities

Unlike the Chinese, the Portuguese displayed tremendous industry as plantation indentured laborers. Like the Chinese, however, they fell victims to tropical pestilences, in particular malaria and filaria. Not only were the Portuguese industrious, but they were also very frugal, denying themselves food and clothing, except where absolutely necessary, in an eager attempt to accumulate savings. Quite a few of them died from malnutrition (Laurence, 1965; Moore, 1975).

Despite the numerical paucity of the Portuguese, their white phenotype endeared them to the British ruling class. Brian Moore observed:

> Yet on account of their racial affinity to the dominant white classes, they enjoyed a social importance out of proportion to their numerical position . . . race was the overriding determinant of the social status of the Portuguese immigrants in British Guiana during the nineteenth century: and . . . this criterion was dictated by the need to preserve and bolster the social supremacy of the small dominant white minority of that plantation civilization in the face of the new challenge occasioned by the emancipation of the slaves. (1975:7)

This was white fear of the aftermath of emancipation, in which

> for the first time in the history of the plantation society, black and white were rendered equal before the law. The ex-slaves were free to dispose of their labor as they wished. This freedom was feared most by the white classes of society. Not only might the blacks, who formed the large majority of the population, withdraw their labor altogether from the plantations and opt for an "independent" and lawless life of "barbarism" in the densely forested interior of the colony; but by extension the plantation economy and, with it, the white civilization in the colony would decay. It was even feared that the freed blacks might run wild and attack the whites and plantations before decamping to the bush. (Moore, 1975:7)

The objectives behind Portuguese immigration, then, were to create a white middle class and to secure a regular and reliable supply of cheap labor to supplement the existing local resources of ex-slaves' labor. Portuguese immigration functioned to bolster the numerical strength of the white sector of the society and was therefore encouraged in the interest of white racial supremacy and the preservation of white civilization in the colony. Governor Light declared, "it is of immense importance to the future prospects of the colony that a large industrious body of whites should be established. . . ." (C.O. 111/235: No. 180). Governor Wood-house similarly asserted that the Portuguese were the only immigrants who "could . . . be advantageously treated . . . in as much as they possess habits of industry, coupled with other qualities calculated to render them peaceful and valuable citizens when set free from artificial control" (C.O. 111/316: No. 69). Brian Moore (1975) pointed out that in 1851 the dominant whites numbered only 3,630, or 2.8 percent, out of a total population of 127,635. The Portuguese immigrants added another 7,928, or 6 percent, to the white population. Further, by 1891 the dominant whites numbered just 4,558 (1.6 percent), while the total population had increased to 278,320. The Portuguese population had increased to 12,166, or 4.3 percent of the population.

The sojourn of Portuguese immigrants in agriculture was, however, to be very brief. Having the phenotypically white Portuguese laboring alongside Indians and blacks in the field would blow apart the myth of white superiority. Thus the Portuguese soon came to be known as "white trash" and, in effect, declared and treated as nonwhite by the dominant white ruling class. Thus until today, the myth is perpetrated that "puttagee" is not white. The cognitive dissonance produced by Portuguese labor on the plantations soon led to a policy to remove them and relocate them in the urban centers and the villages. The Portuguese moved into the retail trade, finding a ready market among the freed blacks. Soon Portuguese retail shops sprang up en masse in the urban centers and the villages. Credit was afforded the Portuguese but denied the blacks. Tax exemptions and other inducements coupled with the industry of the Portuguese immigrants soon resulted in their firm entrenchment in their new, middle-class status.

The Portuguese, however, never really had a geographically distinct community. They lived together in identifiable clusters in the urban centers of Georgetown and New Amsterdam. Charlestown and Alberttown were areas where the Portuguese lived in small clusters. In effect, then, the Portuguese remained an urban-based functional community. Although not so close-knit a community as the Chinese, the Portuguese supported one another in a systematic effort to monopolize retail trade. Like the Chinese, the Portuguese functioned as supportive communities. The Portuguese immigrants were, however, higher up the stratification order than the other immigrants, being placed immediately below the white ruling class.

In time, the Portuguese entered wholesale trade—a sector previously monopolized by dominant whites. As in the retail trade, the Portuguese immigrants were quite successful in this area and presented a threat to the dominant white wholesalers. In time to come, the "sponsored" Portuguese community became very independent and so progressive as to present a challenge to the dominant whites. Anglo-Saxon resentment toward the Portuguese found its curious expression through the blacks who were being exploited by the Portuguese. Blacks felt that the Portuguese were overcharging them in their retail shops and soon developed anti-Portuguese sentiments. Several riots directed against Portuguese businesses broke out in Georgetown, the "Angel Gabriel" riots in 1856 being the most famous. Portuguese business premises were looted and burned, and some of the owners were physically assaulted. Moore described this ethnic antipathy toward the Portuguese:

> As a result of such deep-seated prejudices on all sides, the ill-feeling generated between these two groups from their first encounters never died out, but slumbered, waiting opportunities to break out in open violence, and, indeed anti-Portuguese riots occurred . . . : 1840 in Berbice, 1856 in Essequibo, 1889 in Georgetown and 1956 in Demerara. It is significant that on each occasion the immediate pretext was created by the inefficient practical conduct of affairs by the white ruling classes, which seemed favourable towards the Portuguese. (1975:11)

It is of interest to note, however, that during the 1856 riots the colonial authorities scarcely intervened as blacks looted and burned Portuguese businesses. The police and military firmly intervened only after much damage was done and quite a few Portuguese immigrants were beaten. Incidentally, it was the East Indians in rural villages who fought off the blacks trying to destroy Portuguese shops.

The importation of the Chinese and Portuguese completed the ethnically plural character of Guyanese society and the communities therein. The nonwhite communities were carefully positioned and orchestrated within the social system. The Portuguese and Chinese were the only groups encouraged in economic ventures to the point of obtaining some measure of self-sufficiency. But wherever such development was perceived as competitive by the dominant whites, the other ethnic groups were encouraged to destroy what they had built up.

Urban Village Communities

Georgetown, New Amsterdam, and other urban centers in Guyana grew up initially from plantations turned into villages. While the village background can be easily recognized in places such as Rose Hall and Corriverton, perusal of the historical background and present formation of Georgetown and New Amsterdam would reveal that essentially they are a conglomeration of urbanized villages. Presently, Georgetown has been expanded to include additional villages like McDoom, Agricola, and Kitty Campbellville, to name only a few. It is the heavy concentration of population in these areas and the hive of industrial and commerical activities that earned them the label "urban."

Just like the rural villages, urban villages display ethnic concentration. Invariably, the majority of the population in urban centers tends to be black. Historically, however, within certain sections of those areas the dominant whites and Portuguese live like "big shots" in pockets of ethnic exclusivity. Not unnaturally, urban communities are more developed than rural communities. Commercial activities play a critical role in such development. The concentration of pockets of various ethnic groups in these areas manifests clearly the ethnic segregation and color–class hierarchy of the society.

Mining Towns

Mining towns in Guyana grew up around the establishment by multinationals of large enterprises consciously set up to exploit minerals such as bauxite and manganese. For historical reasons, the population of these mining towns are predominantly black. Prior to nationalization of the bauxite industry, a minority white bourgeois group lived separately from the black communities near the industrial plant. In some respects, mining towns possess some of the same characteristics of East Indian village settlements around sugar plantations. The black communities were conditioned to center their economic activities around extracting and processing a particular ore or mineral. These industries, like bauxite, attracted the blacks more than did the plantations because of higher wages being offered. No care was taken by the white bourgeoisie to assist the development of black communities. Thus until recently, despite the higher wages received, the blacks lived under poor housing and social conditions.

Among the reasons for the lack of development of the black community in mining areas, despite the relatively good wages, is that initially most of the black employees viewed the area as a place exclusively for work and had their families elsewhere. In addition, housing and land-distribution policies did not encourage community-building. Black males moved away from the villages to the mining areas in search of employment. Many of them did not return to their families and instead established relationships of concubinage in the mining towns. Over time, however, as the residents began to perceive the area as their home, efforts were made to develop it. Further, mining industries are now nationalized, and the state is pursuing a policy of assisting the residents in the task of building their communities. The most famous and best-known mining community in Guyana is the town of Linden, which has a population of about 30,000 residents, who are predominantly black. The concentration of blacks in mining areas further testifies to the occupational specialization of the ethnic groups in Guyana.

The picture presented from our brief historical survey of communities in Guyana is that most of these communities emerged as reactions to or derivatives of the dominant institution of the sugar plantation. These communities are ethnically differentiable and kept in a state of underdevelopment by the dominance of the plantation community and the exploitative and racist policies of a white ruling class. The level of repression and underdevelopment was inversely related to the nearness to whiteness of the particular ethnic group that composed the community.

Continuing Underdevelopment and the Postcolonial State

So far, we have traced the historical emergence and development of communities in Guyana, and have identified and discussed six historical types. These communities, with the exception of the Amerindian village communities, were bound to the plantation, and their development or underdevelopment was inevitably determined by the plantation system. The colonial state with its repressive laws and coercive regulatory measures functioned to protect plantation interests and sought as far as possible to maintain a stable social climate for plantation exploitation. The benefits of production of the society during that historical period were channeled toward metropolitan development, while the colony and the communities within it remained largely underdeveloped. While it lasted, the plantation community was very effective as a production mechanism. Had the profits from plantation production been used to diversify the economy and develop the society instead of being exported, Guyana would have attained a higher level of social and economic development. Some efforts were made by the dominant plantation economic sector and the colonial state to improve the lot of the various communities. Such efforts, however, were largely cosmetic and purely instrumental in terms of fostering the dominance of the established order and producing habits of compliance among the masses, who were carefully stratified and orchestrated into more or less dependent communities (Matthews and Danns, 1980).

The orientation toward exploitation and nondevelopment of the colony of the British Guiana by the colonial state and the plantocracy must be attributed in part to the nonresidential nature of the ruling class. The colony was not home but a place of work and temporary sojourn. Apart from the fact that colonial state officials were civil servants of the Colonial Civil Service and therefore could have been assigned to any British colony, the sugar plantations were in large measure owned by absentee proprietors. Without a ruling class that was committed to the society, its failure to develop becomes understandable. Moreover, the ruling class of colonial Guyana was committed to the development of the mother country, Britain, and the consequent exploitation of the colony for that purpose.

How and why does the postcolonial state that has appropriated ownership and control of the sugar plantations and an estimated 80 percent of the economy continue to induce underdevelopment? Several interrelated external and internal factors can explain the failure of the country to develop. Among the external factors are:

1. The socialist posturings of the Guyana government. Guyana is viewed by developed capitalist nations as a poor climate for investment and is being denied capital for self-determined development.

Further, the government complains about the efforts by external agents to destabilize the country's economy.

2. The external control of commodity markets for nationalized industries like bauxite and sugar, upon which the Guyana economy is critically dependent. Low world market prices for both sugar and bauxite have thrown the Guyana economy into a deep recession. With export earnings drastically reduced, economic problems are further exacerbated by the government's having to maintain compensatory payments to former owners of the nationalized industries.

3. The border dispute with neighboring Venezuela, in which a claim is being made to five-eighths of Guyana's territory. The Venezuelan government has discouraged loans and outside investment for development projects in the disputed area. As a consequence, the Guyana government has had to divert resources for development toward a relatively sizable military buildup. Also, much of the foreign policy initiatives of the regime are focused on activating international support for Guyana's cause.

However, the initiative for the development of a society must come from the involvement of its people and its leaders. Consequently, greater weight should be given to those *internal* factors that can influence development. It was, after all, the internal operation of the plantation system and the colonial state that resulted in external dependence and underdevelopment of the society. There are several internal factors that affect Guyana's development:

1. An emergent ruling class whose members are unsure of themselves as a ruling class and therefore incapable of providing leadership. The colonial ruling class withdrew from the society after independence and nationalization.

2. The authoritarian seizure of the state apparatus by the People's National Congress party. The captive state apparatus has become a "party state," in which a narrow group of political elites insensitively and undemocratically dictates to the masses.

3. Ill-trained, untrained, and uncommitted state officials who are responsible for formulating and operationalizing development policies. Inept and inconsistent development plans have resulted.

4. A marked inability by the new rulers to mobilize the people for development. Ethnic conflicts are a key factor militating against mobilization. The crises of confidence, credibility, and legitimacy

being experienced by the rulers of the captive state system are other factors.

During the colonial era the role of the state was not concerned with fostering the development of the colony, but with providing a carefully regulated environment for the domination, subjugation, and exploitation of the colonial people by the plantocracy. The role of the state in relation to the economy was in large measure limited to the control of the recalcitrant labor force, taxation, and regulation. By contrast, the task of planning for and spearheading development efforts in the postcolonial Third World is largely, and in some instances exclusively, the lot of the state in these countries. In Guyana, in particular, the state owns and controls an estimated 80 percent of the economy. As a consequence of this "national responsibility," a holistic approach informs development plans that are expected to provide blueprints for solving the economic and social ills of the society. With an approach to development and nation building that is socialist in orientation, there is a tendency to view the nation as one large community with one common fate and a common orientation. Such an approach justifies the centralizing of authority and decision making within the state system in the "national interest." In the dominant one-party system that obtains in Guyana, such effort must also meet the approval of watchdog party institutions. The peoples in the society are constrained by policy and practice to rely on the state and in increasing measure on the dominant PNC party to mobilize and direct development efforts. Such a trend is, of course, reinforced by an inherited dependency syndrome brought about by the colonizing powers. This "planned change approach" that has been adopted places great emphasis on the paramountcy of the "national interests" and "national development." The notions of "community interests" and "community development" have been ignored or else deemphasized.

Policies of nationalization and control of the economy have led to the unparalleled extension and amplification of the power and authority of the state. The postcolonial state now combines the powers and resources of the defunct plantocracy as well as the colonial state bureaucracy. The state no longer functions as a mediator between the activities of the economy and the rest of the society but as the sole arbiter of the fate of the nation and the lives of the people therein. The dependency of the communities within the society on the colonial state and the plantocracy has been transferred to a dependency on the monolithic and all-embracing postcolonial state system. Nationalization of major industries that were foreign-owned and the appropriation by the state of control and/or ownership of local enterprises have produced no effective transformation of the structures that sustain dependency. The structures of nationalized enterprises remain essentially intact, with the real change being a "circulation of elites." The new state-technocratic elite and its political overlords administer these nationalized enterprises inefficiently, and there has been no discernible qualitative or quantitative improvement in the economic well-being of the society as a consequence of nationalization. Instead, there has been decelerating performance, as evidenced by negative growth rates, galloping inflation, widespread unemployment and underemployment, a foreign exchange deficit, and conspicuous absences or shortages of consumer products of every sort. The policies of nationalization included compensation of the multinationals for their assets. This has added to a massive external debt (Thomas, 1984).

The bottom line is that nationalization and the dominant participation of the centralizing and directing presence of the state in the economy have proved to be not a boon but a bane to development in Guyana. No longer can the plantocracy and the colonial state be blamed for stagnating development. With nationalization, no longer can the blame be squarely laid on the rapacious multinationals for exporting surpluses needed for reinvestment and the generation of new wealth and development. The country obtained political independence from Britain. The regime has promulgated a republican "People's New Constitution," allegedly fashioned to reflect the needs and aspirations of the people and their demands for a revolutionary socialist transformation. It has pursued radical foreign policy initiatives that include a nonaligned international posture. These factors, along with the state's control of the economy, should combine to reduce considerably international dependency relationships that were concretized during the colonial era. In a very real way, the radical decolonization of Guyana has placed the responsibility for its development and its direction in the hands of its government and its people. Yet, instead of development, deepening underdevelopment is a feature of Guyanese society. The logical and factual conclusions are:

1. The postcolonial state is mainly responsible for the dependent underdevelopment of the society.
2. The continued dependency and persistent poverty of the communities within the nation and, therefore, the society as a whole can be directly attributable to the policies and activities of the postcolonial state.
3. None of the policies or activities of the managers of the postcolonial state apparatuses have functioned to reduce external dependency or stimulate economic growth. Apart from the inherited economic enterprises, it is difficult to pinpoint any new enterprise that has been created by the postcolonial state administrators that is generative or productive of economic wealth.
4. There must be a lack of commitment to and appreciation by the peoples in Guyanese society of the state and policies of its managers.
5. The efforts to mobilize the Guyanese people for the purpose of development have been evidently unsuccessful or not tried. People power is crucial for the realization of developmental initiatives.
6. The managers of the postcolonial state must seriously reexamine their approach to development and their attitude toward the people for whom development schemes are being planned. Development will not occur unless the initiative is given or restored to the people.

The position of this paper is that development can occur only if the people are effectively involved and such involvement occurs at the level of the community. This position finds support both in societies that are state-controlled and reputedly socialist and in capitalist societies with restricted state control and participation in the economy. The experience of other societies—such as Cuba, with its "cadre system", China, where the commune is emphasized, and the Israeli kibbutzim—has demonstrated the viability of the community approach to nation building.

A nation is as strong as its communities are organized and developed. The loosening of bonds of dependency with core nations requires strong communities and as a consequence a strong nation, supporting the bargaining tactics of the state. Presently, there exist in Guyana weak and poorly organized communities dominated by and alienated from the state system. The higher the level of community inputs in decision making and community action, the greater the possibility of mobilizing people for the purpose of development. An emerging nation like Guyana would need to experience teething problems in trying to turn around over three centuries of exploitation and underdevelopment. However, a repressive state apparatus that controls the economy is unlikely to make the task an easy one.

References

Adamson, Alan H. (1972). *Sugar Without Slaves: The Political Economy of British Guiana, 1838–1904*. New Haven, Conn.: Yale University Press.

Beckford, George (1972). *Persistent Poverty*. New York: Oxford University Press.

Best, Lloyd (1968). "Outline of a Model of Pure Plantation Economy." *Social and Economic Studies* 3:283–326.

Brewster, Havelock (1973). "Economic Dependence: A Quantitative Interpretation." *Social and Economic Studies*, March, pp. 90–95.

Casanova, Pablo Gonzales (1970). *Democracy in Mexico*. New York: Oxford University Press.

Danns, George (1982). *Domination and Power in Guyana*. New Brunswick, N.J.: Transaction Books.

Demas, William (1965). *The Economics of Development in Small Countries with Special Reference to the Caribbean*. Montreal: McGill University Press.

Frank, Andre Gunder (1969). *Capitalism and Underdevelopment in Latin America*. New York: Monthly Review Press.

Goffman, Erving (1968). *Asylums: Essays on the Social Situation of Mental Patients and Other Inmates*. Harmondsworth: Penguin Books.

Hintzen, Percy (1977). "Myth, Ideology, and Crisis in Plantation Society: The Case of Guyana." Unpublished manuscript: Yale University.

Laurence, K. O. (1965). "The Establishment of the Portuguese Community in British Guyana." *Jamaica Historical Review* 5:2.

Mandle, Jay R. (1973). *The Plantation Economy: Population and Economic Change in Guyana, 1838–1960*. Philadelphia: Temple University Press.

Matthews, Lear K., and George K. Danns (1980). *Communities and Development in the Caribbean: A Neglected Dimension in Nation Building*. Georgetown: University of Guyana, Institute of Development Studies.

McIntyre, Allister (1971). "Some Issues in the Trade Policy of the West Indies." In Girvan and Jefferson, eds., *Readings in the Political Economy of the Caribbean*. Kingston: New World Group.

Menezes, Mary Noel (1977). *British Policy Towards the Amerindians in British Guiana, 1803–1973*. London: Oxford University Press.

Moore, Brian (1975). "The Social Impact of Portuguese Immigration into British Guiana after Emancipation." *Journal of Latin American and Caribbean Studies*, December, p. 19.

Nath, Dwarka (1950). *History of Indians in British Guiana*. London: Nelson.

Rodney, Walter (1981). "Guyana: The Making of the Labour Force." *Race and Class* (Spring):331–352.

Singh, Paul (1972). *Local Democracy in the Commonwealth Caribbean: A Study of Adaptation and Growth*. Port of Spain: Longman Caribbean.

——— (1976). "The Politics of Local Government Reform 1930–1970." In H. Lutchman et al., eds., *Selected Issues in Guyanese Politics*. London: Oxford University Press.

Smith, R. T. (1956). *The Negro Family in British Guiana*. London: Oxford University Press.

Sukdeo, Fred (1979). *Rural Development in Guyana: A Study of Four Villages*. Georgetown: Institute of Development Studies.

Thomas, Clive (1974). *Dependence and Transformation*. New York: Monthly Review Press.

——— (1984). "Guyana: The Rise and Fall of Cooperative Socialism." In Payne and Sutton, eds., *Dependency Under Challenge*. Manchester: Manchester University Press.

Weber, R. F. (1931). *Centenary History and Handbook of British Guyana*. Georgetown: Argosy.

CHAPTER 7

Establishing the Patterns of Progress and Poverty in Central America

E. Bradford Burns

In Central America after 1860, the rising production and exportation of coffee altered basic institutional structures, particularly those related to land and labor. The new structures enhanced the power and wealth of the few, while impoverishing the overwhelming majority. Coffee production in Central America illustrates how nations can grow economically without developing.

General confusion shrouds the meaning of "growth" and "development." The media as well as many scholars have long treated the two terms as synonymous, at least implying that economic growth signifies development. Nothing could be more erroneous. They differ fundamentally. Economic growth is numerical accumulation. It tells us that something within the economy, or perhaps the economy as a whole, has increased in size. The term alone does not specify what has increased. Was it beans for the masses, the amount of coffee exported, or profits for foreign investors? Nor do growth figures customarily reveal who benefited from the growth, although use of per capita figures, as long as they increase, seems to imply that everyone might have, an implication more illusory than real. Growth is a crude, often deceptive standard of judgment. Unless accompanied by considerations of what grew and who benefited, talk of economic growth causes more confusion than clarification.

The definitions of development vary widely. I define it as the utilization of a nation's potential for the greatest benefit of the largest number of inhabitants. Such a definition recognizes the relativity of development, relative to a nation's natural and human resources, and eschews any absolute. However, it does emphasize that no nation can consider itself developed if less than a majority of its inhabitants enjoy the benefits of society. Furthermore, development can be differentiated from growth by its concern with consumption levels, rather than the traditional emphasis on production. Who consumes what and how much become primary questions, a social concern missing from discussions of growth.

The Central American elites also confused development with modernization or, to use the word in vogue during the nineteenth and early twentieth centuries, progress. For them, progress meant the replication of Europe or the United States in Central America. Progress, under their nurturing, was most evident in the export sector of the economy and in the core of the capital cities. Economic growth financed those manifestations of progress. However, the veneer of progress did not make nations "modern." Neither did it promote development. In fact, just the opposite occurred in Central America, where economic growth, measured almost exclusively by the sale of coffee to a few European nations and particularly to the United States, subjected the economy of the small republics to the whims of a fickle marketplace. Such a situation fostered economic dependency, which in turn imposed political subordination, cultural imitation, and social inequity.

El Salvador offers a particularly thought-provoking study of the establishment of economic patterns through which growth and progress generated prosperity for a privileged few but poverty for the overwhelming majority. The economy grew, but El Salvador did not develop. The rise of coffee exports after 1860 propelled rapid change in that small Central American nation. A largely self-sufficient folk society became a dependent, neocapitalist state in which a few either enjoyed the wealth earned from coffee or exercised the political power wealth conferred.

As late as the 1850s, El Salvador remained relatively isolated and more closely linked to its Indian past than to Europe. Five foreign visitors left accounts of the simple but seemingly satisfactory life styles they observed during that decade. Mrs. Henry Grant Foote, wife of a British diplomat, lived most of that decade in El Salvador and wrote the most complete and articulate account. She noted, "What strikes me on arriving from Europe is the absence of all extreme poverty" (Foote, 1869:101). She concluded that southern

Europe and the major cities of England suffered far worse poverty and human misery. She explained the relative well-being of the Salvadorans by the fact that everyone enjoyed access to land. Most of the large Indian population still possessed at least a part of its communal land. The large hacienda existed, but it did not monopolize the rural economy. Other travelers corroborated the observations of Mrs. Foote (Bailey, 1850; Squier, 1855; Scherzer, 1857; von Tempsky, 1858).

Whatever the turbulent political problems of El Salvador during its early decades of independence, the inhabitants enjoyed some economic benefits. The land was reasonably well distributed. Food was produced in sufficient quantity to feed the population. In a varied economy, little emphasis fell on the export sector. The foreign debt was low. An absence of the extremes of poverty and wealth bespoke a vague degree of equality.

By the end of the 1850s, new socioeconomic patterns began to take shape as Salvadoran elites realized that their soil grew a mild, delicious coffee bean that would command impressive prices in Europe and the United States. After a trip to Europe, President Gerardo Barrios (1858–63) vowed to "regenerate" the nation. He announced a governmental program that would promote agriculture, industry, and commerce; introduce El Salvador to the progress that distinguished Europe; encourage immigration; reform the educational system in accordance with the latest European ideas; construct roads and ports to facilitate international communication and transportation; and promote coffee culture. He anticipated that coffee sales would finance the regeneration he envisioned. Indeed, coffee had a profound effect, more perhaps than he dared to anticipate. Its growth and export during the 1860 to 1890 period altered old institutions and well-established life styles.

Impressed with the lucrative profits to be earned from coffee sales, the few Salvadorans with capital or access to foreign capital invested in coffee production, whose complexity also required skill and patience. Coffee trees did not bear fruit until three to five years after planting. Land suitable for coffee culture appreciated in value, and as the profits from coffee exports rose, demand for that land increased. Inevitably, coffee plantations encroached on communal lands and peasant plots. Barrios and his successors promoted sustained legal attacks to force those lands onto the market. No president was more energetic in that regard than Rafael Zaldivar (1876–85), who oversaw the final dispossession of the Indians of their land. He abolished the *tierras comunales*, municipally owned and worked lands, in 1881, rationalizing, "The existence of lands under the ownership of *comunidades* impedes agricultural development, obstructs the circulation of wealth, and weakens family bonds and the independence of the individual. Their existence is contrary to the economic and social principles that the Republic has accepted" (Durham, 1979:42). Two years later, he abolished the *ejidos*, land-holding communities. He also declared them to be "an obstacle to our agricultural development and contrary to our economic principles" (Durham, 1979:42). Both laws facilitated the concentration of land into ever fewer hands.

The new coffee class proved its efficiency. Coffee composed 1 percent of the exports in 1860 and 50 percent in 1880, and at no time during the 1922 to 1935 period did coffee represent less than 88 percent. After 1880, El Salvador was a monoagricultural exporting nation, dependent not only on a single export, but also on only two or three markets for that export. The situation contrasted sharply with the variety of exports prior to 1880: maize, tobacco, sugar, balsam, cacao, coffee, cotton, tropical fruits, and indigo.

The Indians and peasants dispossessed of their land were expected to labor on the expanding coffee plantations. The government assured the planters of their labor with the Vagrancy Laws of 1881, which required the populace to work under threats of fines, arrests, and punishments. The Agrarian Law of 1907 further regulated the rural working class. It authorized special agricultural judges—in a fashion reminiscent of the Spanish *repartimiento* system of the colonial period—to make certain that a labor force responded when the planters called. Further, the 1881 laws authorized the organization of a rural constabulary to enforce the judges' decisions and to provide protection for the landowners. Rural protests exploded in 1872, 1875, 1880, and 1898 in response to land seizures and forced labor.

The planters imposed order and enjoyed a remarkable period of political tranquility between 1903 and 1931, the heyday of coffee "democracy." During that period the presidents served for four years, as stipulated in the constitution of 1886, and then peacefully left office, although not without selecting a successor for whom the very limited electorate dutifully voted. The prosperity and order of the period promoted the rebuilding of the ports, the expansion of the railroad line, the rise of banking, the increase of foreign investment, and the modernization of San Salvador. The planters appreciated the importance of a modern capital, the symbol of their prosperity, a tribute to their "progressive" inclinations, and the focal point of their political authority. The coffee elite prospered. It exercised politcal power, held the small but aggressive middle class at bay, repressed or manipulated the impoverished majority, and neutralized the military. In short, it succeeded in restructuring El Salvador to complement its interests.

While the new institutional structures benefited the coffee planters and their closest allies, they endangered the well-being of the vast majority as well as compromised national independence. By 1930, El Salvador's economy had become acutely dependent for its well-being on one export, concentrated in the hands of 350 growers; on one major market for its coffee exports, the United States; and on one primary source of investments, U.S. capitalists. As coffee exports grew impressively, food production could no longer keep up with an expanding population. Lands that once grew corn, the staple of the national diet, produced coffee. People who once farmed their own land intensively worked only a few months of the year in the coffee harvests. Studies of the 1920s reveal food shortages, the skyrocketing prices of basic foods, the increased need to import food, high living costs, and low wages (Anderson, 1971:83, 84; Wilson, 1969:29–115, 112; Durham, 1979:36; Marroquin, 1977:118).

The El Salvador of the 1920s was far different from the El Salvador of the 1850s. The El Salvador observed by Mrs. Foote, with a well-fed population, the coexistence of large estates, small farms, and communal lands, and a varied export sector, no longer existed. In its place was a country dominated by coffee exports and subjugated by dependency. The new institutions had elevated the quality of life of a minority, while inflicting penury on the overwhelming majority. One observer in 1931 estimated that approximately 0.5 percent of the population held 90 percent of the nation's wealth (Anderson, 1971:83–84).

The economic, social, and political imbalances caught the attention of Alberto Masferrer, a nationalist whose insights have made him one of the most provocative Salvadoran intellectuals of the twentieth century. He assessed the state of Salvadoran society in 1928 in this way:

> El Salvador no longer has wild fruits and vegetables that once everyone could harvest, or even cultivated fruits that once were inexpensive. . . . Today there are the coffee estates and they grow only coffee. . . . Where there is now a voracious estate that consumes hundreds and hundreds of acres, before there were two hundred small farmers whose plots produced corn, rice, beans, fruits, and vegetables. Now the highlands support only coffee estates and the lowlands cattle ranches. The cornfields are disappearing. And where will the corn come from? The coffee planter is not going to grow it because his profits are greater growing coffee. If he harvests enough coffee and it sells for a good price, he can import corn and it will cost him less than if he sacrifices coffee trees in order to grow it. . . . Who will grow corn and where? . . . Any nation that cannot assure the production and regulate the price of the most vital crop, the daily food of the people, has no right to regard itself as sovereign. . . . Such has become the case of our nation. (1960:179–82)

In vivid contrast to Mrs. Foote's earlier observations, Masferrer saw a hungry population with limited access to the use of land, a population whose basic need for food was subordinated to the demands of an export-oriented economy. The contrasts between Foote's and Masferrer's observations suggest that little or no development had taken place, although remarkable economic growth had been recorded.

Similar trends occurred elsewhere in Central America. Nicaragua, too, had been only marginally incorporated into Spain's trading network. Independence brought few changes to remote Nicaragua, at least for the first half century. The French scientist, Paul Lévy visited Nicaragua at the end of the 1860s and wrote an exhaustively detailed account of the land and its people. The pervasive poverty of the people impressed Lévy. Yet, as he commented more than once, debt peonage did not exist—nor did a wealthy, privileged class. Everyone had access to land on which to grow food.

> Thus, this system is perfect as a political institution and for individual liberty. . . . Nicaragua offers the phenomenon of a country in

which food is both plentiful and cheap and the hired worker expensive; perhaps it is the only country in which a worker receives a salary more than four times the cost of his maintenance. (Lévy, 1873:447)

Like Foote, Lévy examined a society on the cusp of change. Again, coffee culture propelled that change.

During the 1870s, coffee production began to spread slowly in the more populous western portion of the country. It encroached on communal and peasant lands, not only dispossessing the former claimants, but pressing them into forced labor. The newly emerging coffee planters found in the constitution of 1857 appropriate passages to legalize the new land and labor systems they imposed. The increase of coffee culture and the dispossession of peasants coincided with the government's program of modernization. Officials in Managua took advantage of the increasing number of landless workers pressing them into the construction of railroads, telegraph lines, and public buildings.

The shift to new land and labor institutions accompanied by the pressures of modernization disrupted the rural masses. Social disturbances erupted. Growing demands on their land and labor caused the Indians in Matagalpa to revolt in 1881. The army fought for nine months to restore order. The soldiers repressed the Indians so cruelly that the president finally interceded to remove the commander of the army, but he had already accomplished his task, making it possible as well as safe for the coffee estates to expand (Wheelock Roman, 1981).

In the twentieth century, the Nicaraguan capitalists became closely intertwined with the expansion of the United States into the Caribbean and Central America. They involved the United States in the overthrow of the highly nationalistic President José Santos Zelaya in 1909 and welcomed the U.S. occupation from 1912 to 1933. Two decades of occupation weakened the economy and forged heavy chains of dependency (Biderman, 1983). The journalist (and later historian) Carleton Beals judged the occupation ruinous for Nicaragua, a political hug from the metropolis so tight that it literally cut off the economic circulation of the client:

Nicaragua at the time of my visit, after eighteen years of almost constant American meddling, much of which was attended by American financial, military and political control and by the employment of high-priced experts, was in a truly miserable condition. The argument for or against intervention cannot be based on its material benefits, actual or supposed, to a people; yet it is significant that when I was there, its cities were dilapidated, its public buildings run down and dirty; that it had fewer miles of railway and roads than under Zelaya, whom Knox, because of personal investments, overthrew in 1910; there are fewer schools. The north coast in Zelaya's time had over forty Government schools; today it hasn't half a dozen. The flourishing traffic of Zelaya's time up and down the great artery, the San Juan River and Lake Nicaragua, is today practically nonexistent. I later made the trip at the risk of my life. The post office service, and in fact nearly every public service, was a joke. Nicaragua, under our paternal tutelage for so many years, had become the most backward and miserable of all Central American Republics. (1932:300–301)

The physical intervention of the metropolis brought no advantages to the impoverished majority of the Nicaraguans.

More closely integrated into the Spanish colonial system than any other part of Central America, Guatemala followed a different course during its first half century of independence. Well organized, the Liberals acted vigorously in the 1830s to modernize Guatemala. They helped to remake the country as quickly as possible in the image of Europe north of the Pyrenees and to Westernize the Indians both through law and influence and through ambitious programs encouraging European immigration. The Indians, as well as the Conservatives, protested. Under the leadership of Rafael Carrera, a mestizo with deep roots in the Indian communities, the Indians rose up in 1838 to 1839 to challenge the Liberals and the "progress" they had attempted to impose. In what was one of Latin America's major Indian rebellions of the nineteenth century, the Guatemalan Indians triumphed. As a result, Carrera dominated the government until his death in 1865. He respected the native cultures, protected the Indians, and sought to incorporate them into his goverment. His strength lay in his ability to instantly raise armies of loyal Indians who recognized him as a sympathetic protector.

Carrera set out to improve the living conditions of the Indians, the overwhelming majority of Guatemalans. He ordered the translation of governmental decrees into Indian languages and appointed "protectors" to serve the Indian communities. As president, he regularly received Indian delegations and traveled frequently throughout the republic to visit the Indians. To relieve some of their economic burden, he reduced taxes on foodstuffs and abolished the head tax. Very importantly, he excused the Indians from contributing to the loans which the government levied to meet fiscal emergencies. By removing many of the taxes on the Indians, which were paid in the official currency circulating in Europeanized Guatemala, the government reduced the need for them to enter the monetary economy. Thereby the pressue on them to work on the estates diminished, and the Indians could spend more time and energy cultivating their own lands or attending to the needs of their own communities.

Of all the efforts Carrera made on behalf of the Indians, none surpassed the protection he accorded the Indian lands. His government returned land to the Indian communities and settled disputes in their favor. The government declared in 1845 that all who worked unclaimed lands should receive them. What was even more unusual, it enforced the decree. It was decided in 1848 and repeated the following year that all *pueblos* without *ejidos* were to be granted them without cost, and if the population exceeded available lands, then lands elsewhere were to be made available to any persons who voluntarily decided to move to take possession of them. In 1851, Carrera decreed that "the Indians are not to be dispossessed of their communal lands on any pretext of selling them," a decree strengthened a few months later by prohibiting the divestment of any *pueblos* of their *ejidos* for any reason. In that way, Carrera spoke forcefully and effectively to the most pressing problem of Latin America: the overconcentration of land in the hands of the elite and the need for the rural masses to have land to cultivate (Coronado Aguilar, 1975:4382–486; Woodward, 1971:68; Moorhead, 1942:92, 190). From the evidence at hand, it would seem that the quality of life for the Indian majority improved during the Carrera years.

The well-being of the Indians proved to be transitory. Carrera died in 1865, and the landed elites regained power in 1871. Under the banner of Liberal reforms, capitalism made its definitive entry into Guatemala. Its triumph signified large-scale cultivation and exportation of coffee, with all the attendant consequences for that agrarian economy. The government imported foreign technology, ideas, and manufactured goods. It contracted foreign loans and invited foreign investments. The improvement of roads from the highland plantations to the ports and then the construction of the much-desired railroads, first to the Pacific and later to the Atlantic, accelerated coffee production and integrated Guatemala into the world market system more closely than ever. The new railroads were owned and operated by foreigners and paid considerable profits to overseas investors. The burden of financing the accoutrements of progress fell on the local poor.

Like El Salvador and Nicaragua, Guatemala experienced several long-range negative consequences from coffee production. It diminished the amount of land, labor, and capital available to produce food for local consumption. Wheat harvests especially declined. Monoculture dominated the economy. To create the necessary work force on the coffee estates, the Indians were forced, under the burdensome system of *mandamientos* (orders), to become wage laborers. Meanwhile, the government did not hesitate to concede to private landowners many lands on which the Indians had lived and worked for generations. By a variety of means, the large estates encroached on the Indians' communal lands. As a consequence, the economic and social position of the Indian majority declined. In his novel *Edmundo* (1896), José A. Beteta includes a lament for the degradation of the "miserable Indians bent beneath the weight of their rude work . . . who seemed to cry over the loss of the adored land that belonged to their grandfathers and to sigh for the liberty robbed from them" (23–24).

Judgments of the long period of Liberal governments after 1871 inevitably point to material changes: improved roads and ports, railroads, telegraphs, and the transformation of Guatemala City into a modern, more Europeanized city. Coffee exports rose. The elites prospered, and a small middle class thrived in the largest cities. The other side of "progress" at the end of the nineteenth century was a growing dependence on monoagriculture and a single export, declining food production for local consumption, a rising foreign debt, forced labor, debt peonage, the growth of the latifundia, and the greater impoverishment of the majority.

For a variety of special reasons, access to land remained more open in Honduras and Costa Rica than in Guatemala, El Salvador, and Nicaragua. The major links of Honduras to the capitalist world in the late nineteenth century were, first, the New York and Honduras Rosario Mining Company and, second, the incipient banana exports from the Caribbean coast. In Costa Rica, coffee exerted a powerful influence after the highland growers began exporting the beans in the 1840s. The government sank deeply into foreign debt, financing the railroad from the highlands, the center of both population and coffee culture, to the Caribbean port, Puerto Limón, between 1870 and 1890. Coffee estates grew in both number and size, but an impressive number of small producers also characterized coffee culture. Partially because of very small populations and an abundance of available land, neither Costa Rica nor Honduras experienced the sharp edge of poverty and wealth that became the dominant characteristics of the other three coffee-exporting nations in the final decades of the nineteenth century.

In sharp contrast to its historical trajectory prior to 1860, much of Central America entered intensely into international trade during the last decades of the nineteenth century. The major product for the world's market place was coffee. It came to dominate the exports of Costa Rica, Guatemàla, El Salvador, and Nicaragua. In the last three, it sharply altered old institutions and behavioral patterns, giving rise to new ones, which in turn have shaped contemporary Central America. A few planters concentrated lands in their hands, radically altering landowning systems once balanced among large estates, communal lands, and peasant holdings. Dispossessed peasants and communal members became a rural proletariat, underpaid and periodically unemployed. Nations self-sufficient in food and production in the nineteenth century resorted to food importation in the twentieth. Dependency deepened as the nations concentrated on a single crop for export to two or three markets. A direct correlation existed between rising coffee exports and falling quality of life for the majority in Guatemala, El Salvador, and Nicaragua.

Prior to the world financial collapse of 1929, the export-oriented elites imposed political order to complement and protect their economic prosperity. Despite rural uprisings to protest harsh economic conditions and growing social inequity, relative political tranquility reigned. When and where necessary, the elites unhesitatingly used force to counter any opposition. They both dominated and strengthened the military. Professionalism of the military got under way in the early twentieth century, and the officers quickly demonstrated an awareness of their own corporate interest. These included support of the elites, whose life style they aspired to emulate. When the financial disaster of 1929 to 1931 exposed all the weaknesses of the export-dominated economy and the political institutions that supported it, the military did not throw the elites from power but joined them in the exercise of it. The officers relegated the management of the economy to the export-oriented elites, while they exercised political control in El Salvador, Nicaragua, and Guatemala.

By the opening of the twentieth century, the elites exercised power from the capital cities. The major planters either had moved to the cities or spent part of the year there. Bureaucrats, bankers, and merchants, who, of course, resided in the capitals, played increasingly important roles. They made far-reaching decisions that increasingly shaped life in the countryside. Integrated into the export economy, beholden to its well-being, they sought to modernize the economic system, to improve its efficiency, rather than to challenge or change it. The shift of the locus of power from the individual estates to the capitals did nothing to initiate development.

The role of economic growth in Central America during the 1860 to 1930 period has been accepted rather than questioned, seemingly approved as some preliminary and necessary step toward development. Yet even a superficial investigation of that growth suggests that it created more problems than it solved. It established institutions and patterns antithetical to development. Statistics abound on the rising tonnage of coffee exports, railroad mileage, efficiency of ports, and investments. Yet social scientists have provided few statistics on caloric intake, longevity, the real purchasing power of rural wages, corn and bean production, and infant mortality rates. Statistical emphasis on growth rather than development demonstrates the imbalance in the studies of the Central American past. The selection of thematic topics reveals similar prejudices. Peasant uprisings for the 1860 to 1930 period have not even been fully identified, certainly not studied. Life styles of the rural workers remain unchronicled. Little has been written about the quality of life for the majority. The preference for elitist themes and growth statistics has masked social realities, distorting rather than clarifying the past. Also, social scientists have been slow to question the modernization path selected and imposed by the Central American elites. The question of whom it benefited has not been boldly confronted. Consequently, its impact on the majority has not been understood. Social scientists must ask why so little development occurred in Central America or, more daringly, why the development that once existed was reversed after 1860 in the name of "progress."

A critical questioning of growth, development, and modernization promises a fuller understanding of the Central American past as well as insight into the crisis besetting the region in the 1980s. Such questions might provoke inquiry casting doubt on the wisdom of the decisions made by the governing elites in the nineteenth century. Those decisions ignored the well-being of the majority of the citizenry. They bequeathed a legacy of poverty, dependency, and class conflict that succeeding generations of generals, politicians, and planters have exacerbated rather than resolved.

References

Anderson, Thomas P. (1971). *Matanza: El Salvador's Communist Revolt of 1932*. Lincoln: University of Nebraska Press.

Baily, John (1850). *Central America: Describing Each of the States of Guatemala, Honduras, Salvador, Nicaragua, and Costa Rica*. London: Saunders.

Beals, Carleton (1932). *Banana Gold*. Philadelphia: Lippincott.

Biderman, Jaime (1983). "The Development of Capitalism in Nicaragua: A Political Economic History." *Latin American Perspectives* 36: 7–32.

Coronado Aguilar, Manuel (1975). *Apuntes Históricos-Guatemalenses*. Guatemala City: Editorial José de Pineda Ibarra.

Durham, William H. (1979). *Scarcity and Survival in Central America: Ecological Origins of the Soccer War*. Stanford, Calif.: Stanford University Press.

Foote, Mrs. Henry Grant (1869). *Recollections of Central America and the West Coast of Africa*. London: Newby.

Lévy, Paul (1873). *Notas Geográficas y Económicas sobre la República de Nicaragua*. Paris: Libreria Española de E. Denne Schmitz.

Marroquin, Alejandro R. (1977). "Estudio sobre la Crisis de los Años Trenta en El Salvador." *Anuario de Estudios Centroamericanos* 3:118.

Masferrer, Alberto (1960). *Patria*. San Salvador: Editorial Universitaria.

Moorhead, Max Leon (1942). "Rafael Carrera of Guatemala; His Life and Times." Ph.D. diss., University of California, Berkeley.

Scherzer, Carl (1857). *Travels in the Free States of Central America: Nicaragua, Honduras, and San Salvador*. London: Longman.

Squier, E. G. (1855). *Notes on Central America, Particularly the States of Honduras and Salvador.* New York: Harper.

Tempsky, G. F. von (1858). *Mitla. A Narrative of Incidents and Personal Adventures on a Journey in Mexico, Guatemala, and Salvador in the Years 1853–1855.* London: Longman.

Wheelock Roman, Jaime (1981). *Raíces Indígenas de la Lucha Anticolonialista en Nicaragua.* Managua: Editorial Nueva Nicaragua.

Wilson, Everett A. (1969). "The Crisis of the National Integration in El Salvador, 1919–1935." Ph.D. diss., Stanford University.

Woodward, Ralph Lee, Jr. (1971). *Social Revolution in Guatemala: The Carrera Revolt.* New Orleans: Tulane University Press.

CHAPTER 8

Prerevolutionary Nicaraguan Agricultural Development

John Brohman

The analysis of a society's farming policies and its road toward agricultural development is a powerful method of illuminating the overall effectiveness of its development policies and the priorities of its political leadership. This is particularly true of agrarian Third World countries such as Nicaragua, in which the livelihood of the majority of the population and the structure of national economic growth are so intimately intertwined with developments within the dominant agricultural sector. Presently, the Nicaraguan revolutionary government is faced with the challenge of transforming an agrarian structure whose mode of development traditionally has been dictated by the "logic of the minority." This has meant that the overwhelming majority of Nicaraguans have been systematically excluded from access to the benefits of agricultural development, while a small socioeconomic and political elite has skewed growth in the agrarian sector to serve its own interests.

In Nicaragua, the legacy of widespread agrarian underdevelopment and of sharply uneven development among regions, sectors, and social classes serves as a powerful indictment of its prerevolutionary agricultural structure. Arable land and wealth were increasingly concentrated among a minority of large rural landholders, while the impoverished rural majority was dispossessed of its land or driven into ever-more agriculturally marginal areas. The most fertile sections of the country were dominated by the large estates of the agricultural export sector, whose methods of production were characterized by severe underuse of good soils, low levels of productivity, technological backwardness, and growing environmental destruction. At the same time, domestic food production by the peasant majority remained stagnant at an abysmally low level due to the persistence of an archaic rural production and marketing structure and to discriminatory government policies that favored capitalist development among the agrarian oligarchy. In a country blessed with one of the highest ratios of arable land to population in Latin America, two-thirds of the rural population had been deprived of enough land to feed themselves, 60 percent of the nation's children were suffering from first-degree malnutrition, and domestic food consumption had become increasingly dependent on costly imports which aggravated worsening balance-of-payments problems.

The agrarian structure that the Sandinistas inherited in 1979 had deep historical roots: some elements of rural labor relations and common production techniques were first established by the Spanish colonists in the preindependence era. However, this agrarian structure was decisively shaped by the consolidation of capitalist social relations in the large-scale modern agricultural export sectors in the post-1870 era, and particularly by the rapid acceleration of capitalist development following World War II. Moreover, capitalist development in Nicaraguan agriculture acted to underdevelop the traditional peasant sector at the same time that development was accelerating in the modern export sectors. Overall, agrarian development was marked by growing inequalities both over time and space and among social classes; the patterns of development and underdevelopment that evolved were the consequence of a single dialectical unity involving the penetration of capitalism into both the traditional and the modern agricultural sectors. Growth and accelerated accumulation of the modern large-scale capitalist farms were, in part, consequent on the stagnation, impoverishment, and destruction of much of the traditional peasant sphere.

Two Routes to Capitalist Agriculture

The uneven pattern of Nicaraguan capitalist agrarian development was quite similar to that of many other countries in Latin America (especially Guatemala, El Salvador, and Colombia, in which feudal estates were gradually transformed into capitalist enterprises along the "Junker" road of agricultural development). In this respect, Nicaraguan growth was consistent with classical interpretations of the law of unequal development (Sweezy, 1942; Amin, 1976; Desai, 1974) and theoretical work of the "development of underdevelopment" school (Frank, 1969; Kay, 1975; Dos Santos, 1979). However, Nicaraguan agriculture, especially in the era prior to World War II, was structured to a much greater extent by the internal dynamics of domestic class formation and conflict than by the growth of dependent relationships of international exchange with America and Western Europe. Critiques of the "dependency" and "development of underdevelopment" schools (e.g., Laclau, 1971; Brenner, 1977; Weeks and Dore, 1979) have deemphasized external dependent metropolis–satellite relationships and have stressed the importance of the internal class structure of peripheral countries in determining the development of productive forces and social relations, both for agriculture and for the economy as a whole. In addition, other writers have recently begun to note the rise of class conflict in Third World rural areas, exacerbated by the unstable manner by which the peasant masses are articulated to the dominant (class) mode of production (e.g., Beaucage, 1974; Foster-Carter, 1978; Havens, 1982; Seddon, 1978). According to this theory, the laws of social reproduction of the classic Third World latinfundia–minifundia complex systematically destabilizes the peasantry, leading to increasing class conflict and opening up possibilities for revolution.

In contrast to some other Latin American countries (e.g., Mexico, Peru, Chile), large-scale capitalist farms did not become a significant factor in Nicaraguan agriculture until the late nineteenth century. In addition, direct foreign ownership within the modern capitalist agriculture sector has remained low, and a domestic agrarian-based oligarchy has traditionally exerted control over the Nicaraguan state. Thus Nicaraguan agricultural development (or lack thereof) was decisively dependent on the actions of a growing national agrarian bourgeoisie, while foreign capital and some foreign governments (especially the United States) played a supportive role in the consolidation of economic and political power by this powerful domestic ruling class.

The development of capitalism in Nicaraguan agriculture, particularly in the post-1870 period, has closely followed the Junker road of agricultural growth (as first outlined by Lenin [1936] in an analysis of prerevolutionary Russian agriculture). The Junker road is characterized by the slow transformation of feudal estates (first established in Nicaragua by the Spanish colonists) into large-scale capitalist farms (which began to predominate following the coffee boom during the 1870s). On the Junker road, the development of capitalism among the peasantry is blocked by the economic, political, and coercive power of the large-estate owners. The Junker road is highly regressive in income and land distribution; it usually blocks development of a (nonelite) domestic market for agricultural goods; and it almost always is associated with repressive, nondemocratic forms of government.

This Junker road may be contrasted with the other dominant road toward capitalist agricultural development—the "farmer" or "American" road. In contrast to the Junker road, the farmer road is characterized by a multiplicity of small to medium farms (at least in its initial stages) and the growth of a large class of small to medium farmers (or rural petty bourgeoisie). This road may be created by revolution or by land reform or through colonization and homesteading of new territory. Along the farmer road, many farmers eventually go bankrupt and are forced to migrate, but a few develop very efficient capitalist agricultural enterprises. The farmer road is generally regarded as economically and politically superior for capitalist agricultural growth—it enlarges the domestic market to allow for the development of economies of scale in the production of wage-foods, and it frees individual creative initiative to pursue advanced agricultural techniques. In addition, it favors the development of patterns of accumulation articulated to the local domestic economy instead of overseas markets, and the creation of democratic forms of government. The principal area in which the farmer road became significant in Nicaragua was in the northeast highlands of the Matagalpa-Jinotega area, and stand in stark contrast to the latifundia–minifundia pattern, which dominates the remainder of the country.

A key difference between the Junker and the farmer roads, which is vital to the form and pace of agricultural development, is the geographic and social location of the market for products of the modern agricultural sector. Following Amin (1976), de Janvry (1981) has developed models of "articulated" economies (favored by the farmer road) and "disarticulated" economies (favored by the Junker road and characteristic of Latin America and much of the Third World). In an articulated economy (e.g., the United States, Western Europe), the market for agricultural products is located across a broad spectrum of social classes within the domestic economy. A socially and sectorally articulated economy has an objective relationship between rates of profit and real wages, between development of the forces of production and the rate of surplus value, and between the rate of economic growth and income distribution. The market for a large portion of its agricultural products originates in rising national wages (which tend to increase in relationship to productivity increases). There is, therefore, every incentive for capitalist agrarian enterprises to produce wage-foods to meet the high effective domestic demand created by a proletarianized (but relatively well-paid) work force.

In a socially and sectorally disarticulated economy (e.g., prerevolutionary Nicaragua), the market for agricultural products of the modern capitalist sector does not originate in the domestic wages of the working class, but is generated either abroad or in the profits and/or rents of the national agricultural bourgeoisie. Accumulation in this form of capitalist agriculture is determined by the performance of the export sector (particularly the terms of trade on the international market) and by the continuing luxury consumption of the domestic elite. Under social disarticulation, local consumption (based on real wage levels) does not have to be joined with production. Low wages are perpetuated, most often by regressive and repressive labor policies. The main motive for the proletarianization of labor is reducing labor costs (not creating a home market out of rising wages). The link between productivity and wages (present in articulated economies) is severed, so that a continuing source of cheap labor becomes the chief determinant of high rates of profit. A disarticulated socioeconomic system has a twofold effect on the agricultural sector. First, production in the modern capitalist sector will tend to concentrate on luxury goods for the domestic elite and exportables for the foreign market. Second, links of "functional dualism" are established between modern capitalist farms and the traditional peasant sector—which allow for the continuing production of inexpensive foodstuffs in order to keep real wage levels low.

Functional dualism is the contradictory mechanism whereby the disarticulated economy satisfies its need for cheap labor by taking advantage of large masses of semiproletarianized peasants (de Janvry, 1981). The process of semiproletarianization begins with the dispossession of much of the peasantry from subsistence plots in the traditional, more fertile farming areas by the expansion of the latifundias. The peasantry is forced onto minifundias, which are often too small to allow subsistence to take place, or are in more marginal agricultural areas. In this position, the peasants may work their small plots to provide for part of their own subsistence, but are forced to seek outside wage labor on the latifundias to make up the remainder of their subsistence income. The peasantry becomes semiproletarianized (part wage laborer, part subsistence farmer), a process that functionalizes peasants to the needs of disarticulated accumulation in the large estates, and negates the possibility of stable reproduction of peasants as independent agriculturalists. The latifundistas are able to "overexploit" these semiproletarianized workers by paying them lower wages than would be required to maintain and reproduce the labor power of a fully proletarianized work force. Because these semiproletarians grow some of their own food on small plots of land, this part of their reproduction needs does not need to originate out of wages paid for working on the latifundias. Thus they can subsist at a minimal level, which allows their labor power to be reproduced while receiving relatively lower wages than their proletarianized counterparts, who are fully dependent on wages for their livelihood.

This relationship of functional dualism between the peasantry and the modern agricultural sector becomes the ultimate embodiment of the contradictions of accumulation in disarticulated economies. A steady source of cheap labor is maintained, while the capitalist estates enjoy high profits by marketing their produce either abroad or to the domestic bourgeoisie. However, functional dualism is ultimately contradictory and therefore only a transitional phase of agricultural development. It does not have its own laws of stable reprodution (Batra, 1974; Amin, 1976). The transitory articulation that is developed through functional dualism between the peasantry and the dominant capitalist mode of production (i.e., the large estates) gradually breaks. The semiproletarianized peasants become increasingly unable to sustain their own reproduction through subsistence food production, as they are constantly shifted onto smaller plots of less fertile land by means of a combination of large-estate expansion and rural population growth. The counterparts of growth and high profits for the latifundistas are growing social inequalities, severe impoverishment of the peasantry, and stagnation of domestic foodstuff production—which, in turn, bring about the liquidation of functional dualism by demographic explosion, rural-to-urban migration, further exploitation, growing environmental destruction, and generally increased rural (and then urban) unrest.

The Formative Period:
The Colonial Legacy Until 1870

As elsewhere in Latin America, the establishment of a latifundia-minifundia agrarian structure by the Spanish colonists played a role in the future development of social relations and the forces of production within Nicaraguan agriculture (Wheelock, 1975). However, agricultural development (and economic growth in general) is a markedly uneven process; it arises at particular points, propagates itself with greater or lesser facility in different areas, acquires greater vigor and sustained growth in some places, and stagnates or is aborted in others. Each agricultural area in Latin America has its particular cluster of resources and growth factors that helped to determine the pace and direction of development. In a relatively small, severely isolated community such as colonial Nicaragua, capital could not be absorbed into agricultural expansion without developing new techniques and opening up new markets (Furtado, 1976).

Nicaragua was virtually neglected by Spain during much of the colonial era; internal strife and political instability prevented the consolidation of state power by any one faction of the emerging agrarian oligarchy (West and Augelli, 1966). Although a small landed oligarchy was established among the Spanish colonists, and commercial links were created with an incipient class of merchant capitalists in the towns, Nicaraguan agriculture failed to establish strong external economic links that would have allowed it to flourish. Thus during the colonial era and much of the nineteenth century, Nicaragua remained an isolated "backwater" in comparison with other Latin American centers, such as Peru and Mexico. Ties of external dependency were only weakly established in the agricultural export sector, and rural differentiation and capitalist class formation had begun on only a very limited scale.

Thus in contrast to the analysis of the early "dependency" and "development of underdevelopment" schools (Frank, 1969; Dos Santos, 1970; Sunkel, 1969), which focused on the sphere of circulation and assumed Latin America to be thoroughly capitalist from the initial stages of colonialism, capitalist social relations developed only slowly and unevenly in Nicaraguan colonial agriculture. Haciendas were established by the Spanish colonists in scattered areas along the Pacific coast and in the Nicaraguan lake region. With fertile volcanic soils and plentiful seasonal rainfall, this region is regarded as the agricultural heartland of Nicaragua. Until the Spanish arrived, it had supported a fairly dense population of Chorotegan Indians (the southernmost extension of the high Mesoamerican native culture) for approximately two thousand years (West and Augelli, 1966).

However, disease brought on by the Spanish conquest and the sixteenth-century slave trade in Nicaraguan natives rapidly depleted the population of Indians in this area, forcing the latifundistas to adopt labor-saving, extensive agricultural techniques (MacLeod, 1971; Radell, 1969). Semifeudal and authoritarian internal relations of production were established between the natives and the Spanish agrarian oligarchy. The native peasantry was tied to the large estates by the presence of internal subsistence plots (*chacras*), for which they paid rents to the landlord in the form of labor services (Collins, 1981). The peasantry was further bonded to the large estates by systems of labor servitude, debt peonage, and extraeconomic coercion.

In addition to bonding scarce native labor to their estates by semifeudal, authoritarian productive relations, the latifundistas adopted extensive agricultural techniques that had relatively low labor requirements and could be combined with native food production on the peasants' internal subsistence plots. The relative isolation of these semifeudal estates from the forces of outside capitalist competition allowed for their survival despite low investment levels, technological backwardness, low productivity, and rampant waste and mismanagement. Widespread stagnation of the development of the agrarian forces of production was exacerbated further by the high rate of absentee landlordism. Many large-estate owners typically lived in towns, took only a marginal interest in increasing the productivity and profitability of their farms, and left rather ill-trained, technologically backward *majordomos* (foremen) in charge of day-to-day operations.

Because capitalist relations of production developed only slowly and haphazardly until the late nineteenth century, the legacy of colonial agriculture continued to have a significant and lasting influence on the Nicaraguan farming sector, which has continued until the present. A system of haciendas using extensive cultivation practices was gradually established on the most fertile volcanic soils along the Pacific coast and lake lowlands and has endured to the present. Coercive social relations of production that were formed during the colonial period, including surplus extraction mechanisms such as rent in labor (*colonato*) and rent in kind (*mediería* or *aparcería*), persisted in various forms of debt peonage until the 1979 revolution (Biderman, 1983). The relative scarcity of labor and abundance of land per capita in Nicaragua has traditionally made it necessary to bond peasant labor to the large estate through coercive, noncapitalist, semifeudal means. Finally, the persistence of absentee landlordism from the early colonial period to the present has exacerbated problems in Nicaraguan agriculture of low productivity, technological stagnation, waste and mismanagement of some of the country's best agricultural resources, and growing ecological destruction (especially soil depletion and erosion) caused by neglect and the use of technologically backward farming practices.

Unlike the 1870s, then, Nicaragua's commercial agrarian economy was dominated by a relatively small landed and merchant oligarchy based in the cities of Granada and León. Large cattle ranches had been established on a limited scale early in the colonial period to supply the local market in the towns. By the seventeenth century, cattle-related activities had become the main basis of Nicaragua's colonial economy (Radell, 1969), and extensive cattle latifundias still dominated the Nicaraguan economy until the introduction of large-scale coffee production in the last third of the nineteenth century (Biderman, 1983). Cacao, which had been cultivated commercially in the sixteenth century, had suffered a rapid demise because of primitive cultivation techniques, competition from cheaper foreign sources (especially Ecuador), labor shortages, and British pirate raids in the seventeenth century. Indigo, which had quickly become the most important colonial cash crop following its commercial introduction in the seventeenth century, had likewise suffered a steep decline owing to labor shortages, credit and transportation problems, increased foreign competition, and the introduction of synthetic dyes (Radell, 1969; MacLeod, 1973). Before the advent of coffee cultivation in the 1870s, then, Nicaraguan commercial agriculture continued to produce primarily for the internal market, and external economic links (mainly with Britain) had been developed on only a very limited basis.

1870 to World War II: Coffee Boom Followed by Stagnation

The transformation of Nicaragua's precapitalist estates into more modern, large-scale, export-oriented capitalist farms began in earnest as a result of the coffee boom, which commenced during the 1870s and continued at an accelerating pace until the turn of the twentieth century. The rise of economic liberalism and of the agricultural export sector, both of which facilitated the transition to capitalist farming practices, was similar to that of many other Latin American countries, except in its relative lateness. In other Central American nations the coffee boom was already well under way by the 1870s, and the wealthy new coffee bourgeoisies had consolidated control over their respective state structures much earlier (Biderman, 1983). For most Latin American countries, the era of economic liberalism, which integrated their economies into the global process of accumulation as agroexporters to the core capitalist nations (i.e., the United States and Western Europe), began during the 1820s and had been virtually completed by the late nineteenth century (de Janvry, 1981).

The relatively slow integration of Nicaragua's commercial agricultural sector into the world economy has been attributed to the continuing dominance of the traditional (inward-looking) landed oligarchy through most of the nineteenth century (Biderman, 1983). The consolidation of Nicaragua's coffee export structure did not take place until the ascendancy of the administration of José Santos Zelaya (representing the most "reformist" elements among the coffee entrepreneurs) to state power in the late nineteenth century

(Wheelock, 1975). The impact of the Zelaya administration on coffee production was dramatic—coffee production doubled after 1899 (Tores-Rivas, 1973). Most of the expansion of coffee acreage occurred in the central uplands of Managua-Carazo on large capitalist farms, which still produce a large part of Nicaragua's coffee crop (International Bank for Reconstruction and Development [IBRD], 1953).

Under Zelaya, a number of significant changes took place that greatly aided in the consolidation of capitalist social relations and the expansion of acreage in the modern agricultural sector. A Law of Agrarian Reform and other legislation were passed that allowed the coffee entrepreneurs to acquire new lands through auctions of native communal territory and much of the public and church lands in Nicaragua's agricultural core (Collins, 1982). The confiscation of many remaining subsistence plots from the peasantry by these "liberal" Zelaya reforms quickened the process of semiproletarianization, ensuring a steady supply of cheap labor at harvest time on the large coffee estates. Moreover, vagrancy laws were decreed which required *campesinos* to show proof of employment on demand during the coffee harvests. In addition to these measures, direct incentives were provided for coffee cultivation and foreign immigration, a rudimentary road infrastructure was constructed in the large coffee areas to aid in marketing, and the incorporation and sale of coffee lands were facilitated by land reorganization laws (Biderman, 1983). The effect of these changes under Zelaya was a slow but steady rise in the profitability of commercial agriculture, both absolutely and relative to other domestic economic sectors. The result was an expansion and consolidation of the economic and political power of the agroexporter and commercial oligarchies in association with foreign capital, and a massive new concentration of landownership causing further dispossession and semiproletarianization of the peasantry.

With few exceptions, the rise of the capitalist coffee estates in Nicaragua followed the Junker road of agricultural development. The landowning dominant class retained its political and economic power by exercising control over both the production and realization of profit by means of monopoly relations in primary agricultural production and in commercial exchange, especially foreign trade. In the process, a class of semiproletarianized rural workers (often with subsistence plots adjacent to the large estates) emerged more fully. The penetration of commodity relations, with regard to both land and labor, coupled with the retention of various means of precapitalist coercion, was used to break the reproduction cycle of systems of traditional peasant economies. The landed elite still retained control over the state—but had strengthened their class alliance with export-oriented elements of their own agrarian oligarchy, the emerging commercial bourgeoisie (*compradores*), and foreign capital.

The foreign element of this alliance was further strengthened in the early twentieth century by direct U.S. military intervention to forestall the rising nationalism of the Zelaya regime and to dampen internecine struggles that had developed between factions of the Nicaraguan oligarchy. Following the disposal of Zelaya by U.S. Marines, U.S. capital assumed direct control over the operation of the Nicaraguan central bank. From this time until the late 1920s, the U.S. Marines were in almost constant occupation of Nicaragua, providing the military might to allow U.S. manipulation of the Nicaraguan political system to suit its own interests.

The most serious challenge to U.S. military intervention during this period came from a peasant rebellion concentrated in the mountainous north-central section of the country, led by a fervent nationalist and antiimperialist by the name of Augusto César Sandino. Despite having an overwhelming advantage in firepower, the U.S. Marines were unable to defeat the rebels, who used classic guerrilla tactics to sap the strength of the U.S. forces, leading to their removal from Nicaragua in the late 1920s. The growing political influence of Sandino (from whom the present-day Sandinistas take their name) following the departure of the U.S. Marines was quickly snuffed out by his assassination and the ascendancy of Anastasio Somoza-García to power in 1933 following a coup by the U.S.–created National Guard. The Somocistas moved quickly to further consolidate the alliance between the Nicaraguan export-oriented agrarian bourgeoisie and international capital. This regime made liberal use of the powers of the state to encourage modernization and diversification of the commercial agriculture sector, thus stimulating and deepening new sources of accumulation. Anastasio Somoza himself (followed by his son Tacho) played a large and direct role in this agricultural expansion, and in 1979, when the Sandinistas assumed power, the Somocistas directly owned more than 20 percent of Nicaraguan farmland and, even more important, had achieved monopolistic control over food processing and commercialization, particularly for agroexports.

The rise to dominance of this alliance among international capital (metropolitan bourgeoisie), the domestic dependent and commercial bourgeoisies, and the landed elites of a Third World country, such as Nicaragua, typically implies that the logic of disarticulated accumulation will prevail (de Janvry, 1981). With its characteristics of deepening penetration of capitalist relations, cheap labor and an impoverished peasantry, agroexports and stagnation of domestic food production, and heavy repression by the state, this model of disarticulation is dominant in Latin America.

However, despite the intensified penetration of capitalist social relations into the agrarian section within this model, it must also take into account a pervasive tendency toward stagnation. In a disarticulated economy competitive pressures for the monopoly Junker class to modernize are typically weak, and profits/rents are often spent on luxury consumption instead of prudent reinvestment in capital assets. Although there was some minor commercial expansion (particularly of cotton and sesame acreage) and some machinery and agrochemical inputs were introduced, Nicaraguan agriculture between World War I and World War II was largely stagnant. An IBRD report issued in 1953 severely castigated the backward conditions which prevailed in the Nicaraguan commercial agriculture sector:

> As a general rule, lands other than subsistence farms are held for investment purposes. Few large owners live on the land and direct day-to-day operations. Instead, they live in town and leave the management to poorly paid majordomos. Some owners prefer to rent their land for cash and thus are relieved of any management problems. (1953:310)

The IBRD report found that less than a quarter of Nicaragua's cultivable land was in productive use. Productivity of both land and labor remained very low. Much land was being seriously misused (e.g., cattle grazing on fertile, level soils and intensive food production on poor, less fertile soils and steep slopes). Serious problems of soil depletion and soil erosion had resulted in a growing number of areas. Growing problems of environmental degradation were being exacerbated by the misuse of mechanized equipment, particularly in the expanding cotton region of fertile (but easily eroded) volcanic soils. Primitive production techniques, low labor productivity, neglect, and mismanagement had severely limited yields per acre. The IBRD found little knowledge or appreciation of what might be accomplished by the use of measures such as fertilization, crop rotation, soil conservation, seed selection, improved breeding practices, and the adoption of proper storage techniques. Even in the primary coffee sector, there was found to be little appreciation of rudimentary pruning, terracing, or fertilizing techniques. As a result, yields per coffee tree lagged far behind those of El Salvador, Guatemala, and Costa Rica, despite similar soils and climate.

Moreover, in spite of the direct involvement of the Somocistas in some agriculture sectors, involvement of the state in overall agrarian development was found to be inadequate and haphazard. Lack of access to credit (especially for small and medium producers) was seen as a particular problem: "Credits have been restricted to current production loans which go, for the most part, to a relatively small number of large landowners" (IBRD, 1953:29). No banking facilities were in existence at all for small credits, and the cost of short-term private credit ranged from 18 to 60 percent *per annum*. Further problems included low standards of health and education, an archaic fiscal system, an inadequate transportation and communications infrastructure, and the absence of long-range government planning or investment programs.

Overall, the IBRD's report represented a serious indictment of Nicaragua's commercial agriculture sector—and particularly the role that the state, the domestic bourgeoisie, and the landed oligarchy had played in overseeing its continuing stagnation, despite the presence of considerable potential for acreage expansion and productivity increases. Although commodity relations had begun to penetrate Nicaraguan agriculture, and the agroexport sector had greatly increased in importance, the prevalence of the Junker road in Nicaragua had severely limited the possibilities for articulated growth and sustained capitalist development.

World War II to 1979: Acceleration of Capitalist Agricultural Development

In contrast to the previous era of relative stagnation, the Nicaraguan commercial agriculture sector, and the economy in general, grew at an accelerated pace in the postwar period. This rapid development is indicated by the aggregate growth figures. Between 1950 and 1955, the annual growth rate of Nicaragua's total product was 9.3 percent, making it the highest in Central America (IASI, 1960). After a sharp cyclical downturn in the late 1950s, rapid growth resumed in the early 1960s. Per capita real income also showed a steady advance—from $170 in 1949 to $245 in 1955 to $288 in 1961 (U.N., 1964). The figures for the value of Nicaraguan exports are even more impressive—from $14 million in 1945 to $34 million in 1950 to $65 million in 1956 and $106 million in 1963 (Banco Central, 1972). Although another cyclical downturn hit the Nicaraguan economy in the late 1960s, the export sector continued to show phenomenal growth: from $106 million in 1963 to $179 million in 1970 and $250 million in 1972 (Banco Central, 1972). In summary, from 1950 to 1960, the value of Nicaraguan exports grew by 225 percent, and from 1960 to 1970, the value grew by 275 percent (Banco Central, 1972). These figures indicate that the postwar period in general was the most economically dynamic in Nicaraguan history.

The rapid development of capitalist agriculture following the war continued to follow the Junker road. The transformation of the social relations of production (toward increasing semiproletarianization) was accompanied neither by a change in the social or geographic location of the market nor in the distribution of assets nor in the control over the state. By the mid-1970s, almost 70 percent of Nicaragua's gross national product (GNP) was taken up by export production in contrast to 10 percent for Mexico and 18 percent for Chile (Collins, 1982). Exports expanded not only to the core capitalist countries, but also to other Central American countries (e.g., powdered milk) within the framework of the Central American Common Market. In 1979, a survey by the Sandinistas found that non-Somocista large and medium farmers controlled over two-thirds of all agricultural land, while the Somocistas directly controlled a further one-fifth of the total, leaving approximately two-fifteenths of Nicaragua's total agricultural land for its multitude of small peasant producers (two-thirds of the population). Under Somoza during the 1970s, the minimum wage for agricultural workers was supposedly $2.10 per day, but in practice the going rate was $0.80 to $1.70 per day (except for skilled workers such as machine operators). Despite widespread neglect of the minimum-wage laws (as well as other mandatory fringe benefits such as meals and transportation), the Somoza regime was loath to pursue its allies among the agrarian bourgeoisie. Supposedly, only those few growers who somehow crossed Somoza and had to be "taught a lesson" were selected for enforcement of the national labor laws (Collins, 1982: 70).

The export-oriented boom in production of cotton (beginning in the 1950s) and beef (in the late 1960s) signified the rapid development of capitalist relations in Nicaraguan agriculture in the postwar era. Although much land continued to be held primarily for investment and speculative purposes, many large-estate owners began to adopt capitalist production criteria (e.g., adopting new production techniques and altering uses of their land according to profitability criteria). By 1954–55, cotton acreage had expanded to five times its 1950 level, and cotton production exceeded one million *quintals* of ginned cotton (one quintal equals approximately 100 pounds). Cotton exports soared from $1.8 million (5 percent of total exports) in 1950 to $31 million (39 percent of total exports) in 1955, displacing coffee as Nicaragua's principal export product (Banco Central, 1972; FAO, 1956). Despite declines in production in the late 1950s caused by a drop in international prices, by 1965 cotton acreage had reached 340,000 acres (Biderman, 1983), production exceeded 2.5 million quintals, and exports had risen to $66 million (44 percent of total export) (Banco Central, 1972). Following another downswing in the late 1960s and early 1970s, cotton acreage and production once again assumed a high growth rate (Banco Central, 1979). Since 1950, the growth rate of Nicaraguan cotton has been among the highest in the world.

The steep rise in cotton production and export figures during this period can be attributed to the adoption of large-scale capitalist production techniques and increasing state involvement in the agroexport sector. Responding to new possibilities for accumulation offered by higher international prices, the state provided credit to the cotton entrepreneur for an expansion of acreage, the purchase of agrochemicals, and investments in laborsaving machinery. As early as the mid-1950s, two-thirds of all agricultural bank credit was allocated to the cotton sector (Banco Central, 1970). The combined effects of credit, agrochemical inputs, research and extension, and other government-subsidized service became evident not only in increased production figures, but also in steep rises in yields per acre, which were among the highest yield levels in the world for rain-fed cotton by 1964 to 1965 (Biderman, 1983). Moreover, the widespread use of laborsaving production inputs (e.g., herbicides, tractors and other machinery) allowed cotton growers to reduce their labor costs and increase their profitability. A small work force could take care of year-round operations, while a cheap source of seasonal labor could be found for the harvest (which remained labor-intensive) from among the burgeoning ranks of the impoverished semiproletarianized peasantry. By the 1970s, the number of seasonal cotton workers averaged from 150,000 to 200,000 people (one-half of the economically active agricultural population), and they constituted 90 percent of the annual work force, earning 60 to 70 percent of the annual wages in the cotton sector (PREALC, 1973).

Although the expansion of acreage and lowering of labor costs relative to productivity were the most important factors in the growth of cotton production, the accumulation process was further strengthened by both horizontal and vertical integration. Not only was land concentrated and centralized among a few large producers, but virtually all activities involved in the cotton industry (e.g., cotton processing, marketing, banking and financial services, input distribution, and cotton-related services) were controlled by the same members of the cotton oligarchy. Private financial groups, such as the Banco Nicaraguense, were created to handle credit and other financial matters. Powerful regional associations were formed to influence the allocation of state resources and the general direction of cotton-related state policy. An estimated seventy commercial firms supplying cotton inputs and equipment were controlled by the cotton oligarchy, as were some thirty gins to process cotton (Biderman, 1983). Some large growers also were involved in the manufacturing and marketing of domestically produced insecticides and the domestic processing of cottonseed into vegetable oil. But the monopolization tendency in the cotton industry was particularly evident with regard to the export sector—fewer than twenty exporters (mostly owned by or affiliated with foreign corporations) controlled all cotton exports, and five of these dominated most of the trade (Biderman, 1983).

In addition to the cotton boom in the postwar period, other

agrarian-dominated and export-oriented agrarian activities grew rapidly during the 1960s and 1970s. Beef exports in particular, and to a lesser extent dairy products, poultry, sugar, tobacco, bananas, and irrigated rice, became important sources of income and foreign exchange. Although extensive cattle ranches were present in Nicaragua from colonial times, exports had been confined to limited quantities of live cattle before the 1950s. In the late 1950s, significant quantities of chilled boneless beef began to be exported, primarily to the United States and Puerto Rico. Beef exports rose from a negligible level prior to 1958, to $5 million in 1963 and $34 million in 1970 (15 percent of total exports). A further expansion took place in the early 1970s, with exports reaching $63 million by 1972 (Banco Central, 1972). Despite some efforts by the state to promote intensification and modernization, cattle production continued to be dominated by traditional, extensive grazing practices. Expanded beef production meant as a consequence that a tremendous expansion in acreage devoted to cattle grazing was also needed. After 1960, a doubling of the area in cattle pasture occurred; by the 1970s, 10 out of 11 million acres used for export production were devoted to cattle grazing (Collins, 1982).

The cattle industry was not as concentrated as other major agroexport sectors (e.g., cotton, coffee, sugar), owing to continuing beef production by traditional small and medium-sized producers, which accounted for two-thirds of the cattle stock in 1971. However, the largest cattle ranchers (2 percent of the total number) still owned 27 percent of the cattle and more than 50 percent of the area in pasture (Biderman, 1983). Moreover, through coercive and monopolistic marketing practices, small producers were dominated by intermediate merchants, processors, and exporters. By the late 1970s, there were only seven export slaughterhouses in Nicaragua, and most of these were directly or indirectly controlled by the Somoza family. Likewise, the bulk of Nicaragua's market for dairy products was controlled by five pasteurizing plants in Managua and a Nestlé subsidiary (PROLACSA) in Matagalpa that produced powdered milk.

As has been indicated, the Somoza regime greatly increased its role during the postwar period (relative to the prewar era) in facilitating the development of the forces of production, capitalist social relations, and an increasingly concentrated productive and distribution structure in Nicaraguan agriculture. Both direct and indirect state actions reinforced tendencies toward monopolization and uneven agricultural development. State resources devoted to agriculture were almost exclusively channeled to further the accumulation interests of a select group of large-scale, export-oriented capitalist producers. State activities that disproportionately benefited the agrarian oligarchy included selective road construction to facilitate access to the large estates; discriminatory credit, tariff, pricing, and exchange-rate policies favoring agroexports and agrarian production inputs; and the provision of publicly subsidized irrigation, research and extension, storage, and processing/marketing facilities.

Not coincidentally, the Somocistas were often directly involved in many of the activities that were receiving state assistance, particularly processing and marketing. Somoza and his associates controlled most of the six large vertically integrated enterprises that dominated the sugar industry. The Somocistas were also heavily involved in tobacco production, operating a string of large plantations using some of the most advanced capitalist production techniques in Nicaraguan agriculture (Wheelock and Carrion, 1980). In total, the Somocistas controlled approximately 20 percent of Nicaragua's agricultural land (and 25 percent of the land in large estates) by the late 1970s (Collins, 1982). Two-thirds of these estates were larger than 4,350 acres, and the bulk of Somocista property could be characterized as highly modernized export-oriented farms and cattle ranches. These agrarian estates occupied land with some of the best soils in Nicaragua and made use of highly developed agrarian forces and relations of production. Furthermore, and perhaps even more important, the Somoza state controlled development of the processing industry and marketing (especially of agroexports) for the bulk of the capitalist agricultural sector through state agencies such as FONAC (Instituto de Fomento Nacional) and BNN (Banco Nacional de Nicaragua). Thus the Somoza state, whether directly or indirectly, was instrumental in promoting rapid capitalist agricultural development in the postwar era. Its actions were very much directed toward further consolidation of the Junker road of disarticulated development, leading to an increasing concentration and centralization of the country's land and wealth and to a solidification of the politicoeconomic power of an alliance among the emergent commercial-agro/industrial bourgeoisie, foreign interests, and the landed oligarchy.

The Consequences of Disarticulated Capitalist Growth

As is typical in Third World nations, the development of capitalism in Nicaraguan agriculture caused serious problems of inequality and unevenness in social, sectoral, and regional terms. The widespread displacement, semiproletarianization, and increasing impoverishment of the small producers was in sharp contrast to the high growth and profitability rates of the large export-oriented capitalist farmers. The boom of the modern agroexport sector contrasted with the stagnation of domestic food production in the traditional peasant sector. And finally, this social/sectoral unevenness was manifested in concomitant severe regional imbalance. The development of modern capitalist forces of production was most advanced in the area of large export-oriented estates in the Pacific coastal region, while much of the interior and mountainous central regions stagnated in very backward conditions. Much of the peasantry not only was displaced over the years from the most fertile, level areas to less accessible, more mountainous, and less fertile regions, but also was denied access to the state's resources through discriminatory policies.

The displacement of the peasantry from Nicaragua's most fertile and level land is a process that dates back to the establishment of extensive precapitalist estates in the colonial era. However, good land was readily available at that time, and a large-scale migration of peasants into the more mountainous interior did not occur until the expansion of more capitalistic coffee estates along the Pacific coastal region during the late nineteenth century. By the 1890s, a large number of small and medium peasant holdings had been cleared out of the rugged hardwood forests of Matagalpa and Jinotega (West and Augelli, 1966). Throughout the twentieth century, much of the independent and small peasantry has been pushed farther and farther north and east along the constantly expanding agricultural "frontier," often being forced off their newly cleared lots several times in one generation by expansions in extensive farming and grazing activities of the large estates (Collins, 1982). This displacement of small producers became particularly intense following World War II. The expansion of cotton acreage forced many peasants from the Pacific coastal zone into the central region. Slash-and-burn agriculture was typically carried on in increasingly remote areas, until this land too was occupied for pasture during the cattle and beef boom. Thus, many peasants were progressively forced onto smaller plots in more remote and less fertile, rugged areas.

The forced concentration of the peasantry onto plots of diminishing quantity and quality created a growing class of semiproletarians, occupying subfamily farms not large enough to support a subsistence living without some outside employment. The number of subfamily farms (less than 10 *manzanas* or 7 hectares) increased from 17,943 in 1952 to 51,936 in 1963. By 1976, subfamily farms represented 61 percent of all farms in Nicaragua but occupied less than 4 percent of the total cultivated area (Collins, 1982). Meanwhile, the largest farms (more than 500 *manzanas*, or 350 hectares) represented less than 2 percent of total farms but controlled nearly half of the agricultural land. As an increasing share of Nicaragua's land became concentrated among the rural elite, two rural classes of land-poor workers grew in numbers. A class of landless workers who also lacked stable employment represented an estimated 32 percent of the economically active populaton (EAP) in agriculture in 1978. But the largest rural class was the semi-proletarian group, which formed 38 percent of the agricultural EAP. Only 13 percent of the agricultural EAP had access to enough land to satisfy family requirements (Deere and Marchetti, 1981).

As the peasantry was forced onto ever smaller plots in more marginal agricultural areas, a serious stagnation of Nicaraguan food production was created relative to effective demand (which was growing quickly because of high rates of population growth). The breakdown of peasant agriculture gravely affected food production, as the small peasantry traditionally had supplied the bulk of Nicaragua's foodstuffs. In the 1970s, small farms (less than 34 acres, and often much less) represented 76 percent of the total number of farms, used only 14 percent of the farmland, and produced 60 percent of the country's staples of corn and beans (Collins, 1982). The only staple food that was not produced primarily on small peasant plots was rice, which was cultivated chiefly on large mechanized capitalist farms. The expansion of the large cotton and cattle estates in the postwar period was largely at the expense of small plots of land previously devoted to beans, corn, sorghum, and other basic food crops. By the 1970s, twenty-two times as much land (including farmland and pasture) was being used for export production as for growing food for Nicaraguans (Collins, 1982).

The actions of the state further exacerbated problems of stagnant food production. While the state took elaborate measures to ensure the profitability of the agroexporters, little support was afforded to the small food producers. Access to public credit was generally blocked, forcing small farmers to seek private credit at usurious rates that often required payment in crops at extremely low prices during the harvest period. Even a U.S. AID (Agency for International Development) program credit scheme specifically designed to help small farmers had 80 percent of its total credit distributed to the big export producers by the Somocistas. Lack of adequate storage and transportation facilities, compulsory rental arrangements with large landowners, monopolistic pricing of agricultural inputs, and disadvantages presented by the growing insecurity and impoverishment further increased opportunities for abuse of the peasantry by rural middlemen offering coercive marketing arrangements.

In addition to its lack of support for small producers, the Somoza regime further compounded food production problems by its pricing policies. In contrast to the Sandinistas (who substantially raised prices offered food producers following the revolution), the Somoza administration had consistently encouraged the maintenance of low food prices through its policies. Low food prices, however, form a very important component of the logic of a disarticulated, export-oriented agrarian economy—low food prices permit lower wages to be paid by the agroexport sector and thereby facilitate higher profitability without expensive technical inputs. The state agency (INCEI) that was ostensibly created to offer reasonable support prices for food crops concentrated its purchasing efforts within the large-scale capitalist rice sector. This left rural intermediaries free to pursue their pattern of historical abuse of the peasantry.

As a result of the state's food policies (which stagnated domestic food production while encouraging agroexports), Nicaragua was forced to import increasing quantities of basic foods in the postwar era, exacerbating its growing balance-of-payments problems. Despite being rich in potential farmland, Nicaragua imported 21,000 tons of grain in 1955; by 1978, it was forced to import ten times this amount (Collins, 1982). As a result, Nicaragua's debt problem worsened, particularly during the 1970s (when it was compounded by the Managua earthquake). In 1972, 9 percent of annual export revenues were taken up by external debt-service payments; by 1977, the figure was 18 percent and by 1978, it was 30 percent (Deere, 1981). Thus, Nicaragua's food policies not only systematically impoverished the peasantry and urban proletariat, causing widespread malnutrition and increasing unrest, but also caused balance-of-payments and external debt problems that limited the ability to purchase needed imports.

Conclusion

Nicaragua's prerevolutionary agricultural development closely followed the theoretical model of the Junker road of agrarian growth associated with a disarticulated Third World economy. Although capitalist relations of production developed only very slowly until the late nineteenth century, agricultural development before this time left an enduring legacy of coercive labor relations, extensive agricultural techniques on large estates, and absentee landlordism that has traditionally compounded problems of resource misuse and economic mismanagement. Following the coffee boom of the late nineteenth century, Nicaragua's semifeudal estates were slowly transformed into large-scale capitalist farms. Opportunities for the development of capitalism among the peasantry, however, were blocked by the economic, political and coercive power of the large-estate owners. A socially and sectorally disarticulated economy was consolidated in which production in the modern agricultural sector was concentrated on exportables for the foreign market. Links of functional dualism between the peasantry and the large capitalist estates acted to ensure the latter's profitability by keeping both wages and food prices low.

In labor-scarce and land-abundant Nicaragua, a key component of the process of disarticulated development was the progressive semiproletarianization of the peasantry. The displacement of peasants onto ever smaller plots in more marginal agricultural areas forced them to seek employment on the large estates to meet their subsistence needs. This semiproletarianization process was greatly strengthened in the postwar period by the expansion of large-scale capitalist farms (particularly cattle and cotton) over much of the most fertile soils in the Pacific coastal zone and lake lowlands, thereby forcing many peasants into the more rugged and less fertile interior region. The Somocistas played an active role through manipulation of state policy in order to facilitate the growth in exports and profitability of the agrarian oligarchy. A dualistic latinfundia–minifundia agrarian system was consolidated, characterized by extreme inequality between social classes and uneven development of economic sectors and between geographic regions. However, such a system is highly contradictory; it does not have its own stable laws of systemic reproduction. Generalized economic growth is stagnated due to the concentration of resources and wealth among a severely limited export-oriented bourgeoisie and the perpetuation of abysmally low wage levels which restrict internal effective demand. This economic instability is eventually reflected in the growth of serious class conflict—both among bourgeois and petty bourgeois factions that are competing for state influence or have seen their development possibilities blocked by the agroexport model, and between the ruling class and the impoverished peasantry, semiproletarians, and working class. Ultimately (as was the case in Nicaragua), widening social inequalities exacerbated by increasing landlessness, unemployment, and a stagnation of domestic food production led to growing unrest among the disadvantaged and the creation of a revolutionary situation. Thus increasing class conflict and, eventually, revolution may be seen as consequences of the dynamics of disarticulated capitalist development in the Third World—whose laws of reproduction systematically undermine broadly based internal economic growth and inexorably lead to the immiseration of the overwhelming majority of the population.

References

Amin, S. (1976). *Unequal Development*. New York: Monthly Review Press.

Banco Central de Nicaragua (1970, 1972, 1979). *Principales Indicadores Económicas*. Managua: Banco Central.

Bartha, R. (1974). *Estructura Agraria y Clases Sociales en México*. Mexico City: Ediciones Era.

Beaucage, Pierre (1974). "Modos de Producción Articulados o Lucha de Clases?" *Historia y Sociedad* 51:37–58.

Biderman, J. (1983). "The Development of Capitalism in Nicaragua: A Political Economic History." *Latin American Perspectives* 101 (Winter).

Brenner, R. (1977). "The Origins of Capitalist Development: A Critique of Neo-Smithian Marxism." *New Left Review* 104 (July–August).

Collins, J. (1982). *What Difference Could a Revolution Make? Food and Farming in the New Nicargua.* San Francisco: Institute for Food and Development Policy.

Deere, C. (1982). "A Comparative Analysis of Agrarian Reform in El Salvador and Nicaragua, 1971–1981." *Development and Change* 13 (January).

Deere C., and P. Marchetti (1981). "The Worker–Peasant Alliance in the Year of the Nicaraguan Agrarian Reform." *Latin American Perspectives* 8 (Spring).

de Janvry, A. (1981). *The Agrarian Question and Reformism in Latin America.* Baltimore: Johns Hopkins University Press.

Dos Santos, T. (1970). "The Stucture of Dependence." *American Economic Review* 60:2.

FAO (Food and Agriculture Organization) (1956). *FAO Production Yearbook.* Rome.

FIDA (Fondo Internacional Desarrollo Agrícola) (1980). "Informe de la mision especial de programación a Nicaragua." Rome.

Foster-Carter, A. (1978). "The Modes of Production Controversy." *New Left Review* 107:47–77.

Frank, A. G. (1969). *Capitalism and Underdevelopment in Latin America.* New York: Modern Reader.

Furtado, C. (1974). *Obstacles to Development in Latin America.* Garden City, N.Y.: Anchor Books.

—— (1976). *Economic Development of Latin America: A Survey from Colonial Times to the Cuban Revolution.* Cambridge: Cambridge University Press.

Havens, A. Eugene (1982). "La Cuestion Agraria: El Papel de las Luchas Campesinas en la Reproducción y Transformación del Capitalismo." In *CIERA: Reforma Agraria y Revolución Popular en América Latina.* Managua: CIERA.

IASI (Inter-American Statistical Institute) (1960). *América en Cifras.* Mexico City: Estadisticas Demográficas.

IBRD (International Bank for Reconstruction and Development) (1953). *The Economic Development of Nicaragua.* Baltimore: Johns Hopkins University Press.

Kay, G. (1975). *Development and Underdevelopment: A Marxist Analysis.* New York: St. Martin's Press.

Laclau, E. (1971). "Feudalism and Capitalism in Latin America." *New Left Review* 67 (May–June).

Lenin, V. I. (1936). "The Agrarian Programme of Social Democracy in the First Russian Revolution." In *Seclected Works*, vol. 3. London: Laurence and Wishart.

Macleod, M. (1973). *Spanish Central America: A Socioeconomic History*, 1520–1720. Berkeley: University of California Press.

PREALC (Program Regional del Empleo para America Latina [of ILO]. (1973). "Situación y perspectives en Nicaragua." Santiago.

Radell, D. (1969). "Historical Geography of Western Nicaragua: The Spheres of Influence of Léon, Granada, and Managua, 1519–1965." Master's thesis, University of California, Berkeley.

Seddon, David, ed. (1978). *Relations of Production*. London: Frank Cass.

Sunkel, O. (1969). "National Development of Policy and External Dependence in Latin America." *Journal of Development Studies*, October.

Sweezy, P. (1942). *The Theory of Capitalist Development*. New York: Modern Reader.

Torres-Rivas, E. (1974). *Interpretación del desarrollo social centroamericano: Procesos y estructuras de una sociedad dependiente*. Costa Rica: Editorial Universidad Centroamericano (EDUCA).

UN (United Nations) (1964). *The Economic Development of Latin America in the Postwar Period*. New York: United Nations Publications.

Weeks, John, and Elizabeth Dore (1979). "International Exchange and the Causes of Backwardness." *Latin American Perspectives* 6:62–87.

West, R., and J. Augelli (1966). *Middle America*. Englewood Cliffs, N.J.: Prentice-Hall.

Wheelock J. (1975). *Imperialismo y dictadura*. Mexico City, Siglo XXI.

Wheelock, J., and L. Carrion (1980). "Apuntes sobre el desarrollo económico y social de Nicaragua." Managua: Secretaria Nacional de Propaganda y Educación Política del FSLN.

CHAPTER 9

Surplus Labor, Unequal Exchange, and Merchant Capital: Rethinking Caribbean Migration Theory

Hilbourne A. Watson

Historically, the origin, development, and reproduction of the capital–wage labor relation in the Caribbean has been shaped by the phenomenon of migration. Although the problem of migration has received considerable attention from the state sector, scholars, the media, nonprofit organizations, and others, most existing studies tend to be theoretically weak and inadequate. This applies to research that has evolved within the tradition of neoclassical economic analysis and underdevelopment/dependency theory. Neoclassical economic theory fixates on the factors-of-production thesis and attempts to explain international migration as a function of the mobility–immobility of these "factors of production." The mobility of capital is contrasted with the relative immobility of labor. Countries with a high endowment of productive resources and rapid and all-around development of their productive forces are contrasted with countries that have a low endowment of productive resources and underdevelopment. Capital as a "factor of production" is said to migrate to those areas where it is in scarce supply, and labor is said to migrate away from those areas where it is in relative superabundance.

Of course, the reality is that capital circulates within and between the countries of developed capitalism at a much higher rate than that at which it flows to the underdeveloped countries. But capital also circulates between the developed and underdeveloped countries on a large scale, as the statistics on foreign investments, profit flows, and technological rents amply demonstrate. On the other hand, the bulk of international migration on a world scale has been from the underdeveloped countries to the developed countries. In neoclassical theory, it is asserted that it is the scarcity of capital and the failure of the underdeveloped countries to develop their productive resources that account for their high levels of participation in international migration.

Neoclassical theory represents an intellectual miscarriage when it comes to explaining international migration. In essence, neoclassical theory lacks a concept of migration as a social process that reflects "the incessant motion of the circuits of capital" within which "labor power is thrust and repelled in response to the rhythm and dynamic" of the requirements of accumulation (Watson, 1981:5). Populations exist in the modern world as "population for capital," and it is this capital which at the different stages of its operation distributes and allocates labor according to the requirements of exploitation and accumulation. Migration of labor and capital accumulation are inseparable in the capitalist world economy. To begin with population pressure, migration, or other demographic characteristics is to ignore the "systems of social relations of production that incorporate and give meaning to production, distribution and exchange around which classes, capital, wage labor, value, surplus value, accumulation, valorization, and expanded reproduction take place" (Watson, 1981:6).

For its part, underdevelopment/dependency theory has failed to explain migration within and from the underdeveloped countries in a satisfactory manner, although its contributions are superior to those of neoclassical economic theory (Amin, 1976; Watson, 1976). The basic problem with underdevelopment/dependency theory — the theoretical and methodological bases of which have been analyzed and evaluated by Palma (1978) — is that it departed from the "logic of capital" as developed in Marx's *Capital*. It abandoned the labor theory of value, the theory of surplus value, and the primacy of the production relations in the political economy of social formations. Exchange (trade) and commercial relations, specialization within the international division of labor, and external relations as a whole have tended to dominate the dependency/underdevelopment paradigm. Thus, migration has been seen primarily as a response to or consequence of foreign domination and the imperialist division of labor. It is not possible to explain migration from the "Third World" without giving due consideration to these factors, but this is not the correct starting point. Attempts to integrate unequal exchange theory into one or another variant of dependency analysis have not fared much better.

My objective is to go beyond dependency/underdevelopment analysis in all its variants, including the "*Monthly Review* school" tendency typified by the works of Samir Amin (1974, 1976), the "World-System Model" represented by Immanuel Wallerstein (1974), and the "Latin American school," expressed in the journal *Latin American Perspectives,* which reflects economic nationalism and neo-marxism. To do this, it is necessary to return to the "logic of capital," so to speak (Watson, 1984b). This is not to say that I will discuss the works of Amin, Wallerstein, and the Latin American school per se; it means that by returning to Marx, I will attempt to provide a more adequate and approximate conceptual framework for explaining Caribbean migration as part of international migration.

By going beyond these theoretical frameworks, it is possible to overcome the limitations of the ideology of economic nationalism, the eclecticism of neo-Marxism, and the general bankruptcy of neoclassical theory. From this departure it can be shown (1) what have been the main problems in the relationship between capital and wage labor in the Caribbean; (2) what has given rise to the reserve army of labor; and (3) how the historical tendency of capital accumulation is mediated by the backward forms of domestic capital, foreign capital, unskilled labor specialization in the international division of labor, and labor migration. In a basic way, I am attempting to rethink and reexamine some of the basic premises of my earlier work on the political economy of the Commonwealth Caribbean, including the work on migration (Watson, 1975, 1976, 1981, 1982). Most of that work was developed within the framework of dependency/underdevelopment theory and is subject to some of the criticisms that will be directed at that theory.

Underdevelopment/Accumulation
and the Logic of Capital

In a major statement made in the *Grundrisse*, Marx emphasized the importance of going beyond the appearances of social phenomena. The methodological importance of that assertion cannot be overstated:

It seems to be correct to begin with the real and the concrete, with the real precondition, thus to begin, in economics, with, e.g., the population, which is the foundation and the subject of the entire social act of production. However, on closer examination this process proves false. The population is an abstraction if I leave out, for example, the classes of which it is composed. These classes are in turn an empty phrase if I am not familiar with the elements on which they rest, e.g., wage labor, capital, etc. The latter in turn presuppose exchange, division of labor, capital, etc. For example, capital is nothing without wage labor, without value, money, price, etc. Thus, if I were to begin with population this would be a chaotic conception . . . of the whole and I would then by means of further determination move analytically toward even more simple concepts . . . until I had arrived at population again, but this time . . . as a rich totality of many determinations. (1973:100)

Recognition that the concept of population represents "a rich totality of many determinations" under capitalism should not blind us to the fact that the development of capitalism is itself subject to historical laws and existing social conditions. According to Marx and Engels:

It is not the want of productive power which creates a suprlus population. It is the increase of productive power which demands a diminution of the population and drives away the surplus population by emigration. It is not population that presses on productive power, it is productive power that presses on population. (1971:51)

This brings us back to the "logic of capital." The development of capitalism under the auspices of productive capital (industrial capital and the industrial bourgeoisie) is based on the ongoing development of the wage labor–capital relation. This requires the ongoing development and transformation of the productive forces as the rational way to increase the exploitation of labor power in order to increase the rate of profit and counter "the tendency of the rate of profit to fall."

However, while this approach has been characteristic of productive capital, the development of capitalism has not always taken place with productive capital at the helm. The relationship between productive power and population that Marx and Engels established above would appear to be contradicted by the experience of Third World economies of the Caribbean. When the domestic sector and the so-called enclave foreign sector of this economy are examined and related, it appears that it is both the lack of productive power in the domestic sector—which is dominated by agriculture, commerce, and other services such as government and tourism—and the external (enclave) sector—which is made up of extractive activity, export agriculture, light manufacturing, and services such as banking, insurance, and tourism—that expel the so-called surplus population. There is truth in this; yet Marx and Engels were addressing the problem of nineteenth-century capitalism: the period of the Industrial Revolution and the industrialization of agriculture, the consolidation of the home market, and the subjection of commercial (circulation) capital to productive capital: in other words, the period in which industrial capital overthrew the rule of merchant capital. The development/underdevelopment of capitalism in the Caribbean throughout its history, and particularly since the end of World War II, has been characterized by a fundamental tension in the coexistence between backward agrocommercial capital and foreign capital. In many respects, the production and reproduction of the "surplus population" in the Caribbean is the undeniable product of this phenomenon.

The failure to develop an "autocentric" capitalism is not the fault of foreign capital, but it is traceable to the relative independence of backward forms of agrarian and commercial capital in the domestic economy under the control of an agrocommercial bourgeoisie. Marx (1967:328) noted that "independent development of merchant's capital. . . . stands in inverse proportion to the general economic development of society." Commerce does not independently prevent the expansion of the market. On the contrary, it is the quantity of employed capital and the productivity of capital that are determinative. When manufacture remains undeveloped or underdeveloped, it fails to develop large-scale industry and cannot, under these conditions, create its own market through the production and circulation of commodities. Thus, it fails to subject commerce to its rule, and commerce escapes being transformed into a special phase of investment capital. It is this phenomenon that equates the "independent and predominant development of capital as merchant's capital . . . [with] the nonsubjection of production to capital" (Marx, 1967:327–28, 331).

The composition of capital precedes its forms. In the West Indies, for the most part, preindustrial agricultural capital and merchant capital merged to produce agrocommercial capital. This union produced profound consequences for the development of the productive forces and the productivity of labor. In preindustrial economies, the merger of merchant's capital and agricultural capital has tended to put the former in command over the latter, mainly because of merchant capital's control over the circulation process. It is this fact that allows it to act "as a medium through which the law of value is brought to bear on all parts of the economy, particularly the sphere of production" (Kay, 1975:94). Therefore, the failure of merchant capital to break out of "the sphere of circulation to impose the law of value directly on the sphere of production" (Kay, 1975:97) is a key factor in the riddle of underdevelopment in the periphery.

The composition of capital in plantation agriculture also requires specific characterization. This sector of the economy has been, for the most part, represented by a low organic composition of capital. This has been reflected in the preindustrial character of its organization, techniques of production, and surplus extraction: small amounts of fixed capital have been combined with large quantities of unskilled labor in the production process. This low ratio of constant capital to working capital on sugar plantations and the "capital widening character of the fixed capital" has been "antithetical to the advancement of the capitalist mode of production. . . . It is this situation which undermines the production of labor power and value" (de Silva, 1982:470; Watson, 1984a:15–16). The fixed assets of sugar plantations in the Caribbean have been held mainly in land, roads, estates, housing, and direct investment in agriculture. A higher level of productive forces as reflected in technological development through machinery has been mainly confined to the processing of output rather than the actual production process. Any attempt to increase the level of production has generally required a large outlay of capital given the existing organic composition of capital. The incidence of semislavery of Haitian labor in the foreign-owned capitalist plantation of Gulf and Western in the Dominican Republic is ample evidence in support of this argument. The operations of Tate and Lyle and Bookers Brothers, McConnell in the Commonwealth Caribbean are other cases in point.[1] Thus "the initial absence of increasing returns to scale was/is due not merely to a low ratio of fixed capital to working capital but also to the nature of fixed capital itself which is mostly of a non–labor saving type" (de Silva, 1982: 466–467).

However, it is also the case that the noncompetitive nature of this capital and the problems of competition that output (sugar) constantly faces in the world market force it to modernize the production process. It is the latter that, assuming the form of mechanization and the retirement of labor, leads to the swelling of the ranks of the reserve army. Of course, land ownership, distribution, tenure, and use patterns are part of this problem. When this labor turns to the urban manufacturing sector, where one exists, it finds an organization of production based mainly upon small-scale light-manufacturing enterprise and imported technology. Here the problem is "neither capital intensity nor labor intensity per se that characterizes the production technologies in use in the Caribbean manufacturing industries; the main characteristic is import intensity [where] imports dominate manufacturing production [and] where neither capital nor labor is important in relation to output" (Watson, 1984b:31).[2] Agrocommercial capital, foreign capital, and the high import content of export-oriented production in economies that have not yet carried out their agricultural revolution have systematically undermined any possibility of transforming the wage labor–capital relation and developing the productive forces.[3]

Foreign capital and domestic capital operate in separate but related spheres of activity. Foreign capital bears the imprint of exchange value, whereas domestic capital is tied primarily to the sphere of use value. Both are subject to the law of value. Together, they generate contradictions that act as solvents upon the accumulation process. Girvan, Gomes, and Sangster (1983:102–103) have explained how foreign capital and foreign technologies that dominate manufacturing production where neither capital nor labor is important in relation to output reinforce the import-intensity of this production. It is because manufacturing activity in the Caribbean is limited to processes

> such as mixing, blending assembly, packaging and other final stage processes [that] the requirements for plant, machinery and labor (especially skilled labor) are far lower than for activities in which complex chemical transformation processes and physical mechanical processes involving the use of machine tools, precision equipment and other skill intensive processes are important. If manufacturing activities were

carried backwards to the stages of processing primary or raw materials . . . and the manufacture of intermediate products for final processing and packaging, then this would increase the requirements for both labor and capital in relation to final output and correspondingly reduce the foreign exchange cost of the material component of final output. In such a case, the average capital/labor ratio in manufacturing might be higher but—and this is what is important—the average labor/final output ratio would be higher. The employment impact of the gross value of manufacturing production would be correspondingly greater. (1983:102–103)

The so-called surplus population/unlimited supplies of labor— that is, reserve army—is traceable to these just-mentioned phenomena in the case of the Caribbean. It is this reality that neither the neoclassical tradition represented by W. Arthur Lewis (1951,1954) nor the two-sector model of economic development, on one hand, and the dependency/underdevelopment theory, on the other, has fully grasped. Industrial capital is not disposed to organize its global accumulation activities "with the underdevelopment of the periphery as its primary goal: that goal is production of exchange value according to necessary and feasible organic composition of capital, and the political and cultural arrangements that can facilitate that process" (Watson, 1984b:6). Because dependency theory is fundamentally wedded to the ideology of economic nationalism, which it imposes on historical materialism in eclectic ways, it

assumes both explicitly and implicitly that the main mechanism of world accumulation is primitive accumulation which is also considered to be the most effective way to increase the rate of surplus value. The logic behind this assertion, . . . is that capitalism especially under the auspices of metropolitan capital is detrimental to or unable to develop the periphery. . . . Thus we are left with the interpretation that the metropole must rely upon the exploitation of the periphery via primitive accumulation in order to resolve the contradiction of advanced capitalism. (Watson, 1984b:5)

This outlook is inconsistent with the logic of capital developed by Marx in the "critique of political economy."

Of course, the notion of imperialism as a system of empire rather than as a stage in the history of capitalism is also deeply embedded in the ideology of dependency analysis. But underdevelopment is not the result of imperialism as a system of empire but of the modes of production existing within periphery social formations, the relation of the state to the dominant social classes in these formations, the composition of capital, the structure of the productive forces, class formation process and so forth. (Watson, 1984b:6)

The mode of production "constrained the surplus generating capacity and . . . together the capital-widening regimes of plantation capital and merchant capital produced technological stagnation and restricted the surplus generating capacity of the economy" (de Silva, 1982:424). It is not surprising, then, that the most acute problem facing Caribbean economies has been the problem of labor productivity. They have failed to develop or sustain the production of a skilled proletariat, which is the foundation for the creation of exchange value.

As I have already argued, agriculture has failed to sustain an expanding labor force; commerce is not the domain of exchange value; and foreign investment operates according to the logic of productive capital. But both the colonial and neocolonial state and local capital need foreign investment, not for the purposes of underdeveloping the economy, but for the express purpose of creating the conditions for increasing production, raising productivity, and augmenting their respective share of the surplus product.[4]

Thus it is not foreign capital per se, nor the question of the legality or nationality of ownership nor trade or technological dependence, financial or structural openness of the economy nor even the export of the so-called mechanisms of transformation, that are the causes of underdevelopment. These are its symptoms. There is no intention on my part to absolve imperialism from responsibility for the role it plays in this process. But the key question. . . . is whether imperialism can rationally and systematically underdevelop an economy by keeping it tied to primitive accumulation and to the norms peculiar to absolute surplus value in order to exploit it for accumulation on an expanded scale. (Watson, 1984b:9)

The answer to this question is "No." This does not mean that past strategies of colonial and imperialist accumulation in the colonies and neocolonies did not rest on primitive accumulation at previous historical junctures. What it means is that it is necessary to begin with the periodization of capitalism's development in order to understand the connection and relationship between accumulation strategies and historical processes.

The fact that Caribbean economies also specialize in the export of labor power as a commodity is indicative of the internationalization of capital and creation of an *international* proletariat. The failure of Caribbean economies to provide necessary levels of employment at home is the consequence of their failure to solve the problems raised in the following questions:

> To what extent have the Caribbean bourgeoisie and state undermined the pervasiveness of preindustrial and semi-industrial capital in the economy? Have they successfully competed with international capital and consolidated the economic spheres in which the law of value imposes its will upon production? Have they facilitated the development and reproduction of a skilled proletariat? Have they carried out an agrarian revolution? Has the home market been captured for industrial capital? Has the industrialization of agriculture been effected? What is the relationship between imports and production? In other words, has the Caribbean bourgeoisie carried through a capitalist revolution based upon the ascendancy of modern industry? Clearly, the answer is "No." (Watson, 1984b:11)

Unequal Exchange, Accumulation, and Migration Theory

The answers to the questions raised above are the starting point for resolving the riddle of migration from the Caribbean.[5] The structural problems of productivity and unemployment that are found in Caribbean economies force them to specialize in primary production, light manufacturing, and the export of labor. Value transfers take place in direct form through large amounts of labor in their exports and indirectly in the form of professional, technical, and kindred labor exports to the metropoles. (Levels of emigration are influenced by the population and immigration policies of the metropolitan countries.) It is capital that produces a world market for labor and internationalizes labor forces and the reserve army. In this way "commodity production is being increasingly subdivided into fragments which can be assigned to whichever part of the world can provide the most profitable contribution of capital and labor" (Frobel, Heinrichs, and Kreye, 1980:13–14). While it is in the interests of this global market that unequal exchange takes place, the roots of this phenomenon of unequal exchange are traceable to the processes of production and the composition of capital in the various production zones of the world economy: "The labor of a country with a higher productivity of labor is valued as more intense so that the product of one day's work in such a nation is exchanged for the product of more than a day's work in an underdeveloped country" (Mandel, 1978:71–72). Migration is the characteristic form assumed by the international deployment and allocation of labor power. Labor power is the producer of value. The phenomenon of migration must, therefore, be explained through the mechanism of the law of value. This demystifies migration.

There is a lack of consensus on the question of the application of the law of value to the analysis of international trade and the equalization of the rate of profit at the level of international economy. For example, Mandel (1978:66–67, 346, 361–62) argues that because capital is not perfectly mobile at the international level, rates of profit are not equalized at the level of the international economy. Shaikh (1980:53–57) does not believe that this argument is to be taken seriously. Earlier on, I argued that imperialism does not conspire to tie economies of the periphery to primitive accumulation in order to exploit them. "The transfer of surplus value through international exchange is an expression of uneven development" (Watson, 1981:18) at the global level. Shaikh argues: "It is not monopoly or conspiracy upon which uneven development rests but free competition itself: free trade is as much a mechanism of the concentration and centralization of international capital as free exchange within a capitalist nation is for the concentration and centralization of capital" (1980:41).

Thus the transfer of surplus value from the neocolonial economies to the metropole is a feature of underdevelopment, not a cause of it.[6] (Migration from the neocolonies may also be seen in this same light.) Unequal exchange theory is a theory "of the transfer of value from low wage periphery countries to high wage center countries." As such, unequal exchange is to be distinguished from

other forms of value transfer caused by trade restriction (the result of interference with the market, e.g., quotas, tariffs, taxation, exchange rates, etc.) and differential profit rates caused by monopoly activities in production and investments such as lead to unequal accumulation between periphery and center (as a result of the transfer of profits by MNCs). As such unequal exchange assumes conditions of free trade competition and the equalization of rates of profit on a world scale. In essence, then, unequal exchange refers to the exchange of unequal amounts of social value between the periphery and the center primarily through the production of commodities in each zone and which enter into international circulation. (Watson, 1981:79–80)

As formulated by Emmanuel (1973), unequal exchange theory assumes that labor is immobile between countries. Yet industrial migration represents a challenge to this particular assumption of unequal exchange theory, although migration does not take place according to free-trade norms. De Janvry and Kramer (1979:4–12) and Shaikh (1980) distinguished between specific and nonspecific commodities in Third World trade: the basic staples on which periphery economies rely for employment, and foreign exchange and the secondary commodities. Both these categories of commodities have substitutes that are produced in the core. The Third World commodities are generally produced under conditions of monopoly production. Free-trade conditions are not the ones that condition the absorption and expulsion of Caribbean labor: the nature of the mode of production, the composition and forms of capital, the objectives of the capitalists, and the imperialist division of labor are the places we should examine when we look for the answers. We now know why cheap labor exists in the Caribbean. Foreign and domestic capital needs this kind of labor. Given the low average productivity of this labor, both forms of capital rely on it as the means by which to produce cheap commodities. The predicament for the Caribbean is that it must sell its commodities cheap relative to the low productivity of its labor. The paradox is that these commodities are unable to compete with those that incorporate intense labor of the metropolitan economies.

The conditions of unequal exchange that were assumed by Emmanuel (1973) do not characterize the form of value transfer from the Caribbean to the United States[7] Therefore, this means that "the relationship between migration and underdevelopment must be sought beyond the theory of unequal exchange" (Watson, 1981:82). Caribbean exports have generally been produced behind protectionist barriers, and some staples, such as sugar, have been sold under special agreements. Bauxite and petroleum products markets have been controlled by the handful of vertically integrated monopolies that own and/or control the resources, technologies, and markets. Manufactured exports from these countries have invariably faced tariff and other entry restrictions in the North American markets. The forms of value transfer from the Caribbean include those that result from unequal trade relations, state intervention in taxes, tariffs and related restrictions, and the transfer of surplus through the activities of transnational corporations, or TNCs (Watson, 1981:83). Increasingly, Caribbean emigration has been conditioned by these economic factors and the increasing incidence of political repression and authoritarianism in the state and society. Current patterns of instability in the region place emphasis on the development of national security instruments, and the rising tide of economic and political refugees from several avowedly anticommunist Caribbean states have thrown U.S. immigration and refugee policy into a state of confusion and chaos. New thinking and analysis are greatly needed.

Imperialism, the Logic of Capital, and Caribbean Migration

We have seen that the relative immobility of labor at the international level is largely a function of the population and accumulation policies of governments. As each government attempts to implement policies necessary for the reproduction of its social order, it must consider the implications of the flow of labor within and across its borders for these policies. The countries of the Caribbean with "surplus labor" have made emigration into a basic plank in their development strategies. The countries of immigration are concerned about how to regulate the international flow and circulation of this labor power. While it is clear that the internationalization of capital has produced an international proletariat, the relationship between, say, the international labor requirements of capital accumulation and immigration policy is not very obvious or consistent. The political and security needs of imperialism mediate this relationship in different ways. For example, in the early postwar period, when the United States was consolidating its hegemony over the capitalist world order, it was stressed that American immigration policy should reflect the needs of this country for persons who have specialized skills or cultural accomplishments, close family relationships, the population and immigration policies of countries sending immigrants to this country, their past immigration and trade relationships with this country and their assistance to the defense of the friendly and free nations of the World. (Congressional Research Service 1979:16, quoted in Watson, 1981:25)

Throughout the period between 1952 and 1965 these criteria were consistently stressed in American immigration policy.

After 1965 to 1968, when the postwar economic expansion of the U.S. economy was beginning to contract and as America's hegemony was being challenged throughout the Third World, the question of imposing a numerical ceiling on Western Hemisphere immigration soon became predominant in American immigration policy debates. For example, in 1965 a House Judiciary Committee report stated: "The most compelling reason for placing a numerical ceiling upon the Western Hemisphere relates to the worldwide population explosion and the possibility of a sharp increase in immigration from the Western Hemisphere. Testimony before the Judiciary Comittee identified Latin America as the area of the greatest future population growth" (quoted in Watson, 1981:26).

Labor certification provisions and numerical ceilings for the Western Hemisphere were incorporated into the 1965 amendments to the Immigration and Nationality Act. The changing economic situation was at the center of this shift in U.S. immigration policy toward the Caribbean. The 1965 amendments "closed the door" to the alien, and it was only the Secretary of Labor who could open it (Congressional Research Service 1979:58). But competing interests within the state and among different sections of capital played a major role in determining policy outcomes toward migrant labor from Mexico and the Caribbean. In this context, the agricultural interests in the South and Southwest of the United Sates have played a significant and major role in shaping U.S. immigration policy.

The present period of economic crisis has forced U.S. capitalism to embark on a new scientific and technological revolution in an attempt to solve its accumulation crisis. Computers and information processing are two central features of this new revolution in science and technology. Both the production process and the labor process are being restructured. Capitalism as a global system is also being restructured through the international division of labor. This means that new specializations are emerging between and across countries. U.S. capital is on the cutting edge of this global restructuring process. The Caribbean Basin Initiative (CBI) represents a twin program of "security" and "economics" for the obvious purpose of rationalizing and reshaping the relationship between the United States and the Caribbean. In other words, the CBI is the U.S. response to the impact of the economic and political crisis upon Caribbean–U.S. economic and security relations (Watson 1984b:15–42).

New patterns are developing alongside the traditional specializations of the Caribbean Basin countries that provide the United States with large numbers of immigrants. The Reagan administration has established a connection between the regional crisis, immigration, and U.S. "national security interests." The administration argues that the solution of the economic and security problem should stem the flow of immigrants and refugees into the United States. As I have pointed out (Watson, 1984b), this is wishful thinking given the provisions and objectives of the CBI on the one hand and the realities of Caribbean Basin political economies on the other.

While the Reagan administration would like to keep the Caribbean people "where they belong"—in the Caribbean—countries like Haiti, the Dominican Republic, and Jamaica are rapidly developing new specializations tied to the U.S. economy. Haiti is the largest producer of baseballs, although baseball is not played in that country. The Dominican Republic is rapidly becoming a recruitment market for new baseball players for the major league clubs in the United States (*Wall Street Journal,* April 3 and October 12, 1984). This development has profound and ominous implications for the future of Afro-American baseball players in the major leagues. *The Wall Street Journal* of April 3, 1984, reported that there were 110 Latinos in the majors that year. Jamaica is exporting large quantities of marijuana to the United States (*Jamaican Weekly Gleaner,* February 6, 1984), a specialization that has become Jamaica's leading source of foreign exchange. Elements in the state apparatus are said to be deeply involved in this marijuana trade. Barbados has been jockeying for a slot as a major international financial center for offshore banking, while other islands, including

Jamaica (*Wall Street Journal,* May 3, 1984), are catering to the entertainment needs of U.S. capitalists. Jamaica offered the California movie industry a 100-acre site to relocate part of its production structures in order to lower production costs.

According to the U.S. Drug Enforcement Administration, Jamaica exported 1,750 metric tons of marijuana (ganja) to the United States, which amounted to 14 percent of the American market. The wholesale value of this quantity of marijuana was U.S.$2.3 billion. Other estimates place the annual cash crop value of Jamaican ganja at $3.5 billion, which is larger than Jamaica's official GNP. The economy of Jamaica is clearly in a transition based on the ascendancy of marijuana as the primary source of foreign exchange, and of some employment. Tourism and sugar, bauxite, bananas, and other exports, are fading in relative importance to ganja. Entire communities have already made this transition. According to Jeff Stein in an article in the Outlook section of *The Washington Post* of November 11, 1984: "Travelling around Jamaica I found whole villages which had made the transition from dependence on legal commodities to a vast and lawless economy based on marijuana. One might say that the Jamaican marijuana production is a shining example of the free trade market at work"—the very kind that the Reagan administration extols ("Free Market Magic: Jamaica Has Gone to Ganja," p. D1). In other words, many Jamaicans are pulling themselves up by their own "free enterprise" marijuana "bootstraps" and supplying the tourist market in Jamaica and part of the ganja market in the United States with "free enterprise" pot.

Jamaicans are unlikely to return to the low-productivity conditions associated with agriculture and other unskilled activities to try to make a living. When one of the bauxite plants in southwestern Jamaica closed down in 1976, the entire town, which had depended on the bauxite plant for its livelihood, turned to farming ganja because there was nothing else to do there. The ganja crop is "tended so carefully," said Stein, "that it looks like a Japanese rice paddy and the plants—acres upon acres of them—are tended and pruned in long irrigated rows not unlike Florida citrus groves" (p. D2). Low productivity—the failure of the economy to reproduce labor power and value—has forced many Jamaicans, the victims of unemployment, into a new commodity-producing activity on a large scale. When ganja farmers are raided by the police or army, they are known to burn down their neighbors' sugar cane in retaliation. This tends to reduce government pressure against the ganja producers. The structural crisis in the economy of Jamaica finds the World Bank and the International Monetary Fund considering additional devaluation for the Jamaican dollar and additional cuts in social services to create additional foreign exchange to pay for its foreign debt. Stein concludes that "for the Jamaican economic future, it is likely to be rum, ganja and rebellion against drug laws mixed with hopes that tourism can take up some of the slack in currency earnings" (p. D2).

Meanwhile, it is dramatically clear that the Reagan administration cannot provide Seaga with the $3 billion in foreign exchange that Jamaica would need to replace forfeited marijuana revenue, assuming that Seaga would dare to destroy marijuana production. Reagan and Seaga have agreed in principle on the need to interdict the marijuana trade by improving the police and military infrastructure and surveillance techniques. There is no agreement on plans to eliminate ganja production, which is a much more sensitive economic, political, and security issue. Many middle-strata, ruling-class, and lumpen elements associated with the ruling party, the military, and the police may be too closely tied to the marijuana phenomenon for the government to attempt to eliminate it: "The ganja trade is the one, foolproof means to make enough money to get off the island and secure some kind of future." Thus many in Jamaica look to marijuana as the link between rising income and emigration in order to build a future abroad (Stein, pp. D1–2).

There are yet other implications. Jamaica's economy, having failed to sustain the reproduction of labor power and value, is undergoing an unstable restructuring process. Ganja and tourism are not by their nature activities that develop a skilled proletariat. Both are dependent on the international economy and will not yield sustained benefits to the local economy. They do not provide substitutes for foreign imports of food or capital goods. The shift to ganja aggravates the local food production problem and increases the foreign exchange leakage. The ascendancy of ganja to the status of prime mover of the economy is a tragic comment on the degeneration of the social fabric of a society that is Reagan's "showpiece" of a "new Caribbean." Low productivity, tourism, drugs, militarization, emigration, and authoritianism are not cures for underdevelopment. These are concrete expressions of a backward capitalism that has placed itself shamelessly at the service of U.S. imperialism. The way of Jamaica shows the path that the rest of the Commonwealth Caribbean is very likely to follow.

All these developments are in the service sector, which is not a basic producer of exchange value. The CBI provides few prospects for the industrialization of the Caribbean, and none for the transformation of its stagnant agricultural sector (Watson, 1984b). Therefore, the Caribbean reserve army will be reproduced more than before, and the restructuring that is taking place in the world economy will make the labor-absorption problem much more difficult. The increasing visibility of the military and authoritarian politics of the regimes in the national life of all Caribbean neocolonies are features of, and reactions to, the regional economic and security crisis. The Reagan regime has issued an unambiguous message to all Caribbean Basin regimes: whatever they do within and outside their national boundaries will have implications for American security interests. Friends must prove themselves and their reliability by deeds more than by declarations. Friends and allies will be rewarded. Enemies and challengers should expect treatment appropriate to their behavior.

However, the unrestricted access of their skilled labor, unskilled labor, and surplus population to the United States is not one of the rewards that friends and allies can count on. The hard fact is that the accumulation crisis in the United States and the so-called reindustrialization program have left millions of American workers unemployed and many others potentially unemployable. The new model of capital accumulation is based fundamentally upon new labor saving technologies. Some U.S.–based enterprises that rely on unskilled cheap labor may find Caribbean labor very attractive, because of the lower average cost of its social reproduction, but they will also find it easier to rely on abundant unskilled cheap labor supplies at home.

Very little of the productive capital that immigrated to the Third World during the 1970s and early 1980s ended up in the Caribbean. The countries of the Pacific rim and a small number in Latin America were the major beneficiaries of this expansion. Those countries that have not modernized their agriculture (e.g., much of Latin America) have experienced industrial growth combined with agricultural stagnation, ballooning external debt, and rising levels of political repression. Unable to feed their labor forces at lower cost per capita, these countries have found that the potential gains from industrialization were eaten up by the higher cost of imported food, capital goods, and energy resources. This targeted expansion has resulted from the global accumulation strategies of transnational capital. The leading beneficiary countries were able to satisfy the necessary economic, technical, political, and broad cultural requirements for accumulation: an adequate resource base, abundant supplies of labor, a favorable investment climate, and conducive labor relations.

Caribbean regimes have essentially placed themselves at the disposal of the U.S. state and private capital. They have requested and/or have been offered U.S. military assistance to protect them from their own populations in the face of the protracted economic crisis and mounting class struggles. But no extent of expansion of the defense and security forces in the Caribbean will be sufficient to offset chronic levels of unemployment and the propensity to migrate. Caribbean migration is as much an economic expression of, as it is a cultural statement on, the social reality in the region. Migration is a central component of the political economy of development of Caribbean regimes. If there were no foreign exchange problems, unemployment, and the so-called population pressure to propel individuals to emigrate from the Caribbean, there still would be political factors and family reunification bonds that link Caribbean populations to urban centers in the metropolitan countries. The Caribbean is inextricably linked to the metropoles via the international division of labor as a zone of "labor reserves," investment, and trade, as well as recreation. The Caribbean is an area whose populations and social systems are totally penetrated as much by the U.S. communications media, presenting American cultural lifestyles, as by the circular flow of large numbers of Caribbean people, who are residents in North America and Western Europe. Thus the psychological motives of West Indians who migrate to the metropoles are anchored in the history and immediacy of the contrast between acute deprivation of the masses of the Caribbean people and the increasing levels of authoritarianism, relative to the affluence of the bourgeoisie and the middle strata, and the representation and appearance of North American societies as centers of opportunity, affluence, and liberal democratic culture. The wave of Haitian refugees ("boat people") is the most dramatic reaction and response to this contradiction.

Today, the resident population of Jamaica is slightly over 2 million people. Between World War II and the present, approximately 750,000 Jamaicans emigrated to the United States alone. More than 250,000 Jamaicans emigrated to the United Kingdom between the end of World War II and the middle of the 1960s. When other receiving countries such as Canada are considered, it is not inconceivable that there are close to 1 million Jamaicans living abroad. The direct and indirect contribution of Jamaica to the development of labor resources in the metropoles has been immense for a country of its size and standing in the world. Between one-fourth and one-half of Jamaica's population is unemployed. Emigration continues to be a sociocultural and economic response to backward capitalism.

Conclusion

Thinking about migration theory requires new points of departure that break with the conventional wisdom. Neither neoclassical theory nor dependency analysis and unequal exchange theory has proven to be very helpful.[8] The return to the logic of capital, modes of production analysis, organic composition of capital, and accumulation objectives of ruling classes and their respective strata are more fruitful areas for investigation. The postwar period of capitalist expansion and rapid accumulation was fueled, in part, by massive migration flows into the advanced capitalist countries. This partially softened the impact of the unemployment problem in the Caribbean. The persistence of high levels of unemployment was nonetheless the result of the forms and composition of capital that have dominated economic activity in the region. The tendency of these economies to export both skilled and unskilled labor influenced the formulation of the productivity problem in association with migration. For example, it was customary to argue that migration was a cause of underdevelopment because Caribbean economies exported much of their limited supply of skilled labor even in periods of considerable economic expansion (Watson, 1976,1982). The present reality is different, and our knowledge of the historical roots of the problems

of productivity and accumulation in the colonies and neocolonies
has improved. Economic crisis in the capitalist world economy,
class struggles, national liberation struggles, and the emergence of
new models of capital accumulation require new thinking and new
analyses about the migration problem. I have tried to show in a
preliminary way that the critique of political economy provides a
very fruitful path to an understanding of Caribbean migration, not
as a technical problem that results from the disproportionality of
factor endowments, but as a social phenomenon associated with
capitalism as a global system.

Notes

This article is based on a paper originally prepared for a presentation at
the Round Table on International Migration Theory, Illinois Council on
Latin American Studies Conference on Migration from Latin America and
the Caribbean. University of Illinois at Chicago, November 16–17, 1985.

1. In recent years, a number of important transnational corporations (TNCs) have either cut back or terminated their operations in
the Caribbean. Cases include British Petroleum (BP) and Texaco in
Trinidad and Tobago; Caroni Limited (Tate and Lyle) also in Trinidad
and Tobago. A few years ago, the bauxite TNCs closed their operations in Haiti. In the Netherlands Antilles, the operations of Exxon are
closing or about to close. Alcoa, Reynolds, and others no longer consider it viable to operate in Jamaica. Gulf and Western has sold its
operations in the Dominican Republic. As usual, the assembly industries migrate from one island to another in search of new and profitable short-term tax holidays. The Caribbean is no longer attractive
to the TNCs. It is not simply that Caribbean labor is unproductive.
It is the clear result of the global restructuring of the world economy through the international division of labor. New techniques of production and surplus extraction have emerged. Computers and information processing are central to this process. In the world economy, the
mechanisms for incorporating labor into production have been changing rapidly. Industrial relocation within the core economies, and from
the core economies to certain neocolonies, is part of the restructuring
process. For details see Watson (1984b) and Frobel, Heinrichs, and Kreye
(1980).

2. A large amount of empirical data may be found in Watson (1981).
See also Girvan (1983).

3. I have traced the historical development of this phenomenon from 1838 to 1937 in the case of Barbados. Considerable attention was paid to the economic and political formation of the agrocommercial bourgeoisie, the petty bourgeoisie, and the preindustrial rural and urban working class. The role of merchant capital and agrarian capital and their merger and transformation into agrocommercial capital are also detailed. See for details (1985) passim.

4. Among very useful studies on Barbados in the postwar years see, for example, Celia Karch, "The Transformation and Consolidation of the Corporate Plantation Economy in Barbados, 1860–1977" (Ph. D. diss., Rutgers University, 1979), and J. E. Greene and Christine Barrow, *Small Business in Barbados: A Case of Survival* (Cave Hill, Barbados; ISER University of the West Indies, 1979).

5. A few comments are in order about a general theory of international migration and Caribbean migration, on the one hand, and dependency analysis, on the other. It was beyond the scope of this project to generate a general theory of international migration, although it is clear that such a theory is needed in which to situate the study of Caribbean migration. I attempted to suggest the outlines of such a general theory in Watson (1982). But such a general theory cannot be built on unequal exchange theory and dependency analysis as we know them. Both elevate predetermined specialization and exchange relations to the status of theory. They undervalue production relations. Unequal specialization is central to the dependency analysis of Frank, Wallerstein, and Amin. Development is "blocked" in the periphery largely because of the competition from the core capitalist economies. Migration from the colonies and neocolonies becomes a consequence of this process, we are told. As such, migration of labor becomes a "specialization" of the periphery in this predetermined context. This is not an explanation of the causes of migration. The case of Barbados detailed in Watson (1985) challenges the fundamental premises of dependency and world-system analyses.

6. Positivistic Marxism such as is reflected in the writings of Bill Warren, for example, asserts that capitalism and imperialism have not contributed to underdevelopment and backwardness in the colonies and neocolonies. I do not accept this formulation in spite of the fact that I have not detailed the role of imperialism in this project. I decided to hold as given the role of imperialism and to focus on the internal dynamics of underdevelopment. This may seem contradictory, given the fact that the colonial and neocolonial experiences have been part of the global process of reproduction and accumulation. However, my emphasis was placed upon a concrete analysis of the role of international dynamics in a concrete situation. I am currently working on a framework for the

study of capitalist development in the British West Indies after emancipation. See Watson (1984b,1985).

7. Essentially, unequal exchange theory addresses the special case rather than the general case when it comes to international accumulation and underdevelopment. It has much more to say about the formation of international prices where capital is mobile and labor is immobile. It is silent on international migration. The Caribbean does not constitute a special case, and it is clear that an adequate theory of underdevelopment as well as a theory of migration must be placed within a general theory of capitalist accumulation on a global scale. We have to know why capital does not flow en masse to the colonies and neocolonies. Neither unequal exchange theory nor dependency analysis properly account for this. The proper starting point is with production and production relations.

8. See Watson (1981).

References

Amin, Samir (1974). *Accumulation on a World Scale: A Critique of the Theory of Underdevelopment*. New York: Monthly Review Press.

———— (1976). *Unequal Development: An Essay on the Social Formations of Peripheral Capitalism*. New York: Monthly Review Press.

De Janvry, Alain, and Frank Kramer (1979). "The Limits of Unequal Exchange." *Review of Radical Political Economics* 4:3–15.

De Silva, S. B. D. (1982). *The Political Economy of Underdevelopment*. Boston: Routledge and Kegan Paul.

Frobel, Folker, Jurgen Heinrichs, and Otto Kreye (1980). *The New International Division of Labor*. New York: Cambridge University Press.

Girvan, Norman, P. I. Gomes, and B. G. Sangster (1983). *Technology Policies for Small Developing Economies: A Study of the Caribbean*. Mona, Jamaica: Caribbean Technology Studies Project.

Jamaican Weekly Gleaner (North American edition) (1984). "Illegal Drug Traffic: Jamaica Said Significant Transportation Port." February 6.

Kay, Geoffrey (1975). *Development and Underdevelopment*. New York: St. Martin's Press.

Lewis, Sir W. Arthur (1951). *The Industrialization of the British West Indies:* Bridgetown, Barbados: Advocate Printing.

———— (1954). *Economic Development with Unlimited Supplies of Labor*. Manchester: Manchester University of Economic Research.

Marx, Karl (1967). *Capital: A Critique of Political Economy*. Volume 3 [1894]. Friedrich Engels, ed. New York: International Publishers.

———— (1973). *Grundrisse: Foundation of the Critique of Political Economy* (1857–58). Martin Nicolaus, ed. Harmondsworth: Penguin.

Marx, Karl, and F. Engels (1971). "Forced Emigration." In *Ireland and the Irish Question*. Moscow: Progress Publishers.

Palma, Gabriel (1978). "Dependency: A Formal Theory of Underdevelopment or a Methodology for the Analysis of Concrete Situations of Dependency?" *World Development* 6 (July–August).

Shaikh, Anwar (1980). "Foreign Trade and the Law of Value Part II." *Science and Society* 44:27–57.

United States Immigration Law and Policy 1952–1979 (1979). Report Prepared by the Congressional Research Service at the Request of Senator Edward Kennedy, Chairman, Committee on the Judiciary, United States Senate, Upon the Formation of the Select Commission of Immigration and Refugee Policy. Washington, D.C.: U.S. Government Printing Office.

Wallerstein, Immanuel (1974). *The Modern World-System*. New York: Academic Press.

Wall Street Journal (1984a). "Diamond Sparklers: Burst of Juan Samuel into Baseball Big Time Marks Latins' Uprising: Phillies' Dominican Rookie is Among 110 Latinos in the Majors This Year." April 3.

——— (1984b). "Yanqui Helps Latins Prepare for a Future in or out of Baseball." October 12.

Watson, Hilbourne A. (1976). "International Migration and the Political Economy of Underdevelopment: The Commonwealth Caribbean Experience." In S. Bryce-Laporte and Delores Mortimer, eds., *Caribbean Migration to the United States*. Washington, D.C.: Smithsonian Research Institute on Immigration and Ethnic Studies.

——— (1981). "The United States and the West Indies: International Migration and Unequal Exchange." Presented at the Colloquium on International Relations and International Migration. Sponsored by the Insituto de Investigaciones Sociales, National Autonomous University of México, Mexico City, October 26–29.

——— (1982). "Theoretical and Methodological Problems in Caribbean Migration Research: Conditions and Causality." *Social and Economic Studies*, March, pp. 165–205.

——— (1984a). "Merchant Capital, Transnational Banks and Underdevelopment in the Commonwealth Caribbean." Paper delivered at the Conference on New Perspectives on Caribbean Studies Toward the Twenty-first Century. Hunter College, New York, August 28–September 1.

——— (1984b). "The Caribbean Basin Initiative and Caribbean Development: A Critical Analysis." *Contemporary Marxism* 10 (Spring).

——— (1985a). "Merchant Capital and the Consolidation of Backward Capitalism in Barbados: From Emancipatin to 1937." Paper presented at the XII International Congress of the Latin American Studies Association, Albuquerque, New Mexico, April 17–20.

——— (1985b). "Caribbean Development in the 1970s." *El Caribe Contemporaneo* 2:5.

——— (1985c). "International Migration and Unequal Exchange." In Gerald Pierre Charles, ed., *Capital Transnacional y Ejercito Migrante de Reserva*. Mexico City.

CHAPTER 10

The Consistency of a Revolutionary Movement: Peru's Sendero Luminoso and Its Texts, 1965–1986

Peter T. Johnson

The insurrectional character of a revolutionary movement makes much of its information inaccessible, because of either its oral or clandestine nature. Other types of documentation exist that suggest the substance of such "forbidden" areas or even synthesize aspects of the revolutionaries' concerns. Here one finds the formulation of the plans for revolution as well as the ideological splits and other internal disagreements that characterize most of these groups. To understand a movement's development of political prominence or military might, close attention must be paid to the details of its internal workings. Peru's Sendero Luminoso (Shining Path) is one of various left-wing Latin American guerrilla organizations consisting of compact cells that are difficult for government intelligence services to infiltrate. Given the selectivity with which the revolutionaries grant interviews or release information to what they often perceive as a hostile press, it is difficult to obtain the documentation necessary to understand the movement. Indeed, the ability to identify what constitutes a revolutionary movement is in question: by the time the ideological fights end in schisms, reconciliation, or the elimination of opponents, key ideological and political dimensions for assessing the guerillas could be lost.

Such circumstances do not negate the importance of studying all phases of a guerilla movement's life. Both libraries and scholars can be faulted for not taking seriously those advocating the overthrow of government through violent means. Certainly it is far more difficult for libraries to identify and obtain the pamphlets, broadsides, and short-lived serials that are the bulk of a movement's literature than to rely on the standard secondary accounts and mainline journals, newspapers, and news magazines, which, after all, are thought to satisfy all but the meticulous scholar.

The emergence of yet another guerrilla group forces the researcher to make a comparative assessment, or else to doubt the significance of all movements. Which one holds the promise of maturing, of wielding truly national influence, and of gaining control of the state? Is an assessment of marginal or alienated political minorities worth preparing, or even feasible, given the obscurity of their literature and the likelihood that a topical or longitudinal analysis will not be possible? Such inherent difficulties suggest that revolutionary movements are not considered fully, or at least not at their inception or during the early phases of their regional and national organizing efforts.

What about the guerrillas themselves, when approached from the perspective of their own literature? No other source exists that provides information with this intimacy. Historical objective conditions that are subjectively realized and make revolution possible must serve as the basis for any scholarly analysis. The guerrillas' prescriptions for society merit a careful assessment, taking into consideration their ideological origins, the strategy for achieving them, and the guerrillas' adherence to them. Such analysis is only possible using a representative collection of key publications, such as those that document a movement's meetings, congresses, solidarity groups or otherwise infiltrated interest groups, recruiting literature, and theoretical essays by the leadership.

Sendero Luminoso: Historical Background

The literature on the Sendero Luminoso is but one example among many in Latin American studies of overreliance on secondary sources resulting in flawed interpretations. From the earliest positions of its founder, Abimael Guzmán, to the formal establishment of his Communist party (CP) faction and its subsequent armed engagement of government forces, the movement's objectives were enunciated and refined within a nationalist and ideological context. Much commentary characterizes it as a hermetic group and considers it difficult to discern its real intentions. A review of a cross section of the literature for the fifteen years preceding their first armed attack suggests that Sendero Luminoso leaders were open about their intentions and objectives. The fact that few observers chose to place much credence in their successfully implementing a strategy, especially one defined within a Marxist-Leninist-Maoist context combined with the historical and ideological interpretations of the Peruvian writer and political activist José Carlos Mariátegui (1895–1930), emphasizes the prejudices with which many social scientists operate and which influence the policies of research libraries collecting the publications of such groups.

The early phase of the movement's activities requires attention to the nationalist roots of its ideology. As with other factions of the Communist movement, Mariátegui provided a valuable historical base for Sendero Luminoso. Guzmán and a few associates successfully combined Mariátegui's ideological interpretations of the country's feudal realities with the theoretical elements that proved compatible with Mao's thought, an emphasis on peasantry, and a rural-based revolutionary movement. The ample documentation on Mariátegui and his work enables the movement to be scrutinized more closely than is possible with some other Latin American movements, which use individuals to create a mythology of revolutionary deeds but provide little, if any, political philosophy beyond the necessary call for independence or freedom from foreign economic control. Sendero Luminoso's strong adherence to Mariátegui's teachings, therefore, offers an opportunity to appraise the movement's unique Peruvian elements and those that may be categorized as standard Marxism-Leninism.

From this historical dimension, and using texts long available in Peru, Sendero Luminoso developed a range of media to convey its message. Some material is for mass consumption. Other imprints serve to document the movement's internal debates and, as such, have more limited appeal and availability. Pamphlets, printed slogans, and graffiti augment these more formal imprints. Other forms of communication are more symbolic. Sendero Luminoso began by hanging dead dogs on lampposts and soon established two other symbols of its expanding strength: the urban blackouts due to bombed electric pylons and the burning hammer and sickle on mountainsides overlooking the suddenly darkened cities. The pres-

Table 10.1 Deaths Attributed to Sendero Luminoso Guerrilla Action,
May 1980–July 1987

Victims' Affiliation	1980	1981	1982	1983	1984	1985	1986	1987
Armed forces and police	0	6	32	59	81	45	125	86
Civilians	3	5	52	692	1,785	770	451	245
Presumed Senderistas	9	71	109	1,226	1,721	660	811	170
Total	12	82	193	1,977	3,587	1,475	1,387	501

Sources: Desco–Banco de Datos en base a CARETAS, no. 885, and *Resumen semanal–Desco*, 1987 monthly issues.

ence of the red flag is another well-reported symbol in highland villages temporarily occupied by Sendero Luminoso.

Guerrilla-produced information displays a directness and purity of ideology that no secondary interpretation can offer. If the nature of Sendero Luminoso as a Peruvian revolutionary movement of increasing national significance is to be understood and assessed accurately, then close readings of publications produced over nearly twenty years become necessary. Given the violence and socioeconomic implications of Sendero Luminoso's continuing successes, to dismiss these guerrillas as a fanatical band is not supported by the facts (e.g., between 1980 and mid-1987, at least 9,200 Peruvian civilians, members of the armed forces and police, and presumed Senderistas were reported killed in violence associated with the movement). Failure to account for the origin, inspiration, and endurance of Sendero Luminoso was a serious error in political judgment made by the Belaúnde government. The ample evidence covering CP congresses, position papers, student movement literature, and the like can reveal much of importance for understanding what Sendero Luminoso is, why it prevails, and on what basis it might succeed.

Sendero Luminoso: Refining Its Ideology and Recruiting

The movement now known as Sendero Luminoso traces its origins to the various philosophical tenets of Marx, Lenin, Mao, and Mariátegui. Nearly a half century earlier, Mariátegui had critically analyzed Peruvian society with the help of Marxism. Upon Mariátegui's conclusions, Guzmán elaborated a course of action to address the injustices that Peruvians experienced. As Guzmán demonstrated in his 1961 law school thesis, "El Estado democrático-burgués," his command of Marxist theory was thorough. The inspiration for the Peruvian assessment and prescription came from Mao and his experience in the countryside. Never before had the teachings of Mao figured centrally in a Peruvian political movement. The CP over the years had adhered to the Moscow line and continued to do so throughout the 1960s, when the party experienced the growth of dissident factions. Attracted to the Cuban Revolution and its attempt to influence revolutions in the Andes in the mid-1960s, various CP members began unsuccessful guerrilla actions. Slightly later, the appeal of the Chinese Cultural Revolution as an alternative emphasizing the application of Maoist thought captivated a small group of Marxists. Guzmán and others began to assess its applicability to Peruvian reality. By combining Mariátegui's analysis of Peruvian society's feudal structure and employing strategies for change using Maoist ideology, Guzmán could weld a more dynamic and nationally sensitive political agenda. Guzmán then emphasized mastery of ideology, which would be employed successfully to exercise control over the movement, rather than terror tactics, which lacked any philosophical foundation.

The emergence of Sendero Luminoso as a virulent guerrilla movement in 1980 caught Peruvians and foreign observers alike by surprise. While the military's opponents were diverse, none appeared to reject adamantly the return to democratic rule that the elections promised. Judging from Sendero Luminoso's attacks on polling centers in Ayacucho, the political transaction as they interpreted it would only perpetuate peasant subjugation and capitalist control over the economy.

Why was such a position taken? A review of the preceding fifteen years indicates why and how Sendero Luminoso evolved through a series of disagreements and breaks within the CP, ultimately to build its own power base in Ayacucho. Much of the documentation consists of different CP publications, few of which had mass-circulation potential or were intended for a broad readership.

During much of this time, the party had to operate clandestinely, which further complicated distribution. Yet the atmosphere of Peru never approached the repression in Argentina or Chile under military rule. In those countries, CP publications constituted a forbidden literature. In Peru, the CP did not represent a threat to the military comparable with that perceived by the dictators of the Southern Cone countries. However, with the 1980s bombing campaign, Sendero Luminoso reemerged nationally as a small but dangerously transformed CP splinter movement previously known only to CP members. Possessing their literature became an invitation to incarceration. The amount of documentation that can be correctly attributed to the Sendero Luminoso decreased, yet the variety increased. Prior to 1980, ideological tracts designed for internal consumption, reports on meetings, and recruiting materials directed at students or women predominated. As of 1980, the organizational literature devoted to party meetings virtually ceased, and training manuals, simplified translations of Mao's works couched in a Peruvian idiom, and recruiting propaganda written for the masses came to dominate Sendero Luminoso's production.

Much of the literature about Sendero Luminoso begins its discussion of the movement with its first armed action in 1980 or makes only sporadic references to the preceding fifteen years of the movement's growth.[1] This failure to consult the earlier literature, which provides great detail about the ideological position, strategy, and objectives of the movement, results in many articles professing the novelty of the Sendero Luminoso. Scrutiny of the texts issued by the CP, as well as those issued by groups controlled by the Sendero Luminoso leadership, indicates a clear and consistent perception of what was necessary to transform in Peru and why an armed struggle originating in rural areas was the only acceptable course to pursue. At the Fifth National Conference of the CP, held in 1965, the ideas of Mao figured prominently, at the expense of Moscow and Havana. Here the strategy for the party is delineated: (1) the emphasis by the party on organizing the countryside: (2) the formation of a popular army for the armed struggle; (3) the reorganization and strengthening of national commissions of workers; (4) the creation of corresponding clandestine organs to involve the masses and direct their attention to the liberation of the countryside; and (5) the establishment and support of links among students, workers, and peasants (Partido Comunista Peruano [PCP], 1965a:100; 1965b:1–14). Each element of their program became incorporated into the organizing efforts of the 1970s and the actions of the 1980s.

A key to understanding Sendero Luminoso's survival in the years of intraparty disputes is recognizing how firmly party leadership believed in the strategy announced at the Fifth National Conference. Its development required a laboratory relatively free from the ideological impurities present in Lima. The reopened Universidad Nacional de San Cristóbal de Huamanga (UNSCH) offered such a setting, and Guzmán retreated to it, soon to be joined by like-minded Maoists fluent in the works of Marx, Lenin, and Mariátegui. Debate continued among intellectuals, but the dominant view generally reflected that of earlier statements on the vitality of armed struggle originating in the countryside, the encirclement of the cities, and the ultimate control of the country by the party as a result of this peasant-based (albeit intellectual-led) revolution. At the Ayacuchan Seminario de Reforma Universitaria "José Carlos Mariátegui," which ended in November 1968, emphasis first appears on the importance of active participation in the liberation of the Peruvian people by those connected with the university. The only road to power is the *guerra popular*, which will originate in the countryside and ultimately reach the cities. The necessity of a violent revolution is unquestioned. This demarcated the Sendero Luminoso group from others within the CP who believed that some form of accommodation with non-Communist parties was possible and even desirable in order to achieve the preconditions for a proletarian revolution. The seminar condemned Yankee and Soviet imperialism and, by association, Cuba (as Moscow's puppet state). Class struggle can be advanced successfully only along the ideological lines of Mao's philosophy and Mariátegui's analysis of Peru's socioeconomic conditions combined with Marxism-Leninism.[2]

The belief in the inevitability of armed struggle became a preeminent position between 1973 and 1977. Success depended on preparation, especially the support of the peasants, which required working alongside and with them. Without this level of participation, it would be impossible to gain their assistance. This foresight attested to the leadership's recognition of the crucial importance of the peasantry. Guzmán and other leaders believed that large gains could be realized from such a strategy (PCP, 1965a:72–73). Previous failures, especially of the Movimiento de la Izquierda Revolucionaria (MIR) in La Convención, illustrated the futility of not forming a single wide front to wage a prolonged armed struggle. MIR's error of not securing peasant support, and operating with the government's knowledge of its location and military objectives, could not be repeated.[3] Thorough preparation and success in the countryside would enable urban workers to link themselves with the armed struggle.[4] This type of strategy, carefully developed and systematically propagandized among university students, highland peasants, and workers, succeeded in adding to the ranks of adherents. Their conviction of the "correctness" of the armed struggle as delineated by Sendero Luminoso leaders owes a great deal to the refinement of the policy in the period 1965 to 1968. The successful meshing of Mariátegui's assessment of the country's weaknesses and the type of measures required to alleviate the injustices combined well with Maoist thought on the central importance of the peasantry to revolution.

Revisionism remained a party concern for the last half of the 1960s, which reflects the international impact of the Sino-Soviet split. Central to the factionalism was a 1966 adoption by the Comisión Política of the CP of Maoism as the "instrumento de trabajo revolucionario y como guía de sus luchas, aplicado a la realidad concreta de nuestro país . . ." (PCP, 1969a:91–92). This resulted in a pro-peasant revisionist position that contributed to the splits that occurred later. Ample discussions of the *revisionismo criollo* provide insights into the growing disagreements within the party. José Sotomayor, as representative of the Comité Regional de Ayacucho (CRA), is attacked for his concurrence with the Chinese Central Committee's position on questions of the international Communist movement. As close associates of Guzmán, the party's national leaders became the subject of attack, which ultimately led to the CRA's rejecting a centralized direction in the party. The perceived domination of the CP's Comisión Política by Lima's representatives was also important to the disagreements. The hard sacrifices that CRA members anticipated having to make for the revolution to succeed were not thought compatible with the preferred comforts of city life (PCP, 1968:51–58). While there were other reasons for the split, those noted provide insights into the concerns that become the dominant features of the Sendero Luminoso's strategy during the 1970s and 1980s. By challenging national leadership yet failing to gain control of the party's administration, the CRA effectively removed itself from the national organization. The party recognized that the weight of its work in the countryside was minimal and in the end had to relinquish the area to the "sectarians" (PCP, 1968:48).

The conference proceedings from this period reveal an extraordinarily doctrinaire group among several CP factions. They survived by severing themselves from Central Committee and General Secretariat control, which the remoteness of Ayacucho helped accomplish. Guzmán and his colleagues' assurance of the "correctness" of armed struggle growing out of the countryside led to concentrated efforts to strengthen the movement's ideological-political base. This required infiltrating existing organizations catering to students', peasants', and women's interests to recruit members with propaganda. Although much of the literature produced by these groups in the next decade is scarce, there is enough to give an idea of the consistency of adherence to the ideological lines set forth in the mid-1960s. The opposition to the various factions favoring all or selected aspects of the Sendero Luminoso ideology also provide criticism and critiques of the errors of these groups. In short, the record is not as thin as has been thought.

By 1968, Sendero's leadership had retreated almost exclusively to its Ayacuchan stronghold and engaged in various public and semiclandestine organizing efforts. Referring to the fact that Mariátegui had not appeared publicly as a Communist, Sendero Luminoso leaders charged the *liquidacionistas* with trying to eliminate the essence of the partisan organization, which was its clandestine and, by extension, regionalist character (Bandera Roja [BR], 1970a:10–11). With the country under a military junta, the CP discerned its route to political power as one of revolutionary violence and a *guerra popular*. Its strategy was to organize the countryside into *fuerzas armadas populares* (PCP, 1969b:5–6). As Mariátegui had instructed, recruiting propaganda would be directed toward workers and peasants, thus introducing a class emphasis to politics and emphasizing Marxist-Leninist, and Maoist thought (BR, 1969:14). By the end of 1969, with fully a decade remaining before Sendero Luminoso leadership would activate its plans for armed struggle, the basis for the revolution had been debated widely among CP members and rejected by some for its strong Maoist influences. The documents of the period leave no doubt that a hard-core group based in Ayacucho (but with sympathizers in Lima's universities) had analyzed Peru's problems and arrived at the conclusion that a complete reordering of the country along the lines Mariátegui had advocated a half century before had to be accomplished. By moving into clandestine organizing efforts directed at ultimately seizing power through a violent revolution originating in the countryside, the Sendero Luminoso leadership established an intransigent position. The mainstream of the CP failed to concur with this strategy. Nonetheless, splinter groups emerged in the early 1970s that enabled a strengthening through the addition of ideologues and cadres in both rural and urban areas.

The literature at this point begins shifting from primarily CP documents to works that are the movement's recruiting literature. Several national events enabled Sendero Luminoso's positions to be advocated publicly under the general guise of opposing the military government. Both the education and the agrarian reform laws provoked much discussion in various publications. By opposing these measures, Sendero Luminoso could criticize and condemn the government as fascist and beholden to the capitalist (i.e., bourgeois) and landowner interests, as well as to the U.S. imperialists. By constant repetition in meetings (as reported in proceedings) and in propaganda leaflets for a wider readership, Sendero Luminoso claimed that the problems of Peru could not be resolved by the military government or by parliamentary democracies based on coalitions. Sendero Luminoso presented its solution: a violent, peasant-based revolution as the only means for a thorough national transformation. To emphasize the nationalist quality of its movement, Mariátegui figured prominently in Sendero Luminoso's illustrations and quotations. The juxtaposition of his thought with Mao's further strengthened the association between the two in the minds of the populace. This legitimizing tactic enabled Mao's ideology and revolutionary strategy to be accepted as valid and appropriate for Peru. Superficial comparisons between the two men and their countries also appeared, but to sophisticated readers these must have been somewhat less than convincing. However, to the general reader, at whom this literature was directed, the parallels seemed convincing. One had only to consider the great advances that China had achieved under Maoism to realize that Peru, following the same illuminated path, could also elevate peasants to the positions of respect and power while overthrowing the foreign capitalists and native bourgeoisie who controlled and exploited the country. Recruitment and training in the 1970s derived their inspiration from this approach.

The linkage of Mariátegui to the revolutionary strategy appears to increase in the literature of the early 1970s. Declaring that the organization's independence or separation from revolutionary violence was now impossible, and that clandestine work will strengthen the movement because counterrevolutionaries never destroy a people so organized, Sendero Luminoso leaders proceeded to interweave their interpretation of Mariátegui into all aspects of the propaganda. A *guerra popular* is "la guerra del pueblo entero" and, as such, requires the unity in thought, action, spirit, and faith that only Mariátegui gives. Within the mass organizations, a small directing nucleus, agile and dynamic, must be built to lead the masses. Great attention must be given to the possibility of infiltration by counterrevolutionary forces. The ideological reconstruction and policies of the mass organizations will also derive their inspiration from Mariátegui (BR, 1970b:13–16). It is abundantly clear that neither Moscow nor Havana has anything to offer these revolutionaries: reconciliation with their revisionist Partido Comunista Peruano was impossible.

By incorporating student and peasant interests into the debate about the legal changes in agrarian reform and education, an excellent mobilizing potential was exploited. The Ley Agraria came under repeated attack for failing to destroy the landowner class. Expropriation of excess lands and limits and regulations on land use were counterrevolutionary measures and actively beneficial to landowners, Sendero Luminoso leaders charged. Only confiscation would be a revolutionary measure, and that was not part of the military's intentions (Federación Universitaria Huamanga, 1972b: 1; Ley, n.d.).

Student organizing efforts left a substantial body of documentation at universities in Ayacucho and Lima. Once again, the military proposal for reform provided the best circumstances for political mobilization. At the UNSCH, the student Federación advocated the university's serving the masses; such a transformation could be built only within a revolutionary context. It charged the Comisión Estatutaria Nacional with attempting to destroy the university through its legal measures. The Federación called for a series of modifications to the Ley General de Educación and a general freeing of the university from influences by the Church and the military. If these demands were not met, the university would become a force of reaction and then the people would destroy it. The university should be in the service of the revolution, and a university alliance with the masses would ensure its future (Federación Universitaria de San Cristóbal, 1972a:1–3; Peru. Comisión de Reforma, 1971: 36–50).

At the same time, the Frente Estudiantil Revolucionario (FER), a Marxist-Leninist-Maoist group with strong acceptance of the Declaration of Principles of FER de Ayacucho (1965), was engaged in a process of reconstruction (until mid-1972) after embracing Mariátegui and rejecting the military junta, the Havana and Moscow lines, American Popular Revolutionary Alliance (APRA), and the Christian Democrats. In its rebuilding, FER recognized that one of its chief deficiencies was its lack of written materials, especially fliers and documents for the masses, so that little propaganda was available on such important questions as the reconstruction of the representative organs through and with class bases. FER's limited integration in legal and semilegal organizations of the universities indicated that at this stage its contacts with other revolutionary student groups and nonstudent organizations caused concern to the leadership (FER, 1972a:5; 1972b:11–14).[5] By 1974, FER had consolidated and operated openly as it continued rebuilding along the lines of Mariátegui's teachings. FER perceives itself not only as *the* university's organization against the military government, but also as the movement that gained its legitimacy from originating in class struggle and in organizing the masses. As part of such a process, the leadership notes the particular importance of the politicization of university women. Secciones Femeninas began to appear by late 1974 (Federación Estudiantil Revolucionaria, 1974:7–13; Frente Estudiantil, 1974:unpaginated). These activities further demonstrate Sendero Luminoso's careful organizing efforts and effectiveness in broadening its base of support to include students and women especially. With such political exposure, students became recruits and supporters then and in the 1980s. The military's failure to make significant improvements in the socioeconomic conditions of the Department of Ayacucho further strengthened Sendero Luminoso's position as a political option for peasants and disaffected educated youth.

It was also in 1974 that Guzmán and his colleagues increased their power over the student movement, in part by advocating such popular measures as increased enrollment (in five years, UNSCH had gone from 900 to 4,000 students), larger dining facilities (from serving 500 to 2,000, accompanied by a price freeze), the suspension of entrance exams, and the formation of the Asociación de Docentes-SUTE-UNSCH (Frente Democrático, 1974:1–10). The opposition to these and other measures that Sendero Luminoso advocated made the UNSCH a combative setting during these years (Palmer, 1986:127–146). As a previously outlined organizing strategy, the systematic work with students at the UNSCH and to a lesser extent in Lima established the legitimacy and viability of Sendero Luminoso, thereby enabling it to retain and increase the participation of university-trained youth in the post-1980 revolutionary phase. While much of the literature of the period is repetitive, the concepts—always advanced within a nationalist setting—succeeded in attracting the youth to the ranks of Sendero Luminoso. Much of this documentation emphasizes the unity of the different groups composing the rural population. By accentuating the concept of class solidarity among the literate, Sendero Luminoso was assured of a cadre for transmitting propaganda to the substantially illiterate masses, which became a major target for recruitment during the 1970s. This phase of activity involves far more oral work, particularly by village schoolteachers (many trained in UNSCH), and small printed fliers augmented by wall graffiti. While one may surmise that the message was identical or similar for the *comuneros* (villagers), little printed evidence exists. The success in recruiting among these groups in the early 1980s does suggest that visions of a rural-based revolution were commonly endorsed.

What appears to be a remarkable presence of women in leadership positions and within the Sendero Luminoso cells is frequently noted by journalists in the 1980s.[6] Peruvians stress the equality and leadership capacity demonstrated by these women.[7] Mariátegui recognized the importance of women to Peru, arguing that a liberation movement should be one of women and not feminists. The Movimiento Femenino Popular (MFP) emerged with this background, and its Declaración de Principios (Ayacucho, September 1973) recognized women as an oppressed group because of the class nature of society. For the MFP, women were militant fighters rather than apolitical human beings. Mobilization and organizing efforts drew upon research and brought a need to make propaganda. The development of the means of revolutionary agitation and propaganda became a continuing commitment for the MFP, which fully expected to participate in all forms of worker-organizing efforts. The responsibility of women, as the oppressed majority, became that of unifying the people into class organizations of the masses. Adherence to Mariátegui's thought and democratic centralism was believed to ensure ultimately a change in the status of Peruvian women (Centro Femenino, 1974:64–68; MFP, 1975:54–59, 66–69; 1977:1–4).[8]

The Era of the *Guerra Popular*

In retrospect, the 1970s were confrontational years for Sendero Luminoso leaders. They had been expelled from the country's Moscow-line CP and left with only their conviction that a new party had to be built around the ideology of Mao and Mariátegui. Certain aspects of reconstruction required secrecy, thereby leaving documentation only of the results of internal debates for the researcher, only the possibility of attempting to isolate these discussions among the issues covered in publications from various front organizations. Both sources provide evidence of the group's unswerving commitment to achieving national control by applying the teachings of Mao, Mariátegui, Marx, and Lenin. As the 1980s approached, it became clear that Guzmán was the unquestioned interpreter or, as proclaimed, "fourth sword of Marxism." The *guerra popular* was the consecration of revolutionary violence, with peasants providing the class base, albeit with mestizo or white intellectuals holding the top ideological leadership. Since Mariátegui had emphasized peasant participation and the countryside as the launching point of the revolution, Sendero Luminoso can be considered as an attempt to fulfill a historic agenda (*BR*, 1976:5). This adherence to armed struggle required the party to reject participation in the forthcoming elections. Change could not come through "parliamentary cretinism" (*Impulsemos*, 1978:5–6). Since the emergence of Sendero Luminoso as the Partido Comunista del Perú–por el Sendero Luminoso de José Carlos Mariátegui in 1970, Guzmán had unified various CP factions that believed in the peasants' central role in the revolution and the fact that the countryside had to be seized and secured before engaging in the city. This revolution's course is portrayed as one in stages, with interruptions, yet always ideologically consistent with national, democratic, and popular principles (*Forjemonos,* 1978:2).[9]

The literature of the 1980s shifts its focus to become more "consumer oriented," with its vocabulary, message, and format designed for mass appeal and distribution. By continually emphasizing the same points and linking them to contemporary matters (e.g., national elections and guerrilla warfare), these publications, often of no more than one or two pages, can be quickly produced and distributed. By stressing the unified nature of classes in this struggle for "life," Sendero Luminoso successfully combines Marxist-Leninist doctrine with Mariátegui's focus on Peruvian conditions. The creation of this promising future with bread, education, rights, liberties, and freedom from want results from armed struggle (Partido Comunista del Perú [PCdelP], 1–2; 1981b:13, 22–25).

This phase of the literature provides limited information on the nature of the state to be created, how it will be governed, and other pragmatic public policy considerations. In 1981 and 1982, the Comités Populares originated and constituted the initial forms of *Nuevo Poder.* From 1983 to 1985, the government's opposition to the imposition of *Nuevo Poder* in the highlands resulted in 20,000 Sendero Luminoso actions, which revealed the strength of the Ejército Guerrillero Popular. Sendero Luminoso's claim that the *Nuevo Poder* now operates with state functions could be true, given the broad scale of activities throughout the southern and central highlands. Literature of this period also refers to the formation of the República Popular de Nueva Democracia, in which the Comités Populares are central bases of support (PCdelP, 1985a:2, 1985b:12; 1987:46–47). Given the attraction of "true" participation in a government, there should be no reason to support the existing one by voting, so the literature associates voting with an endorsement of the misery, genocide, and state violence that Ayacuchanos experienced during the preceding parliamentary democracy and continue to experience. To vote would be a betrayal of those who have sacrificed themselves in building the *Nuevo Poder* (PCdelP, 1985a:6–7).[10]

Practical and Methodological Problems
of Studying the Sendero Luminoso

This revolutionary group is imbued with a range of survival mechanisms developed with considerable care by what appears to be an extraordinarily able and dedicated leadership. Sheer tenacity and clarity of vision contribute to their organizational successes, as nationally coordinated actions have demonstrated repeatedly. Their unswerving faith in the correctness of Marxist-Leninist-Maoist philosophy, Mariátegui's analysis of Peru, and Guzmán's strategy utilizing their principles of revolution merit recognition and much greater study. A key to understanding how these different ideologies were adapted to the Peruvian situation is to be found in the Sendero Luminoso leadership. Fortunately, several leaders have written works that prove germane to understanding the evolution of the movement.[11] Tracing the small band of Maoists through the CP internal squabbles of the 1960s and early 1970s is feasible because of their uncompromising adherence to Maoism and vitriolic denunciations of Moscow, Havana, and Washington as revisionist and imperialist, respectively. While the full proceedings of the national conferences are the publicly known documents for conveying these interpretations, consideration must also be given to the various position papers, statements, and accounts of conferences that deal with revisionism. These documents reveal strategy that naturally leads to the literature produced for and by interest groups created by the Sendero Luminoso to advance their objectives, or infiltrated by them to gain control. The nature of these organizations varies. Those serving students tend to be the most sophisticated in structure and to publish literature best characterized by its lengthy sections on ideology or doctrinaire attacks on government policies. Other publications meeting the needs of local interests discuss issues within fewer pages and with a simpler vocabulary. In both, readers are reminded continually of the leading position that peasants hold in the Maoist-Mariátegui–inspired movement.

This literature is one of several records of the Sendero Luminoso. The others are the empirical tests of their theorizing and, as such, are amply reported in the daily press. Interviews are extremely rare and usually conducted under the conditions of incarceration. Hence, one must return to the printed texts to understand the relationship between the now historic analysis of Peruvian conditions made by Mariátegui and the contemporary emphasis on a blend of a variety of Marxist ideologies. The selecting certain themes that consistently appear— a peasant-led violent revolution, armed struggle as the only option, rejection of other interpretations of Marxism-Leninism—and following them through the literature reveal how self-serving of its strategy Sendero Luminoso's beliefs have been. Given the breadth of documentation, neither the government nor journalists should find it surprising that particularly spectacular or bloody actions will not cease regardless of the fatalities either side sustains. Although the movement's silence reflects the principle of clandestineness dictated by the cellular configurations that restrict knowledge of membership, the operations, targets, and ideological premises have proven consistent. To understand the future in more realistic terms, especially the governing intentions of Sendero, proves far more difficult.

Despite all of Sendero's literature devoted to ideological debates or directed toward interest groups throughout the years, only the most vague and general vision of Peru under Sendero's rule is discernible. The failure to go beyond the rhetorical slogans casts doubt on what the leadership intends this peasant movement to become after the military objectives are achieved. How will this semi-industrialized, urban country reconfigure itself? Where does Peru fit in the scheme of world revolution that Sendero claims it instigated and Guzmán heads (PCdelP, 1986:4)? At the simplest of levels, violence is the instrument that will eliminate resistance. The Peru that emerges could be characterized as a nation with few international links, operating with Marxist-Maoist and Indian premises. Certainly the successful recruiting among educated youth from Lima's squatter settlements underscores the Andean cultural dimensions that this population still recognizes. Given the continual movement between the highlands and the coast, and the generalized failure of the urban environment to fulfill migrants' economic expectations, Sendero's program to destroy this exploitative society recruits increasing numbers of adherents. For many of the urban residents, the memories of a simpler, albeit no less harsh environment, are easily recalled. Sendero strengthens such associations by insisting that urban recruits train in the rural areas. What results is an acceptance not only from conviction but also from anger or resignation. Demands on leadership to debate detailed governing plans that posit the public policy options apparently do not occur. The fact that hundreds of pages of documents fail to raise such an important dimension is enlightening. Critiques of the Belaúnde and García governments' agrarian, economic, and social policies provide only indirect suggestions of Sendero's specific public-policy intentions (PCdelP, 1987:68–92). Does this silence suggest that Sendero is yet another movement capturing ethnic sensibilities (i.e., *indigenismo* [Indian identity]), directed by a small clique of elitist white and mestizo intellectuals, that has no intention of establishing a socialist democracy? The arcane matters of overall leadership apparently are to remain in the purview of the select few.

Since the years of the Velasco Alvarado and Morales Bermúdez military rule (1968–80) to the present Aprista government (1985–   ), various parties or movements have succeeded in mobilizing the peasantry and, by extension, the urbanized migrant peasants surrounding all of Peru's cities. By whatever measures employed, Sendero's impact continues for the state and the political Left. As the extremes of the Left intensify their violence, the Moscow-aligned Partido Comunista Peruano and its Izquierda Unidad coalition partners appear less radical, although not more appealing than the Apristas, judging from the results of the 1986 elections (PCdelP, 1987:48–65). Apra's attempts to capture the initiative in the countryside with the Rimanacuy (1986–   ) remain unproven.[12] The peasantry in areas under Sendero's sway is left with only the continuing violence and the *Nuevo Poder* employing its Comités Populares in the exercise of state functions. But as the effectiveness and extent of their governing cannot be appraised critically due to the clandestine nature of the República Popular de Nueva Democracia, a clear vision of Peru wholly under Sendero Luminoso control remains highly obscure. The socioeconomic and political conditions criticized since the late 1960s remain, and so long as they do, Sendero's message will reach enough Peruvians to ensure the movement's continuation.[13]

Notes

Various trips to Peru received the support of Princeton University and in 1985 of the Fulbright Commission. This and other essays on the Sendero Luminoso benefited from comments by Antonio Annino, José Alvarez,

Forrest Colburn, Ronald Berg, David Scott Palmer, and Michael Martin, and discussions with Gustavo Gorriti Ellenbogen. Information and cited publications come largely from Peruvian sources. The appendix was prepared with the assistance of María Cecilia Arissó.

1. The principal sources about Sendero Luminoso actions are Peruvian news magazines. Most important and easily accessible are *Caretas, Que-Hacer, Oiga, Debate, Resumen semanal-Desco* (all published in Lima), and the British *Latin American Regional Report: Andes.* Polemical literature by Peruvian ideologues comprises another segment of information. The more reasoned and scholarly accounts include Alan Angell, "Classroom Maoists: The politics of Peruvian Schoolteachers under Military Government," *Bulletin of Latin American Research* 1:2 (May 1982):1–20; Vera Gianotten, Tom de Wit, and Hans de Wit, "The Impact of Sendero Luminoso on Regional and National Politics in Peru," in David Slater, ed., *New Social Movements and the State in Latin America* (Amsterdam: Centrum voor Studie en Documentatie van Latijns Amerika, 1985), pp. 171–202; Cynthia McClintock, "Sendero Luminoso: Peru's Maoist Guerrillas," *Problems of Communism* 32 (September–October 1983):19–34, and "Why Peasants Rebel: the Case of Peru's Sendero Luminoso," *World Politics* 37:1 (October 1984):48–84; and Lewis Taylor, *Maoism in the Andes: Sendero Luminoso and the Contemporary Guerrilla Movement in Peru* (Liverpool: Center for Latin American Studies, University of Liverpool, 1983), all of which rely almost exclusively on the reports appearing in Peruvian news sources. Only David Scott Palmer emphasizes field study and familiarity with Sendero Luminoso's literature, feasible because of Palmer's presence in Ayacucho in 1962 to 1964, 1970, 1972, 1977, and 1979. See his "Rebellion in Rural Peru: The Origins and Evolution of Sendero Luminoso," *Comparative Politics* 18:2 (January 1986):127–46. Fundamental to the movement is the Peruvian Marxist philosopher José Carlos Mariátegui (1894–1930). His works assessing Peru remain important sources for the Peruvian left. See *Obras completas* (Lima: Editora Amauta, 1959–   ), 20 vols., and *Seven Essays* (Austin: University of Texas Press, 1971).

2. The Seminario receives coverage in the Frente Estudiantil Revolucionario's *Crítica y preparación,* April 1973, pp. 10–12. Such reprinting of internal documents in a publicly circulated source occurs wth various Senderista publications.

3. Hugo Blanco (Trotskyist) established a base in Cuzco's La Convención valley at this time, but the MIR adoption of Che Guevara's strategy emphasizing small armed groups to begin a rural revolution proved unacceptable to Blanco. MIR's bases there and in the Department of Junín succumbed to government forces. The cause of failure—using leadership and cadres from the urban middle classes to wage a revolution in the

name of peasant masses—was not lost on Sendero Luminoso's leaders. For elaboration on the period see Aníbal Quijano, *Problema agrario y movimientos campesinos* (Lima: Mosca Azul Editores, 1979), and Héctor Bejar Rivera, *Peru 1965: Notes on a Guerrilla Experience* (New York: Monthly Review Press, 1970).

4. The literature issued after 1974 emphasizes much less urban participation.

5. FER began in the 1950s in Arequipa as an expression of popular struggle against the dictatorship of Odría. *FER por el luminoso sendero de Mariátegui. Organo del Comité Nacional* 1:1 (January 1974):2.

6. Among these women figure Catalina Arianzén (wife of Antonio Díaz Martínez), Elizabeth Cárdenas, Nelly Cárdenez, Judith Galván, Ondina González, Carmen Rosa Julca Rivas, Edith Lagos, Isabel Beatriz Reynoso (niece of Abimael Guzmán), Juana Saavedra Galvez, Carlota Tello, Augusta de la Torre Guzmán, and Laura Zambrano Padilla.

8. Piedad Pareja Pflucker, *Terrorismo y sindicalismo en Ayacucho* (Lima, 1981) provides some relevant documentation. This useful study on strikes by miners captures the class tensions in the Department. Pareja Pflucker comes from a mine-owning family.

9. The orthodox Maoist party also maintained this line; see Partido Comunista del Perú (Patria Roja), *El C. R. Tupac Amaru: El problema campesino y la campaña de rectificación* (N. p., 1978), p. 5.

10. Voter participation in the 1985 presidential elections—departments with the greatest Sendero Luminoso presence:

Department	Registered Voters	Valid Cast Votes	Blank and Void Votes; Absentee Percentage of Registered Voters
Apurímac	113,914	73,019	40,895/36%
Ayacucho	182,019	116,674	65,345/36
Cuzco	352,217	225,771	126,446/36
Huancavelica	140,865	90,294	50,571/36
Junín	423,098	271,206	151,892/36
Puno	384,995	246,782	138,213/36
Total	1,597,108	1,023,746	573,362
Six Department Totals	—	64%	36%

Source: Resumen semanal—Desco 8:311 (April 5–12, 1985):4, as cited in *El Nacional*, April 8, 1985. PCdelP, 1987:56 provides figures for Apurímac, Ayacucho, and Huancavelica; percentages for column 3 range up to 3.2% higher.

11. In Arequipa Guzmán's theses were "La Teoría del espacio en Kant" (1961) and 'El Estado democrático burgués" (1961), both submitted to and accepted by the Universidad Nacional San Agustín. Díaz Martínez's works include *China, la revolución agraria* (Lima: Mosca Azul Editores, 1978) and *Ayacucho; hambre y esperanza* (Ayacucho: Ediciones "Waman Puna," 1969).

12. An effort of the National Institute of Planning, the Rimanacuy (Quechua for "hand of stone") attempts to suggest a revival of the Incan system of agrarian organization. It consists of a general assembly of representatives of indigenous communities brought together by government officials to discuss difficulties in agriculture, credit, land titles, and the like. Begun in May 1986, it is Apra's idea to decentralize the country's economy.

13. Foreign scholars confront several problems, not the least of which is access to and availability of documentation, which generally is mimeographed and exists in relatively few copies. Research libraries should acquire such material, but relatively few do because of policies excluding such formats, the inability of book dealers to supply it, and the high costs associated with buying and processing it. Fieldwork becomes necessary, yet with the clandestine nature of the Sendero Luminoso and the physical dangers involved, site visits do not offer many promising leads. In the right quarters of most cities and in certain types of bookstores, literature of the type discussed in this paper exists. Scholarly life would be easier if such imprints were gathered *as issued,* and this too can be arranged for a price. While most revolutionary groups would place library collections of their literature as a low priority, if one at all, members of the movement may hold an historic perception of their activities and desire that a record be preserved. Regardless of circumstances, however, scholars and bibliographers should attempt to coordinate their fieldwork in order to ensure that the essential types of documentation to trace a popular revolution are obtained and preserved. Such collecting efforts must include the literature from the inception of the movement and continue throughout its life. The early years especially hold great importance for ideological positions and strategies for achieving power. With key documents on the movement's intentions, comparisons with results become possible. The ideals, objectives, and deeds of guerrillas will acquire a new analytical context through the analysis of their writings.

References

Bandera Roja (BR) (1969). "La Base unitaria y el desarrollo de la propaganda." 7 (October):42.

———— (1970a). "Contra el fascismo, contra el liquidacionismo, llevar la lucha hasta el fin." 8 (May):44.

———— (1970b). "Reconstituir las organizaciones populares." 88 (May): 44.

———— (1976). "Quinto Pleno del C.C. ¡Retomar plenamente a Mariátegui e impulsar la reconstitución:" 9 (May):45.

Centro Femenino Popular (1974). *El Marxismo, Mariátegui y el movimiento femenino.* Peru.

Federación Estudiantil Revolucionaria, Convención Nacional, 2 (1974). *Circular.* N.p.

Federación Universitaria de San Cristóbal de Huamanga (1972a). *Posición ante la Comisión Estatutaria Nacional.* Ayacucho.

Federación Universitaria Huamanga (1972b). *Sobre la situación política nacional.* Huamanga.

Forjemonos (1978). *¡Forjemonos como organizadores de la revolución!* N.p.: Ediciones M.O.T.C.

Frente Democrático de Docentes de la UNSCH (1974). *Manifesto.* Huamanga.

Frente Estudiantil Revolucionario de la Universidad Nacional de Ingeniería, Comisión Política (FER) (1972a). *Documento de trabajo para el plenario de FER de la UNI.* Lima.

———— Convención (FER) (1972b). *Informe político.* Lima(?).

Frente Estudiantil Revolucionario por el Luminoso Sendero de Mariátegui, Convención Nacional, 2. (1974). *Manifesto.* N.p.

Impulsemos (1978). *¡Impulsemos la movilización!* N.p. (citation from the September 1977 Reunión del Buró Político Ampliado).

Ley (n.d.). *Ley de reforma agraria, Decreto Ley No. 17716.* Lima.

Movimiento Femenino Popular (MFP) (1975). *El Marxismo, Mariátegui y el movimiento feminino.* 2d ed. Lima.

———— (1977). *Gloria a las madres del pueblo.* N.p.

Palmer, David Scott (1986). "Rebellion in Rural Peru: The Origins and Evolution of Sendero Luminoso." *Comparative Politics* 18 (January):2.

Partido Comunista del Perú (PCdelP) (1981a). *¡A nuestro heróico pueblo combatiente!* N.p.: Comité Central.

———— (1981b). *¡Desarrollemos la guerra de guerrillas!* N.p.: Comité Central.

———— (1985a). *¡Combatir y resistir, repudiar las elecciones del régimen genocida y desarrollar más la lucha armada!* N.p.: Bases.

———— (1985b). *¡No votar! Sino, ¡generalizar la guerra de guerrillas para conquistar el poder para el pueblo!* N.p.: Ediciones Bandera Roja.

———— (1986). *Día de la heroicidad.* Peru.

———— (1987). *Desarrollar la guerra popular siviendo a la revolución mundial.* N.p.: Ediciones Bandera Roja.

Partido Comunista Peruano (PCP) (n.d.). *Análisis de los puntos de vista erróneos del c.A. con motivo de una entrevista con dos cc. del C.R. de Ayacucho.* N.p.

(1965a). *La Situación política y tareas del partido.* Lima: Ediciones Trabajo y Lucha.

———— Conferencia Nacional, 5. (1965b). *Resoluciones y conclusiones.* Peru.

———— Conferencia Nacional, 6. (1968). *Informe complementario. Deslinde de posiciones con el oportunismo de derecha disfrazado de "izquierda."* Lima(?).

———— (1969a). *Informe político. El Triunfo de la linea proletaria y el falso "Marxismo-leninismo" de los grupos antipartido.* Lima(?): Ediciones "Bandera Roja."

———— (1969b). *Resoluciones.* Lima.

Peru. Comisión de Reforma de la Educación (1971). *Reforma de la educación peruana: informe general.* Lima.

Sendero Luminoso
Basic Chronology

1894–1930	José Carlos Mariátegui
1934	Abimael Guzmán Reynoso born in Mollendo; later known as "Camarada Gonzalo"
1961	Guzman graduates from Universidad Nacional San Augustín (Arequipa) after completing his two theses: "Acerca de la teoría Kantiana del espacio" in January and, for law, "El Estado democratico-burgues" in November.
1963	Guzmán joins the faculty of the Universidad Nacional San Cristóbal de Huamanga (UNSCH).
1964	Partido Comunista Peruano, Conferencia, 4th, Guzmán splits from national leadership (Moscow line) and with others forms the Partido Comunista Peruano–Bandera Roja; Mariátegui emphasized.
1968	Military seizes power from the civilian government.
1970	Partido Comunista Peruano–Bandera Roja, Pleno, 2d. Central Committee condemns Guzmán as "leftist opportunist" and expels him.
1970–77	Recruitment conducted at UNSCH; *Voz popular* issued.
1971–72	Verbal attacks on MIR, Vanguardia, Patria Roja, and other leftist groups.
1974–75	Strengthening of the women's movement but beginning of decline in influence at UNSCH.
1976	Sendero Luminoso begins *escuelas populares* (popular schools) in the barrios (districts) of Ayacucho Department.

1978	Sendero Luminoso leadership leaves UNSCH and goes underground; relies on cell structure rather than mass organizations.
1979	Partido Comunista del Perú–Sendero Luminoso holds its first National Conference.
1980	
May	First violent action by Sendero Luminoso: burning of ballot boxes, Plaza of Cangallo (Ayacucho), in a symbolic demonstration against the electoral process.
1981	
March	Anti-terrorism law enacted.
August	Sinchis (military unit) combat Sendero Luminoso in five of Ayacucho's provinces.
October	State of emergency declared by the government in five provinces of Ayacucho.
1982	
March	Ayacucho prison break releases 230 Sendero Luminoso suspects; Edith Lagos freed. Largest offensive to date. First blackout in Lima, which demonstrates Sendero Luminoso's planning capacity and knowledge of electrical grids.
March–May	Conferencia Nacional, 2d.
July	Sendero Luminoso initiates public executions of government officials, merchants, peasant and labor leaders.
August	Raid on Allpachaca (experimental farm connected with UNSCH); destruction of livestock and grains for local production evokes strong reaction by local peasants against Sendero Luminoso.
	Second Lima blackout.
September	Government security forces kill Edith Lagos; major funeral in Ayacucho demonstrates local support for Sendero Luminoso.
December	Execution of 21 civilians and government officials in Ayacucho results in declaration of martial law and entry of the army.

1983

January — Government's counterinsurgency offensive begins.

Eight Lima journalists massacred at Uchuraccay.

March — Partido Comunista del Perú–Sendero Luminoso, Congreso, 8th, attended by delegates from central and southern Peru; no northern representatives reported.

Decision to expand operations in the departments of Lima, Junín, Cuzco, and Apurimac.

Twenty-one Senderistas killed by Guardia Civil in the sector of Victor Fajardo (eighteen between March 20 and 22 and three on March 27).

July — Partido Comunista del Perú–Sendero Luminoso, Conferencia Nacional, 3d. Evaluation of past actions and future plans set.

Lima blackout accompanied by individual attacks on political party, private sector, and government offices.

August — Twenty-seven Sendero Luminoso members of the Comité Político-Militar Regional del Centro responsible for most of the terrorist action in Cerro de Pasco, Huancayo, La Oroya, Tarma, and Norococha are captured.

September — Sendero Luminoso members burn and sack the Palacio Municipal de Lomas.

September 29 — Up to now, confrontations with Sendero Luminoso have resulted in more than 1,000 dead, of whom 150 are from government security forces and approximately 2,000 captured countrywide.

November — Sendero Luminoso kills the populist mayor Victor Arias in Cerro de Pasco and attacks four hamlets in the department.

Sendero Luminoso confiscates many students' *libretas electorales* at la Ciudad Universitaria de Ayacucho.

Seven actions, including one electric high-tension tower destroyed and two damaged and some damage at the Honduran embassy.

More than fifty Senderistas killed by the Guardia Civil, Guardia Republicana, and PIP in Huancavelica.

Ayacucho: Dynamite explosion near the offices of the Policía de Investigaciones; a blackout that affects three-quarters of the population; strong explosions afterward in different parts of the city.

November 12 Lima: Sendero Luminoso tries to scare the people against voting by bombing the headquarters of the PCP and the Acción Popular (AP), producing five deaths.

November 13 An election registrar in Huancavelica killed by Senderistas.

Fifty Senderistas kill fifteen peasants in Huanta—men, women, the aged, and children; Sendero Luminoso cuts some peasants' fingers for having voted (in Huancavelica).

November 17 Blackout in Ayacucho.

November 18 One hundred Senderistas assault a police post in Ocros, Cangallo, and rob it completely of arms and uniforms without firing a single shot.

Many political candidates resign out of fear of Sendero Luminoso. State of emergency for sixty days in Lucanas and Huancavelica.

1984

April Arrest of Antonio Díaz Martínez, head of the *comando político-militar* of Sendero Luminoso.

July Army given direct control over combating internal subversion.

1985

April Senderistas kill the AP mayor for the district of San Juan de Salinas in Azangaro, along with other actions.

1985 (*continued*)

May	Sendero Luminoso attacks diplomatic missions of the United States, the Soviet Union, China, and Cuba in Lima.
May 15	Sendero Luminoso kills the Aprista mayor of Sanagorán and kidnaps twenty children between the ages of twelve and sixteen.
July	Lieutenant governor in Ayacucho (Chilcaccassa) is decapitated after a "public trial" in which he was accused of being a *soplón* (informer) and a traitor.
August	"Camarada Pablo," one of the principal *cabecillas* (rebel leaders) is captured—a strong blow to the Sendero Luminoso's structure.
	Leader of the command of Iquitos, "Camarada Pancho," is captured—another major loss.
September	Sendero Luminoso remembers the third anniversary of the death of Edith Lagos with three alarming explosions in Ayacucho.

1986

January	Huge blackout in Huanta. One of the principal heads of Sendero Luminoso, José M. Alvites Pariona, is captured.
	Torching of the Ministerio de Agricultura results in the death of a worker.
April	Sendero Luminoso kills Aprista mayor of Churubamba.
May	Sendero Luminoso kills Aprista mayor of Sanagorán, on the anniversary of APRA (Department of La Libertad).
June	Government slaughter of suspected Senderistas in Lurigancho, Frontón, and Santa Barbara (for women) prisons.
	Governor of Gorgon (province of Cajatambo) assassinated by Sendero Luminoso in the public plaza.
July	Aprista party leader and candidate of the Secretaría Departmental Benjamín Castillo de Flor shot.

	Sendero Luminoso blows up four electric power towers, cutting off electricity to parts of Huanta and Ayacucho.
August	"Camarada Yolanda," one of the principal *cabecillas* of Sendero Luminoso is captured.
	Sendero Luminoso blows up the antenna of the radio station Onda Azul and electric pylons, leaving Puno without electricity and telephone service.
	Sendero Luminoso dynamites the agencies of Cooperación Popular and APRA (provincia de Canchis).
	Blackout in Huanta.
September	Huge blackout in Trujillo.
	Blackout in Huanta and Ayacucho.
	Total blackout in Huancayo and provinces of Concepción and Jauja.
October	Bombing of an Aprista party local in Lima.
October 5	Bombing of another Aprista local in Chiclayo.
October 8	Another bombing in Chiclayo takes the lives of three Aprista political operatives: the candidate for district mayor of Villa de Armas, the general secretary of Peruvian Aprista Party (PAP) for the Department of Huancavelica, and his wife.
November	Blackout for six hours in Ayacucho and Huanta.
December	The longest and most extensive blackout in 1986 in Huancayo; similar actions in Ayacucho and Huanta.
1987	
January	Mayor of the district of Hongos, province of Yauyos, is captured by twenty Senderistas and later traded for food.
March	Senderistas behead the Aprist governor of Trebolini Alta, 175 kilometers east of Ayacucho.
	Senderistas shoot the Aprista mayor of the district of Hermilio Valdizán, province of Leoncio Prado.

1987 (*continued*)

April   The secretary general of the PAP for the district of
                 Corpangui is shot to death by Senderistas, who then
                 force all authorities, professors, and businessmen
                 to leave town.

May   The PIP of Ayacucho captures the head of a *célula
                 de aniquilamiento* (annihilation cell) of Sendero
                 Luminoso of Huamanga, along with five other
                 members, including a minor.

June   For the second time this year, Senderistas *irrumpen*
                 (invade by force) the jail of Paucartambo to free
                 prisoners convicted of terrorist acts.

                 Three Senderistas die and four are captured in
                 Andarapa (Andahuaylas).

                 After intercepting a group of boats in Sanambari,
                 Senderistas kill nineteen people following a *juicio
                 popular* (popular judgment) and kidnap seven busi-
                 nessmen.

August   Senderistas blow up three high-tension towers,
                 leaving Ayacucho and Huanta in the dark.

Prepared by Peter T. Johnson and María Cecilia Arissó, Princeton University, April 1987. Sources include the Lima weeklies *Resumen semanal-
Desco, Caretas,* and *Oiga,* as well as Sendero Luminoso publications.

PART III

Studies of the Semiperiphery and Core

CHAPTER 11

Class and Political-Economic Development in the Mediterranean: An Overview

James F. Petras

Perhaps the best approach to discussing such a broad and disparate region as the Mediterranean is to attempt to provide a synoptic perspective on major structural and state developments through a set of telegraphic propositions. In the subsequent sections an attempt will be made to describe some of the salient features of class formation and at the same time try to provide a periodization of the processes of class conflicts. The discussion will conclude with a brief commentary on the new political directions, in particular neoliberal economics and the perspective it brings to bear on Mediterranean class politics.

Twelve Theses on Mediterranean Political Economy

Structural Changes

Profound changes in the nature of the productive system, class structure, and the state characterize Mediterranean development after World War II. A brief identification of these changes follows.

First, the massive population shift from rural to urban centers and the movement from agrarian to industrial and service activities express broad demographic and economic transformations. These changes accompanied the region's growing integration into the world economy and the concomitant decline of subsistence production.

Second, these transformations have never been consummated to the point of rupturing the relations with previous economic activity, social behavior, and kinship relations. Accordingly, "proletarians" still own or have access to units of petty-commodity production; extended-family linkages lead to the circulation of income back into petty-commodity forms; the savings of overseas proletarians finance their return and reproduction as "self-employed" rentiers and petty distributors. The reproduction of precapitalist relations and forms of production and distribution accompany the process of capitalist modernization.

Third, enduring inequalities in the distribution system have accompanied the rapid and widespread increases in growth of personal income, consumption, and property ownership. While rising new social strata with higher living standards have emerged in the social economy, their frame of reference no longer is the previous standard of living of the rural poor, but rather the current standard of living of upper-income groups. For them, progress is measured not by retrospective but by present and future standards, and shapes the ambiguous "radicalism" characterizing the new "middle strata" — a radicalism that challenges the elites, but does not seek to level the hierarchy for the benefit of those below.

Fourth, the Mediterranean region has experienced accelerating integration into a new European division of labor with specificities distinct from those of the past. International circulation of labor and capital characterizes the new configuration: the Mediterranean exported labor power and imported consumer-tourists from the North; the South became a site for the "reproduction" of northern labor power. The convergence and divergence of northern European and Mediterranean countries is contained in the homogenization of consumer life styles while maintaining differentiation in the levels and the depth of the productive system. The uneven extension of industrialization into the Mediterranean has reproduced, within both the region and the countries, the same polarities as previously existed between the North and South. Uneven development, in turn, has brought about the absorption of labor power from the less-developed regions, leading to urban and social concentrations of labor and capital on a scale and scope without historical precedent.

Fifth, maintenance of preindustrial forms of production and distribution have accompanied the integration of the Mediterranean economies into the European division of labor. The continued reproduction of old, and expansion of new, petty-commodity distributors and producers alongside advanced technological structures has brought about a heterogeneous social formation whose unevenness has hindered the homogeneous spread of effects that might arise from the introduction of new technology.

External Linkages and Internal Development

Sixth, the external linkages that have, to degrees varying by country, been central to the dynamic reproduction of both large-scale and petty-commodity production have severely fragmented the processes of production and distribution. This, in turn, has accentuated internal competition within and between classes for favorable access to the state—namely, access to foreign exchange, to import licenses, to credit, and so forth. The lack of internal coherence and the economic dependence upon external sources for financing national and enterprise expansion and individual aggrandizement (as well as the intense competition for limited state resources) have decreased communication between local producers and distributors. This, in turn, has caused delays in decisions, systematic evasion of responsibility in the state bureaucracy, and behavior that maximizes short-term gain. Overall, there has been a general lack of sustained focus on strategic objectives, accompanied by continued investment in nonproductive areas and transfers of capital abroad.

Seventh, during the 1960s and 1970s massive remittances from migrant labor and mass tourism led to the growth of the real-estate market and to the overdevelopment of nonproductive activity. In many Mediterranean countries, this stimulated particular areas of industrial development (construction-related), but ultimately it limited the deepening of the industrial process. The aggregate industrial growth figures obscure the uneven character of the industrial structure, its fragile financial base, and its weak competition.

State and Political Change

Eighth, the process of social change and economic development has occurred not through a rupture with previous political institutions, but rather through adding, over time, new functional agencies with varying degrees of autonomy. This incremental additive style incorporates innovative institutions (that is, ones capable of innovation) into the existing state structure, creating, in effect, "multiple states":

1. The state as that conglomerate of new autonomous parastate agencies that serve as vehicles for the financing, marketing, and restructuring of industrial development. This is the state of technocrats and of the development-oriented bourgeoisie.
2. The "historic state"—the bureaucratic apparatus that functions as a vehicle for political patronage and as the employment agency of last resort. This state is subject to the claims of the political class and the dominant ensemble of political parties.
3. The repressive state—the self-contained caste that directs the repressive organs and that at times stands "over" society and acts as the protector of the propertied class.

The overlay of these states leads to contradictory processes within "the" state, and to a constant process of bargaining and coalition building that extends into the organization of parties and social classes. The recruitment process, the objects, and the organizational functioning of each sector of the state unify the different line and staff into relatively self-contained units, which for analytical purposes allows us to speak of "different" states. The "several" states, of course, operate in the same space, and they converge on specific issues—especially in reaction to political challenges to the structural underpinning of society.

Ninth, overdevelopment of the state vis-à-vis the underdevelopment of the productive forces reflects the weakness of the logic of industrial capital (the weakness of the process of sustained production and reproduction of capital) and the strength of the clientelist logic as a mechanism for containing class conflict (Stambouli).

Tenth, state bureaucracy proliferates in response to the problems engendered by the growth of nonproductive capital. Yet, at the same time, the state as general employment agency is unable to provide solutions to development problems (Cerase). This incapacity reflects the power of nonproductive capital and the limits that it places on the systematic recruitment of technically trained personnel and the effective implementation of economic programs. Because of its dominance, nonproductive capital tends to reproduce itself in the state structure according to the precepts of patrimonial domination, thus blocking new initiatives.

Eleventh, the fragmented economy, the patterns of limited political accessibility, the weak links of communication, the overdevelopment of nonproductive consumers as against a limited productive base, the monumental inefficiency of the state, and the state's permeation through society all engender widespread disaffection and the broad circulation of radical ideologies. The radicalism of the overdeveloped nonproductive classes expresses the accumulated resentment of the newly rising middle classes over their lack of political representation, social recognition, and economic access to the state dominated by established, traditional configurations of power.

Twelfth, the politics of resentment focuses on the distribution of resources within the system—not on the principle of hierarchy. The basic structural features and relations that characterize the system and engender the blockages and disparities are not challenged. Indeed, the very effort by the oppositions to change society is counterbalanced by deep commitment to sustain it. Hence, the basic feature of southern European radicalism is the oscillation between the politics of change and the exigencies of conformity: the need to affirm the principle of autonomy of action and the need to become a part of the state to secure economic resources.

Class Formation

The formation of the class structure in the Mediterranean presents particular features that require specific analysis. First is the multiple class positions that individuals occupy and the implications this has for social, economic, and political behavior. It is commonplace to note that individuals employed in multiple types of economic activity are located in different class positions. For example, owners of small farm holdings also are employed in construction or factory work in the provincial towns; a skilled wage laborer employed by state electrical enterprise also works as a self-employed household repairer; agricultural merchants frequently double as labor contractors, financiers, and transport owners. More generally, substantial proportions of most classes own real estate and derive some portion of their income from rent. Multiple class membership may not hinder demand making on the state and on opposing classes, but it probably does lead to resistance to claims by the state and others that affect one or another of the multiple positions that these same individuals occupy. Thus while most workers and farmers may support increased welfare expenditures, they may also join large real-estate interests in opposing land or property taxes if rentals are a portion of their income.

The second characteristic of the class structure that needs to be emphasized is the reproduction of petty-commodity producers and distributors rather than their dissolution (Moschonas, Paci). The Mediterranean economies have been incorporated into the international division of labor in part as a labor reserve: the dynamic expansion of northern and central Europe and the absorption of their surplus rural labor force led to the massive importation of Mediterranean labor. The process of labor migration and return led to the dual process of externally induced proletarianization and return petty-bourgeoisification. The insertion of Mediterranean labor into the modern dynamic industrial sectors of northern Europe and the massive growth of tourism in the South led to the proliferation of petty-commodity distributors and producers. The dynamic expansion of capital in the North expanded the petty bourgeoisie in the Mediterranean precisely because of the absence of centrally organized capital markets capable of channeling the large-scale but dispersed earnings into alternative strategic sectors; the reproduction of petty-commodity producers and distributors within the tourist-related services was not incompatible with the concentration and centralization of capital in other sectors. This dual process, however, suggests that attempts to reduce the social process to the capitalist logic is likely to miss the complexities of class formation and, more important, to lose sight of the multiple points of departure for class political action and the divergent sets of social claims that ensue.

The larger issue that confronts social analysts of the Mediterranean is the mosaic of social forms and social action contained within the parameters of the social formation. The interlocking of different types of productive systems, levels of technology, and social relations and their physical proximity suggest that the process of development in the Mediterranean is much more incremental and additive than in northern and central Europe and the United States, which are more likely to rupture and replace past practices. In that sense, contrary to the image of the unstable and volatile South and the stable North, the Mediterranean regions exhibit a kind of organic conservatism that is much more flexible in adapting to changes, but also resistant to blanket transformations. The result is that new technologies, productive units, and political and social organizations are juxtaposed to preexisting ones defining a whole area of society that at one and the same time exacerbates conflicts but limits their consequences—at least in the absence of an all-inclusive political organization and overarching political crisis capable of unifying the heterogeneous forces.

In the last three decades, homogenizing forces have been operating in the Mediterranean: capitalist social relations, commercialization, bureaucratization, and consumerism have spread throughout the region. Yet the resilience of locally based institutions, social values, familial ties, and class relations continues to manifest itself (Farsoun). Moreover, the conflict engendered by the rapid growth of large-scale organization (class conflicts in the major industrial centers), the decomposition of the cities, and the impotence of the central state has led to a movement back to provincial areas, to small-scale units of production, and to the resurgence of "decentralist politics" (Capecchi). The dominant megalocentralist logic of capital is faced with an undercurrent that has roots in the continuing viability, real or imagined, of the provincial areas. No doubt, the viability of this decentralizing movement will be based not on romantic nostalgia seeking to reconstruct the village, but on integrating the local economies with the new centers of economic and social action. The specificities and continuities of the Mediterranean region, however, are confronted by a set of powerful forces that have significantly transformed the class structure during the past thirty years.

Capitalist Agriculture and Class Structure

Agricultural production and class structure have been profoundly affected by the increasing expansion of capitalist production, spreading transportation and communication networks, the mechanization of production, and the increasing direct linkages to industrial production (Huerta Carbonell, Allaire, Cabral, Moisides). While family farms continue to dominate the economic terrain, this type of production has increasingly shifted toward capitalist forms of production, characterized by expanding investment in farm machinery, pesticides and fertilizers, links to regional, national, and international markets, increasing ties to formal banking services, and increased networks of industrial food-processing centers. The emergence of the capitalist farmer and the decline of subsistence agriculture have been accompanied by the increasing marginalization of women from production and the massive exodus of redundant farm labor—in particular, poor young farmers and farm laborers to the cities and to the industrialized countries (Gourdomichalis, First-Dilic). Capitalist farming's increasing linkages to the market and increasing dependence on the state (for subsidies, financing, price support) have been decisive in shaping political struggle—one in which the adverse decisions in the marketplace are translated into militant claims upon the state (Papandreou). Recent confrontations involving farmers in southern Europe increasingly pit them against the state, especially in those countries where new industrial development strategies involve channeling funds away from maintaining farm incomes and toward funding the restructuring of capital (Petras, 1984).

Industrialization and the Stratification of the Working Class

The range of industrial development in the Mediterranean is immense with countries found in all stages from light-consumer industries and capital-goods industries to new high-technology enterprises (Stamatopoulos, Pamuk). Nowhere is the pattern of development in the Mediterranean more highly differentiated than in the level and depth of industrial and technical development. Moreover, within some countries there are the same substantial disparities, with large-scale modern firms juxtaposed to a sea of small enterprises. Increasingly, however, in some countries of southern Europe the level of efficiency and competitiveness of an industrial enterprise is not necessarily associated with size (Capecchi). Moreover, with the tendency toward deconcentration and decentralization of industry—accompanying the shift from heavy industry to high technology—there is a decline in working-class concentration, unionization, and militancy (Capecchi). The different levels of industrialization are evident in the attempts to industrialize in some countries, while others restructure existing industry, confronting an industrial structure wracked by financial crisis. The result is a mass of young unemployable workers excluded from industrial employment in declining regions, older employed workers facing redundancy in traditional heavy industries, and new low-paid, nonunionized assembly workers in the new growth sectors. Throughout the region, a profound cleavage exists between workers in problematic industries threatened with redundancy through state-promoted restructuring and stable, skilled, unionized workers in strategic enterprises (Loannou). The sporadic violent demonstrations and unruly strikers reflect the desperation of the former and contrast with the ritualistic militant action in pursuit of corporate demands of the latter.

The notion "industrialization" thus incorporates the ingredients of three industrial revolutions, reflecting the coexistence of simple mechanically powered textile looms, heavy industry, and high-technology electronic and information enterprises. The growing differentiation and the deepening cleavage of the productivity capacity of different industrial enterprises strongly suggest that the common classification of wage workers (rooted in the capital-wage distinction) obscures the tremendous differences in cultural, social, political, and economic existence. No doubt there will emerge overarching issues—inflation, repressive regimes or laws—that may serve to unify the disparate segments of the working class across the widening chasm of technological and economic differentiation. Be that as it may, the intellectual task is to explore the social and political implications of the growing internal differentiation of the working class, reflecting the profound unevenness in development that increasingly characterizes industrial development.

The Mediterranean region is witnessing a race between crisis-wracked, declining older industries (textiles, steel, shipyards) and the beginning (in some countries) of high-technology industries. This "transition" is problematic in several senses: the decline of the old industries occurs independently of the capacity of a country to create the new pattern of development; there is no necessary fit between the geographic location, levels and types of skills, income, and trade-union rights in the declining industries and the new; there is no assurance of the viability of the new industries, as the shift is taking place in a number of countries, with some ahead of others; finally, the rate of decline of old industries seems to have far exceeded the development of the new, creating high levels of unemployment and labor marginalization despite some state efforts to cushion the effects through early retirement, increased unemployment benefits, transfers to state enterprises, and the like (Petras, 1984).

The increasing number of displaced workers and the high number of unemployed young workers, particularly women (in Italy 50 percent of women workers under twenty-five are unemployed), have created a large "subproletariat" whose relations to the means of production either has been ruptured or never existed, and whose potential for organization at workplaces is thus absent (Capecchi, Fernandez de Castro). This "available mass" has weakened allegiances to traditional forms of labor organization, yet its growing size and increasing malaise suggest that it might lend itself to new styles of political and social action or inaction. Among the unemployed, class organizations may decline in importance, giving rise to the growing importance of kinship, neighborhood and informal peer-group associations—and perhaps, in some cases, increase the importance of spontaneous "street politics"—movements, and other loosely organized forms of collective action with few of the traditional constraints.

In summary, when we disaggregate the notion of "industrialization" and examine its impact on class formation, the high level of internal stratification of the working class becomes evident: (1) the older, declining, light-consumer goods industries with their low pay and heavy concentration of women; (2) the "middle-aged" heavy industries—heavily indebted and increasingly operating far below capacity—with heavily unionized, better-paid male workers; (3) the new high-technology industries, with both low-paid, semiskilled workers and high-paid skilled technicians; (4) the closed factories and the displaced workers joining unemployed young workers. In this context the notion of a single working class itself becomes a basis for further debate and elaboration.

Old and New Petty-Commodity Producers and Distributors

The existence of a vast army of petty-commodity producers and distributors (self-employed merchants, manufacturers, farmers, and so on) is one of the striking characteristics of the Mediterranean region (Moschonas, Paci). The size and scope of their activity and its impact on economic development, technology, politics, and state revenue have been noted over the years. The contradictory conclusions that have emerged from these discussions suggest that the simple formulas set forth to encapsulate this class are inadequate: most structural-historical analysis has underestimated the internal dynamics of these strata, and the impact of events and specific conjunctures in shaping the changing and continuing allegiances of this class. More important, the internal differentiation of this class has in recent years taken on increasing importance. The 1970s witnessed the emergence of increasingly efficient, competitive, and dynamic small and medium-size enterprises—particularly in Italy—linked to "subcontracts" with larger firms (seeking to lower labor costs and to minimize class conflict) or developing their own set of products and developing market "competitiveness" (Capecchi). The emergence of specialized, technologically advanced small firms alongside the traditional small-scale manufacturers and distributors requires greater empirical specification of the meaning and consequence of the term "petty-commodity production." The neofunctional discovery and celebration of the underground economy based on a rather narrowly conceived notion of its successful operation was premature. Locked into a world of occasional affluence and the poverty of public service, this perspective takes for granted that other classes and productive activity will provide the wherewithal to sustain the basic investments, taxes, and technology upon which the "underground economy" can function. But what would happen if the behavior of the "underground economy" became the norm? The shift from traditional to modern petty-commodity production is also a shift from the underground to the overground: the development of an economy linking private gain with the need for public-sector services.

Real-Estate Capital: The Mediterranean Road to Development?

Real-estate capital has assumed major significance in the expansion of southern European development, absorbing substantial amounts of savings and influencing investment and development patterns (Petras, 1985). Several aspects of the growth of real-estate capital require analysis: the importance of rent income (both urban and rural) for households and its impact on national productive activity; the combining of real-estate holdings with other class and occupational positions (multiple class positions); the "massification" of real-estate investment—from an elite phenomenon to one permeating the whole social structure; the interrelationship between the dynamic growth of real-estate capital and the central role that tourism and immigrant remittance play in the expansion of southern European economies.

The implications of the growth and pervasiveness of real-estate capital on class formation, the state, and cultural values depend on their relation with other forms of capital: we can hypothesize that where real-estate capital is dominant, it would tend to limit the prospects for industrial and agricultural development.

Class Conflict and the Shifting Terrain of Struggle

While it is difficult to group all the Mediterranean countries into a uniform sequence, there appears to be a "weighted" pattern that can be divided into three phases. (1) The early 1960s to early 1970s was a period in which the labor and popular movements were on the offensive. In Spain and Greece, the struggle took the form of democratizing dictatorial states; in North Africa, the Algerian liberation movement overthrew colonial rule; in Portugal, a mass movement instituted democratic and far-reaching social changes; in France, the popular movement of the spring of 1968 created a near-revolutionary situation; in Italy, the "hot autumn" initiated a period of active mobilization of entire sectors of the working class and advancement of a whole series of reforms. (2) The mid-1970s to early 1980s was a period of economic crisis and loss of political momentum of the mass movements, in which the working-class movements failed to develop an alternative to capitalist rationalization and fell back to defending the "welfare" gains of the previous period. The basic terrain of struggle shifted from the streets to the parliaments and ministries. As the crisis deepened in the early 1980s, and in a context of greater competitiveness, capital pressed forward by squeezing labor and peripheral regions of surplus to finance the new technologies and models of development. (3) The present phase, beginning in 1985, witnesses the return of the politics of the movements and street politics. Rising waves of strikes are evident, particularly in France, Italy, Spain, and Tunisia.

The movements in southern Europe, however, are caught in the bind of defending employment in declining industries or losing employment. In the context of capitalist restructuring of the economy, the "corporate vision" (employment, wages, welfare, and so forth) of the traditional trade union movement is demonstrating its limitations. The positive side of the strike movement is its rejection of technocratic planning resulting in the systematic exclusion of those directly affected by capital restructuring. Even in the growing number of less-structured young working people's protests there is at least a recognition that the technocratic planners provide no future for them in the new development models.

Nevertheless, the new movements in their early phase exhibit several limitations. There does not appear yet a new political perspective: there is no political-economic alternative to the current drive by capital to rationalize and restructure production. Currently, most of the debate takes place on the terrain of the "market," and on this terrain the logic of the market involves meeting the competitive terms of international capital. Second, no political organization has appeared that is capable of harnessing the disparate activities, sectors, and fragments into a coherent political movement. Third, few organic intellectuals (Gramsci) are present to synthesize the experiences and codify the movements of the struggle, linking defensive tactics with offensive strategies. The generation of the 1960s and early 1970s has in part been "institutionalized" (professionalized), privatized, or incorporated into the bureaucratic apparatus.

The result is a condition of "dynamic immobilism," in which rising movements within existing societies limit excesses but are incapable of breaking out of the logic of the restructuring of capital. Whether these movements will regroup with older forces in a new coalition to stabilize the status quo, or deepen the process of radicalization, is a subject worthy of empirical research.

The Neo-Liberal Revival: Rejecting Old Socialist Dogmas for Ancient Liberal Ones

The most dramatic shift in recent years has been the embrace by a significant part of the Left of neo-liberal doctrines: reduced support for state enterprises, cuts in welfare state spending, and the reduction or elimination of price and rent controls as well as in the indexing of wages have been in recent years led by sectors of the "historic Left." In its place there has been an uncritical promotion of the market, of large-scale private enterprises, of increasing state incentives, financing, and research for new private investments. The movement in the Mediterranean (with some exceptions) is not toward a more radical version of welfare state politics but toward orthodox liberal market economics.

As in other parts of the world economy, there is in the Mediterranean a movement toward creation of a new model of accumulation. This movement is directed toward the conversion of capitalist production from areas of low profitability to those of high profitability. In effect, several regimes in the region have become the engines for the creation of a new model of capitalist accumulation, and as such assumed the burden of shutting down old industries, breaking down labor control over employment, creating "labor flexibility" (downward pressures on labor to make it more adaptable to the lower wage level of new industries, increasing labor's geographical mobility, and so forth). This process involves a policy of "restructuring" of capital, as the new model of accumulation is described. The transition period between models of accumulation is, however, fraught with conflict, particularly where important sectors of the working class are not tightly controlled by the state-aligned trade union leaderships.

The second broad historical trend apparent in the neo-liberal pattern of Mediterranean development is the move to broaden the scope of market forces and in general to denationalize and reprivatize the economy. The intellectual currents that are most influential among governing circles have taken up the political terrain held by liberal-centrist forces. There is increasingly a detached critical distance from any measures that promote state intervention in favor of redistributive measures. The new posture emphasizes the importance of the "discipline of the marketplace," the adaptation of labor to the changing demands of the marketplace. This neo-liberal movement has taken as its major target the deficit-generating state-owned enterprises (Parboni). The whole burden for the deficit and losses is identified with the diffuse entity known as "the state." The neo-liberal critique of the "inefficient state" provides virtually no analysis of the burdens foisted on the state by the bourgeois political machines (to solve their patronage problems), by the capitalist class in search of lower costs for state services, or by the political exchanges that resulted in disadvantageous contracts for the state enterprises. Instead of an analysis of the serious problems engendered by the unequal relation between the state and the market in a capitalist political economy, the neo-liberals have embraced the free-market doctrine in the service of facilitating the privatization of long-standing state activities. In response to the growth of neo-liberalism, the remains of the Left have adopted a conservative position (in the generic sense of the term), defending the existing standard of living, the importance of state-owned enterprises for national development, and the treatment of labor as something other than a commodity.

Conclusion

The rich mosaic of conflicting social forces, the complex articulation of a range of modes of production, the increasing differentiation of distinct subsets of interests within the same class categories, and the various layers of state organization strongly suggest that many of the old categories describing the Mediterranean region are no longer adequate, whatever value they possessed in the past. The pervasive demands for autonomous social and political organization and the decay of state-imposed associations suggest that the older notions concerning the affinity of Mediterranean social strata with corporatist forms of organization are not always useful. To the degree that state-technocratic development has gained ascendancy, and the demands for restructuring of industry and agriculture have gained momentum, the state has ceased to be exclusively an area of patronage and clientelism. No doubt, there persist strong undercurrents of what are loosely described as corporatist and clientelist practices. But they increasingly compete with, and in many cases have been overtaken by, the emergence of class and independent interest-group politics. The appearance of dynamic social and political forces in declining industries and regions, as well as those located on the cutting edge of new development models, suggests that the political and social outcome of the present transitional period is still indeterminate. By this I mean that the kind of social system and productive system that will emerge will not be an inevitable consequence of any of the forces now in contention.

References

This essay relies in part on a series of papers presented at an international conference organized by the author under the auspices of the Foundation for Mediterranean Studies, Athens. The conference, "Social Classes, Social Change and Economic Development in the Mediterranean," took place in Athens on May 3–6, 1984. This essay also draws on a series of monographs by Greek scholars on class structures that he directed during his residence as director of sociopolitical studies at the foundation.

Conference Papers

Allaire, Gilles. "The Mediterranean Face of France: Rural Development and Crises."

Boleic, Silvano. "Class Interests and Post-War Economic Development in Yugoslavia." (Belgrade).

Capecchi, Vittorio. "Small Industries and the New Working Class in Italy." (Bologna).

Cerase, Francesco. "State Employees in the Italian Socio-economic System: Trends and Perspective of Their Changing Nature and Role."

Farsoun, Samih. "Class and Sect: The Role of Bank and Merchant Capital in the Political Economy of Lebanon."

Fernandez de Castro, Ignacio. "The Process of Industrialization and the Working Class in Spain." (Madrid, IEPALA).

First-Dilic, Ruza. "Changing Economic Role of Rural Women in SFR Yugoslavia." (Zagreb).

Hurta Carbonell, Jesus Ruiz. "La Agricultura en el Proceno de Desarollo Económico Español."

Paci, Massimo. "Self-Employment in the Italian Class Structure: Old and New Trends."

Pamuk, Senket. "Industrialization and the Industrial Bourgeoisie in Turkey."

Parboni, Ricardo. "The Shipwreck of Italian State Shareholdings: Conflict Between Public and Private Capital."

Stambouli, Frej. "État et la dynamique des classes moyennes en Tunisie."

Villaverde Cabral, Manuel. "State and Peasantry: Agricultural Policy and Strategies in Portugal Since World War II."

Monograph Series: Foundation for Mediterranean Studies

Gourdomichalis, Alike. *The Participation of Women in the Agricultural Labor Force.*

Loannou, Christos. *Greek Trade Unionism: 1974–1981*.
Metaxas, Babis, and Chryssi Vitsilakis. *The Greek Labor Tradition: Elements of Structural Permanence and Attitudinal Change*.
Moisides, Antonis. *Social Stratification in Greek Agriculture: 1951–1984*.
Moschonas, Andreas. *Self-Employment in Greek Development*.
Papandreou, Nicholas. *Markets and Power in Greek Agriculture*.
Stamatopoulos, Dimitris. *The Evolution of Industry in Greece*.

Articles Cited

Petras, James (1984). "Rise and Decline of Southern European Socialism." *New Left Review* (July–August).
———— (1985). "Rentier Capital: Dynamic Growth and Industrial Underdevelopment." *Journal of the Hellenic Diaspora* (Winter).

CHAPTER 12

Development Policy in the 1980s: The Twin Plants, a Lesson for the Enterprise Zone Proposal?

Devon G. Peña

> . . . the traditional differentiation between affluent developed countries and impoverished underdeveloped countries no longer is clear-cut and mutually exclusive. Distinctive Third World conditions and institutions are becoming widespread in the First World. The underlying reason for this dimming of dividing lines is that all regions of the globe are becoming ever more tightly integrated components of the international market economy. . . . With Third World conditions sprouting within the metropolitan centers, the history of the Third World is no longer a history of distant and exotic peoples with whom we have only tenuous contact. It is now an integral part of our own history. (Stavarianos, 1981:26–27)

In a recent article Phillip Mattera (1981) explores one of the latest strategies developed by capital to deal with the decline of the inner cities: the enterprise zone proposal. The enterprise zone proposal is part and parcel of the so-called nouveau supply-side economics. The zones would presumably stimulate private sector investments in declining urban areas through tax reductions and curtailed regulations, the twin pillars of supply-side ideology. Among the concessions that would be granted to capital are the elimination of property taxes, 100 percent capital allowances, and simplified planning requirements.

The enterprise zone concept has been strongly advocated by the Reagan think tank, the Heritage Foundation. The foundation has gone on record stating that the proposal would "provide an attractive climate for private money and business" (as cited in Mattera, 1981:18; also see Butler, 1980). What concerns Mattera is that the enterprise zone proposal embraces a policy that "aside from possible encroachments on the minimum wage . . . [would generate] jobs [that] will be not only low-paying but probably dirty, unsafe, and non-union . . . any new economic activity in the inner cities will be limited to marginal enterprises employing workers from the lower rungs of the labor market hierarchy . . ." (1981:19). This policy, Mattera points out, is based on the notion that "a bad job is better than no job at all" (1981:19). Just as unsettling to Mattera is that the policy is a reflection of the "unquestioned principle . . . that in a crisis, business gets incentives and the people get austerity" (1981:20).

The enterprise zone concept, Mattera explains, "furthers the reversal of fiscal power relations that has characterized the response to the social struggles of the 1960s. In that period, public workers and the poor forced the state—at both the federal and local levels—to improve the conditions of their lives by expanding public expenditures . . . " (1981:21). The enterprise zone concept signifies a culmination of a "fiscal counter-revolution," Reaganomics in one of its forms of attack on the gains of prior working-class struggles.

What is significant here is the striking similarity of the enterprise zone proposal and the export-processing zone (EPZ) concept.[1] The EPZ has been the cornerstone of development policies in Third World countries like Mexico since the 1960s. The EPZ involves a policy calling for massive investments by transnational companies in return for a packaging of fiscal incentives, subsidies, and rigidly controlled industrial relations. One might be inclined to characterize the enterprise zone concept as representing a policy for the "underdevelopment" of the United States via the imposition of a Third World–styled productivity deal: *bad jobs for less pay*.

Mexico's Border Industry Program (BIP), our southern neighbor's version of the EPZ development strategy, has many of the features that will characterize the enterprise zones. These features include: (1) tax reductions and exemptions, (2) curtailed regulatory mechanisms and controls, (3) low-wage, high-productivity work, (4) hazardous working conditions, (5) abnormally high labor-force turnover rates, and (6) an entrenched antiunion atmosphere. The twin plants (*maquiladoras*) are labor-intensive in-process assembly operations, the backbone of the BIP.[2] Such assembly plants may be representative of the type of industrial development that will be promoted under the auspices of the enterprise zone proposal. The twin plants may offer a glimpse of our own immediate future.

The sunbelt states are a primary locus of the emergent capitalist restructuration of U.S. labor markets and the imposition of a new productivity deal. As Mattera states, "the sunbelt states [are in] a national bidding contest for investment. . . . So aggressive [is this bidding] that sunbelt states are presenting the local work force as disciplined, productive, and willing to work for subsistence wages . . ." (1981:20). Advertisements by sunbelt states in the national press use the exact same sales pitch that Mexico's Minister of Industry and Commerce was making to Wall Street in the mid-1960s to attract investors to the BIP. The emphasis, then as now, was on low wages, high productivity, and the absence of strong independent labor organizations.[3] The transnationalization of capital appears to have turned full circle: from the runaway shop we are witnessing the return of the sweatshop via the enterprise zone.

This paper examines the twin-plant program as the basis for an evaluation of the enterprise zone proposal, particularly as it may apply in the sunbelt region. An attempt is made to assess the potential political and economic impact of the enterprise zone proposal on the population of Mexican origin in the sunbelt states. The enterprise zone proposal is also examined in the context of the interregional forces which have led to the current phase of capitalist geopolitical mobility and restructuration.

The Interregional Context of Capitalist Mobility

Bluestone and Harrison (1980) have made a major contribution to our understanding of the causes and consequences of the mobility of capital in the present period. They offer the following observation to explain the increasing level of plant shutdowns and relocations:

> The long-standing resistance of Southern [and some western and border] states to raising the social wage has produced quite extraordinary interregional differences in workers' standards of living in the United States . . . workers and their families are better off in the states where

Table 12.1 Selected Indicators of Standard of Living in 1977: States with and without Right-to-work Laws

Indicator	Right-to-work States	Other States
Average wages of manufacturing production workers: hourly	$ 4.64	$ 5.38
weekly	186.00	216.00
Average weekly unemployment benefits	$ 67.46	$ 75.23
Percentage of states in the group with minimum wage law	55	97
Percentage of states with fair employment practices law	40	100
Corporate income tax as a percentage of total state tax collections	5.5	7.6
Percentage of states with equal pay laws for women	60	84
Percentage of families in poverty	11.4	8
Average monthly payments to families with dependent children	$ 58	$236

Source: U.S. Bureau of the Census, *Statistical Abstract of the U.S.* (1977), as cited in Bluestone and Harrison (1980).

union shops are legal than in the [right-to-work] states where they are prohibited. . . . (1980:183)

Therefore, a major force behind the process of capital relocation to the sunbelt states is the absence of strong labor organizations there. The absence of a strong, unionized work force is characteristic of those states with "right-to-work" laws and a low social wage. The social wage is the package of nonwage benefits that governments provide workers in order to maintain their health and purchasing power when they are unable to work (Bluestone and Harrison, 1980:183). Interregional (North–South) differences in the social wage, the authors argue, are a primary motive for capital flight to the sunbelt states.

Data collected by the U.S. Bureau of the Census (1977) on selected indicators of living standards for 1975 demonstrate significant interregional differences in the basic aspects of living standards (see Table 12.1). The sunbelt (right-to-work) states are seriously lagging behind the northern (frostbelt) states in social wage levels. Average hourly and weekly wages of manufacturing production workers, average weekly unemployment benefits, and average monthly payments to families with dependent children are all significantly lower in the right-to-work sunbelt states.

By comparison, tax-related and regulatory laws that favor business provide a much stronger investment climate in the sunbelt states. Corporate income taxes, for example, are significantly lower in these states. Likewise, regulations and laws governing employment practices, discrimination, and equal pay are less evident in the right-to-work states than in the northern states. To this, one can add the higher incidence of poverty in right-to-work states, and the result is a highly favorable climate for private investment, unfettered by a high social wage.

A poverty-stricken population is more likely to accept low wages and the absence of union organization than is a labor force with lower unemployment and higher relative income. This can be seen from data on the unionization rates of the nonagricultural work force. Right-to-work states in the sunbelt have consistently lower rates of unionization and a higher relative incidence of families living below the poverty level. For example, unionization rates for right-to-work states include Arizona (16.0 percent), Arkansas (16.8 percent), Florida (12.5 percent), Mississippi (12.9 percent), North Carolina (6.9 percent), South Carolina (8.0 percent), and Texas (13.0 percent) (U.S. Bureau of the Census, 1977:74). By comparison, unionization rates in union-shop states include Alaska (26.4 percent), California (28.2 percent), Hawaii (36.2 percent), Illinois (34.9 percent), Indiana (33.2 percent), Michigan (38.4 percent), Missouri (32.3 percent), New York (38.0 percent), Pennsylvania (37.5 percent), and West Virginia (38.2 percent) (U.S. Bureau of the Census, 1977:74ff).

A recent study by the Conference of State Manufacturers' Association (COSMA) applauds the probusiness, antiunion character of the sunbelt states. Not surprisingly, three of the four southwestern border states were ranked in the top ten most favorable business regions. Texas was ranked second (behind Florida); New Mexico, seventh; and Arizona, eighth (*El Paso Times*, 1982b:G3). The high ranking attributed to Texas was based on the following factors. Unemployment compensation benefits, averaging $32 paid weekly per worker covered, are the lowest in the nation. Population increase over three years (1974–77) amounted to 1.427 million, second in the nation and first in the south-central region. Value added by manufacturing employees (a productivity index) was $4.99 for each dollar of production payroll, the third highest nationally and second regionally. The average hours worked per week was 41.2, a tie with Louisiana for third nationally, first in the region. The proportion of labor union members per 100 nonagricultural workers was 11 percent, the fourth lowest nationally and first regionally. State and local government public welfare expenditures averaged $105 per capita, the fifth lowest nationally and lowest regionally. Maximum weekly payments of $133 for temporary total disability workers' compensation insurance were the fifth lowest nationally and second lowest regionally (*El Paso Times*, 1982b:G3).

The same study applauded Texas for a two-year change in non-agricultural union membership per 100 workers. Between 1974 and 1977, Texas experienced a decline of 8.33 percent in nonagricul-tural unionization. Related to this was a decline in hours lost to work stoppages. Texas experienced a rate of only 0.055 person-hour lost per 1,000 workers during the same period. Finally, the study found that Texas experienced a 7.66 percent decline per $1,000 of personal income. In a word, Texas is the epitome of a probusi-ness environment. It offers an attractive package of tax breaks and exemptions, low labor costs, and low unionization. Its social wage is among the lowest in the nation. Moreover, it offers a long work week, high productivity, and a disciplined work force.

It is in this context of interregional living-standard discrepan-cies that the shift of capital from the high-wage, high-unionization northern states to the low-wage, low-unionization sunbelt states has occurred. It is also in this context that we must begin to analyze the political and economic implications of the enterprise zone proposal.

Enterprise zones in the northern states could effectively reduce wages and unionization rates by lowering workers' wages and curb-ing unionization efforts. Enterprise zones in the sunbelt states could ensure continuity in the region's tendency for low wages and an antiunion atmosphere. The net result could be a convergence in north–south living-standard differentials.[4]

Underlying these interregional differences is the fact that the northern states have experienced a higher level of working-class militancy, as expressed in hours lost to work stoppages. Northern states have been subject to a more intense level of strike activity compared with the sunbelt states.[5] Thus the movement of capital from the northern to the sunbelt states represents a basic expression of capital flight from worker unrest.[6] The reconstruction of U.S. labor markets may be a process intimately linked with the cycles of working-class struggle that have characterized the past twenty years. We thus see the dismantling of industrial investments in the northern states and their relocation to the Third World and the sunbelt region. This has been a particularly acute phenomenon in the electronics, textile, automotive, and machine manufacturing sectors.[7]

While supporters of the enterprise zone envision a program that would help rejuvenate urban ghettos like the South Bronx and Chicago's West Side, the program would also apply to the sunbelt region. In particular, the poverty-stricken, yet energy-rich, southwestern border region could be included in the enterprise zone initiatives. In the case of the sunbelt states, the enterprise zone is not without antecedents. Sunbelt states have long promoted supply-side incentives in an effort to attract industrial investments to their areas. Rural areas have been particularly active in these efforts.[8] More recently, individual cities and counties have joined the supply-side incentive bandwagon. Through preexisting political ties between local elites and the business community, cities and counties have been organizing industrial development foundations. These foundations have been active since the early 1970s in efforts to consolidate and coordinate the efforts of municipal governments, chambers of commerce, and financial institutions.[9]

Local versions of the enterprise zone are springing up in cities from Tucson, Arizona, to McAllen, Texas.[10] National Semiconductor, for example, began construction on a new $15 million facility in southwest Tucson where workers will assemble high-reliability, military-spec semiconductors. The firm received a $750,000 loan from the city of Tucson. In addition, the corporation will finance the project through $10 million in *tax-exempt* industrial bonds. In return for the assistance, National Semiconductor has promised to hire half of its employees from within a twelve-square-mile poverty pocket in southwest Tucson (Pacific Studies Center, 1981:3).

These local versions of the enterprise zone are the embodiment of Reagan's "New Federalism." The "New Federalism" promotes the *localization* of investment incentives and severe reduction of direct federal involvement, with the exception of minimal financial assistance.[11] A basic question to be resolved is whether these new efforts to attract industry will have a negative impact on those workers occupying the lower strata of the labor market, particularly the Mexican-origin population concentrated in the southwestern border states, where these experiments are likely to occur. Enterprise zones could augment the segmented character of the labor market. This would involve creation of disadvantaged, dead-end jobs for unemployed and underemployed Mexican workers. Enterprise zones would also open the door for the revival or extension of nonunion, low-wage, and hazardous working conditions in many southwestern border region cities.

Criticisms of the Twin Plants

What follows is a brief analysis of criticisms directed against the twin-plant program. These criticisms are important since they highlight the character of a development policy that, we hope to show, portends things to come in the United States under the enterprise zone proposal. The critique of the twin plants is then followed by an analysis of the similarities between the enterprise zone proposal and the twin-plant program.

Mexico's twin-plant program has numerous critics, ranging from the AFL-CIO and protectionist politicians to self-styled activists and social scientists of all persuasions.[12] The most penetrating critiques of the twin plants have come from social scientists. Sociologists and labor economists on both sides of the U.S.–Mexico border have pointed to serious structural and policy problems associated with the program.

A leading critic of the twin plants is the Mexican sociologist Jorge Bustamante. Bustamante (1975) has attacked the program by pointing to its failure in resolving Mexico's border region unemployment problem, as was originally intended. While the *maquiladoras* have increased manufacturing employment among younger Mexican women, they have not provided jobs for the large pool of unemployed male workers and may have also increased the migratory flow from the Mexican interior to the border region. The twin plants, Bustamante and others argue, have attracted large numbers of immigrants in search of work with a simultaneous and absolute rise in unemployment among young Mexican males.[13]

Bustamante (1975) also argues that the twin plants have merely increased Mexico's dependence on U.S. capital. This implies that the Mexican government is losing ground in its struggle to gain greater control over the planning and decision-making processes that shape industrial development policy. The twin-plant program reduces the government's degree of autonomy in its basic programming decisions by removing policy making to corporate headquarters far removed from the locations where those decisions have an impact.

Raul Fernandez (1973, 1977) has joined Bustamante in criticizing the twin-plant program for its failure to improve the technical skill levels and standard of living of Mexican workers. Both authors argue that the BIP may actually be depressing living standards in the border region by increasing the size of the labor force (through migration and increasing female labor-force participation) at a faster pace than the creation of jobs.[14] The *maquilas*, they point out, place a heavier burden on border municipalities to meet the increased demand for energy, water, and social services attendant on demographic growth. The foreign-based transnationals operating twin plants are offered short- and long-term tax exemptions and other subsidies. Thus local governments are facing higher levels of demand for basic services without a corresponding increase in public revenues.

Other critics (Carrillo, 1980; Hernandez, 1980; Carrillo and Hernandez, 1982; and Peña, 1980, 1983) have pointed to the adverse working conditions, low wages, high production pressures, and abnormally high labor-force turnover rates as indications that the twin plants have failed to provide quality, *long-term* employment for workers in the border region. Research on *maquiladora* industrial relations reveals a pattern of autocratic labor control, high production standards, and managerially induced turnover. These features of the BIP are representative of the instability of employment and line speedup characteristic of the Fordist organizational form.[15]

Carrillo's (1980) research indicates that management purposely implements employment, seniority, and promotion policies that guarantee the existence of a *temporary* work force that can be replaced at will. This, Carrillo argues, is possible because of the large mass of surplus labor and because of the relative ease with which workers can be trained for highly de-skilled assembly-line jobs (also see Carrillo and Hernandez, 1982; Peña, 1980, 1983).

Hernandez (1980), de la Rosa Hickerson (1979), and Van Waas (1981) have produced similar findings in their analyses of collective bargaining and trade unionism in the BIP. Van Waas makes reference to the nature of labor control:

> . . . this tight, autocratic union control can and does have advantages for management. It not only simplifies contract negotiations and policy implementation, since worker input is excluded from both, but for managers willing to adopt such a policy, union leaders can and will take over traditional management responsibilities such as hiring, firing, internal plant discipline, and worker control. (1981:110)

In another vein, Peña (1983) points to wage and productivity data that indicate that *maquila* workers, while perhaps better off than many Mexicans, have suffered serious and repeated setbacks in wage levels. These setbacks have been rooted in inflationary pressures, monetary and exchange policies (the peso devaluations), and the not uncommon imposition of fixed wages for extended periods of employment. The February 1982 peso devaluation, for example, reduced *maquila* workers' wages by nearly 50 percent, from $70 to $40 a week (U.S. equivalent).[16] Moreover, officials at the Centro Patronal del Norte have indicated the the BIP companies will likely resist the federal government's call for 10 to 30 percent wage increases (*El Diario de Juarez*, 1982:A1).[17]

Wage problems are compounded by the sporadic and seasonal character of production scheduling in many twin plants.[18] While this is principally a sectorally specific phenomenon (i.e., mainly garment operations), workers often suffer through numerous weeks of unemployment or reduced weeks in accordance with the fluctuations of market demand. This undermines the overall earning potential of *maquila* workers. Evidence of this tendency is currently widespread. For example, several Juarez-based twin plants recently implemented large-scale layoffs, staggered work shifts, and two-week furloughs in response to recessionary conditions in the U.S. economy.[19]

Since *maquiladoras* pay workers in pesos but realize market earnings in dollars, one must also point to the problem of extremely unequal exchange relations. Another important issue concerns the *relative value added by maquila* work compared with work in other sectors. Here the evidence suggests that the Fordist assembly line of the twin plants subjects workers to higher levels of productivity pressures, with consequences of high stress and turnover (Fernandez-Kelly, 1980: Peña, 1983). While twin-plant workers may earn higher wages relative to other Mexican workers, they are also subject to higher levels of productivity. In a word, earnings may be somewhat higher, but the workers' relative output is still much higher, so that proportionately their wages are a minimal part of the value their labor power creates (see Peña, 1984b:3).

The problem of occupational health and safety in the twin plants has also attracted the concern of critics.[20] Many electronics and textile (garment) operations have relocated hazardous, labor-intensive production to foreign EPZs to escape OSHA regulations. Mexico's BIP has received its share of these "runaway hazards" (North American Congress on Latin America [NACLA], 1977c). These occupational health and safety problems are perpetuated by government policies that negligently accept industrial hazards and environmental pollution as a price to pay for the generation of jobs and attraction of capital investments. As NACLA researchers assert: "Reluctantly it is being admitted that a certain level of pollution and a certain percentage of injured or diseased workers is socially affordable. . ." (1977c:9).

One of the least understood aspects of the occupational health and safety problem is the relationship between high productivity quotas, outmoded equipment, and the incidence of optical nerve disorders and psychogenic illness among assembly-line workers (see, e.g., Gettman and Peña, 1984). The problem of optical nerve disorders is one of the most widespread of occupationally related diseases in electronics twin plants. Disorders and weakening of the optical nerves affect nearly 60 percent of the workers in the sector with three or more years of employment, according to one independent (unofficial) estimate.[21] As these disorders take their toll, the workers' productivity diminishes and they are terminated, further compounding the problem of high labor-force turnover (also see Carrillo, 1980).

The problem in identifying and understanding these occupational hazards lies, in part, in the fact that the electronics sector (particularly semiconductors) is widely regarded as a "clean, light" industry (NACLA, 1977b; Talbot et al., 1977). This misconception persists despite increasing evidence to the contrary. Workers in the electronics sector face very stressful working conditions (e.g., high productivity demands) and risk exposure to hundreds of toxic and potentially carcinogenic substances (Talbot et al., 1977; PHASE, 1979; ECOSH, 1979). Moreover, the psychogenic, stress-related afflictions documented among U.S., Southeast Asian, and British assembly-line workers are also evident among *maquiladora* workers.[22]

Critics of the twin plants have based their analyses on rigorous survey data and extensive case histories. The criticisms are thus empirically based and not ideologically derived conclusions. In fact, some Mexican officials have recently expressed dismay over the problems afflicting the twin plant program. They have stopped short of suggesting or implementing policies to deal with the problems outlined above.[23] It is difficult, nonetheless, to ignore the current situation surrounding the twin plants, which are affected by labor unrest, cyclical and seasonal layoffs, reduced output, and political criticism within Mexico and the United States. It is also difficult not to recognize the seriousness of the continual displacement of workers: for example, between September 1981 and March 1982, five thousand workers were laid off in the Juarez sector, and 20 to 30 percent of the work force was given reduced work loads.[24]

Enterprise Zones: A Form of Core Underdevelopment?

Most of the problems that characterize the twin-plant program are likely to occur in the enterprise zones that may soon dot the industrial landscape of U.S. inner cities. In January 1982, the Reagan administration announced plans to establish an initial set of twenty-five such zones as part of its urban policy package for the 1982/83 fiscal year (*El Paso Times*, 1982a:A1). A total of seventy-five zones were proposed over the next three fiscal years. As of fiscal 1983/84, the initiative had not yet been implemented. However, at least one of the primary congressional sponsors of the legislation (Jack Kemp) had acknowledged plans to reintroduce the plan on the floor during the spring 1985 session of Congress.[25] Except for the expected opposition of organized labor, support for this policy is widespread.

For example, at a December 1981 meeting in Tijuana the Overseas Development Council (ODC) drafted a consensus report that included endorsement of the enterprise zone proposal for use in future border region development plans.[26]

What will the enterprise zones look like? Some features of the proposed zones may be readily extrapolated from the statements of officials and consultants responsible for the concept.[27] Besides the package of fiscal incentives (tax exemptions, reduced planning and zoning requirements, 100 percent capital allowances), the zones in all likelihood will be characterized by the absence of unions. In the right-to-work states, enterprise zones will capitalize on preexisting constraints on union organizing. In regions with union shops—which are precisely the regions most devastated by the current flight of capital—we may expect renewed attempts to legislate unions out of the zones (as originally planned by the Kemp-Garcia version of the proposal). Additionally, where attempts to constrain union organizing through legislation or arbitration are difficult, we may expect zone employers to utilize the high labor-force turnover employment policies that have thus far weakened independent unionism in the twin plants. This will have multiple ramifications. Wages could be kept at or below subsistence levels. As Felix Rohatyn, a staunch supporter, has remarked: "Sacrifice [will be] demanded from all the different elements among our citizens and if, as is inevitable, sacrifice is always greater among our underprivileged. . . ."

The absence of unions also implies that workplace conditions will remain largely uncontested and unregulated and, hence, hazardous. Labor-force turnover rates can be expected to remain at a high level, given the low wages, hazardous working conditions, speedup, and high employment rates characteristic of targeted areas.

Another important feature of the zones will be the marginal character of the industries established therein. We might expect enterprise zone business to be limited to small and medium-size employers. These may include garment shops, toy manufacturers, auxiliary assembly plants servicing already established industries in electronics, machine tools, and construction materials, and a variety of service-oriented operations (Mattera 1981; also see U.S. Congress, 1980). These businesses would be marginal in the sense that their existence would largely depend on contracting with larger, more stable industries in the monopoly sector of the economy.

Hence, they would constitute part of the current process of restructuration among monopoly sector firms. This involves automation, transnationalization, and decentralization of production processes through subcontracting. Traditionally, the subcontracting firms of the so-called competitive sector offer lower wages, fewer benefits, poorer workplace conditions, and dead-end jobs lacking opportunity for occupational and income mobility. The net result could be the imposition of low-wage, nonunion, and hazardous jobs that further fragment an already severely segmented labor market. The working poor, women, and ethnic minorities could be channeled into the enterprise zones (as Representative Garcia, co-sponsor of the original bill, envisions), furthering their entrenchment at the bottom of a sexually and racially segmented labor market.

The enterprise zone proposal, as Mattera (1981:23) has observed, "tolerates the uncontrolled mobility of capital at the same time it encourages marginal industry." Can we, therefore, expect an uninterrupted ebb and flow of "fly-by-night" businesses that will relocate to a more favorable site at the first sign of labor unrest or marketing problems? Mattera sums it up best when he observes:

> . . . the enterprise zone proposal is . . . an attempt to rationalize and institutionalize the underground economy. Instead of the current situation, in which fly-by-night businesses exploit workers in sweatshops and through home labor for a while and then disappear, small entrepreneurs could do the same in a more orderly way. (1981:23)

Even more striking about the enterprise zone concept is that it encourages a policy favoring a return to small-scale, decentralized, and even primitive production strategies. This at a time when the United States is heading in the direction of great advances in large-scale, automated technologies like microprocessors, biotechnology (genetic engineering), integrated transnational production, and robotics. While seemingly contradictory, the enterprise zones would have their place, as Mattera points out, in the emerging international division of labor:

> It may seem odd to speak of sweatshops and marginal jobs at a time when the media are ballyhooing a new technological revolution and a new wave of automation. . . . Both tendencies are real: there are simultaneous moves towards labor-intensive primitive forms of production and toward an advanced electronics, genetic engineering,

and the like. What this implies is an increasing polarization of both forms of production and the conditions of work and life of the people involved in each. . . . The largest number of people will find themselves [facing] . . . grossly reduced social services, irregular employment, poor wages and working conditions, and inadequate and deteriorating housing and transportation. A smaller number of industrial workers and technicians will be relatively privileged. . . . this reduced labor force will be permitted good wages, benefits, and job security in exchange for loyalty and discipline. (1981:23)

Viewed from this perpective, the enterprise zones will play a significant role in the restructuration of the (class) division of labor within the United States. The zones may signal the return of familiar forms of labor control: low-wage, unorganized workers held captive in unregulated sweatshops. The zones will involve the imposition of shop floor conditions not unlike those of the EPZs. But they may also utilize a labor force composed of workers with a Third World background: *marginalized labor from the periphery working in marginalized industrial zones in the core of advanced capitalism* (see Sassen-Koob, 1984, for related commentary). Already there is a tendency in certain sectors of the U.S. economy toward the use, for example, of undocumented workers from Mexico: from the automotive plants of Van Nuys and Fremont to the garment sweatshops of East Los Angeles, El Paso, and Chicago (see e.g., Morales, 1984).[28]

For the Mexican-origin population of the sunbelt border region, this prospect is far from positive. Mexican workers are already devastated by their concentration in the secondary labor market and by the current rounds of budgetary cutbacks and planned austerity. Now Mexican workers will be asked to make a choice between continuing unemployment and welfare rolls or bad jobs for less pay. Numerous studies have already documented the fact that Mexican workers—both U.S. and foreign-born—take the jobs rejected by other U.S. native-born workers (see, e.g., Cardenas, Shelton, and Peña, 1983; Flores, 1983; Bustamante, 1981).

There is a strong possibility, in light of the above, that *all* native-born workers (Chicanos included) will reject employment in the enterprise zones. If the zones are established in border cities, then undocumented and green-card Mexican workers will in all likelihood be strongly recruited by businesses located in the zones.

The historical antecedents for this are not difficult to see. Labor recruiters from the United States have made forays into Mexico in search of labor power since the period of the Porfiriato (1880s–1910) and the days of the Alien Contract Labor Laws. These workers have historically been destined not only for agriculture—as is often assumed—but also for steel mills, packing and slaughter houses, mining operations, textile factories, rail construction, and the like. Green-card ("commuter") workers have a long-standing presence in the border region work force. The use of these workers has shifted from rural to urban, agricultural to industrial activities, where they have often displaced Chicano workers. Use of green-card workers as strikebreakers is well known (e.g., the Farah strike in El Paso and the onion harvest strike of the Texas Farmworkers' Union). Undocumented and green-card workers may, in fact, be preferred by enterprise zone businesses. In the case of the undocumented, their status as "illegal" workers would increase their vulnerability to exploitation and deportation in the event of organizing efforts. In the case of green-card workers, their residence in Mexico implies that their reproduction as labor power comes at reduced or no cost to captial. In such a situation, capital would benefit from greater flexibility and less resistance in determining the employment conditions of a "subclass" of workers. In such a scenario, enterprise zones would not alleviate unemployment but would rationalize the utilization of undocumented and green-card workers.

From the vantage point of municipal revenues, the enterprise zones will contribute to the further erosion of local tax bases. This will create or aggravate problems for municipalities in their efforts to meet already strenuous demands for residential and social services for the working population and demands for infrastructure improvements for the new industrial interests. EPZs have affected municipalities in the same manner from the Bataan Export Zone to the northern Mexican border. City and county authorities are faced with a reduction of federal assistance and are on the verge of fiscal insolvency or political suicide by hiking property taxes for homeowners in order to compensate for the shortfalls induced by Reagan's austerity measures. It may prove difficult for local public officials to justify tax hikes for property owners at the same time business is granted enormous tax reductions and exemptions. Whether these officials can convince their local constituencies that reduced taxes for business and higher taxes for homeowners is not too severe a price to pay for jobs remains to be seen. In the long run, their failure to gain support for supply-side incentive schemes at the *local* level may undermine the viability of the enterprise zone proposal as an urban redevelopment strategy in the advanced core of industrial capitalism.[29]

Possible Responses of the Working Class

This section focuses on the possible responses of the working class in the United States to the process of "core underdevelopment," discussed above. The U.S. working class (including both native- and foreign-born sectors) has historically engaged in intense offensives in the face of capitalist restructuring and repression. One need only recall the great strike waves and organizing efforts associated with the Great Depression to recognize this historical possibility.[30] Faced with imposed austerity and the erosion of wage gains and social benefits, one might expect workers to launch a new series of offensives against capital.

However, in the present political-economic conjuncture, labor unions are making wage and benefit concessions in return for job security.[31] Such is the response of a work force threatened by the patterns of plant shutdowns, relocations, and layoffs discussed earlier. The pattern of concessions has generated sharp divisions within organized labor: for example, the emergence of a rank-and-file anticoncessions movement in 1981 and 1982. Moreover, concessions have not prevented capital flight; in many cases, they have only delayed plant closures and layoffs. Nevertheless, it seems unlikely that workers will accept imposed austerity in the form of wage reductions and layoffs over the *long term*. The response of organized sectors of the U.S. working class to the enterprise zone proposal has not yet been determined. The response will nevertheless provide a strong indication of the direction the U.S. labor movement will take in the coming decades. There are a number of possibilities worthy of speculation here.

Native-born, U.S. workers may reject the bad jobs for less pay that will characterize the enterprise zones. There is already evidence that supports this speculation: research on the impact of undocumented workers on the U.S. labor market clearly indicates that the undocumented occupy jobs rejected by native workers (see, e.g., Bustamante, 1981; Cardenas, 1980; Cardenas, Shelton, and Peña, 1983; Flores, 1982, 1984). The types of jobs rejected by native workers and accepted by the undocumented are precisely those that would characterize enterprise zone businesses (garment work, food processing and packaging, electronics assembly, etc.). If this pattern develops—in which native-born workers reject and foreign-born workers accept enterprise zone employment—we may thus witness an increasing polarization of the working class in the United States along racial, national origin, skill, and gender lines. Mattera's prediction of increasing polarization will clearly be exacerbated by the enterprise zones.

However, there are other political possibilities. Accompanying the increasing role of undocumented workers in automotive, assembly, garment, and other manufacturing sectors is an increasing level of organizing efforts by unions. For example, in Van Nuys, the United Autoworkers Union (UAW) local has had a membership including close to 40 percent undocumented workers (see Morales, 1984). Similar organizing efforts are evident in the International Ladies' Garment Workers Union (ILGWU), the Amalgamated Clothing and Textile Workers (ACTW), the International Association of Machinists (IAM), the International Brotherhood of Electrical Workers (IBEW), the Teamsters (truck drivers), and the International Longshore Workers Association (ILA), among many others (see Gomez-Quiñones, 1981; Mora, 1981; Flores, 1982; Morales, 1984).[32] These organizing efforts are a response to the declining membership levels experienced among the traditional (white male) unionists and to the realities of the use of "transitional labor" in declining industries. Nevertheless, these organizing efforts, should they persist, may cushion and eventually reduce the divisive consequences of increasing polarization. Of course, it remains to be seen if these organizing efforts can be extended into enterprise zones.

Another possible response may involve strengthening and extending the so-called experiments in "workplace democracy" which have emerged in the United States over the past decade and a half (see Zwerding, 1978). This includes the establishment of worker- and community-owned, self-managed enterprises, worker and community buyouts of plants closing, and the less acceptable alterna-

tive of ESOPs (Employee Stock Option Plans). Recent initiatives
in places as far-flung as Youngstown, Ohio, and Maricopa County, Arizona, indicate that working-class alternatives to economic
development are being undertaken.[33] However, the results have
certainly been mixed: as in the case of the Youngstown buyout,
few experiments in workplace democracy have succeeded over the
long term.[34]

The fundamental political question may be posed as a struggle between "planned underdevelopment of the core," as a means
for disciplining the U.S. working class, and workers' autonomy
expressed as the refusal to accept the imposition of austerity. In the
words of W.W. Goldsmith: "In effect, the enterprise zones would
keep American jobs from being exported—by bringing the Third
World home to the United States" (1982:25). This underdevelopment or "Third Worldization" of U.S. labor markets via the enterprise zones is one of capital's possible responses to the increased
power and autonomy of the working class produced by decades of
difficult struggle. The U.S. working class now faces the formidable
task of developing new forms of organization and struggle. These
new forms must possess the ability to confront capitalist geopolitical mobility. It is precisely this mobility that currently gives capital greater power and flexibility. The enterprise zones, as Mattera
notes, will increase and rationalize this mobility. However, new
forms of organization must also confront the increasing polarization
induced by the combination of enterprise zones and high-technology
development efforts.

Whether or not the enterprise zones become a salient feature
of industrial development in the sunbelt border region or other
regions is not the heart of the matter. Given interregional differences
in living standards, in the social wage, and in unionization, *the
entire sunbelt border region can be seen as a massive enterprise
zone already.* More at the heart of the matter is the possibility
that whatever form capitalist restructuration takes, working-class
response may not materialize with sufficient force or timeliness.
Nevertheless, if the enterprise zone concept becomes an aspect of
capitalist restructuring, then it is difficult to find a more strategic
issue to be reckoned with by organizers and activist scholars. As
Goldsmith has noted:

The danger . . . is that enterprise zones would not stay contained. Once industry became accustomed to lower wages, lower taxes, and limits on workers' rights in enterprise zones, these provisions would tend to spill over elsewhere. Why should GM tolerate a high wage, unionized workforce in Detroit when a government-approved domestic Third World is available [elsewhere]? (1982:30)

Conclusion

The future direction of urban development strategy as well as the future development of the U.S. labor movement will be increasingly affected by the transnational character of capitalist production. International differentials in working-class power and thus in wage and productivity differentials figure prominently in determining the particular patterns of capital investment. This is also true of interregional patterns of investment within the United States: as we have seen, frostbelt–sunbelt differentials in the social wage, unionization, and investment incentives have encouraged the movement of capital into the sunbelt region.

The enterprise zone proposal has been analyzed as a case of "underdevelopment in the core." What is most striking in this analysis is the similarity of conditions in export-processing zones (EPZs) like Mexico's twin-plant program and the conditions that are likely to exist in the enterprise zones: low wages, high productivity and turnover, and the absence of independent unions and regulations governing occupational health and safety. I have argued that the enterprise zone proposal therefore involves "peripheralization" of select regions of the United States.

There are a number of unresolved issues that require further inquiry and analysis. Two issues of fundamental importance are: (1) further analysis of the impact of peripheralization strategies on the internal divisions of the working class—that is, polarization along racial, national origin, skill, and gender lines; (2) analysis and refinement of alternatives models of economic development and their prospects of success (i.e., worker and community ownership of enterprises, producer co-ops, self-management experiments, etc.).

The emerging capitalist restructuring of industrial development will have a negative impact on all sectors of the U.S. working class. However, if historical patterns repeat themselves, the urban

working poor, women, and national and ethnic minority groups will
be most adversely affected. Future scholarship on this issue must not
lose sight of the international dimensions of the process. Enterprise
zones are merely the transference of the export-processing zone
strategy from the Third World to the United States. Therefore,
an assessment of the current struggles of workers in the EPZs
of Mexico, Malaysia, Taiwan, the Philippines, Singapore, and
other Third World countries should provide an indication of likely
consequences and organizing strategies.

What the workers of Mexico's *maquiladoras* do in the manner of
workplace and political struggles may hold important lessons for an
understanding of what we may expect in the enterprise zones. But
there is another important consideration. The emergence of Third
World conditions in the United States through enterprise zones is
only one aspect of the overall process. Another, equally important
aspect has to do with the possibility that increasing numbers of
Third World workers will be brought into the United States to labor
in these "peripheralized enclaves." Such is already the case in
California's "Silicon Valley," where over half of the assembly-line
work force consists of foreign-born (Mexican and Southeast Asian)
women. Thus whether traditional workers in the United States refuse
to accept less pay and more work, or they remain on the path of
underdevelopment and austerity, may well be determined by the
outcome of the struggles of Third World workers in the periphery
and core regions of the international economic system.

Notes

This is a revised version of a paper prepared for the 1982 Annual Meetings of the Western Social Science Association, April 22–23, Denver,
Colorado. The author acknowledges the comments and assistance of Gilber
Cardenas, Estevan Flores, and Harry Cleaver. The author is also grateful
to W.W. Goldsmith for crucial correspondence.

1. The EPZ has been promoted in Third World countries since
the 1960s as an alternative path to development, replacing the "import-substitution" strategies implemented during the 1950s. The EPZs,
also known as platform economies, free production zones, and export-
manufacturing zones, involve "in-process" assembly operation linked
through subsidiaries, subcontractors, or *prestanombres* to transnational corporations. As "in-process," operations of the industries in the EPZs are

involved only in the primary and secondary assembly phases of an internationally dispersed production apparatus. Ordinarily, the EPZ operations assemble components manufactured in the home bases of transnational corporations for reexport to the home base markets. For further commentary and analysis, see Trajtenberg (1978), Bonifaz (1975), Froebel et al. (1980), Peña (1980).

2. The *maquiladoras*, or "twin plants" as they are known in business and official circles, are assembly operations involved in export-processing for transnational corporations. They are the primary industries promoted under the auspices of Mexico's Border Industry Program (BIP) and function under the legal framework of Article 321 of the Mexican Customs Code and tariff items 806.30 and 807.00 of the Tariff Schedules of the United States. The predominant sector of the BIP is electronics, which includes over 40 percent of all BIP operations and employs close to 70 percent of all BIP workers. Most twin plants in the electronics sector are foreign subsidiaries of U.S.-based transnationals like RCA, GTE-Sylvania, General Electric, Westinghouse, and Motorola. For further discussion and analysis, see Peña (1980, 1981, 1983). Also see Konig (1975). The term "twin plants" is a misnomer: the term derives from the fact that the program involves two facilities, one on each side of a given border locale. However, the U.S. operation is normally a warehousing, transport, and technical support facility. All production processes are on the Mexican side. For purposes of this paper, the term "twin plant" is used interchangeably with the term "*maquiladora*" (which is derived from *maquilar*, "to manufacture").

3. For the comments by Campos-Salas, Mexico's Minister of Industry and Commerce during the Diaz-Ordaz administration, see the *Wall Street Journal* of May 25, 1967. Advertisements promoting the favorable business climate of the sunbelt states can be found in the *Wall Street Journal, Business Week, Fortune, Texas Business Review, Arizona Business*, and other business-oriented publications. I know of at least one local development foundation (The Greater Laredo Development Foundation) that has published brochures exalting the low cost and the unorganized state of the local labor force. This brochure was distributed to corporations based in northeastern and midwestern states. Such brochures, and the promotional tours for prospective investors financed by the chamber of commerce and the foundation, are quite common. The Organization of U.S. Border Cities and Counties has also published brochures and reports, as has the American Chamber of Commerce of Mexico (AMCHAM-COMEX), a major representative of *maquiladora* interests in Mexico.

4. For further discussion, see Bluestone and Harrison (1980). Organized workers in the northern, northeastern, and midwestern regions

of the country are already hard pressed to provide substantive wage concessions in order to protect their jobs. The 1982 UAW–Ford contract and various contracts between the United Steelworkers Union of America (USWA) and steel mill operators contain such concessions. The trend toward concessions and wage constraints continues largely unabated. For example, wage increases throughout 1984 averaged 2 percent, the lowest in seventeen years. If the tendency toward concessions and givebacks continues unabated, the north–south wage differentials will be significantly reduced.

5. For sectoral statistics on work stoppages by state and region, see U.S. Department of Labor, Bureau of Labor Statistics (1975).

6. For an analysis of capital mobility in the textile and electronics sectors, see NACLA (1975, 1977a, 1977b) and Peña (1980).

7. This problem has been serious enough that union representatives from both sides of the border recently met in Mexico City to discuss problems and possible responses. The First U.S.–Mexico Conference on International Capital Mobility and Binational Labor Organizing, held in July 1984, was an attempt to establish linkages and working groups among U.S. and Mexican unions in automotive, electrical parts, steel, and agricultural sectors. Among the unions represented at the conference were the UAW, USWA, Arizona Farm Workers Union, Teamsters, and International Confederation of Free Trade Unions.

8. Interview with Victor Nelson Cisneros, former senior research associate at the National Rural Center, Austin, Texas (March 1980).

9. For a directory of development foundations active in the southwestern border region, see Jamail (1980).

10. In the case of McAllen, the development efforts are labeled "free-trade zones." The free-trade zone concept has been used in a variety of ways on both sides of the border since the 1800s. For a relevant discussion, see Martinez (1979). As used in the context of recent development efforts in south Texas, the free-trade zone involves policies similar to the enterprise zone concept, including tax and planning concessions, tariff exemptions for those businesses involved in import-export activities, and the issuance of tax-exempt bonds for the construction of facilities and infrastructure.

11. For a critique of the "New Federalism," see Margolis (1981).

12. For an extensive review of the relevant literature on the border industries, see Peña (1981).

13. For another view, which argues that the *maquiladoras* have not increased migration to the border region, see Selligson and Williams (1981). Research by Fernandez-Kelly (1980) and Peña (1983) suggests that twin-plant managers prefer to hire workers with at least three or more

years of residence in the area, although more than half of the workers surveyed in these studies had a migratory background.

14. For extensive theoretical commentary on the growth of the labor force in the border region and the significance of the sexual recomposition of the work force, see Van Waas (1981) and Peña (1983).

15. For an analysis of Fordist and Taylorist organizational forms in the twin plants, see Peña (1983). Fordism basically involves (1) the use of automated conveyance of materials (which provides management greater control over the speed and intensity of work), (2) the imposition of day wages based on productivity and quality performance patterns, (3) the introduction of quality-control supervision, (4) hierarchical controls over planning and execution, (5) "preconceptualization" of the entire process of production, and (6) the continual division and redivision of tasks, resulting in deskilling and fragmentation of informal work groups through line and work-shift reassignments.

16. Figures are based on calculations by the author. The minimum wage paid to *maquiladora* workers was at the time of this study 1,960 pesos per week. At the then effective peso–dollar exchange rate, this amounted to approximately $70 U.S. Prior to the 1981 devaluation, the peso exchange rate was approximately 27:1; after the 1981 devaluation, it fluctuated between 40:1 and 47:1; currently (January 1985), the rate is approximately 205–225:1 (after the 1982 and 1983 devaluations and the adoption of a daily "mini-devaluation" of about 13 Mexican cents).

17. In fact, the first plants to agree to the governmental wage increases were those threatened by informal work stoppages. For a comprehensive analysis of wage policies in the BIP, see Van Waas (1981).

18. See Peña (1980, 1983). Interview with Guillerminia Valdez de Villalva, Director, Center for the Orientation of Women Workers (COMO), Cd. Juarez, Chihuahua, Mexico (October 1981).

19. Among the plants implementing these layoffs, staggered work shifts, and two-week furloughs were RCA, Subensambles Electronicos, General Instruments, General Electrics, Electrocomponentes, Spectronics, and Allen Bradley.

20. Chief among the critics of health hazards in the electronics industry are NACLA, the Electronics Committee on Health and Safety (ECOSH), and the Project for Health and Safety in Electronics (PHASE), the latter two based in California's Silicon Valley. The American Friends Service Committee (AFSC) has also been involved in a worker-education project designed to alert *maquiladora* workers to the dangers of toxic and carcinogenic substances used in electronics assembly processes.

21. Interview with staff, Center for the Orientation of Women Workers (COMO), Cd. Juarez, Chihuahua, Mexico (May 1980).

22. See, for example, Levine and Scotch (1970), Paglaban (1978), Bernstein et al. (1980), Makower (1981).

23. Interview with staff member of the Secretary for Patrimoney and Industrial Promotion (SEPAFIN), Cd. Juarez, Chihuahua, Mexico (February 1982).

24. Data compiled by the author and COMO. In the aftermath of the 1981 and 1982 and 1983 peso devaluations, employment in the BIP has once again boomed. By the end of 1984, over 160,000 workers were employed in the twin plants, an increase from 140,000 during 1983.

25. Telephone interview with staff member, Senator Jack Kemp's office, Washington, D.C. (January 1985).

26. Mayors in San Antonio and El Paso, Texas, and San Diego and Los Angeles, California, among many others, have been credited with public statements in support of enterprise zones for their respective cities.

27. See, for example, Butler (1980), U.S. Congress, House of Representatives (1980). For a useful analysis of the various approaches to "reindustrialization," see Wolff (1981).

28. The importance of the presence of undocumented workers in these sectors has not escaped the attention of union organizers. At the First U.S.–Mexico Conference on International Capital Mobility and Binational Labor Organizing (see note 7 above) labor organizers outlined the importance attached to organizing efforts among these workers and the need for binational coordination of workers in auto plants on both sides of the border. For commentary, see Peña (1984a).

29. Opposition to such measures has already materialized in a number of sunbelt border cities. For example, EPISO (El Paso Interreligions Sponsoring Organization), COPS (Citizens Organized for Public Service, San Antonio), Valley Interfaith (McAllen and Brownsville), and various other grass-roots organizing efforts under the auspices of the Industrial Areas Foundation (IAF) have all spearheaded efforts to oppose tax hikes for property owners and tax breaks for relocating businesses, and have made demands for better public services in poorer neighborhoods (including home revitalization loans and water supplies to marginal areas). On strategies for local (neighborhood) organizing, see Simpson (1981).

30. For analyses of the "cycles" of working-class struggle in the United States, see Baldi (1972), Bologna (1972), Bock, Carpignano, and Ramirez (1976), Cisneros and Peña (1981). On Chicano/Mexicano workers' struggles, see Arroyo et al. (1975).

31. Examples of this trade-off are the recent contracts between the UAW and Ford, and between the USWA and steel mill operators in Pennsylvania and West Virginia. See Labor Education and Research Project (1981a, b, c) for commentary and analysis.

32. See note 28 above.

33. I am referring to community–worker efforts to take over manufacturing plants facing shutdowns (e.g., Youngstown, Ohio) and to the efforts by migrant farmworkers in Maricopa County, Arizona, to gain a contract that includes an economic development fund paid for by growers and used for development projects in the Mexican villages that are the originating sending points for the union members. See Lynd (1981) and Arizona Farm Workers Union (1981). For further case studies, see Zwerdling (1978).

34. For the definitve analysis of the struggle against shutdowns, see Lynd (1982).

References

Arizona Farm Workers Union (1981). "Introductory Proposal of the Arizona Farmworkers' Economic Development Fund." Mimeo.

Arroyo, L., and V. Nelson-Cisneros, eds. (1975). "Special Issue on Labor History and the Chicano." *Aztlan: International Journal of Chicano Studies Research* 6:2 (Summer).

Baldi, G. (1972). "Theses on the Mass Worker and Social Capital." *Radical America*. 6:1 (May–June).

Bernstein, A., et al. (1980). "Silicon Valley: Paradise or Paradox?" In *Mexican Women in the United States: Struggles Past and Present*. M. Mora and A. del Castillo, eds., Los Angeles: Chicano Studies Research Center Publications.

Bluestone, B., and B. Harrison (1980). *Capital and Communities: The Causes and Consequences of Private Disinvestment*. Washington, D.C.: The Progressive Alliance. Republished as *The Reindustrialization of America*. New York: Harper/Colphon, 1982.

Bock, G., Carpignano, and B. Ramirez (1976). *La formazione dell'operaio massa negli USA, 1898–1922*. Milan: Feltrinelli.

Bologna, S. (1972). "Class Composition and the Theory of the Party at the Origins of the Workers-Councils Movement." *Telos* 13 (Fall).

Bonifaz, A. C. (1975). *Empresas multinacionales*. Mexico City: Ediciones El Caballito.

Bustamante, J. (1975). "El progama fronterizo de maquiladoras: observaciones para una evaluación." *Foro Internacional* 16:2 (October–December).

——— (1981). "The Immigrant Worker: A Social Problem or a Human Resource?" In *Mexican Immigrant Workers in the U.S.* A. Rios-Bustamante, ed., Los Angeles: Chicano Studies Research Center Publications.

Butler, S. M. (1980). *Enterprise Zones*. Washington, D.C.: Heritage Foundation.

Cardenas, G. (1980). "Immigrant Women in the Labor Force." Report prepared for the Women's Bureau, U.S. Department of Labor. Austin: Department of Sociology, University of Texas.

Cardenas, G., B. Shelton, and D. Peña (1983). "Undocumented Immigrant Women in the Houston Labor Force." *California Sociologist* 5:2 (Fall).

Carrillo, J. (1980). "La utilización de la mano de obra femenina en la industria maquiladora: el caso de Ciudad Juarez." Mexico, D.F.: unpublished report, Centro de Estudios Sociológicos, El Colegio de Mexico.

Carrillo, J., and A. Hernandez (1982). "La mujer obrera en la industria maquiladora: el caso de Ciudad Juarez." Mexico, D.F.: professional thesis, Facultad de Ciencias Políticas y Sociales, Universidad Nacional Autónoma de México.

Cisneros, V., and D. Peña (1981). "Los Viejos Topos: Mexican Workers' Struggles North of the Border, 1880–1980." Paper presented at the First International Symposium on United States–Mexico Relations: A Focus on the Mexican–American Community. Santa Monica, Calif. (April).

de la Rosa Hickerson, G. (1979). "La contratación colectiva en las maquiladoras." Chihuahua, Mexico: professional thesis, Escuela de Derecho, Universidad Autónoma de Juarez, Ciudad Juarez.

El Diario de Juarez (1982). "Compas de espera en maquiladoras, aumentaran salarios todas las empresas: Centro Patronal." March 31, p. A1.

Electronics Committee on Safety and Health (ECOSH) (1979). "You Are Not a Hypochondriac." Information bulletin. Mountain View, Calif.:ECOSH.

El Paso Times (1982a). "Reagan Bows to High Excise Tax." January 21, p. A1.

——— (1982b). "Study Shows Texas Rates Second in Business Climate." March 14, p. G3.

Fernandez, R. (1973). "The Border Industrial Program on the United States–Mexico Border." *Review of Radical Political Economics* 5:1 (Spring).

——— (1977). *The United States–Mexico Border: A Politico-Economic Profile*. South Bend, Ind.: Notre Dame Press.

Flores, E. (1982). "Post-Bracero Undocumented Mexican Immigration to the United States and Political Recomposition." Ph.D. diss., Department of Sociology, Univerity of Texas, Austin.

———— (1983). "The Impact of Undocumented Migration of the U.S. Labor Market." Unpublished paper.

———— (1984). *Houston Journal of International Law* 5:2 (Summer).

Froebel, F., et al. (1980). *The New International Division of Labor.* Cambridge: Cambridge University Press.

Gettman, D., and D. Peña (1984). "Women, Mental Health, and the Workplace: Research Issues and Challenges in a Transnational Setting." Paper presented at the National Association of Social Workers First National Conference of Health and Public Policy, Washington, D.C. (June).

Goldsmith, W. W. (1982). "Bringing the Third World Home." *Working Papers for a New Society* 9:3 (March–April).

Gomez-Quinones, J. (1981). "Mexican Immigration to the United States and the Internationalization of Labor, 1848–1980: An Overview." In A. Rios-Bustamante, ed., *Mexican Immigrant Workers in the U.S.* Los Angeles: Chicano Studies Research Center Publications.

Hernandez, A. (1980). "Política y práctica laboral en la industria maquiladora: el caso de Ciudad Juarez." Mexico, D.F.: unpublished report, Centro de Estudios Sociológicos, El Colegio de Mexico.

Jamail, M. (1980). *The United States–Mexico Border: A Guide to Institutions, Organizations, and Scholars.* Tucson: Latin America Area Center, University of Arizona.

Konig, W. (1975). "La economia de la subcontratación international." *Foro Internacional* 16:2 (October–December).

Labor Education and Research Project (1981a). "Ford's Foot in the Concessions Door: Steel Division Workers Take Pay Cut." *Labor Notes* 26 (March 25).

———— (1981b). "Ford Demands 50% Wage Cut." *Labor Notes* 33 (October 27).

———— (1981c). "Teamsters Reformers Meeting Maps Fight Against Contract Concessions." *Labor Notes* 34 (November 23).

Levine, S., and N. Scotch (1970). *Social Stress.* Chicago: Aldine.

Lynd, S. (1981). "What Happened in Youngstown: An Outline." *Radical America* 15:4 (July–August).

———— (1982). *The Fight Against Shutdowns: Youngstown's Fight Against Steelmill Closings.* Boston: Single Jack Books.

Makower, J. (1981). *Office Hazards: How Your Job Can Make You Sick.* Washington, D.C.: Tilden.

Margolis, R. J. (1981). "The Limits of Localism." *Working Papers for a New Society* 8:4 (July–August).

Martinex, O. (1979). *Border Boom Town: Cuidad Juarez Since 1848.* Austin: University of Texas Press.

Mattera, P. (1981). "From the Runaway to the Sweatshop: 'Enterprise Zones' and the Redevelopment of the Cities." *Radical America* 15:5 (September–October).

Mora, M. (1981). "The Tolteca Strike: Mexican Women and the Struggle for Union Representation." In *Mexican Immigrant Workers in the U.S.* A. Rios-Bustamante, ed., Los Angeles: Chicano Studies Research Center Publications.

Morales, R. (1984). "Transitional Labor: Undocumented Workers in the Los Angeles Automobile Industry." *International Migration Review.*

North American Congress on Latin America (NACLA) (1975). "Hit and Run: U.S. Runaway Shops on the Mexican Border." *Latin America and Empire Report* 9:5 (July–August).

——— (1977a). "Capital's Flight: The Apparel Industry Moves South." *Latin America and Empire Report* 11:3 (March).

——— (1977b). "Electronics: The Global Industry." *Latin America and Empire Report* 11:4 (April).

——— (1977c). "Dying for Work." *Latin America and Empire Report* 11:6 (June).

Overseas Development Council (ODC) (1981). "Consensus Report." Tijuana, Baja California (December).

Pacific Studies Center (1981). "National in Tucson." *Global Electronics Information Newsletter* 8 (March–April).

Paglaban, E. (1978). "Philippines: Workers in the Export Industries." *Pacific Research* 9:3–4 (March–June).

Peña, D. G. (1980). "*Las Maquiladoras*: Mexican Women and Class Struggle in the Border Industries." *Aztlan: International Journal of Chicano Studies Research* 11:2 (Fall).

——— (1981). *Maquiladoras: A Select Annotated Bibliography and Critical Commentary on the United States–Mexico Border Industry Program.* Austin, Tex.: Center for the Study of Human Resources.

——— (1983). "The Class Politics of Abstract Labor: Organizational Forms and Industrial Relations in the Mexican *Maquiladoras.*" Ph.D. diss., Department of Sociology, University of Texas, Austin.

——— (1984a). "Autonomous Worker Organizing on the Mexico–U.S. Border: A Political Geography." Paper presented at the First U.S.–Mexico Conference on International Capital Mobility and Binational Labor Organizing. Mexico City (July).

——— (1984b). "*Maquiladoras* and Migration: Review of Seligson and Williams." *La Red/The Net* (July).

Project on Health and Safety in Electronics (PHASE) (1979). "Reproductive Hazards in the Electronics Industry." PHASE *Factsheet* 2.

Sassen-Koob, S. (1984). "The International Division of Labor: U.S./Mexico Capital and Labor Flows." Paper presented at the First U.S.–Mexico Conference on International Capital Mobility and Binational Labor Organizing. Mexico City (July).

Seligson, M., and E. Williams (1981). *Maquiladoras and Migration.* Austin: Mexico–United States Program, Institute of Latin America Studies.

Simpson, D. (1981). "Neighborhood Action." *Social Policy* 11:5 (March–April).

Stavarianos, L. S. (1981). *Global Rift: The Third World Comes of Age.* New York: William Morrow.

Talbot, C., et al. (1979). "Hazards of the Electronics Industry." *Labor Occupational Health Program Monitor* 8 (October).

Trajtenberg, R. (1977). *Transnacionales y fureza de trabajo en la periferia: tendencias recientes en la internacionalizacion de la producción.* Mexico, D.F.: Instituto Latinamericano de Estudio Transacionales (ILET).

U.S. Bureau of the Census (1977). *Statistical Abstract of the United States, 1975.* Washington, D.C.: Government Printing Office.

U.S. Congress, House of Representatives (1980). *Urban Revitalization and Industrial Policy.* Hearings Before the Subcommittee on the City, 96th Congress, 2nd Session (September 16–17).

U.S. Department of Labor, Bureau of Labor Statistics (1975). *Handbook of Labor Statistics, Reference Edition.* Washington, D.C.: Department of Labor.

Wolff, G. (1981). "Reindustrialization: A Debate Among Capitalists," *Radical America* 15:5 (September–October).

Zwerdling, D. (1978). *Workplace Democracy.* New York: Harper/Colophon.

PART IV

Toward a Reformulation of Models, Processes, and the Future Direction of the World Economy

CHAPTER 13

Is Historical Sociology of Peripheral Regions Peripheral?

Thomas D. Hall

In this paper I argue that historical sociology, the study of long-term social change, in peripheral areas is vital to the development of an adequate theory of historical processes of social change. The reason is simple, harking back to the first lessons of any methods course: to understand a phenomenon, one must examine its full range of variation. When little is known about a phenomenon, sampling is perforce haphazard, but not necessarily random. Until the universe of discourse is at least crudely known, temporal and geographical diversity are reasonable, if temporary, guides to sampling. Failure to sample the full variance of social change is not only method-ologically unsound, but also leads to distorted theorizing and to the misunderstanding of substantive issues.

A single case study, of course, cannot establish a general pattern. It can, however, demonstrate the existence of a phenomenon and suggest theoretical and empirical issues worthy of further attention. With them, questions about generality inevitably are raised. These can be answered only by further sampling to assess the relative fre-quencies of a newly discovered phenomenon. After such an assess-ment, intelligent comparisons can be designed both to uncover the causes and distribution of a phenomenon and to test theoretical generalizations suggested by its discovery. The examples used in this paper are only the first step of this research process. They do illustrate, however, the necessity for a wider variety of studies of peripheral areas for further theoretical and empirical understanding of the rise of the "modern world-system."

My own work[1] examines the processes of social change in the American Southwest,[2] the area of modern New Mexico and Arizona, focusing on the interactions between local groups and their various external contexts. There are a number of reasons for choosing the Southwest for such a study. Primary among them are the broad variance in the processes of change and the variety of indigenous groups in the region. Indigenous populations range, in Lenski's terms (1966; Lenski and Lenski, 1982), from hunting and gathering groups through advanced horticultural societies.[3] State intrusions vary from early Mesoamerican states through Spain and Mexico to the United States. The impact of Mesoamerica on the Southwest is the most controversial issue, since the very existence of the "Mesoamerican connection" is hotly debated.[4] The Spanish invaders who first explored the region in the 1530s and founded the first permanent colony in 1598 exemplify several types of agrarian society. The American invaders (1846–48) exemplify various types of industrial society. Furthermore, the serial invasions offer an opportunity to compare the consequences of invasions by distinct types of core powers. Since at least the fifteenth century, the region has been "peripheral," or marginal to larger, more central, or "core" areas, such as the Spanish Empire, the Mexican State, and the American state.[5]

The following discussion begins with the problems of doing historical sociology in a peripheral area, moving from practical to theoretical issues. I then discuss some of the benefits derived from such study, drawing illustrations from my study of the Southwest. I conclude by sketching some lessons to be gained from the study of peripheral areas and suggesting comparative strategies for developing broader theories of social change.

Problems Inherent in the Study of the Periphery

There are a number of problems inherent in the study of peripheral areas. While "the periphery" has long been the home of anthropologists, it remains less familiar to sociologists. Sociologists are aware of the significant roles of England, France, and Russia in shaping the modern world, but not many are familiar with the roles of Ute, Navajo, Comanche, Apache, or Pueblo Native American societies in the history of the American Southwest.[6] Thus a sociologist interested in peripheral social change must devote time and pages to describing "basics" that students of core areas can reasonably assume. But this is a minor problem.

More serious is the fact that a periphery is peripheral and from a core point of view is relatively unimportant. "Garden variety" core "ethnocentrism" holds that the periphery and all things in it or associated with it are inconsequential. Western American history, like the region itself, is often considered "a colorfully quaint retreat from the rigors of mainstream American life, but in the end unsophisticated." Thus "western historical works are too often provincial and devoid of conceptual frames of reference" (Steffen, 1979:4). A few historians (e.g., Spicer, 1962; Bannon, 1974; Weber, 1982:ch. 13) have attempted to place southwestern history in broader geographical and theoretical contexts. If I disagree with Steffen, it is only in his implicit limitation of this parochialism to history.

Sociologists often evince a similar ethnocentric elitism. They, however, are bolstered by the fact that the mercantile and industrial revolutions did begin in Europe. Sociologists "into" mainstream sociological analyses, such as survey or census analysis, wonder, is this sociology? or, what can you count? or, more important, why is this sociology? Anthropologists, on the contrary, sometimes fall victim to a different variety of ethnocentrism. They often pursue exotic locations for fieldwork[7] or concentrate on major "native" centers. Still, there are many anthropological contributions to the study of peripheral areas *qua* peripheral areas (see literature reviews by Cole [1977] and Nash [1981]). These problems, nevertheless, are only irritants.

The tendency to ignore the active role of the periphery in social change, both locally in the periphery and in the core, is more serious. This is in part a consequence of peripherality and in part a consequence of the various ethnocentrisms just noted. Peripheral areas have contributed many of the modern staples of human nutrition: corn and potatoes from the New World, rice from Asia, and many other products. The role of New World gold and silver and of African slaves in the development of Europe is well known (Crosby, 1972; Wallerstein, 1974a; Wolf, 1982). But the periphery has made other contributions. Eric Wolf's work, *Europe and the People Without History* (1982) summarizes much of the anthropological work on peripheral areas and has done much to correct this bias.

The key problem is the paucity of work in historical sociology on peripheral areas *qua* peripheral areas. Substantive and theoretical distortions in the study of social change have been introduced by the nonrandom, biased sampling that has overemphasized the study of the core in both "traditional" studies and within world-system theory itself. Both Hechter (1975) and Chirot (1976) have written well-known, excellent world-system studies of core–periphery interactions, but both focus on European areas — the "Celtic Fringe" and Romania. While these works have contributed much to our understanding of the growth of the "modern world-system," much work remains to be done. The distortions that result from a limited sampling of peripheral areas are serious obstacles to building a theory of social change and understanding the origins of the "modern world-system." Some portion of this lack of attention is due to the unavailability or inaccessibility of relevant data. But some of it, too, is due to an excessive focus on Europe. The problem is not one of error, but one of emphasis.

This history of world-system theory is itself doubly ironic. Dependency theory was developed by scholars native to semi-peripheral areas. It did not become "respectable" until it was "mined" and taken to the core, where it was transformed into world-system theory and was reexported to the periphery (Chirot and Hall, 1982:90). Second, Wallerstein found his inspiration for world-system analysis in attempting to untangle these very processes in Africa. To understand Africa, he found it necessary to understand Europe. While that search is far from complete, it is now necessary to return to the periphery to understand the core. The dialectic moves by irony as much as contradiction (see Brown, 1977).

It has been argued, reasonably, that since capitalism arose in Western Europe and engulfed the rest of the planet, Europe is the proper place to study its origin and growth. But without comparison, how can one know what is unique, or even only special, about Western Europe? Since capitalism was a major force behind European expansion and was responsible, at least in part, for the massive transformations that have occurred in the peripheral areas, it follows that the transformations in and of various peripheral areas are also part of the development of capitalism.[8] The periphery is the only location where these problems can be studied, because that is where they have taken place. The examination of this aspect of the growth and spread of capitalism is one of the benefits of the study of the periphery.

The problems I have mentioned so far—lack of familiarity with the history of peripheral areas, inattention to the active role of the periphery in social change, and the paucity of studies of the periphery—all contribute to the fundamental problem. The empirical range of variations of the processes of social change in the periphery is not known. Whether a given process of social change is rare or common is uncertain. Fried's (1967, 1975) argument that tribes are the product of interaction of state societies with band societies is persuasive. My work on the Southwest supports his position (Hall, 1981, 1982, 1983, 1986, 1988), as does Phillips's (1975). But the study of the Southwest also shows that the process is neither simple nor irreversible. State pressure can also cause fragmentation. Sahlins's (1961) study of the Nuer suggests that "tribes" may also be produced by competition with outsiders. Further, he argues that certain forms of social organization, such as the segmentary lineage, are special adaptive arrangements to situations in which there is considerable competition for resources with other band and "tribal" societies. Depending on the social and ecological context, either tribalization or fragmentation may augment or hinder group survival. The segmentary lineage is a form of social organization that can easily adapt to either tribalization or fragmentation.

The absence of general knowledge of all the types and variations of processes of change means that generalizations are necessarily limited. Without knowledge of the empirical variation in processes of change, how can one make theoretical statements? In some cases, such as the study of revolutions (Skocpol, 1970; Skocpol and Somers, 1980), there is little choice. There are only a few cases to use.[9] But this is not so for the study of social change in the periphery—there is almost the entire world to use. It is not that limited generalizations are bad. They are not. Theory building proceeds by generalizing, and then testing the limits of the generalization. The problem is not the examination of only a sample of cases. That is standard procedure. The problem is that the correct type of sample is unknown, although it is certainly neither random nor representative. Presumably, this problem will decline in significance as more studies of historical processes in peripheral areas appear. In the meantime, cautious generalization must be accompanied by an assessment of how each case is limited, and supported with sufficient detail that subsequent workers can discover useful criteria for comparisons.[10]

As the caveats in the preceding discussion indicate, these criticisms of "mainstream" trends in the various social sciences are not new. In history, Frederick Teggart (1918, 1925) long ago advocated the study of areas of contact between societies as an especially fruitful location for the study of social change. Owen Lattimore (1962) continued that trend, noting that it was on the frontier that "civilization" created "barbarians." Among anthropologists, the debates over the culture area concept (see Harris, 1968:ch. 14) raised many of these same issues. Finally, virtually all anthropological studies of "culture change" are studies of peripheral social change, although they are not cast in the terminology of world-system or dependency theory (see Cole, 1977; Nash, 1981).

Two factors warrant raising these criticisms still another time. Obviously, admonitions to study "peripheral areas" or "frontiers" have been honored primarily in the breach. Second, world-system theory offers a paradigm for how such studies may be integrated into a coherent framework. With its formulation, the criticism of the failure to sample widely throughout the periphery is given added force. As I hope the following discussion will indicate, it is now possible and appropriate to begin pulling the extant studies of peripheral areas into a coherent framework. This paper, then, is a call to begin that work. The following discussion both indicates the potential benefits of such an effort and makes some modest suggestions as to how it might begin.

Benefits of the Study of the Periphery

In addition to the obvious benefit of being an antidote to the various ethnocentrisms, the study of the periphery is vital to exploring the interaction of the core and the periphery, for the periphery is where that interaction takes place. It is only in the periphery that questions about how and to what extent the periphery is used by the core may be examined. This is not to say that such "use" does not have important consequences for the core. It does. Rather, I am emphasizing that core exploitation of the periphery actually occurs in the periphery. It is necessary to distinguish between the periphery, meaning all areas in more or less dependent relations with the core, and a particular peripheral region. Thus there are two distinct issues in regard to core exploitation of the periphery: (1) how does the core, as a whole or in part, exploit the periphery? Accepting for the moment that it does exploit the periphery, (2) does the core, or any part of it, profit from every peripheral area? The study of the Southwest shows the answer to be "No" to the latter question. In the late eighteenth century, the New Mexican colony cost New Spain (and hence the Spanish crown) some 55 million pesos annually (Simmons, 1968:88).[11] Why, then, was the province maintained as a colony?

Briefly, there are several political and ideological reasons why the region was kept under Spanish control. First, it was a buffer zone against expansion by other European powers (Bolton, 1929). Second, it was also a buffer against further inroads by surrounding hostile nomads. This was not an unrealistic policy. In the nineteenth century, Comanche and Apache bands from this area raided areas within a hundred miles of Mexico City (Smith, 1963). Third, ecclesiastic authorities wanted to ensure continued attention to the spiritual needs of the Indian converts in the region. Indeed, this was one of the major justifications for the reconquest of the region in 1692, after the Pueblo revolt in 1680 had expelled the Spaniards from New Mexico. Fourth, local elites wanted the area maintained: those in the area for obvious reasons, those from neighboring provinces because their wealth depended in part on trade with New Mexico. The broader question of how typical this situation was, both within the Spanish Empire and in other peripheral areas, remains unanswered. This case, though, underscores the care that must be exercised when examining such issues. Two generally relevant questions in terms of social class, power, and inequality, are who pays these costs and who benefits?

Subtleties and wrinkles in the processes of social change that are often obscure in the core are sometimes manifest in the periphery. Expressed in a statistical idiom, main effects are sometimes weaker in the periphery, and hence interaction effects are more readily observed there. In the core, main effects are frequently so strong that subtler interaction effects are masked. For instance, in both Hechter's (1975) and Chirot's (1976) studies, economic exploitation of the periphery by the core region is so strong that it tends to obscure concurrent political and ideological sources of dependency. On the frontier of northern New Spain, the absence of economic interests serves to highlight these factors. To be sure, a major political concern in New Spain was to protect the silver mines farther south, around Zacatecas, from northern nomadic raiders and potential European rivals. But incorporation of an area into peripheral dependence in order to extract silver (Bakewell, 1971; Brading, 1971, 1978) is significantly different from incorporation of an area to protect another mineral-rich area from marauding raiders or external rivals. The consequences of shifts in the world-system in relative core status on interactions both between the core and the periphery and among groups within the periphery can be studied only in peripheral regions. For instance, the process of incorporation and degree of peripheralization seem to vary, albeit not simply, with different core powers (Hall, 1983).[12] Of greater significance are the consequences of shifts in core power for interactions among, and changes within, local groups. An example will illuminate this point.

Comparisons among three initially similar groups, Apaches, Comanches, and Navajos—all band-level nomadic groups—show that relatively small differences in state power have profound consequences for subsequent social change. For instance, shifts in power in Europe, specifically the Bourbon displacement of the Hapsburg monarchy in Spain in the early eighteenth century, gave rise to the Bourbon reforms (Herr, 1958). By the late eighteenth century, these reforms were felt in the colonies and led to alterations in the administrative structure of New Spain. New vigor was instilled in Spanish America by these changes (Lang, 1975). This was manifested in economic growth and increased prosperity. The northern provinces of New Spain were reorganized politically and militarily for more efficient administration and military protection, primarily from raiding nomads, but also from possible encroachment by Russia, Britain, or France. The latter threat waxed and waned as Louisiana changed hands between Spain and France.

In New Mexico (which throughout the Spanish and Mexican eras included what is now both New Mexico and Arizona and contiguous areas), a concerted effort was made to subdue the hostile nomadic bands (John, 1975; Moorhead, 1968; Simmons, 1968). In 1779,

Governor Anza destroyed a noted Comanche leader, Cuerno Verde, and his band. In 1786, several Comanche band leaders appeared in Santa Fe requesting the Governor Anza distribute food and supplies to them, since they had maintained peace and the hunting had been poor that season. For nearly two centuries, Spanish administrators had used such "gifts" to promote peace and to induce dependency. This time, Governor Anza required that these leaders elect one supreme leader for all the Comanche bands. The petitioning Comanche leaders appeared at his palace the next day with a candidate. Governor Anza refused to accept their candidate until they returned to the Plains and consulted all Comanche bands. Some months later, Ecueracapa, one of the original supplicants, was officially recognized as chief of all Comanches.

In this case, state pressure, exerted through Governor Anza, pushed band organization toward more political centralization, toward a tribal organization. This reactive tribalization (see Fried, 1967, 1975; Hall, 1983, 1986, 1988) was not extreme or permanent, nor was it restricted to Comanche bands. Within a few years, a similar chief was appointed for the Navajo bands. Both chiefs eventually suffered a similar fate: they died in battle leading their warriors, fighting as Spanish auxiliaries, against hostile Apache bands. Here the similarity between Comanches and Navajos ends. The Navajo chief was not replaced. The Navajos remained a group of loosely connected bands. The Comanches elected a new chief, and a lasting peace between Comanches and New Mexicans was established.

This peace was not without its strains, though, for Comanche bands continued to raid in other parts of New Spain, especially in the province of Texas. This raiding persisted after Mexican independence (1821), included raids on the Santa Fe Trail, and continued through the independence of Texas (1836) and until after the American conquest (1846–48). Throughout this time, the Comanche bands remained faithful allies of the New Mexicans and ardent Apache-hunters. Indeed, they sometimes had to be restrained when New Mexico sought to make treaties with various Apache bands (Moorhead, 1968).

State pressure can also work against political centralization, and contribute to increased fragmentation of band-level societies. This becomes apparent in the divergent fates of Apache and Comanche bands.[13] The continual harassment of Apache bands by both Hispanic settlers and their Comanche allies forced them southwest from the Plains to the Basin and Range Province, semiarid regions of southern New Mexico. This region of low desert basins interrupted with relatively small mountain ranges made amassing a large number of raider-foragers difficult, but facilitated a mobile, fluid social organization. Apaches were fragmented into many small, fluid bands. Comanches became the celebrated "Lords of the South Plains" (Wallace and Hoebel, 1952). They were able to maintain large bands, which could readily congregate and disperse on the relatively undifferentiated plains. For a while, Comanches prospered and Apaches declined—until the United States took over.

After the conquest, Americans viewed Comanches as a major threat, due to their constant raiding in Texas and Mexico and their harassment of the Santa Fe Trail trade. They were systematically pursued and subdued. By 1882, when they were permanently settled on a reservation in what is now Oklahoma, they were reduced to 1,382 (Wallace and Hoebel, 1952:32) from an estimated 4,700 in 1866. In the late eighteenth and early nineteenth centuries, they had numbered between 10,000 and 30,000 (Thornton, 1978; Wallace and Hoebel, 1952). The Apaches, by contrast, continued to resist, and were not "pacified" until 1886 (Utley, 1984:201). By 1910, they numbered 14,000 (U.S. Census, 1915). It is not certain whether there was a reduction or an increase in Apache population through this time, but they certainly did not decline like the Comanches.

Finally, the fate of the Navajos contrasts with that of both the Comanches and the Apaches. After an abortive attempt to settle the Navajos on a southern New Mexico reservation, the U.S. government allowed them to return to a reservation on their traditional land in 1868. For the next several decades, they attracted little attention, since they lived in an area that no one wanted. They prospered (relatively), and numbered about 20,000 by 1910 (U.S. Census, 1915).

There are many lessons here, but for our purposes the divergent fates of initially similar groups are of interest. Administrative policy in combination with differences in geographical location and adaptation are important factors behind these variations. Such variation adds new wrinkles to the rule of thumb that in the New World the British colonists destroyed indigenes, while the Spanish enslaved them (Lang, 1975, 1979). That generality holds, but there are important exceptions. Some are found on the northern periphery of New Spain.

Several other points may be drawn from this example. First, the same state—the viceroyalty of New Spain—may have opposite effects on initially similar groups, as shown by the relative political centralization of the Comanche bands and the relative fragmentation of the Apache bands. Second, different states may have nearly opposite effects on the same group through time. Under Spain, Comanches prospered while Apaches suffered; under the United States, the pattern was nearly reversed. Thus there is a clear interaction effect in the consequences of state action for nonstate societies. The level of sociocultural development of both the state and the nonstate societies shaped the result of their contact. Furthermore, geopolitical location is an important mediating factor in state–nonstate interaction.

Third, the process of incorporation is both variable and reversible. At the regional level, New Mexico experienced changes in degree of incorporation into the state systems of Spain, Mexico, and the United States. The Bourbon reforms and the American conquest increased its articulation with the dominant state. The Mexican rebellion and the American Civil War loosened that dominance. These changes had important consequences at the local group level. For nearly two hundred years, nomadic groups were only marginally incorporated into the state system on the northern frontier. With the Bourbon reforms, they were more tightly drawn into the system, ranging in descending order of incorporation from Comanche to Navajo to Apache. With Mexican independence, the connection was loosened. With the American conquest, all were drawn more tightly into the new state system. At the end of the American Civil War, relative incorporation again changed. Navajos were given an isolated reservation on their traditional lands, and their bonds to the state system loosened somewhat. Comanches were forced onto a reservation on a small fraction of their former land (Haga, 1976). Apaches were the last to be reduced to reservations. They were more tightly incorporated than the Navajos, but less than the Comanches. The degree of incorporation for these three groups is a function, in part, of their geopolitical location, and the degree of their threat to surrounding capitalist enterprises. Finally, there is no simple correlation between degree of incorporation and degree of prosperity. Rather, prosperity is a consequence of the interaction of a number of factors, not the least of which—although the least obvious—is a relatively low degree of incorporation. In other areas (e.g., the eastern United States and the Great Plains) full incorporation of nomadic foragers generally led to their destruction (Lang, 1975; Utley, 1984).

The differential survival of nonstate societies within state systems suggests another southwestern example of potentially broader interest. In the last several years, there has been a resurgence of interest in ethnicity and ethnic mobilization (e.g., Olzak, 1983; Nagel and Olzak, 1982), which parallels the recent worldwide resurgence in ethnic mobilization. Among the salient issues addressed in this renascent interest in ethnicity are those of group formation, persistence, and demise and the interpretation of ethnicity as a process rather than a state or attribute (e.g., Barth, 1969; Hannan, 1979). Explanations for changes in, and timing of, such processes have not been adequate. The Southwest offers an example of a group that traversed the entire trajectory from formation to persistence to demise. The changes and timing of these processes appear to be consequences of the impacts of changes in the worldsystem on this peripheral region.

The *Genízaros* were a social category, and subsequently a group composed of "detribalized" Indians (Chavez, 1955, 1956, 1979; Horvath, 1977, 1979; Swadesh, 1974). The origin of the term *Genízaros* is obscure. *Genízaros* came from a variety of sources, but were predominantly captives or individuals forced from their native Pueblo villages for various reasons, not infrequently for becoming overly assimilated to Spanish ways. Captives and livestock were the primary spoils of intergroup raiding. In addition to a lively trade in booty, there was a lively trade in stolen livestock and captives or "slaves" throughout northern New Spain. These "slaves" were typically women or children. Captives were "ransomed" or sold back and forth among groups. Hispanic settlers in New Mexico used them as servants. When taken as children, they were sometimes adopted into the "host" family. At other times, they were pushed into separate *Genízaro* communities.

Two aspects of the *Genízaro* are of interest. First, *Genízaro* as a social, indeed, ethnic distinction was temporary. *Genízaro* communities were located on the frontier of the region, where they bore the brunt of the attacks by hostile nomads. If an individual, through skill, bravery, and luck, became a prominent and wealthy fighter, he, or his offspring, would pass into the Hispanic community. This could take place in one to three generations. Second, once the nomads were "pacified" by the Americans in the late nineteenth century, such raiding stopped and *Genízaro* communities disappeared. The designation and the group were a product of particular social structures and processes on the frontier. Once these structures and processes changed, the group ceased to exist.

This example illustrates the interpretation of ethnicity as a process rather than a state or an attribute. The *Genízaro* example also suggests that the rise and demise of ethnic groups is in part a function of the position of a region in the surrounding world-system. In particular, groups are created at the boundaries of systems (Barth, 1969; Hannan, 1979), but shifts in those boundaries are a function of changes in the world-system (Hall, 1984). The U.S. annexation of the Southwest led to massive changes in patterns of trade and intergroup conflict (e.g., "pacification" of nomadic raiders), which changed boundaries between systems and groups and altered the distribution of available occupational niches for groups and individuals to fill. Once New Mexico became a part of the United States and nomads were pacified, the need for frontier traders or smugglers and for Indian fighters was eliminated. Along with that need, the *raison d'être* for the group that had filled it was eliminated. While the connection between the world-system and local changes is relatively clear for the *Genízaros*, other interesting questions remain unanswered. Is the *Genízaro* experience typical or unusual? If such processes are at least "not unusual," how typical is the *Genízaro* case of such processes? Is their experience an artifact of their peculiar geographical and historical location on the frontier, or is it a typical part of the process of incorporation and peripheralization? These and other important questions can be answered only comparatively. They do serve, however, as examples of issues to be addressed in comparative historical analysis of the periphery.

Some Lessons from the Study of the Periphery

These musings are, of necessity, tentative. They are based on the study of one region by one analyst. Hence, the idiosyncrasies of the

analyst, the peculiarities of the region, and the general consequences of focusing on a peripheral region versus a core region
cannot be completely disentagled. Still, without presenting even one
limited case, there can be no base for comparison and no hope for
sorting out these tangled threads. Furthermore, even this one case
serves to highlight both the problems and the benefits of studying
social change in peripheral areas, and strongly supports the case for
sampling widely in the periphery in attempts to develop theoretical
and empirical accounts of social change and the rise of the "modern
world-system."

At the most basic level, there is a need for careful microcompar-
isons between regions of the northern frontier of New Spain/Mexico
to discover local variations and factors involved in those variations.
Then there is a need to compare this region with other frontiers
in Latin America to discover if the patterns found here repeat
elsewhere. Henessey's (1978) study of Latin American frontiers
offer some guidance in this task. At a global level, there is a need
to compare both this frontier and other frontiers in Latin America
with other frontiers created by the expansion of modern European
powers to discover how much is peculiar to Spain and how much
is general.[14] Finally, there is a need to compare the impact of
European expansion on nonstate societies with other cases of state–
nonstate frontiers before the European expansion to discover just
what is unique about the European processes. There is much that
remains unknown, but this analysis suggests that some answers may
be found in further study of even one case, New Mexico.

There have been a number of attempts to analyze and prescribe
the appropriate methods for studying and theorizing about historical
social processes. Ragin and Zaret (1982) suggest complementary
use of Durkeimian, or variable-based, analyses with Weberian, or
case-based, studies. It would seem at this juncture that the study
of the periphery must be restricted primarily to the latter. Simply
too little is known about the periphery to test theories. They must
be built first, from case-based studies. The salient point of Ragin
and Zaret's discussion is that theory building and theory testing
require different research strategies, styles of analysis, and styles
of presentation.

In conducting "Weberian" studies, Stinchcombe's (1978) prescription to delve into the details is appropriate. The lessons and

potential generalizations about reactive tribalization (or, more broadly, state pressures on nonstate societies for centralization of political organization) and fragmentation (or decentralization) may be found only by a close examination of actual cases such as the Comanche peace, by comparison of the treatment by different states over time, say, of Comanches with that of Navajos and Apaches. A fuller understanding of ethnic processes may be found in a close analysis of communities like those of the *Genízaro*, and by examining the history of other groups over centuries.

In studying social change, it is imperative to locate any social event or process in space and time. As Tilly (1981) points out, "where" and especially "when" are the vital coordinates of an event. "Where" and "when" may be seen as proxies—dummy variables— for stage of development or position within an evolving world-system. These "wheres" and "whens"—whether or not they are cast in world-system terms—locate events and thus facilitate intelligent comparisons. If historical sociology has taught us anything, it is surely that social processes vary through both time and space. Furthermore, contextual data guide the choice of comparisons. While something may be learned by comparing seventeenth-century slave trade in the Southwest with sixteenth-century slave trade in Africa, or by comparing the "pacification" and sedentarization of indigenous groups in eighteenth-century New Spain, nineteenth-century United States, and twentieth-century Brazil, these are obviously different types of comparisons. Different comparisons will yield different sorts of knowledge. The point is not that some comparisons are legitimate and others are not, but that they are different.

Tilly (1984:60–61) distinguishes four types of comparisons. First, there are "individualizing" comparisons, aimed at demonstrating the uniqueness of a specific case. Second are "universalizing" comparisons, aimed at demonstrating that a given case is an exemplar of some general process. Third, there are "generalizing" comparisons, which examine variations within a given phenomenon. Fourth, there are "encompassing" comparisons, which explain variations in phenomena by locating them within a larger context. World-system theory is one such comparative framework. There is clearly a need for all four types of comparisons in historical sociology. In order to build a theory, or theories, of social change it is necessary to move toward "generalizing" *and* "encompassing" comparisons.

Even the one example of the American Southwest indicates both the need for and the potential benefits of such comparisons. The "generalizing" and "encompassing" comparative strategies require many detailed case studies. Such studies should sample widely in space and time. Since the "long sixteenth century" (Wallerstein, 1974a, 1974b), virtually all the world, except Western Europe, has been one or another type of peripheral region. There is much work to be done. Without such divergent studies, generalizations about change, about development, or about the origin, growth, and processes of capitalism will remain distorted. In short, both more studies and more theories are required. The two should be developed simultaneously and self-consciously, drawing as widely as possible from the diversity of human history.

Notes

An earlier version of this paper was presented at the Midwest Sociological Society, Chicago, April 1984. I thank Scott McNall for originally suggesting a paper on this topic, and Theda Skocpol for encouraging comments when it was first presented. Nancy Langton, Leslie Laczko, John Markoff, Gary McClelland, John Packham, and the reviewers for the *California Sociologist* all made helpful comments. That I did not heed all of them is not their fault. Randall McGuire has been very generous in sharing unpublished papers.

1. In Hall (1981, 1982, 1983) I discuss social change in the American Southwest at some length. Specifically, I have concentrated on the effects of states on social change in nonstate societies (Hall, 1983). Hall (1986, 1988) provides more detail and documentation for the examples used in this paper. As is inevitable when several manuscripts reach completion over an extended period of time, which point was first expressed where becomes an unanswerable question. This paper draws heavily on various parts of the book in building the argument presented here.

2. Apropos of the following comments on ethnocentrism, the American Southwest, for most of the time it was known to Europeans, was the northwest of New Spain and then Mexico, and became the "Southwest" only after it was annexed by the United States in 1848. The pervasive use of the term "Southwest" as a name for the region is an indication of the hegemony of the American state.

3. These groups encompass many of the types of societies delineated in various evolutionary classification schemes. Moseley and Wallerstein

(1978) provide a useful summary and comparison of these schemes. The significant feature is the range of types of society, not the specific typology used to classify them.

4. Minnis (1985) and McGuire (1980) critique the "Mesoamerican connection" thesis. The thesis itself is quite old. Early powerful statements of it are found in Kelley (1966), Kelley and Kelley (1975), Riley and Hedricks (1978), and Riley (1982). Others (Pailes and Reff, 1980; Pailes and Whitecotton, 1979; Whitecotton & Pailes, 1978, 1983) have elaborated this theme. Blanton and Feinman (1984) have recently argued for the existence of a Mesoamerican world-system. Mathien and McGuire (1986) include a number of papers from a 1983 symposium at the Society for American Archaeology on this topic. McGuire's paper (included in Mathien and McGuire, 1986), which reverses his earlier position, argues that while Braudel and Wallerstein offer useful insights and strategies for the study of the "Mesoamerican connection," the theoretical and empirical details remain to be developed. Chapter 2 of Hall provides an overview of this debate and offers a modified world-system theoretical account for the effects of the "Mesoamerican connection." Archaelogical evidence for the "protohistoric period" (1450–1650), the period immediately preceding and overlapping with Spanish contact, provides considerable evidence of important contact with Mesoamerica (Riley and Manson, 1983; Wilcox and Masse, 1981). While shaky, the evidence does support two points. First, "precapitalist" states have shaped the evolutionary trajectories of indigenous societies in the Southwest. Second, Spanish contact and conquest dramatically altered dynamic processes, not static conditions.

5. I use the terms "core" and "periphery" metaphorically. Their use does not require a wholesale acceptance of the Wallersteinian model; rather, they provide a convenient vocabulary for the following discussion. There is an irony here. I may, by my own argument, be accused of committing the same error. I have restricted myself to the "modern" era, the last five hundred years or so. A *full* sampling of social change would require examination of earlier eras. The current task itself verges on the overwhelming, hence the restriction. The discussions of the "Mesoamerican connection" reviewed above provide some indication of the complexity of earlier comparisons.

6. These groups are sometimes mistaken either for a new model truck or "quaint" New Mexican villages. Those who know of Taos think of skiing, D. H. Lawrence, or Georgia O'Keefe, but not a centuries-old center of Plains–New Mexican trade (Kenner, 1969). While the comment may seem flippant, such mistakes have occurred in more than one professional presentation of this research. The point, as stated in the text, is that

the presentation of research findings on peripheral areas requires explicit discussion of more background material than research on core areas.

7. Among anthropologists, the rite of passage into the discipline requires field-work in an exotic setting. The Southwest is a pedestrian location, since it is right here in the United States. That Clyde Kluckhohn, Leslie White, Karl Wittfogel, and many others did some of their most important work in the Southwest attentuates this reaction considerably. Despite this, though, anthropologists and archaeologists have tended to concentrate either on the American Southwest, which affords easy access for research, or on the spectacular "civilizations" of Mesoamerica or their contemporary heirs. They have tended to leap over the "Gran Chichimeca"—the vast area between the American Southwest and central Mexico (see Woodbury, 1979:22–23; Hinton, 1983:318).

8. These problems remain irrespective of the defining characteristic of capitalism, production for exchange (Wallerstein, 1974a, 1974b, 1979), or control of labor power (Tilly, 1981; Wolf, 1982). The fundamental problem remains the rise and expansion of Europe and the attendant massive social changes: the growing hegemony of world capitalism and the Industrial Revolution. These phenomena are as yet poorly understood. They must be grasped as wholes, not studied piecemeal (Bach, 1980; Braudel, 1977, 1980; Wallerstein, 1974a, 1974b; Hall, 1984).

9. Even here, there are problems. If the issue is what makes for a successful revolution, then unsuccessful revolutions are as useful as successful ones for studying the problem. The latter, however, are notoriously difficult to locate. Intelligent conceptualization of the unit of analysis may expand the number of available cases (e.g., Paige, 1975).

10. Stephen Bunker's (1984a, 1984b) work is a recent example of what I am advocating. He has conducted a careful study of the effects of extractive economies on the development of the Brazilian Amazon, and used this case study to begin building a theory of development in extractive economies.

11. At that time one peso was worth one dollar (Turlington, 1930).

12. Barbosa (1985) makes a parallel argument about changes in the rates of manumission in colonial Brazil. He argues that as Portugal's position in the world-economy changed, Brazil's economy changed, and hence the economic value of slaves and rates of manumission.

13. Shoshoni Indians in the Great Basin, northwest of New Mexico, experienced similar pressures for fragmentation directly from Spanish contacts, but more forcefully through indirect contact via competition with other indigenous groups (see Steward, 1955: Chs. 6, 9; 1977:ch. 17).

14. Lang (1979) has begun this process by his careful comparison of British, Spanish, and Portuguese colonial patterns. His analysis is not cast in these terms, but lends itself to such an interpretation.

References

Bach, Robert L. (1980). "On the Holism of a World-System Perspective." In T. K. Hopkins and I. Wallerstein, eds., *Processes on the World-System*. Beverly Hills, Calif.: Sage, pp. 289–318.

Bakewell, P. J. (1971). *Silver Mining and Society in Colonial Mexico, Zacatecas 1546–1700*. Cambridge: Cambridge University Press.

Bannon, John Francis (1974 [1963]). *The Spanish Borderlands Frontier, 1513–1832*. Albuquerque: University of New Mexico Press (originally New York: Holt, Rinehart and Winston).

Barbosa, Luiz (1985). "Change in Brazilian Slavery and Changes in the World System." Paper presented at the Southwest Sociological Association Meeting, March, Houston, Tex.

Barth, Frederick (1969). *Ethnic Groups and Boundaries*. Boston: Little, Brown.

Blanton, Richard, and Gary Feinman (1984). "The Mesoamerican World System." *American Anthropologist* 86:3 (September):673–82.

Bolton, Herbert E. (1929). "Defensive Spanish Expansion and the Significance of the Borderlands." In J.F. Willard and C.B. Goodykoontz, eds., *The Trans-Mississippi West*. Boulder: University of Colorado Press, pp. 1–42. Reprinted in Bannon (1964):32–64.

Brading, David A. (1971). *Miners and Merchants in Bourbon Mexico, 1763–1810*. Cambridge: Cambridge University Press.

——— (1978). *Haciendas and Ranchos in the Mexican Bajío: León 1700–1860*. Cambridge: Cambridge University Press.

Braudel, Fernand (1977). *Afterthoughts on Material Civilization and Capitalism*. Baltimore: Johns Hopkins University Press.

——— (1980). *On History*. Sarah Matthews, trans. Chicago: University of Chicago Press.

Brown, Richard (1977). *A Poetic for Sociology: Toward a Logic of Discovery for the Human Sciences*. Cambridge: Cambridge University Press.

Bunker, Stephen G. (1984a). *Underdeveloping the Amazon: Extraction, Unequal Exchange, and the Failure of the Modern State*. Champaign: University of Illinois Press.

——— (1984b). "Modes of Extraction, Unequal Exchange, and the Progressive Underdevelopment of an Extreme Periphery: The Brazilian Amazon, 1600–1980." *American Journal of Sociolgy* 89:5 (March):1017–64.

Chavez, Fray Angelico (1955). "José Gonzales, Genízaro Governor." *New Mexico Historical Review* 30:190–94.

——— (1956). "Tomé and Father JBR." *New Mexico Historical Review* 31:68–71.

―――― (1979). "Genízaros." In Ortiz (1979), pp. 198–200.

Chirot, Daniel (1976). *Social Change in a Peripheral Society: The Creation of a Balkan Colony.* New York: Academic Press.

Chirot, Daniel, and Thomas D. Hall (1982). "World-System Theory." *Annual Review of Sociology* 8:81–106.

Cole, John W. (1977). "Anthropology Comes Part-Way Home: Community Studies in Europe." *Annual Review of Anthropology* 6:349–78.

Crosby, Alfred W., Jr. (1972). *The Columbian Exchange: Biological and Cultural Consequences of 1492.* Westport, Conn.: Greenwood Press.

Fried, Morton (1967). *The Evolution of Political Society.* New York: Random House.

―――― (1975). *The Notion of Tribe.* Menlo Park, Calif.: Cummings.

Hagan, William T. (1976). *United States—Comanche Relations: The Reservation Years.* New Haven, Conn.: Yale University Press.

Hall, Thomas D. (1981). "Varieties of Ethnic Persistence in the American Southwest." Ph.D. diss., Department of Sociology, University of Washington, Seattle.

―――― (1982). "The Effects of Incorporation into the World-System on Ethnic Persistence: The American Conquest of the Southwest." Paper presented at the American Sociological Association, San Francisco, September 1982.

―――― (1983). "Peripheries, Regions of Refuge, and Non-State Societies: Toward a Theory of Reactive Social Change." *Social Science Quarterly* 64 (September): 582–97.

―――― (1984). "Lessons of Long-Term Change for Comparative and Historical Study of Ethnicity." *Current Perspectives in Social Theory* 5:86–103.

―――― (1986). "Incorporation in the World-System: Toward a Critique." *American Sociological Review* 45:3 (June):390–402.

―――― (1988). *Social Change in the Southwest, 1350–1880.* Lawrence: University Press of Kansas.

Hannan, Michael T. (1979). "The Dynamics of Ethnic Boundaries in Modern States." In John W. Meyer and M. T. Hannan, eds., *National Development and the World System: Educational, Economic and Political Change, 1950–1970.* Chicago: University of Chicago Press, pp. 253–75.

Harris, Marvin (1968). *The Rise of Anthropological Theory.* New York: Crowell.

Hechter, Michael (1975). *Internal Colonialism: The Celtic Fringe in British National Development 1536–1966.* Berkeley: University of California Press.

Herr, Richard (1958). *The Eighteenth Century Revolution in Spain.* Princeton, N.J.: Princeton University Press.

Hinton, Thomas (1983). "Southern Periphery: West." In Ortiz (1983), pp. 315–28.

Horvath, Steven (1977). "The Genízaro of Eighteenth-Century New Mexico: A Reexamination." *Discovery,* School of American Research, pp. 25–40.

———— (1979). "The Social and Political Organization of the *Genízaros* of Plaza de Nuestra Señora de los Delores de Belén, New Mexico, 1740–1812." Ph.D. diss., Department of Anthropology, Brown University.

John, Elizabeth A. H. (1975). *Storms Brewed in Other Men's Worlds.* College Station: Texas A & M University Press.

Kelley, J. Charles (1966). "Mesoamerica and the Southwestern United States." In G. F. Ekholm and G. R. Willey, eds., *Archaeological Frontiers and External Connections,* vol. 4, pp. 95–110, of R. Wauchope, gen. ed., *Handbook of Middle American Indians.* Austin: University of Texas Press.

Kelley, J. Charles, and Ellen A. Kelley (1975). "An Alternative Hypothesis to the Explanation of Anasazi Culture History." In Theodore R. Fisbie, ed., *Collected Papers in Honor of Florence Hawley Ellis.* Albuquerque: Papers of the Archaeological Society of New Mexico 2, pp. 178–223.

Kenner, Charles L. (1969). *A History of New Mexican–Plains Indians Relations.* Norman: University of Oklahoma Press.

Lang, James (1975). *Conquest and Commerce: Spain and England in the Americas.* New York: Academic Press.

———— (1979). *Portuguese Brazil: The King's Plantation.* New York: Academic Press.

Lattimore, Owen (1962). *Studies in Frontier History: Collected Papers, 1928–58.* London: Oxford University Press.

Lenski, Gerhard (1966). *Power and Privilege: A Theory of Social Stratification.* New York: McGraw-Hill.

Lenski, Gerhard, and Jean Lenski (1982). *Human Societies,* 4th ed. New York: McGraw-Hill.

Mathien, Frances Joan, and Randall McGuire, eds. (1986). *Ripples in the Chichimec Sea: Consideration of Southwestern-Mesoamerican Interactions.* Carbondale, Ill: Southern Illinois University Press.

McGuire, Randall H. (1980). "The Mesoamerican Connection in the Southwest." *The Kiva* 46:1–2 (Fall–Winter):3–38.

———— (1983). "Economies and Modes of Production in the Prehistoric

Southwestern Periphery." Paper presented at Society for American Archaeology, Pittsburgh, April. In Mathien and McGuire (1986), pp. 243–69.

Minnis, Paul (1984). "Peeking Under the Tortilla Curtain: Regional Interaction and Integration on the Northeastern Periphery of Casas Grandes." *American Archeology* 4:3:181–93.

Moorhead, Max (1968). *The Apache Frontier: Jacobo Ugarte and Spanish–Indian Relations in Northern New Spain, 1769–1791.* Norman: University of Oklahoma Press.

Moseley, K. P., and I. Wallerstein (1978). "Precapitalist Social Structures." *Annual Review of Sociology* 4:259–90.

Nagel, Joan, and Susan Olzak (1982). "Ethnic Mobilization in New and Old States: An Extension of the Competition Model." *Social Problems* 30:127–43.

Nash, June (1982). "Ethnographic Aspects of the World Capitalist System." *Annual Review of Anthropology* 10:393–423.

Olzak, Susan (1980). "Contemporary Ethnic Mobilization." *Annual Review of Sociology* 9:355–74.

Ortiz, Alfonso, ed. (1979). *Handbook of North American Indians*, vol. 9: *Southwest*. Washington, D.C.: Smithsonian.

——— (1983). *Handbook of North American Indians*, vol. 10: *Southwest*. Washington, D.C.: Smithsonian.

Paige, Jeffry M. (1975). *Agrarian Revolution*. New York: Free Press.

Pailes, Richard A., and Daniel T. Reff (1985). "Colonial Exchange Systems and the Decline of Paquime." Paper presented at the Society for American Archaeology meeting, Philadelphia, May. (In Michael Foster and Phil Weigand, eds., *The Archaeology of West and Northwest Mesoamerica*. Boulder, Colo.: Westview Press, pp. 253–63.)

Pailes, Richard A., and Joseph W. Whitecotton (1979). "The Greater Southwest and the Mesoamerican 'World' Systems: An Exploratory Model of Frontier Relationships." In William W. Savage, Jr., and Stephen I. Thompson, eds., *The Frontier: Comparative Studies*, vol. 2, pp. 105–21.

Phillips, George Harwood (1975). *Chiefs and Challengers: Indian Resistance and Cooperation in Southern California*. Berkeley: University of California Press.

Ragin, Charles, and David Zaret (1983). "Theory and Method in Comparative Research: Two Strategies." *Social Forces* 61:731–54.

Riley, Carroll (1982). *The Frontier People: The Greater Southwest in the Prehistoric Period*. Center for Archeological Investigation. Carbondale: Southern Illinois University Press.

Riley, Carroll, and Basic C. Hedrick, eds. (1978). *Across the Chichimeca Sea: Papers in Honor of J. Charles Kelley.* Carbondale: Southern Illinois University Press.

Riley, Carroll, and John L. Manson (1983). "The Cibola-Tiguez Route: Continuity and Change in the Southwest." *New Mexico Historical Review* 58:4 (October):347–67.

Sahlins, Marshall D. (1961). "The Segmentary Lineage: An Organization of Predatory Expansion." *American Anthropologist* 63:2 (April): 322–45.

Simmon, Marc (1968). *Spanish Government in New Mexico.* Albuquerque: University of New Mexico Press.

Skocpol, Theda (1979). *States and Social Revolutions: A Comparative Analysis of France, Russia, and China.* Cambridge: Cambridge University Press.

Skocpol, Theda, and Margaret Somers (1980). "The Uses of Comparative History in Macrosocial Inquiry." *Comparative Study of Society and History* 22:2 (April):174–97.

Smith, Ralph (1963). "Indians in America–Mexican Relations Before the War of 1846." *Hispanic American History Review* 43:34–74.

Spicer, Edward E. (1962). *Cycles of Conquest: The Impact of Spain, Mexico and the United States on the Indians of the Southwest, 1533–1960.* Tucson: University of Arizona Press.

Steffen, Jerome O. (1979). *The American West: New Perpectives, New Dimensions.* Norman: University of Oklahoma Press.

Steward, Julian (1955). *Theory of Culture Change: The Methodology of Multilinear Evolution.* Urbana: University of Illinois Press.

———— (1977). *Evolution and Ecology.* Urbana: University of Illinois Press.

Stinchcombe, Arthur (1978). *Theoretical Methods in Social History.* New York: Academic Press.

Swadesh, Frances Leon (1974). Los Primeros Pobladores: *Hispanic Americans of the Ute Frontier.* Notre Dame, Ind.: University of Notre Dame Press.

Teggart, Frederick (1918). *Theory of History.* New Haven, Conn.: Yale University Press.

———— (1925). *The Process of History.* New Haven, Conn.: Yale University Press. Reprinted as *Theory and Processes of History.* Gloucester, Mass.: Peter Smith, 1972.

Thorton, Russel (1978). "Implications of Catlin's American Indian Population Estimates for Revision of Mooney's Estimate." *American Journal of Physical Anthropology* 49:11–14.

Tilly, Charles (1981). *As Sociology Meets History*. New York: Academic Press.

——— (1984). "Big Structures, Large Processes, Huge Comparisons." New York: Russell Sage Foundation.

Turlington, Edgar (1930). *Mexico and Her Foreign Creditors*. New York: Columbia University Press.

U.S. Bureau of the Census (1915). *Indian Population in the United States and Alaska*. Washington, D.C.: Government Printing Office.

Utley, Robert M. (1984). *The Indian Frontier of the American West 1846–1890*. Albuquerque: University of New Mexico Press.

Wallace, Ernest, and E. Adamson Hoebel (1952). *Lords of the South Plains*. Norman: University of Oklahoma Press.

Wallerstein, Immanuel (1974a). "The Rise and Future Demise of the World Capitalist System: Concepts for Comparative Analysis." *Comparative Studies in Society and History* 16 (September):387–415. Also in Wallerstein (1979): Chap. 1.

——— (1974b). *The Modern World-System: Capitalist Agriculture and the Origins of European World-Economy in the Sixteenth Century*. New York: Academic Press.

——— (1979). *The Capitalist World-Economy*. London: Cambridge University Press.

Weber, David J. (1982). *The Mexican Frontier, 1821–1846*. Albuquerque: University of New Mexico Press.

Whitecotton, Joseph W., and Richard A. Pailes (1979). "Mesoamerica as an Historical Unit: A World-System Model." Paper presented to XLIII International Congress of Americanists, Vancouver, Canada, August.

——— (1986). "New World Pre-Columbian Systems." Paper presented at Society for American Archaeology, Pittsburgh, May. (In Mathien and McGuire, eds., (1986), pp. 183–204.)

Wilcox, David R., and W. Bruce Masse, eds. (1981). *The Protohistoric Period in the North American Southwest, AD 1450–1700*. Tempe: Arizona State University Press, Anthropology Research Papers, No. 24.

Wolf, Eric R. (1982). *Europe and the People Without History*. Berkeley: University of California Press.

Woodbury, Richard B. (1980). "Prehistory: Introduction." in Ortiz (1979), pp. 22–30.

CHAPTER 14

Competing Theories and Third World Political Practice

Perry Mars

The periodic setbacks to the attempts at revolutionary transformation of Third World societies occasioned by both internal and external forces call for serious evaluation in the light of contending theories that presume to explain and predict social change. The primary interest of this paper, therefore, is the relationship between theory and practice, particularly as it affects the realization of necessary social and political changes in the Third World.

Although at the purely epistemological level it is possible to discern a variety of theories competing for recognition and to gain paradigmatic status in terms of explaining Third World change and development, it is the central thesis of this study that the relevance and significance of each of the main theories in the field are determined by both historical and political considerations. Within this perspective, this paper therefore seeks (1) to identify and evaluate the main contending theories in terms of their capacity to explain Third World change, (2) to explore the social bases for their significance or prominence, and (3) to be able to develop some criteria for the identification of the most relevant theory based on the problems that each theory poses in terms of its implications for political practice.

The variety of theories relevant to Third World experience range in importance according to their capacity to explain *and* help the process of social transformation. By these criteria also, it becomes easy to eliminate those that time has proved to be inadequate. The earlier structural-functional framework, for example, which Almond (1960, 1966) utilized to develop a theory of Third World development, has already been found inadequate for its ethnocentric and status quo biases. Again, modernization theories that seek to explain Third World development simply in terms of the absolute negation of traditional practices and values prove to be very limited primarily in terms of their very mechanistic and linear interpretation of political and social processes.[1]

The major theories that can be considered most relevant to the Third World experience, although with varying degrees of significance and impact, are what are called (1) the plural society theory, (2) dependency theory, and (3) the Marxist theory of change based on Marx's conception of the mode of production. That these theories are more relevant than the functionalist and modernization theories is based on the consideration that they are relatively more powerful in their capacity to explain at a more fundamental level social and political change in the Third World. But beyond a basic agreement on the significance of fundamental social change in the Third World, these three theories display a wide variety of fundamental differences with corresponding differential impacts on Third World political practice in general, and the process of political change in particular.

Comparative Assessment of Rival Theories

A comparative assessment of these three rival theories, plural society, dependency, and Marxist, is necessary if we are to understand the extent to which each applies to the Third World experience and is capable of generating insights into the resolution of Third World problems. In keeping with these concerns, we are interested in their mode of explanation of Third World change and their relative potential for providing appropriate guidelines toward the initiation and completion of the process of revolutionary social transformation in Third World countries. In short, we are interested in both their interpretative and their catalytic or revolutionizing potential — the relationship between theory and practice.

Plural society theory claims relevance to the Third World experience in the sense that its analytical focus is on the highly differentiated nature of the Third World universe, characterized as it is by the coexistence of a diversity of peoples and cultures whose roots are not necessarily connected with the particular geographic region within which they exist (Furnivall, 1948; Smith, 1965). Their primary claim to belonging to a single society is the fact that they interact "as cultivators and nothing more" within the same political unit. The major consequences of these polyglot societies are, according to Furnivall (1948), a division of labor in the economic sphere along strict ethnic or racial lines and basic instability as a result of ethnic conflicts.

Furnivall's ideas were significantly extended by M. G. Smith (1965) to embrace other Third World peoples and political units beyond Southeast Asia, in particular the Caribbean and some parts of Africa. Smith's essential contributions to the plural society theory are the observance by each distinct group of basically incompatible cultural-institutional practices, the necessary political dominance of a single cultural section over the rest, and inevitable ethnic and political violence, particularly during times of political crises. Smith's contribution is significant, therefore, from the point of view that it elicits a peculiar explanation of political and social change. The peculiarity of Smith's conception of change, as both implied and expressed in his model of Caribbean and Third World social structure, is its drastic restrictions on the range of alternative choices: change is either catastrophic, violent, and cyclical, or it is highly improbable, if not altogether impossible.

Change is catastrophic, according to Smith, since it must necessarily involve some traumatic war of mutual elimination among the races or ethnic and cultural sections of the society in efforts toward the replacement of one or another of these groups and the ultimate control of political power. Change tends to be cyclical in that the political supersession of one ethnic section by another can repeat itself indefinitely without necessarily entailing progress or development, or any fundamental transformation of the society as a whole. Or else change is impossible, in the sense of the extreme difficulty involved in having intersectional mobility on the part of the individual within his/her lifetime. This difficulty is consequent upon the necessity of the individual to almost transform his/her personality in adopting completely new institutional forms, norms, and practices that were definitely incompatible with his/her original compulsory institutional patterns of life. One of the major consequences of this social trap, as it were, suggested in the plural society model, is

the general tendency toward escapist rituals in which political subservience and dependency on charismatic leadership on the part of
the popular classes are important aspects.

The major problem in the plural society analysis of Third World
conditions is that it deliberately ignores the economic and material
basis in its explanation of social and political process. It is in this
respect that the plural society theory becomes eclipsed and in some
instances superseded by the "dependency" school of thought in the
explanation of Third World reality. But, in addition, there are other
fundamental differences between the two theories that set them apart
as far as the explanation of political and social change is concerned.

With dependency theory, the primary level of analysis tends to
shift from the internal to the external dynamics of change. Whereas
plural society theory locates the source and explanation of change
in the subnational unit—that is, the institutional practice of local
ethnic or cultural groups—dependency theory sees the world capitalist system beyond the national unit as primarily responsible for
the problems within Third World societies. Although there is broad
agreement among dependency theorists on the determinative power
of international capitalism, exemplified by the advanced capitalist
power vis-à-vis "peripheral" Third World countries, there are significant differences about the nature and scope of the impact of capitalist penetration within these Third World social formations. For
example, Baran's (1957) and Frank's (1969) almost totally negative
interpretation of this impact as necessarily and invariably responsible for underdevelopment or backwardness of peripheral societies
is contrasted with the somewhat more positive vision of Cardoso
(1979) and Amin (1976), who see in capitalism the possibilities
of its own regeneration and development even within the dependent Third World context. In this respect, Cardoso speaks of the
possibility of "dependent development," while Amin suggests that
a "radical revision" of capitalism might lead to development, or
transformational prospects, in Third World societies.

In keeping with these differences with regard to the effects of
dependence on peripheral countries, the explanation of change
within the dependency perspective also tends to differ, although
a consensus exists among dependency theorists about the need for
fundamental structural change. The differences in this regard relate
to the particular goals (envisaged by the theorists) toward which

dependent societies should strive, and the particular way in which the relationship between international capital and the formation and development of class forces within the periphery is discerned. While theorists such as Frank and Beckford insist that the entire social fabric established by capitalism must necessarily be completely dismantled in the quest for socialist development, others of the Cardoso and Amin persuasion envision the possibility of development even within an overall capitalist framework. As regards the conception of class developments within the closer periphery, Frank's emphasis would seem to be on a direct linkage between international capital and a local, as he called it, "lumpen" bourgeoisie, which plays essentially a negative role in preventing the development of indigenous capitalism within peripheral social formations. On the other hand, Cardoso and Amin would seem to go further than Frank. Cardoso, for instance, discerns the creation of a national capitalist bourgeoisie with the potential both to resist external capitalist penetration and to create centers of capitalist development within the periphery. Amin sees the creation of a growing peripheral proletariat, not only in developing a dependent industrial work force, but in gradually eroding the independent basis of existence of a peasantry by the incorporation of peasants into a part-time labor force dependent on urban industrial employment, or by the necessity of their producing cash crops for sale in the capitalist market structure.

Although change must necessarily be drastic, fundamental, and far-reaching as far as both the reduction of dependency and the enhancement of development prospects are concerned, dependency theorists have varying interpretations about the necessity of violent struggle. The theorists who see a necessarily violent transformation would seem to be Frank and Marini (1973). Frank's explanation in this regard tends to be based on the somewhat linear assumption that the greater the exploitation, oppression, and impoverishment of the masses in the periphery, the greater the certainty or inevitability of violent revolution, at least in the Latin American context. This position is contrasted, for example, with that of Beckford, who contends that change must start from people's minds. Yet the violent outcome anticipated by Frank differs from plural society theory in that violence for Frank is class violence, and revolutionary to the extent that it is directed toward socialist transformation, rather than simply directed toward the capture of political power, as with the plural society explanation.

Although, of course, dependency theory is an advance over the plural society approach in its fundamental understanding and analysis of the Third World problems—more specifically, the problems of economic exploitation and political domination by externally oriented class interests—it harbors some serious shortcomings that can indeed inhibit its very capacity to explain change and become a weapon or tool to guide successful social transformation. In particular, dependency theory remains weak with regard to generating understanding of the determination and dynamic of the motive forces of change, particularly those related to the subordinate classes such as the peasantry. Its exaggerated economistic emphasis in its analysis of Third World problems tends to inhibit understanding of how and under what conditions class forces take the initiative in political struggle. Classes and corresponding political organizations within the dependency analytic framework are discerned merely as untheorized effects rather than as motive forces for the achievement of desired changes. The stress is on the constraints rather than the facilitating factors in favor of change, and the dynamics of political process would seem to be sacrificed to the elaboration of relatively static structures. In this sense, the important question of political practice becomes subordinated to relatively abstract theoretical constructs and considerations.

Beyond static-structural considerations of both plural society and dependency theories is the alternative posed by Marxist analysis of modes of production, and the attention to class dynamics central to its particular approach. But while this particular aspect of Marxist analysis might represent a decided theoretical advance over its rivals, the question of its relevance and applicability to the Third World conditions is not always obvious, and must therefore be specially discussed.

Marxism's Third World Relevance

A fundamental difference between the Marxist approach and dependency theory relates to the very premises from which each begins its analysis of the problems and issues affecting change and development. Whereas for dependency theory, analysis proceeds from the more general, universal, and relatively abstract consideration of international capital, the Marxist method allows for analysis that proceeds from the concrete considerations of active human and social forces and their dynamic interaction with their material and practical environment. Political and social practice, in particular human productive activity, therefore becomes the basis on which a Marxist theory of developmental change can be constructed. Within this context, the role of classes and such specific motive forces as political organizations supersede the more general, abstract, and holistic factors such as national populations (e.g., core and peripheral countries) as central variables in the explanation of sociopolitical processes. However, the environmental variables, the socioeconomic conditions within which the motive forces operate, are also crucial in understanding the limits and the range of variability of these movements in the quest for fundamental change.

The particular methodological focus of the Marxist approach allows for an appreciation of the crucial significance of internal (as well as external) factors in the determination of fundamental change. It allows further for coming to grips with the specificities of particular social formations, a requirement that is important for understanding such contexts as the very problematic conditions of the Third World. The Marxist conception of the mode of production is in this sense fundamental to the understanding of particular socioeconomic formations. Applying mode of production analysis to the Third World context leads to the discernment of significant variations within the Third World, depending on the specific nature of the combination and interaction of different modes (precapitalist and capitalist) within each particular social formation. This approach naturally challenges such absolute assumptions as the ubiquity and universal dominance of capitalism, as is characteristic of dependency theory.[2]

It is the articulation of precapitalist and capitalist modes that gives to Third World formations their peculiarity as regards class formation and interaction, distinct and different from what obtains in the more clearly developed capitalist centers of the world. And it is the peculiarity of the class forces that underlies the dynamic and relatively volatile nature of revolutionary struggles in these parts — in particular, the rather dynamic role of the peasantry (apart from the other producing classes) in Third World revolutionary processes.

A closer examination of Marx's writings with particular reference to the Third World conditions reveals many of the aforementioned specificities in terms of the explanation of the Third World process of change. In particular, the writings of Marx and Engels on colonialism, although relatively unsystematic and undeveloped compared with their writings on European capitalism, cannot be ignored as one of the bases for our understanding of these specific processes.[3] At least, these writings on colonialism are not inconsistent with Marx's general theory of historical change, and suggest several theses which are definitely contrary to the assumptions of dependency theory. These theses include:

1. The "mutual dependence" between developed capitalist states, on the one hand, and backward Third World countries, on the other hand, rather than the absolutely asymmetrical, zero-sum relations in which the developed countries gain absolutely at the expense of the "periphery," as with dependency theory.
2. The tendency for political factors to be codominant in the determination of socioeconomic processes, in contrast to the almost exclusive determination of the economic as suggested in dependency theory.
3. A nonlinear relationship between economic deprivation (e.g., underdevelopment, poverty, etc.) and the potential for revolutionary mass activity, in contrast, for instance, to Frank's anticipation of imminent revolution on the part of the most exploited, deprived, and underdeveloped Latin American masses.

The validity of Marx's conception of mutual dependence between the developed and the Third World countries is based on several important considerations. First, while, as Marx claimed, societies characterized by what he conceived to be the static, Asiatic mode of production are dependent on the developed colonizing powers for the basic institutions of modernization and laying the infrastructural foundations for future economic development, the latter, in turn, are dependent on the former for the necessary raw materials for capitalist industrial development at the center. There is, however, no suggestion here by Marx that mutual dependence means an essential equality in the relationship between the two.

There is also a second sense in which mutual but unequal dependence could be considered—that is, what could be termed a reciprocity of impact involving both political and economic effects upon both the developed powers and the more disadvantaged Third

World countries. Marx's analysis of colonialism suggests this kind of reciprocity of impact as follows: in terms of the economic consequences, the impact of colonial control tends to be positive for the colonial power or core nations, while tending to be immediately negative for the colonized country or region; and in terms of the political consequences, the reverse is the case, with the impact on the colonial or core power tending to be negative, and that for the colonized tending toward a more positive outcome.

These tendencies are manifested, for example, in the capitalist exploitation of national resources and labor in the peripheral countries for the benefit of industrial development in the colonizing countries. In terms of the political effects, the colonial impact is manifested in increasing corruption and functional disorders within the core nations, while in the peripheral subject nations, colonial control generates the demand for political unification of hitherto disparate and fragmented peoples and at the same time contributes to the development of a higher level of political consciousness on the part of the colonized or ex-colonized peoples (Marx and Engels, 174:26, 54, 82, 168–172).

Similar reciprocity is reflected in the effects of revolutionary struggle. The Marxist argument holds not only that the attainment of genuine independence and socialism in peripheral countries is bound up with proletarian revolutionary struggles in the Third World, but also that it can affect the level of class struggles in the developed metropolitan countries as well. Even more significant is the suggestion by Marx and Engels that these Third World events can supersede in impact the indigenous causes of European revolutionary events. Various statements alluding to this kind of reciprocal interrelationship recur frequently in Marx and Engels's writings on colonialism (e.g., 1974:19).

Closely related to these considerations is the accent that Marxist analysis places on political factors as determinants of Third World revolutionary change and social transformation. For Marx, a political reconstruction of colonized societies is a sine qua non of further economic and social transformation in these peripheral societies. In his analysis of the colonial situation in India, for instance, Marx contended that revolutionary change in this peripheral society was not only a matter of replacement of the English bourgeoisie by the industrial proletariat at the metropole; of equal importance was the necessity for "all the Hindus themselves" to become "strong enough to throw off the English yoke altogether" (1974:85). The pivotal role of this political reconstruction is much in keeping with the general Marxist theory of the conditional paramountcy of the political over the economic in the precipitation of change. This position is reflected, for example, in Engels's contention that under certain conditions, such as are characterized by precapitalist modes, political power "strives for as much independence as possible, and which, have once been established, is also endowed with a movement of its own" (Engels [1890], 1975:53). This argument is reiterated elsewhere in Marxist writing.

The implications of this politically directed process of change for the specificity of class relations and struggle in the Third World are significant, particularly in terms of its distinctions from the nature of class conflict in the more developed capitalist centers of the world. Class conflict in the periphery would then tend to be less empirically clear-cut or directly determined by the domestic economic bases than under conditions where capitalism is more highly developed. This is due in part to the numerical insignificance of the principal economic class forces in Third World countries compared with the more industrialized capitalist nations. Class divisions, therefore, tend to be more submerged and obscured within the process of competition and interaction between rival political organizations in Third World countries. The Third World state itself becomes a product mix of a particular alliance of various class forces, even though it usually represents the interests of the more economically dominant class forces in the society. Thus in Third World countries, particular class interests are best and often represented by deliberate alliances between political organizations with similar ideological orientations. In this respect, it is the ideological orientation more than the empirical determination of economic classes that plays a significant role in the class identification of various political groupings within Third World countries.[4]

It is in this respect also that the level of political conflict and violence tends to be different under Third World conditions. First, the relatively brittle and hence insecure basis of the structure of the Third World state allows for the greater frequency and relatively less intensity of political violence, which is, in turn, a reflection of the myriad competing organizational challenges to its legitimacy.

Second, this is why political conflicts are usually more repetitive, in the sense of changing personnel, than productive as far as advancing the dominance of working-class and peasant interests is concerned. Third, this is why, also, political violence for the advancement of class interests is often diverted into destructive dead ends, such as the mutual elimination contests between tribal, racial, and ethnic groups witnessed in many pluralistic (in M.G. Smith's sense of the term) Third World societies.

The Marxist requirement for intensifying conflict sufficiently to advance the political dominance of working-class interests is based on considerations that are specific to a particular social formation. First, the probability of the outbreak of change-producing conflict in the Third World is, for Marx, dependent on the nature and extent of political oppression by the state apparatus in relation to the particular character of the repressed people as conditioned by its own historical development. Thus, for example, while Marx and Engels attributed to the Irish the potential for increasing resistance against British rule, the nature of Turkish oppressive rule over the Moors in Algeria was such that Engels characterized the latter as "a third race," thereby doubting their ability to resist (1974:156, 258, 262). Second, the Marxist analysis would seem to imply that the ability to resist political oppression is dependent on the relative position one holds in the hierarchy of political control. But it is not necessarily the most repressed who are most likely to initiate rebellion or revolutionary activity; usually it is those who occupy positions closer to the dominant class or political oppressors who tend to strike the first blow. Marx likened this tendency to what he termed "historical retribution." Thus, according to Marx, it was the French nobility rather than the peasants who struck the first blow against the monarchy in 1789, and in the Indian revolt of 1857, it was the sepoys, "clad, fed, fatted and pampered" by the British, who were most instrumental, rather than those elements of the population that were "tortured, dishonored and stripped naked" by them (1974:152).

Thus Marxist theory in relation to the explanation of Third World change is much more dynamic and penetrating than the simple, linear economic determinism of dependency theory. Similarly, the Marxist analysis departs fundamentally from the essentially cultural determinist tendencies of plural society theory. The essentially nonlinear perspective contained in Marxist theory is evidenced, for example, in the tendency at times to subordinate the centrality of the domestic economic base in the explanation of change, in favor of an accent on political factors, particularly under conditions such as are exemplified by Third World social formations. An extension of this line of reasoning suggests what could be discerned as a conditional disjunction between economic exploitation and political oppression, with correspondingly varying effects on class conflict. In this regard, exploitation would tend to have less impact than political oppression on the capability of class forces to initiate revolutionary change. This tendency would seem to be more obvious with regard to the peasantry in Third World social formations, which, as the Chinese and Cuban examples reveal, can become revolutionized less by capitalist exploitation, which applies more to urban and industrial proletarian forces, and more by the oppressive rule of the dominant class, which affects all subordinate groups. It is also within this nonlinear, non-deterministic perspective that proletarian violence itself becomes conditional and possibly dispensable in the Marxist approach, rather than automatic, absolutely necessary, or inevitable in the process of fundamental change, as suggested in both plural society theory and Frank's version of the dependency theory.

Implications for Class and Political Practice

The practical implications of the several theories examined above are closely related both to the historical context in which they are derived and to the class-political interests they tend to protect. Several closely related hypotheses are therefore suggested within this perspective. These could be summarized as follows:

1. The emergence of rival theories is largely determined more by the nature of the political problems generated by the particular historical conjunctures of Third World formations than by crises in the theories themselves.
2. The ability of the particular theory to retain its dominance and gain paradigmatic status is dependent on its ability to support or protect the dominant or controlling political interest in the system.

Plural society theory emerged principally in response to crucial political problems created by colonial rule, particularly over disparate peoples living within colonized society. The very title of Furnivall's work, *Colonial Policy and Practice*, is indicative of the attempt to address this political issue during the particular colonial phase of the historical development of Third World peoples. The primary problem then was the legitimacy of political authority as a foundation for the very conceptionalization and definition of society. M.G. Smith in particular was concerned with the crucial element that holds a society together in the context of conflicting political loyalties, such as are exemplified among the different peoples in artificially created political units like the Dutch colonies of Southeast Asia and the British colonies in the Caribbean. Each of the various ethnic or racial groups in this situation was discerned to display loyalties more to its particular ethnic group or to some foreign "homeland" (such as India for the East Indians and Africa for the African element of the Caribbean) than to the local center of political control.

One of the serious implications of this kind of analysis is to produce justification for the authoritarian type of colonial control often displayed by the external colonial authorities and a variety of colonial governors in these multiracial societies. One such justification for colonial control is exemplified in M. G. Smith's suggestion that without such rule, violent fratricidal conflict will eventually erupt in these contexts. To avoid such an outcome, then, it could be argued that the retention of colonial rule is absolutely necessary, and hence the justification for negation or repression of movements toward political independence. One observation that would seem to mirror this tendency is that of Peter Dodge (1966), who has discovered, for instance, that in Surinam there was a general preference for a retention of the expatriate Dutch presence as an inhibiting factor to the feared domination by one or the other ethnic groups in the system.

Plural society theory is the kind of theory that also can favor the attempts of the colonial masters to ensure an essentially ethnic basis of specific class control favorable to their interests in the event of the granting of independence to their overseas territories. The colonial attempt to resolve the ethnic conflict in Guyana through the introduction in 1964 of proportional representation in electoral politics could be viewed in this light. Although the declared intention of the British was to facilitate cross-racial voting patterns in Guyana, proportional representation had the inevitable effect of cementing traditional racial voting patterns (as the results of the poll showed; see Greene, 1974:25) and precipitated a PNC–UF (People's National Congress and the United Force) coalition government, which tended at least to accommodate British interests against a major political opposition led by the PPP (People's Progressive Party), which represented a more radical political alternative.[5] This conservative outcome of proportional representation in Guyana was commended by Donald Rothchild (1970), who, echoing plural society arguments, suggested that a PNC–UF (Center–Right) coalition government was prefered to a PNC–PPP (Center–Left) coalition since, first, the latter outcome is impossible, given the priority of racial antagonisms that traditionally divided the two parties, and, second, the former gives a better guarantee against continuing racial strife.

What is perhaps the most problematic consequence of plural society theory is its capability of becoming a self-fulfilling prophecy with respect to both the escalation of ethnic conflict and the reinforcement of procolonialist rule. Much of the ethnic voting patterns and violent conflicts manifested in many multiracial or tribal societies, such as Guyana, Surinam, Trinidad, Malaya, and Nigeria, is no doubt a result of ethnic or tribally based political mobilization influenced by the fear of the political dominance of one ethnic group in the system (as predicted by the plural society theoretical insight). As regards the preservation of the dominance of colonialist class interests, plural society perspectives tend at times to complement ideologically colonialist "divide and rule" strategy. This particular approach is manifested, for example, in the Guyana case, where the British preferences for political, military, and administrative personnel in the state apparatus would seem to favor one particular ethnic group over others. The resulting division of labor along strict ethnic lines tended to coincide closely with interests divided along class lines in the system (British Guyana Commission, 1965).

If plural society theory complements colonialist politics, dependency theory becomes important after the attainment of political independence from direct foreign rule, when the problem of economic independence becomes the crucial issue. Dependency theory, as is commonly recognized, grew out of the need to resolve the crucial problems of economic stagnation and backwardness in Latin America, which had realized political independence for well over a century. Starting from the now discredited ECLA (Economic Commission for Latin America) approach, the methodology of dependency theory was more adequately developed into its current form as highlighted and brilliantly defined by Cardoso (1977) in his article "The Consumption of Dependency Theory in the United States." In his article, Cardoso recognized the inherent economistic bias of dependency theory and suggested the need for the complementary development of more thoroughgoing political analysis within the dependency theoretical framework. But it is precisely because of this weakness that dependency analysis tends to restrict political practice to an outcome based either on mass spontaneity, which Frank anticipated in his prescription for violent revolution, or on the almost fatalistic acquiescence of social movements in the as-yet-unfulfilled prospects of restricted capitalist development, as Cardoso predicted.

Also, the question of the increasing proletarianization of the periphery, which Amin and other dependency theorists addressed, tends to displace the initiative of the motive forces of change with an equal resignation in the face of what appears to be the mechanical workings of rather blind and impersonal economic "laws" of development. The fatalistic tendency that this kind of analysis engenders in political practice is largely reflected in a parallel way: what could be described as the aloofness of Latin American Communist parties patiently awaiting the "ripeness" of the time for revolutionary action. It is no coincidence that the Cuban Communist party based its analysis of Cuban conditions on the priority of the universal dominance of international capitalism throughout Latin America—a factor that in the early stages of its development led this party to a "pragmatism" that manifested itself in the support of Batista and the denunciation of the Castroist revolutionary forces as essentially adventurist.[6]

Perhaps the major positive effect of dependency thinking is that it encourages the kind of political mobilization that fosters the political unification of the disparate groups that make up the typical Third World population. At the ideological level, this popular mobilization strategy finds its most appropriate theoretical weapon in nationalism and is in effect a reflection of the populist tendencies evident in many Third World countries. The most radical expression of this populist approach is the anti-imperialist position taken by several Third World political movements, which also see international capitalist intervention as the principal contradiction to be resolved in dependent Third World countries. At the same time, however, the principal class effect of the dependency approach is the consolidation of the political leadership of that class representing or supportive of the interest of local as against foreign capital. It presages a rift and, at times, a conflict between comprador capitalists and a national capitalist class that seeks control of the state apparatus, to be used as an instrument to gain full control of local economic resources. But usually the demand for strengthening the state apparatus against foreign penetration and control, and the consequent consolidation of the leadership of a petty bourgeois class, tends to limit the extent to which nationalization could be utilized as an instrument for social transformation in the sense of increasing the prominence and control of the working and other exploited classes in the Third World formation. It is at this juncture that dependency theory becomes limited in its capability to influence revolutionary practice.

The Marxist relevance to Third World conditions resides precisely in its ability to deal directly with the problem of human emancipation and liberation from native as well as foreign domination. Not only does the Marxist theory specify the class forces that will lead the revolutionary process, but, more important, it explains why this class is necessarily linked to the particular direction change will take. Based on the mode and relations of production thesis, Marxist analysis discerns the dialectical process in which the increasingly exploited and alienated industrial proletariat is destined to become the most important class force in the transformation of capitalist society. Translated into its Third World context, the recognized articulation of both precapitalist and capitalist modes in most of these societies will necessitate an alliance of class forces between the peasantry and the urban workers as the pivotal element in the process of Third World social transformation. The Chinese and Cuban revolutions are examples of the necessity of this type of alliance.

The Chinese example of revolutionary transformation in particular demonstrated both the need for unity of the laboring population and the indispensable fighting capacity of the peasantry—the necessity for simultaneous struggle on two fronts, that is, against both precapitalist relations in the countryside and rising capitalist interest and control in the urban centers. The prospect of such a two-pronged, simultaneous struggle is disallowed in dependency theory, which sees only capitalism as the paramount obstacle to change. It is against this background also that the Leninist thesis of the non-capitalist path demonstrates both its insights and its limitations. It is insightful in the sense that it recognizes the need for struggle against entrenched precapitalist relations in Third World formations. But like dependency theory, it is limited in its ability to give clues as to how to go beyond its advocacy of national capitalist and petty bourgeois leadership to the necessary hegemony of working-class forces in the Third World revolutionary process.

These limitations undoubtedly reflect some problematic weakness in Marxist theory itself as regards the successful transformation of Third World societies beyond the first stage involving the capture of political power on behalf of the working classes' interests. These theoretical problems inhere in the ambiguities about the Marxist interpretation of (1) the emergence of a revolutionary situation in the context of the particular stage of historical development of the particular social formation (except in ex-post facto terms); (2) the necessity or inevitability of physical violence (particularly armed struggle) in the context of relatively weak class forces, as exemplified in Third World countries; and (3) the relationship between class and ethnic divisiveness in the context of the need for working-class unity as a precondition for successful socialist transformation. To a large extent, it is these ambiguities in Marxist theory that allow for both plural society theory's challenges to its authenticity and relevance to Third World situations, and justifications for the attempt or presumption by some dependency theorists to "extend" the applicability of Marxist analysis to the Third World context.

In practical terms, the consequences of these ambiguities often lead to the costly adventurism of some Third World revolutionary organizations or movements reinforced by what are claimed to be Marxist-derived theoretical formulations, such as Debray's (1967) "guerrilla foco" thesis for Latin American revolutionary struggle. Similarly, Frantz Fanon's (1974) unconditional commitment to physical violence in Third World anticolonial liberation struggles is often justified in Marxist terms. But perhaps the most disastrous consequence of these ambiguities is the tendency of some Marxist practitioners to ignore the ethnicity problem in some Third World countries, leading to serious complications, or even reversals, of the class struggle for fundamental change.

Resolving Third World Contradictions

Several criteria for the evaluation and test of theory could be developed. This study is concerned principally with the criteria that aid in the resolution of the contradictions between theory and practice as far as they affect developmental change in the Third World context. That the problems of developmental change and social transformation should constitute the basis of such criteria is founded in the specificities of Third World formations, which are largely characterized by a variety of interrelated contradictions determined by extreme levels of both economic exploitation and political oppression. More specifically, these contradictions, as could be gleaned from the foregoing analysis, in the promises and problems of theories of fundamental change could be characterized as follows: (1) the contradiction between the levels of development of the objective socioeconomic conditions and political structure, on the one hand, and, on the other, the levels of consciousness on the part of the masses in preparation for the initiation of change; (2) contradictions between the desired goals of social transformation and the instrumental means toward the realization of these goals; (3) and contradictions between the necessity of political unification and the tendency toward the political manipulation of the established divisions within the society.

The first contradiction, between stage of development and levels of consciousness, reflects the problem of what could be termed "cultural lag" in the sense that the inertia of tradition and such factors as primordial sentiments, of which sectarian ethnic loyalties are prime examples, tend to undermine the progressive changes introduced by capitalism and colonialism in backward Third World societies. For the same reasons, these sentiments inhibit attempts toward transformation in a socialist direction. Struggle toward socialism then becomes doubly difficult, having to proceed simultaneously against both traditional and capitalist legacies. The struggle for socialism in Tanzania is in this respect inhibited by both traditional values, which resist change, and capitalist tendencies, which were introduced by colonialism (Von Freyhold, 1979).

The second contradiction, between transformation goals and instrumental means, relates to the fundamental objective of reducing or eliminating political oppression and economic exploitation without escalating the level of political violence, which, particularly in a multiethnic and often hostile geopolitical context, can be destructive of the very goals sought. The political expression of this contradiction is reflected in the usual tensions between bureaucratic-authoritarian tendencies and the demand for democratic participation in a variety of socialist-oriented Third World states. The Chinese struggles against bureaucratic authoritarianism during the Cultural Revolution are examples of how to combat the process. At the economic level, this contradiction manifests itself in the international conflict situation and is based on the demand to maximize local sovereignty and control over domestic economic resources and the concomitant necessity of dominant capitalist economic powers to curtail such local autonomy in the interest of the expansion of foreign capital.

The third contradiction, between the demand for political unification and divisive sectional tendencies, manifests itself usually in the problems affecting both national unity in times of peaceful transition processes and working-class unity particularly in times of political crises in many Third World social formations. Naturally, unity tends to be more easily fostered during the times of external threats of intervention than, say, in the interest of political mobilization drives for the attainment of more immediate local objectives when domestic sectarian interests emerge to play a crucial inhibiting role. Working-class unity, necessary in the pursuit of local political and economic objectives, is usually most difficult to achieve when the attainment and control of political power is thought to be bound up with mobilizing sectional or ethnic constituencies, thereby exacerbating ethnic conflicts, as in the case of multiethnic Third World societies such as Guyana, Malaya, and Surinam.

The particular combination of major contradictions tends to determine the nature of the particular course or path of revolutionary change and social transformation adopted in a particular Third World social formation. To a large extent, that path must be characterized by a process of mass mobilization involving several necessary and interconnected elements that are important for the resolution of the overriding contradictions in Third World societies. The process of mass mobilization must be geared toward raising the level of consciousness particularly of the hitherto neglected elements of the population—i.e., the workers and peasants—who also happen to be the most productive classes. Such a consciousness-raising process is best developed from a combination of tactics involving planned political education campaigns at one level and organized political struggles at a more material level of political practice. Political organizations and social movements are critical elements in the conducting of this consciousness-raising praxis. And the orientation or goals sought must combine national interest with the interest of the working class. In this way, the parochial interests that cater to such factors as ethnic divisiveness will be transcended.

Closely related to the consciousness-raising praxis is the necessity for democratization of both political and economic processes. The masses must have direct access to and control the political decision-making process, and political leadership must directly reflect the interest of the working and productive classes in the political sense. In the economic sphere, a movement from private or state control toward workers' participation in and control of the economic enterprises in which they work must be pursued. The effect of this democratization process is to counter the bureaucratic tendencies that usually attend state control of politics and economic enterprises, and thereby liberate the creative initiative of the popular masses.

The realization of democratic political practice is, in turn, intimately connected with the transformation of the state to reflect the interests of the working masses. In this sense, the typical petty bourgeois or middle-class political leadership ubiquitous in Third World formations must eventually yield to political control by the working-class and peasant alliance, which constitutes both the majority and the most productive elements of the population. However, this recommendation is not necessarily synonymous with Cabral's concept of "class suicide" by the petty bourgeoisie, which, given the very nature of the petty bourgeoisie as a class, is most improbable.[7] What is advocated here is a close and consistent but not necessarily unequal alliance between the petty bourgeoisie, on the one hand,

and the working classes and peasants, on the other; such reciprocity and mutual advantages could become the basis of political control at this juncture in the history of Third World struggles for social transformation. The mutual advantages to be derived from such an alliance are, first, that it assumes a popular mass basis of support for the political leadership and state power, and, second, in turn the middle classes can provide an important source for raising the level of both political and economic consciousness on the part of the hitherto neglected masses of the population. In this way, this alliance becomes necessarily a transitional one, in the sense that important elements within the working classes could be trained for eventual political leadership positions within the structure of the Third World state and economic systems.

The successful resolution of these problems is dependent on the ability to purposefully interrelate scientific theory with political practice. In a way, it could be suggested that an additional crucial problem facing the Third World struggle for change is the lack of a scientific theory relevant to Third World conditions. It is with regard to filling this gap that the competing theories examined in this study have emerged. Thus, the extent of the relevance of each of these theories depends on the extent to which each measures up to scientific criteria. In our context, such scientific criteria must also give scope for the development of theory that is capable of explaining for the development of practice the specific conditions that obtain in Third World social formations. It is therefore suggested here that theory relevant to the explanation of Third World specificities must be based on the following criteria: (1) it should facilitate the explanation of, and help further the struggle for, fundamental political and social change; (2) it should be suggestive of the direction or path such a process of change should take depending on the particular conditions or contradictions that obtain in a particular social formation; (3) it should be sufficiently comprehensive and capable of explaining a wider range of variations in the Third World context, compared with rival theories in the field; and (4) it should be closely connected with the concrete political and social practices of the significant movements and forces that struggle for or effect change in these parts.

The extent to which each of the rival theories approximates these criteria is the extent to which each is radical and, therefore, capable of becoming a material force to guide the movements for change and social transformation in Third World social formations. In this way, the theory could be said to be scientific in a special and appropriate sense of the term. Thus the specific nature of Third World problems calls for the development of scientific theory that goes beyond the positivistic assumptions that undervalue the particular as against the universal and rely exclusively on observable empirical as against practical referents as the criteria of scientific truth. Already the structural-functional approach based on positivistic science has been challenged with respect to its relevance to Third World conditions, despite some very ambitious and scholarly attempts toward making it applicable to the Third World. The contributions to epistemology made by Thomas S. Kuhn in *The Structure of Scientific Revolutions* to the effect that scientific knowledge advances not simply by counterfactual falsification of existing theories but by the replacement of one theoretical paradigm by another would seem to imply the significance of practical contextual criteria in changes of scientific theories—which is more appropriate for explanation of particular situations such as obtain in Third World conditions. However, Kuhn's thesis is limited as far as the resolution of concrete conditions is concerned, since the elevation of a particular paradigm is for him dependent essentially on inherent theoretical crises in a dominant paradigm, rather than practical crises in the actual sociopolitical conditions. It is in this regard that the Marxist approach, with its emphasis on practice as a basic criterion of scientific knowledge, becomes most appropriate for the examination of specific conditions such as obtain in the Third World. For the same reason, both dependency theory and plural society theory are limited in that while the one subordinates conscious practice to the deterministic economic process and ends in an unresolvable circle of dependency and stagnation or underdevelopment, the other elevates the observable empirical fact of differences among involuntary groups into an absolute, equally tending toward a deterministic outcome. Both plural society and dependency theories are limited to considerations of the lower levels of political practice in which routine and ritual displace the more creative and purposeful practical activities.

Conclusion

The relevance of theory to Third World political practice is bound up with a necessary shift from theory as a commodity to be bought and sold in the intellectual marketplace, as it were, to theory as a weapon or tool in the struggle for understanding and making change and social transformation. In other words, theory must be directly accessible to and assimilable by the ordinary masses or those sections of the population recognized as the motive forces of change in Third World social formations.

The question, therefore, of whether the rival theories of change— plural society, dependency, and Marxist theories—will attain prominence or paradigmatic status in the Third World is dependent less on epistemological criteria such as inherent theoretical crises, as suggested by Kuhn, and more on the effects of practical political and social crises, which tend to condition the nature of class struggle and determine the class bases of the control of political power. In such circumstances, the ruling ideas then are seen to be what they are, to wit, extensions of the interests of the ruling class.

Conditions in the Third World are sufficiently specific to warrant a particular approach to theorizing based on criteria that focus on fundamental change. Among the theories examined in this paper, the Marxist approach, based on the concept of the mode of production, more closely approximates such criteria, although it remains ambiguous with respect to crucial questions relating to the precise path toward the required changes and social transformations in the Third World. Both plural society and dependency theories are relatively inadequate in the sense that the essentially cultural-determinist character of the former and the economic-determinist emphasis of the latter render these theories incapable of explaining the more complex political element or motive forces in the process of Third World change.

The advantage of the Marxist approach, which allows for the more thoroughgoing analysis of the motive forces of change, is grounded in its recognition of the importance of the political over the economic and cultural in conditions such as obtain in most Third World countries—that is, in which capitalist penetration has not yet clearly or absolutely displaced precapitalist interests and tendencies. However, the incompleteness in the development of

Marxist theory so far is a reflection of the existence of significant gaps in the theory with regard to the resolution of crucial problems within the Third World context. Among the issues that are as yet inadequately theorized with respect to the Third World experience are the rather complex and indeterminate relationships between class and ethnicity; a peaceful transition to socialism, which at the same time ensures the supersession of the most oppressed and exploited classes over the traditional dominance of the more advantaged and privileged classes; and, not least, the transformation of theory itself from an intellectual commodity to a practical tool or weapon in the struggle for change and development under the relatively backward conditions of the Third World. To the extent that these crucial issues are more adequately theorized, it is probable that the prospects for more successful practices within the Third World political process will be greatly enhanced.

Notes

1. Among the theoretical works on modernization that could be subsumed within this perspective, see, for example, Eisenstadt (1966), Apter (1965), Black (1966), and Lerner (1958).

2. For an insightful discussion on this approach, see Taylor (1979).

3. The Marx and Engels work cited below is a collection of their work on colonialism, translated in 1974. For further discussion of Marx on colonialism see Avineri (1969).

4. Although in general one can develop a scheme of the Third World political spectrum based on the expressed ideological commitment of political parties and related organizations, this is not to deny that in some cases the expressed ideology is divorced from political practices. Admittedly, this is a methodological issue that calls for some empirical research.

5. The People's National Congress, the current ruling party in Guyana, is a left-of-center party that initially drew support mainly from the urban black population. The United Force is a right-wing procapitalist party representing essentially big business interests in Guyana. The People's Progressive Party is Marxist and draws support mainly from the rural East Indian population.

6. The reference here is to the Cuban Communist party, which dominated the Cuban labor scene during the 1940s but was totally discredited by its connections with Batista during the 1950s.

7. For an interesting discussion on Cabral's thoughts, see the special issue of *Latin American Perspectives* (Spring 1984).

References

Almond, Gabriel, and James Coleman (1960). *Politics of the Developing Areas*. Princeton, N.J.: Princeton University Press.

Almond, Gabriel, and G. Bingham Powell (1966). *Comparative Politics: A Developmental Approach*. Boston: Little, Brown.

Amin, Samir (1976). *Unequal Development: An Essay on the Social Formations of Peripheral Capitalism*. New York: Monthly Review Press.

Apter, David (1965). *The Politics of Modernization*. Chicago: University of Chicago Press.

Avineri, Shlomo (1969). *Karl Marx on Colonialism and Modernization*. New York: International Publishers.

Baran, Paul (1957). *The Political Economy of Growth*. New York: Monthly Review Press.

Black, C. E. (1966). *The Dynamics of Modernization*. New York: Harper & Row.

British Guyana Commission (1965). "The Racial Problems in the Public Service." *Report of the British Guyana Commission of Inquiry*. Geneva: October.

Cardoso, F. H. (1977). "The Consumption of Dependency Theory in the United States." *Latin American Research Review* 12:7–24.

Cardoso, F. H., and Enzo Faletto (1979). *Dependency and Development in Latin America*. Berkeley: University of California Press.

Debray, Regis (1967). *Revolution in the Revolution?* New York: Monthly Review Press.

Dodge, Peter (1966). "Ethnic Fragmentation and Politics: The Case of Surinam." *Political Science Quarterly* 81:593–601.

Eisenstadt, S. N. (1965). *Modernization, Protest and Change*. Englewood Cliffs, N.J.: Prentice-Hall.

Engels, Frederick (1890). "Letter to Conrad Schmidt." In Howard Selsam, David Goldway, and Henry Martel, eds., *Dynamics of Social Change*. New York: International Publishers, 1975, pp. 53–56.

Fanon, Frantz (1974). *The Wretched of the Earth*. New York: Penguin Books.

Frank, Andre Gunder (1969). *Latin America: Underdevelopment or Revolution?* New York: Monthly Review Press.

Furnivall, John S. (1948). *Colonial Policy and Practice*. London: Cambridge University Press.

Greene, John E. (1974). *Race vs. Politics in Guyana*. Mona, Jamaica: University of West Indies, Institute of Social and Economic Research.

Latin American Perspectives (1984). "Unity and Struggle." Special issue on Amilcar Cabral. *Latin American Perspectives* (Spring):3–96.

Lerner, Daniel (1958). *The Passing of Traditional Society.* Glencoe, Ill.: Free Press.

Marini, Rui Mauro (1973). *La Dialéctica de la Dependencia.* Mexico City.

Marx, Karl, and F. Engels (1974). *On Colonialism.* Moscow: Progress Publishers.

Rothchild, Donald (1970). "Ethnicity and Conflict Resolution." *World Politics* 22:597–616.

Smith, Michael G. (1965). *The Plural Society in the British West Indies.* Berkeley: University of California Press.

Taylor, John (1979). *From Modernization to Modes of Production.* Atlantic Highlands, N.J.: Humanities Press.

Von Freyhold, Michaela (1979). *Ujamaa Villages in Tanzania: An Analysis of a Social Experiment.* New York: Monthly Review Press.

CHAPTER 15

Africa: Time for a New Development Strategy

Robert S. Browne

World Bank figures indicate that twenty-four of the world's thir-ty-seven poorest countries are in sub-Saharan Africa.[1] Poverty, hunger, and disease are endemic there. Africa's illiteracy rates are the highest in the world; its agricultural practices are generally primitive and low-yielding; both physical and social infrastructures are grossly inadequate; the industrial sector is virtually nonexistent; the work force is mainly unskilled; management tends to be inex-perienced; the economies are undiversified and are often single-crop, primary-commodity exporters, heavily dependent on imports of food as well as of consumer goods and capital inputs. During the past decade, most of the countries have experienced chronic balance-of-payment deficits, and about twenty-two of them are car-rying so severe a debt burden that it is unrealistic to expect that they can ever fully repay their debts.

In addition to this litany of debilitating economic problems, much of Africa is plagued with political quarrels and instabilities and with repressive governments, exemplified by the ongoing conflicts within Ethiopia and the Sudan, by the border disputes in various parts of the continent, and, above all, by the nightmare of apart-heid in South Africa and South Africa's attendant subjugation of Namibia.

Clearly, Africa is far behind the rest of the world in terms of almost every measure of welfare; it is handicapped by low levels of productivity, and is largely unfamiliar with and unequipped for much of the new technology; and it is confronting a global competition that it is almost certain to lose unless a change is made in the way in which the game is played. Following World War

II, the developed countries opened the door a crack, and a few of the Third World countries eventually managed to get through—managed to transform themselves into NICs (newly industrializing countries)—and are now providing very serious competition to the developed nations. Korea, for example, not only is beginning to replace Japan as a supplier of many products to America, including steel and autos, but also is providing serious competition within Japan itself. The United States and other developed nations are not happy with this new competition from the Third World, and it is clear that they will make it increasingly difficult for other countries to advance into NIC status.

The evidence of growing protectionism, although directed primarily against the NICs, provides an indication of the obstacles that lie farther down the development path of any country utilizing an export-led development strategy. Regardless of whether a developing country is relying on the export of primary commodities or is attempting to export manufactured goods, it faces a bleak outlook. The greater its success in raising the productivity of its export sector or in diversifying its menu of exports, the greater will be the resistance it can expect to encounter in finding markets. The marketing problem will be further exacerbated by the weakening of prices as increasing numbers of the developing countries attempt to expand their output, thus glutting the market.

Objective circumstances, then, may well oblige Africa to question the wisdom of continuing to pursue the export-led development strategy that the developed countries and the multilateral institutions relentlessly urge on Africa. It seems quite clear that that strategy is not going to take Africa where it wants to go. Africa's practice of channeling the bulk of its efforts into extracting from the ground minerals and crops that it does not consume, shipping them across the ocean for sale, and utilizing the proceeds to purchase consumer goods can increasingly be seen as a no-win strategy. Except for one or two minerals of strategic importance available mainly from Africa, Africa's exports do not provide sufficient leverage to permit the producing country to set the selling price. Rather, Africa must passively accept the price offered for its products, and is equally powerless in setting the prices of the goods it buys. Both the medium- and long-term projections of commodity prices are gloomy, as substitute materials and technologies render some of the traditional primary commodities obsolete for many purposes. The terms of trade shift steadily to Africa's disadvantage, even as the commodity prices exhibit great short-term volatility. Meanwhile, technology speeds ahead, especially in the manufacturing and tradable-services sectors, while Africa, consuming but not producing in these sectors, lags ever farther behind in the technological race. The export-led development strategy thus offers Africa little prospect of ever becoming competitive in the export of manufactured goods, even were the specter of protectionism not so threatening.

Confronted with such a prospect, and saddled as Africa is with debt-servicing obligations that greatly inhibit its ability to import, Africa may finally be forced to search for an alternative to the export-led development strategy. Fortunately, the broad outlines of what such an alternative strategy might be have already been set forth by African technicians. I refer to the Lagos Plan of Action,[2] the historic document jointly published by the Organization of African Unity (OAU) and the Economic Commission for Africa (ECA) in 1980, signed by the fifty African heads of state and government, and promptly ignored.

The Lagos Plan is by no means a perfect document. It is poorly written, uneven, and in places highly unrealistic. In fact, it is not even a true economic plan, as an economist would use the term. It fails to set out clear priorities and timetables; it tends to state goals while remaining silent on exactly how they are to be achieved; and it provides little in the way of quantification—in either volume or monetary terms. The intersectoral linkages that it proposes are vague, and the operational instrumentalities remain largely unspecified. Indeed, it can hardly be considered an operational document at all, which is hardly surprising in that it attempts to shape a path for fifty independent, sovereign nations that are notoriously heterogeneous in their styles and ideologies.

Yet despite these serious flaws, the Lagos Plan stands as a brilliant, if crude, effort to chart a new development approach for an Africa whose economic deterioration had already become palpable. In a challenge to the economic orthodoxy that was being preached by the World Bank and the donor countries, the Lagos Plan rejected the export-led development strategy and called for Africa to use its extensive resource base primarily for its own development rather than for export, to concentrate its efforts on producing the things it consumes rather than items that it does not consume. The call is for collective self-reliance, for developing industry for home consumption and only secondarily for export, for relying principally on Africa's own technical skills and not on those of expatriates, for developing an industrial base and consumption patterns suitable to African needs, customs, and resources rather than blindly adopting models from abroad.

The term "collective self-reliance" is emphasized because the Lagos Plan recognizes that while production for a market of 500 million, or even of 50 to 100 million, is economically viable, production for a market of 10 million is generally not. Because Africa has been chopped up into a number of small entities, most of which boast populations of fewer than 10 million people, the nations are exhorted to gather themselves into effective subregional groupings within which they can cooperate on trade, industrialization, training, technology, monetary matters, communication, the generation of energy, environmental protection, and a host of other issues. Subregional cooperation and integration will gradually be expanded into continentwide efforts, leading eventually to an African Common Market, and by the year 2000 to an African Economic Community. Such, at least, is the vision.

Although the Lagos Plan clearly aims at a substantial reduction in Africa's dependence on external areas, it is certainly not a call for autarky, not a demand for the economic isolation of Africa from the rest of the world. Rather, it is a call for Africans to shift their focus away from what may be an excessive reliance on foreigners and toward a greater reliance on what Africans can do for themselves and with themselves. It is a questioning of whether the comparative advantages assigned to Africa are in fact the inherently correct ones or merely the ones that suited the old colonial pattern. But while Africa is learning the answer to this, it will continue to grow and export its traditional cash crops in order to keep foreign exchange coming in so that necessary capital inputs can be purchased. The Africans will, however, also be growing more food for themselves, and cutting back on food and consumer imports. Manufacturing will focus on import-substitution industries producing the essential goods that the rural populations need, both for consumption and for production, and it was targeted that by 1990 self-sufficiency would be achieved not only in food but also in building materials, clothing, and energy. One may easily be bemused at such ambitious targets now that 1990 is only two years away, but it must be recalled that it was more than a decade in the future at the time of writing, and who could have foreseen the multiplicity of calamities that would befall Africa during the 1980s? And even had they not occurred, the Lagos Plan targets may have been wildly optimistic, but that does not detract from the validity of the objective.

The response to the Lagos Plan has been virtually nil. It is afforded a certain amount of lip service when African heads of state are making economic pronouncements. For example, in the working document that the OAU/ECA prepared for the UN General Assembly Special Session on Africa's economic crisis, the Lagos Plan was cited as the basis for the planning that went into the document, and official statements coming out of OAU summit meetings generally refer to the Lagos Plan as the point of reference for Africa's economic development. The reality, of course, is quite the contrary. One can find only rare instances in which the actions of an African government can be clearly related to the spirit of collective self-reliance as set forth in the Lagos Plan. In fact, the ECA has endeavored to monitor the implementation of the Lagos Plan, and its reports make for very discouraging reading. Apparently, even the call for planning ministers to engage in some discussion with their immediate neighbors in the development of their national plans has elicited little response.

The one area where there has been some significant movement has been in the growth and strengthening of some of the subregional organizations, although even here the picture has been quite mixed. Africa has spawned a plethora of subregional institutions long before the Lagos Plan emerged, most of them underfunded and of dubious effectiveness. The very fact that they had been created was, however, testimony to the need. Southern Africa Development Coordinating Conference (SADCC), Economic Commission of West African States (ECOWAS), and the Preferential Trading Area (PTA) are probably the most significant ones, along with the regional clearinghouses, although the myriad multicountry research agencies, infrastructural undertakings, and monetary unions are all potentially quite important in the drive toward greater self-reliance.

Presently, only about 4 percent of Africa's officially recorded international trade is carried on between African countries, a figure that dramatically illustrates how far Africa is from achieving even the most rudimentary phases of subregional cooperation. There are, of course, a number of reasons why this deplorable situation exists, but to explain is not to excuse.

One of the greatest barriers to inter-African trade is the reluctance of the African countries to accept the currency of other African countries in payment for goods and services. If inter-African trade must be carried out in dollars, francs, or pounds, then self-reliance will obviously remain little more than a vision. For this reason, efforts by the clearing unions to persuade countries to trade "on the books" and settle their balances quarterly is a giant step forward. There is a possibility that the African Development Bank could play a role here by creating a guarantee fund of some sort to relieve the understandable anxieties that attend the acceptance of soft currencies. In the longer run, the objective would be to have the entire continent a free-currency zone. Comparable efforts to create subregional customs unions or common tariff or no-tariff zones and other mechanisms for freer exchange must also be brought to fruition, as the PTA is attempting to do in this region.

In attempting to speculate as to why the Lagos Plan has received such a weak response within Africa one may ask, what has been the response from the developed countries? The Lagos Plan was announced in April 1980, but very little was heard about it until a year later, when the World Bank released its famous report *Accelerated Development in Sub-Saharan Africa*,[3] also known as the Berg Report. The Berg Report, which was released with great fanfare and ultimately became the received wisdom of the donor countries and of the multilateral financial institutions regarding the African economic crisis, made no substantive response to the Lagos Plan, although it did acknowledge that it existed. Instead, by calling for continuing the export-led development strategy that Africa had pursued during and since the colonial era, the Berg Report implicitly rejected the Lagos Plan strategy. The World Bank was apparently unwilling to confront the African heads of state, however, so it chose instead to ignore their document. The donor governments have been equally unresponsive to the Lagos Plan, neither embracing it nor denouncing it, and were it not for a few scholars, the Lagos Plan might have had a quick burial, for within Africa the response was equally restrained. Even today, it is doubtful that any significant number of educated Africans have heard of the Lagos Plan of Action or have any concept of what it means.

The Lagos Plan states that the first call on Africa's natural resources should be Africa itself, with exports limited to whatever surplus production remains after Africa's needs are met. As a long-range plan, this is splendid, but for Africa to develop the capability to utilize its raw materials will require years, if not decades, and with Africa currently drowning in balance-of-payment deficits, exports will remain a major and vital African concern for the foreseeable future.

The absorption within Africa of the continent's raw materials output—its transformation into the consumer and capital goods conversion of iron ore, bauxite, manganese, chromite, sodium, copper, phosphates, and other crude materials into steel, machinery, chemicals, fertilizers, and consumer appliances—requires far more than creative imagination. Training of every imaginable sort, prolonged exposure of the labor force to industrial processes, the acquiring of an industrially disciplined work force, management experience, research, and technology adaptation are just a few of the ingredients that must be vastly expanded within Africa as necessary inputs into an effective program of collective self-reliance.

There are, of course, economic realities that must be addressed, and the ECA might render a real service by providing preliminary analysis of how some of these linkages might in fact be effected. In country-specific terms, and commodity by commodity, it would be helpful to have some tentative idea of what Africa's production profile might look like some years from now, when the Lagos Plan will have begun to approach full implementation. It would also be useful (and the data might already be available to carry it out) to make some preliminary calculation of what might be some of the costs—financial, economic, and social—entailed in attempting a preliminary implementation of an expanded regional trading effort. For example, abolition of customs duties between neighboring countries can result in serious declines in tax revenues if the countries involved depend heavily on customs duties as revenue generators. With what countries is this likely to be a problem, and how serious a problem, are among the questions requiring immediate answers. There are in fact a host of such problems, which the existing subregional organizations are beginning to face, and their experience will certainly provide valuable input into the continuing effort to breathe life into the Lagos Plan. The transformation of the African economies that the Lagos Plan envisions will also require the squeezing of savings from the already meager African economies on an unprecedented scale, even under optimistic assumptions regarding Official Development Assistance. This implies the coercion of a substantial investable surplus from a poverty-stricken population, a challenge perhaps comparable with China's in the 1950s, but without the political and social means enjoyed by China in the form of a unified state directed by a powerful Communist government astride a relatively homogeneous population. How this surplus is to be amassed in Africa is a missing chapter in the Lagos Plan.

Where Africa will fit into the global economy of the twenty-first century is another unexamined avenue for consideration and speculation. It is quite evident that massive shifts are taking place within the world with regard to industrial location. The newly industrializing countries, such as Hong Kong, Singapore, Korea, Taiwan, Brazil, Mexico, Spain, and India, have been rapidly replacing the traditional industrialized nations of Western Europe, the United States, Canada, and Japan, in the production of consumer appliances as well as of such capital-intensive items as autos, ships, and some basic processing industries (e.g., steel). Meanwhile, the low-wage industries that were formerly the province of the NICs, such as clothing, footware, toys, and simple electronics assembly, are now being taken over by countries such as Malaysia, Thailand, Sri Lanka, and the Philippines, where the average wage is about $25 per month. Because African wages are generally higher than wages in other developing areas, a question arises as to whether Africa is better advised to move toward capital-intensive production methods in order to raise labor productivity and be more competitive internationally, or pay greater attention to maximizing employment via labor-intensive production, thereby turning out products that might be undersold by the output of other Third World countries. Will the fact that Africa is the actual producer of so many of the necessary raw material inputs serve to counteract this labor-cost differential? Although definitive answers to such questions are obviously not possible at so early a stage, the assumption by the drafters of the Lagos Plan that Africa can transform its raw materials into intermediate and final goods and capital equipment, and transform them with sufficient efficiency to render it an economically attractive strategy for supplying even an exclusively internal market, may strike some as excessively heroic. Consequently, it becomes imperative that preliminary structuring of internally consistent subregional plans be undertaken as promptly as possible, so that sympathetic observers can evaluate for themselves the feasibility of such an effort.

The short-term outlook for Africa is inescapably grim, regardless of the development strategy or the policy prescriptions that it chooses to pursue. Actually, the options available to it are frighteningly limited. As an immediate strategy, delinkage is not really feasible. Africa's intimate linkages with the industrialized nations cannot be abruptly severed without inflicting unacceptable pain on the continent's fragile economies, for Africa's dependency is all-embracing—for food, for consumer imports, for capital goods, for technology, for technicians, for training. One might even add "for cultural solace," because the foreign-educated African elite has become so indoctrinated with non-African cultural artifacts and life styles that it is unlikely to relinquish them easily. Despite these affinities, however, the harsh economic realities of the 1980s mean that Africa can no longer pay the bill for satisfying its Western tastes.

It would be risky to draw firm conclusions as to how the Lagos Plan is faring in Africa at this time. Genuine cooperation, or even communication, among the countries of Africa has very shallow roots. Most economic relationships run from Africa to the former colonial powers in Europe, a pattern that was firmly fixed during the colonial era. Inter-African telephone and telegraphic communications as well as postal services and even air travel are often most expeditiously accomplished by routing via Europe rather than directly from one African capital to another, thus enhancing the isolation of the African countries from one another. Politicoeconomic commercial arrangements, such as the Lomé agreements, effectively tie Africa to Europe, thereby further discouraging inter-African relationships. Consequently, the development of a thoroughgoing pan-African consciousness is a massive undertaking. In the absence of such a continental outlook, however, the Lagos Plan is not likely to be achievable, especially when one realizes that it requires its participants to veer dramatically from their economic futures to those of their equally fragile neighbors.

Is the plan dead? Despite the paucity of serious implementation, the plan is not dead, nor is it likely to die, because it offers the only real hope for Africa to realize its potential. The document itself is clearly obsolete and admittedly flawed. It would be highly appropriate for it to be reformulated in the light of the almost ten years of experience that have accrued since it was put together. The general thrust would need to be changed very little, because the objective conditions that it addresses have hardly changed at all. What is missing is the will to implement it. The implications of implementing it are not attractive in the short run, but the implications of not implementing it are absolutely disastrous. Implementation would require substantial change in the life styles of Africa's elite class, which would be obliged to forego satisfying its foreign-induced tastes for consumer goods. For a generation or two, Africans would have to consume African-produced goods, fashioned primarily from raw materials found within Africa. Africans would learn to take their vacations in Africa rather than in hard-currency areas. Instead of national airlines and national fertilizer plants, countries, at least the smaller ones, would learn to make do with regional airlines and regional fertilizer plants.

In the even longer run, for Africa to realize its full potential, the fifty countries will have to be replaced, either by a half dozen or so subregional political economic entities or perhaps by a single, continentwide political economic unit. The African Economic Community (AEC) envisioned by the Lagos Plan appears to be modeled after the European Economic Community (EEC), which was a century in the making and even today is still in the process of emerging. Thus the target date of the year 2000 may be unrealistic for the achievement of the AEC, but the AEC is an identifiable goal around which the people of Africa can rally. The journey may prove to be a long one, but the time for taking the first step is long past.

Notes

1. World Bank, *World Development Report, 1987* (Washington, D.C.: World Bank, 1987), p. 202.

2. Organization of African Unity, *The Lagos Plan of Action for the Economic Development of Africa 1980–2000* (Geneva: International Institute for Labor Studies, 1981).

3. World Bank, *Accelerated Development in Sub-Saharan Africa* (Washington, D.C.: World Bank, 1981).

CHAPTER 16

Southern Europe in the World Economy in the Twentieth Century: Implications for Political and Social Transformations

Giovanni Arrighi, Cağlar Keyder, and
Immanuel Wallerstein

The Sunset of Pax Britannica

The acme of British hegemony in the capitalist world economy came in the middle of the nineteenth century. The unquestioned economic primacy of Great Britain had already begun its steady decline with the so-called Great Depression in the last third of the century. The steady rise of Germany and the United States as industrial powers eroded British competitive advantages in many regions of the world economy.

Great Britain, of course, still remained the most powerful country in the world-system. In the colonial scramble of the 1880s, which it did not precipitate but in which it participated actively, Great Britain was able to occupy the largest part of the newly colonized zones and protect and enlarge its de facto privileged position in the peripheral areas of the world economy. Its dominance of the world financial networks, based on the universally accepted gold standard and the centrality of London as a market, met no serious opposition.

This Pax Britannica nonetheless was eaten away by the increasingly acute economic competition among the core powers, which finally resulted, after much delay and hesitation, in World War I. The single most important consequence of this breakdown of the adjustment mechanisms of the interstate system was the Russian Revolution of October 1917, with its dramatic consequences in both the core and the periphery of the world-system. In the core, this political transformation would signal the onset of the period of political turmoil, particularly but not only in central Europe, which would not end until the restabilization of the interstate system under U.S. hegemony after 1945. In the periphery, this political transformation of this most powerful of the peripheral states would signal the speeding up of the process of anti-imperialist revolt, which had already begun and would continue with such intensity throughout the twentieth century.

The Interwar Period

World War I resolved nothing in the struggles within the interstate system. Germany's search for a dominant role was strongly rebuffed without its possibilities of rebound having been eliminated. The continued U.S. economic advance seemed still contingent on its not spending money and energy on the political infrastructure of the world-system. The Soviet Union loomed as an uncertain, troubling force—weak but untamed—in an interstate system for which the new structure of a League of Nations was far too thin to replace the now enfeebled British empire. The world economy lost the regulating utility of the gold standard without any plausible substitute.

The five countries of southern Europe—economically weak but politically sovereign, all relatively small (now that Turkey was stripped of its empire)—faced great uncertainties in the economic and political arenas. The power of Great Britain, and hence the attraction of liberalism, had waned. The power of the United States was yet to be asserted, especially in this region. Germany in the 1920s was struggling to reassert itself as a major power. And the Soviet Union loomed as a menace to the internal order of these states, or at least so it seemed to their ruling classes.

As a consequence, from the point of view of southern Europe, there was in this period unclarity and uncertainty about the interstate system. There was no unchallenged "center." Alliances seemed open. Under such circumstances, when economic difficulties arose, the translation of economic grievances into social movements was more or less immediate in each of the countries. The movements essentially demanded a political construction of propitious economic conditions. State responses had to involve a substantially greater degree of control and guidance over the market than had existed before, the main thrust being the coordination of the accumulation process under political tutelage. The onset of the world economic depression after 1929 reinforced these tendencies toward the rejection of liberalism. Since the countries of southern Europe were primarily agricultural exporters, the precipitous decline in their earnings signaled the necessity for policies to control foreign exchanges. They thereupon attempted to reorient their productive activities away from the international market and toward the domestic. Under the impact of social movements, their reorientation was transformed from a defensive tactic to an assertive strategy aiming at national aggrandizement. This ideology of nationalism and industrial strength is perhaps what distinguished these countries at this time from the majority of peripheral countries, which shared the defensive tactic of control over foreign exchanges. Their ideology may be summarized as a combination of nationalism and mercantilism, not far from the earlier synthesis of Friedrich List. There had been earlier Listian episodes in the history of these countries, notably the Italian Risorgimento. The 1930s version was less insistent on industrial imitation and emphasized the acquisition for national industry of domestic and export markets. It must not be forgotten that while the nineteenth-century model took its blueprint from industrialization through the market (i.e., the British case), the model for the interwar period was inescapably the Soviet one. Depending on the levels of earlier development, northern Mediterranean countries pursued paths of "developmental dictatorship" defined within the Soviet paradigm and mostly in contradistinction to it.

It must be mentioned here that regardless of the character of the regime and the institutional structures designed to legitimate it, the state–economy relationships remained similar. This "Fascist" discourse was most prevalent and was devised earliest in Italy and Portugal, while it arrived in a different form and for a much shorter period in Spain. In Greece and Turkey, there were elements of Fascist discourse, articulated integrally into authoritarian dictatorship. Similarly, institutionalized corporatism was stronger as a definition of the state–society linkage in Italy, while it gave way to more direct oppressive tendencies in other countries. Such diversity was due primarily to the balance between social movements and elite voluntarism obtaining in each country. Other factors were the existence and articulation of rival political organizations, and the degree of radicalness and violence involved in the acquisition of political power.

Nevertheless, in all the regimes, mobilizing ideologies were laid to rest soon after the acquisition of power, and social movements were dismantled in favor of more efficient rule from above. On the eve of World War II, the legitimation of the states derived exclusively from a centrally propagated ideology that fervently rejected class divisions and particularistic interest groupings in favor of an idealized organic solidarity in the service of national pride and aggrandizement. Although class and social conflict were equally anathema to all the regimes, regulation of interest representation was not evenly successful. Italy paved the way for the other regimes, through the handling of state–capital and capital–labor relations within so-called corporations. It is interesting that of the "innovations" that characterized Mussolini's Fascism, the one universally adopted was repressive labor legislation. By 1936, analogous legislation had been enacted in the other four countries, outlawing labor organizations and strikes. Social control was also attempted through similar organizations, based on the *casa* model, although they did not succeed in replacing the more traditional forms of association, and instead remained impositions from above.

The second important world event (in addition to the Depression) was, of course, the emergence of Germany as an economic power willing politically to impose a division of labor on the rest of Europe. In this period, Germany was reasonably successful in attempting to divide a previously united world market into politicoeconomic spheres. By 1937, the foreign trade of southern European countries had come to be oriented predominantly toward Germany. For Spain, Portugal, and Turkey, acquiescence to the German design was a necessary trade-off purchasing nonbelligerence, while Italy and later Greece were more integrally incorporated into the economic policy of the Third Reich. The German model of bilateral trade, with predesignated quotas and a unilateral imposition of the needs and excess industrial supplies of Germany on its trading partners, amounted to a new planned division of labor at the level of Europe. Although the relationship was uneven, subsumption of the market by German planning gave the inferior partners the opportunity to escape the vagaries of earlier liberalism. In other words, external dependency on a dominant European power that sought to supplant the mechanisms of the world market would allow southern European countries to implement more freely their internal economic policies. With the breakdown of accustomed channels of economic transactions during the war, the world market became even less of a constraint on internal policy making and authoritative control dominated the economy—a situation that lasted until the United States was ready to institute a new order in the post-1945 world.

The Post-1945 Period

Before the short-lived era of German domination, southern Europe had been a theater of core-power rivalry. When the war ended, this conflict had been resolved in favor of the United States, which was quick to construct the parameters of a new order, especially through the European Recovery Program. The ERP consisted of unilateral transfers of the international currency (dollar) to European countries, which allowed them to purchase American exports. Since the Bretton Woods agreement had envisaged fixed exchange rates as part of the stable economic environment through which economic reconstruction would proceed, competitive devaluations were out, and the undamaged American economy could export its products only if sufficient demand could be created in Europe through substantial dollar injections. In other words, European economies were allowed to run trade deficits in order to set the American economy and thus the world economy on a growth course. Coincidentally, of course, the injection of aid and grants allowed the U.S. government to wield considerable influence in the internal politics of the recipient countries. Thus the United States came to be directly involved in the construction of social balances in the European countries through the judicious support of certain political parties and personalities, by the attempt to influence the composition and politics of trade unions, and, most important, through the shaping of their economies in a capitalist direction. The United States sought to prepare the recipient countries to participate effectively in the newly reconstructed world market. To be sure, the short-run promotion of American exports was of concern to the United States. But this was in many ways less important than the long-run goal, which was certainly the prevention of the political division of the world economy.

While most of Europe came under the program of economic reconstruction and political molding (this program gaining urgency and greater thrust due to cold war ideology), American leverage was stronger in the case of southern Europe, simply because of the greater economic needs of the countries involved. Thus when northern industrial countries, aided by American direct investment, emerged as a new locus of accumulation in the world economy, southern Europe was still in need of external injections of capital, and therefore closely bound to U.S. assistance. Eventually, however, the economic orientation (and the source of external funds) began to shift. First Italy, then Spain, Greece, and Portugal, and finally Turkey extricated themselves to varying degrees from the privileged relationship with the United States and entered into a new one with northern Europe. Migrants from southern Europe began to work in Germany and France; tourism revenues from primarily northern European tourists became important as a source of foreign exchange; and northern European direct investment entered the scene. By the end of the 1960s, the U.S. share in the external trade and other economic relations of southern Europe was on the decline.

The birth and the growing importance of the European Economic Community (EEC) amounted to an institutionalization of the changing position of Europe vis-à-vis the United States. Although Greece and Turkey were only associate members, and Spain's and Portugal's candidacies were not placed on the agenda until the end of the dictatorships, the EEC, through its legislation on labor mobility and trade, became the most important force shaping the economies of the southern countries. Restrictions on migration and schedules of tariffs designed to regulate trade often had important consequences on the productive structures of southern Europe. At the same time, the issue of "Europe versus America" became important in the determination of political options of governments in the region. While U.S. impositions persisted, especially in the military sphere, the pressure from northern Europe was toward a different set of alternatives. Parliamentary democracy, more even distribution of income, and vaguely socialist policies seemed more in line with the division of labor that would be favored by northern Europe. Not only the customs union (the EEC), but also the political units fashioned in Europe, such as the Council of Europe, employed rewards and sanctions in an attempt to circumscribe the options available to the southern periphery.

However, social-democratic regimes came of age in southern Europe when the northern European "wind," with Thatcherism in the United Kingdom and the crisis of the Liberal–Social Democratic alliance in West Germany, was growing weaker, while the United States under Reagan had turned to a more assertive foreign policy. Only in Turkey was this change reflected in an authoritarian involution. Elsewhere, the social-democratic wave seemed to show a momentum of its own, which in country after country produced Socialist-inspired (Greece), Socialist (Spain), or Socialist-led (Portugal and Italy) governments. This momentum can be traced to two main factors: the increased social and economic power of labor in southern European national locales and the growing impact of world depression on the region.

The first factor has been the long-term outcome of the processes of rapid and extensive proletarianization and of industrialization/tertiarization that have characterized southern Europe since the late 1950s and early 1960s. The large reserves of non-wage-labor, preindustrial, and part-lifetime proletarians with which southern European countries were endowed up through the 1950s had played a double role in their political economy.

On the one hand, they could and were mobilized *politically* to undermine the power of labor organizations and to legitimize labor-repressive state policies. On the other hand, they could and were mobilized economically to enhance competition in the labor market and in the workplace while expanding the supply of wage labor. Fascist regimes in the interwar years stressed the former mobilization at the expense of the latter, particularly in the antidevelopmentalist regimes such as Portugal. Reserves of non-wage labor, preindustrial, and part-lifetime proletarians were thus by and large preserved up through World War II.

The reconstitution of world market competition under U.S. hegemony and the closeness of the region to one of the main and fastest-growing centers of world capital accumulation created strong incentives for the economic mobilization of these reserves — at first through "export" (i.e., emigration with remittances), then increasingly through local productive consumption (i.e., through wage employment) by transnational corporations as well as national industries. The story is complex, each country having reacted to and having been affected by the new situation in different ways. But one common tendency is clearly detectable. First in Italy, and then in the other countries (except Turkey), the reserves of non-wage-labor, preindustrial, and part-lifetime proletarians have been largely exhausted, and the social and economic strength of labor has been greatly enhanced.

The deepening of the world depression, by intensifying competition within and across national borders, has brought the change in the balance of social forces to the fore. In country after country, labor-repressive policies to enhance accumulation have lost their previous legitimacy. It is in this context that social-democratic regimes have been established in southern Europe, with a variety of programs with one common denominator: political power to "socialist" parties in exchange for labor acceptance of the imperatives of accumulation in a capitalist world economy. To what extent the exchange will be successfully implemented, and who will benefit most from it, are still open questions.

American domination during the 1950s was the most important homogenizing force in the region. Its gradual decline has allowed for diverging patterns to reemerge within the region. We may hazard the hypothesis, for example, that the ability of the United States to continue a degree of political control over the five countries has depended on their relative development. Italy, the least dominated, is also closest to core status. Turkey, the most closely controlled, is the most peripheral. The other three countries obviously occupy intermediate positions. Thus the decline of American hegemony has not implied a similarly homogenizing dominance of northern Europe — primarily because the institutional framework of this shift has not yet been established. For this reason, it is possible to trace the similarity of economic policies during the 1950s and the early 1960s. Since then, the diversity of semiperipheral activities, on the one hand, and the varying balance in the "Europe versus America" equation, on the other hand, have led to different sets of economic policies, notwithstanding the apparent similarity in the response to the economic stagnation.

Note

Prepared for the UNITAR Conference, "Alternative Strategies for the Future of the Mediterranean Region," held in Italy on October 25–27, 1983.

CHAPTER 17

Shocks, Deadlocks, and Scorched Earth: Reaganomics and the Decline of U.S. Hegemony

Michael Moffitt

During eight tumultuous weeks in April and May 1987, the witches' brew of Reaganomics finally boiled over. After a long honeymoon blessed by declining interest rates, a gradual but steady drop in the dollar, moderate economic growth, low inflation, and brimming financial confidence, the party suddenly turned sour. The latent but inevitable conflicts and contradictions of the Reagan experiment burst onto the markets and caused a mini-panic that could very well be repeated in the months ahead.

Suddenly, the once powerful dollar collapsed à la Jimmy Carter and Mike Blumenthal. The Fed, as Paul Volcker had long warned, "snugged" monetary policy to protect its international flank despite a fairly weak domestic economy. Long-term interest rates shot up quickly from 7.5 percent to over 9 percent. Wall Street was jolted by huge bond trading losses. The rocket scientists at Merrill Lynch dropped over $250 million trading mortgage-backed securities. First Boston and Salomon each lost another $100 million. The stock market, which had roared past 2,400 in early April, got a kick in the teeth for about 200 points.

In late May, another bombshell was dropped. Citibank, America's largest bank, announced that it would set aside $3 billion to cover potential losses on Third World debt. In effect, Citibank was walking away from billions of dollars' worth of exposure in Latin America, basically admitting that these loans will never be repaid. While Wall Street applauded this belated exercise in accounting candor, the real significance of Citibank's action was bearish, not bullish. By burying Walter Wriston's legacy of lend-today-collect-the-fee-and-worry-about-getting-paid-back-tomorrow, John Reed, his successor, was exhibiting a case of real pessimism about the future of the world economy. Previously, the bank's public position had been that IMF stabilization measures, some new money, and a more robust world economy would nurse the debtors back to economic health. Clearly, John Reed, soon to be followed by others, sees a big storm coming and thinks it wise to provide for the inevitable losses now rather than do it in the midst of the next crisis. Now Citibank has the earnings to cover the mess; then it might not.

Finally, in early June, the man who had been a father figure to financial marketeers for nearly a decade, Paul Volcker, was replaced as Federal Reserve chairman. For years bond traders, currency dealers, and Third World debtniks slept well, knowing that the big fellow was probably up watching the blips on the screens from Tokyo and Bahrain. True, another diehard deflationist, Alan Greenspan, has taken his place. But being president of the world economy, which Volcker really was, is not like model building or equation splitting—Greenspan's specialties. Being a central banker is more like being a linebacker: there is no time to think, only to react. How will Greenspan do the next time Mexico is on the brink or the dollar goes reeling? No one knows.

In fact, economists know a lot less than they pretend to know about where the world economy is headed. Likewise, the bullishness of Wall Street today is based more on wishful thinking than on reality. Only a few months after the shocks of spring, the stock market had shrugged off the problems of Reaganomics as it roared toward 3,000, only to be halted once again by a falling dollar and rising interest rates. Yet the optimism remains; evidently there is a great need to believe that permanent prosperity with low inflation has returned to the United States. On television, before congressional committees, and in expensive financial newsletters, the economic seers confidently predict the future. But, in reality, they are like dart throwers in the dark. It is by now a cliché to say that the world economy is traveling in uncharted waters, but it is no less true for that.

One thing, at least, *is* certain: given the legacy of mounting trade and monetary problems that Reagan will bequeath us, it's going to be a wild ride.

*   *   *

Making sense of the economic history of the past several years is, fortunately, easier than predicting the future. Despite all the confusing crosscurrents, on one hand, and the glib administration propaganda, on the other, it is clear that the world and the U.S. economy have changed in fundamental ways.

For one thing, economic growth is a lot slower in real terms than it used to be, both at home and abroad. Ironically, while one of the justifications for the great war on inflation was to increase real economic growth, the result has been lower inflation *and* lower growth. What *has* increased is unemployment, underemployment, and idle capacity. The Reagan administration, which only a short time ago was predicting 4 percent real growth through 1988, "slowing slightly in 1989–90,"[1] has the worst economic growth record of any U.S. administration since Eisenhower's, and has constantly been forced to lower its GNP estimates. Under Reagan, the U.S. economy has been growing approximately 2.5 percent annually in real terms, compared to average annual growth of 5 percent in the 1960s and 3.5 percent in the 1970s.

The United States is not alone, however. Growth in Western Europe has averaged a dreadful 1.4 percent in this decade. West Germany, Europe's leading economy, has been crawling along at 1.6 percent and showing little improvement this year. Among developed countries, the only genuinely respectable performance in this decade has been by Japan, which has registered growth of 3.5 percent annually, though that's to be expected of a country running such enormous trade surpluses. Still, Japan's growth rate is about 25 percent less than it was in the 1970s and about a third of what it was in the golden 1960s. Growth for all of the less developed countries is, on average, below 2.1 percent a year, and even those that are growing more rapidly, such as Brazil, are exhibiting a dismal performance compared to growth rates of recent decades.[2]

Essentially, what has happened to the United States and much of the rest of the world is that stagflation, that economic scourge of the 1970s, has not disappeared; its composition has simply changed. For the United States this means more stagnation and less inflation. The Reagan administration managed to achieve a cyclical recovery from the 1980 to 1982 recession but nothing more, certainly not the pie-in-the-sky "new generation of prosperity" promised by supply-side windbags. The Reagan expansion has been a long one by postwar standards, but a comparatively weak one in terms of basics like industrial production and investment.

Of course, you won't hear that from the Reaganites. Instead, they applaud the U.S. economy as a great "job creation machine" and boast that "more Americans are working than ever before," naturally taking credit for the numbers. As usual, the reality is much grimmer than the rhetoric. More Americans may be working than ever before, but most of the new jobs are low-paying service jobs. Moreover, many of the new wage earners are women who have entered the work force to compensate for the declining earning power of their husbands in the manufacturing sector or because they head single-parent households. And job losses in manufacturing and mining have forced men to seek additional sources of income. As Alan Sinai, chief economist of Shearson Lehman Brothers, puts it: "As jobs were lost in goods-sector production, services-sector employment picked up more than the jobs lost as workers took on extra positions to generate income lost in the higher paying goods employment. More Americans are working more hours and more jobs now, probably to sustain incomes and the previous standards of living."[3]

In other words, more Americans are expending more labor hours to buy the same basket of goods—as they must: real median family income in late 1986 was less than it was in 1978, which in turn was lower than in 1973.[4] So the vaunted "job creation machine," upon closer inspection, turns out to be a lemon. Since service-sector jobs pay less, on average, than manufacturing jobs, the loss of manufacturing jobs means that more low-paying jobs are being added to offset the drop in incomes. And, in fact, much of the recent growth in jobs has been in retail sales, which offers an average weekly wage of $174, compared to $400 in manufacturing and $472 in construction—in other words, about one-third to one-half as large and growing at about half the rate.[5]

Privately, financial conservatives and Wall Streeters are delighted with slow growth and the shift to a service-based economy. They view slow growth as the best way to avoid inflation and thus protect the value of financial assets. A service economy is also believed to be more stable and less likely to generate "boom–bust" cycles.

There are other, class-based reasons why conservatives and the affluent like slow growth: wages plunge and labor productivity goes up. Tight labor markets encourage job-hopping, strikes, and higher union wage settlements, whereas the decline of our traditional industrial base and the large-scale entry of women, young people, and immigrants into the work force has caused wage growth to stagnate. Productivity, on the other hand, has soared, particularly in mining and manufacturing—the sources of greatest weakness in the domestic macroeconomy and foreign trade picture— mainly as a result of cutting back on labor input and holding down wage gains. Economists who blame the U.S. trade deficit and our economic woes in general on some alleged productivity problem simply don't know the facts, or else ignore them.[6] Manufacturing productivity has grown at an annual rate of 4.8 percent since 1981 and mining productivity by 5.8 percent.[7] Productivity growth rates in those sectors in the last five years have been as great as they were from 1950 to 1965 (though not in the subperiod 1961 to 1965)— the heyday of U.S. industrial hegemony.

At first glance, it may seem that if productivity is up, wage growth is down, and redundant workers have been eliminated in manufacturing, this was just what was needed to make American industry "lean and mean" again. That, at least, is what the Reaganites would have us believe. As I have argued previously,[8] the process of grinding down domestic manufacturing through higher imports, of making fewer workers work harder and longer for less money, was intentional. Recall that as late as the 1984 election, Reagan's Ricardians (Feldstein, Sprinkel, Volcker) argued that the strong dollar was a good thing, that it reflected strength and confidence in the U.S. economy. They saw a strong dollar suppressing inflation generally, but they also saw that rising imports were squeezing domestic producers to get costs and wages down. As a result, manufactured imports surged and domestic wage settlements tumbled.

But is U.S. manufacturing now leaner and meaner, more competitive? In some industries maybe, but with record trade deficits piling up year after year, it is clearly not true for all industries. Any illusions that the trade balance was improving were shattered with the release of trade figures in late August, which showed the second-quarter trade deficit rising to $39.5 billion, up from $38.8

billion the first quarter. At this rate the United States will run a bigger overall deficit in 1987 than in 1986. As Alan Sinai remarked on the release of the second-quarter figures, "There is simply no turn in the [nominal] trade deficit, simply no turn."[9] The question is, why didn't the squeeze work?

The answer is likely to disappoint most economists and politicians, because the problem cannot be fixed by some "policy" or presidential commission on competitiveness. The United States has entered a period of economic and industrial decline that is likely to be permanent, much like the decline in British industrial supremacy that began around 1880. The main difference is that because of technological progress things move much faster these days, so the pace of the decline is likely to accelerate to truly frightening proportions in the years ahead. This decline defies fixing because it is not the result of laziness or budget deficits, but something much more fundamental and irreversible. The proximate cause is the globalization of production created by the multinational corporation and the resulting obsolescence of U.S. manufacturing labor.

The rise of the multinational corporation, I am increasingly convinced, represents the central macroeconomic event of the postwar world,[10] the significance of which neither academic analysis nor policy has fully grasped. While most economists and politicians discuss world trade as if individual nations were engaged in shipping products to and from one another, the rise of multinational corporations has made these conventional concepts of world trade obsolete. Consider the facts: one-third or more of all "trade" in manufactured goods now consists of intracompany transactions by multinationals. In the last five years, foreign direct investment by U.S.–based multinationals has expanded by about 25 percent, a very respectable increase given worldwide gluts in many products. There has also been a real shift away from investment in petroleum and mining toward manufacturing, finance, and banking. Direct investment in manufacturing facilities is up nearly 30 percent since 1983. In certain industries, like machinery, it has soared more than 60 percent.

In manufacturing today, foreign jobs account for about a third of U.S. multinationals' total employment. And, according to business consultant Peter Drucker, around 20 percent of all manufacturing by U.S. multinationals is done outside of the United States. It has been estimated that multinationals import up to 40 to 50 percent of all U.S. imports, with a third of these coming in the form of intracompany transactions. U.S. multinationals are the leading exporters from countries like Taiwan, which is running a $15 billion surplus with the United States. Taiwan and the other Far East dragons—South Korea, Singapore, and Hong Kong—account for about 20 percent of the U.S. trade deficit.

You would never know it from reading the newspapers, but U.S.-based multinationals also do a healthy business inside Japan. Kenichi Ohmae, a management consultant for McKinsey & Co. in Japan, considers total market penetration between the United States and Japan to be more telling than trade deficits and surpluses.[11] In 1984 Japan ran a trade surplus with the United States of approximately $31 billion, but this way of looking at things ignores the $43 billion of products the Japanese bought from U.S. companies operating in Japan. It also ignores the fact that some of "Japan's" exports are foreign sales by Japanese subsidiaries of U.S. multinational corporations. By way of contrast, Japanese firms operating in the United States sold only around $12 billion worth of goods to Americans. As a result, Ohmae calculates that penetration of each other's markets is roughly the same. In fact, he argues, on a per capita basis the Japanese spend two to three times as much on products made by U.S. firms (both imports and made inside Japan) as Americans spend on Japanese goods. The examples of Taiwan and Japan not only shed light on the source of much of the reported U.S. trade deficit, but also reveal how irrelevant conventional discussions of "world trade" are in the age of the multinationals.

Earlier in the postwar period, the U.S. economy clearly benefited from the spread of U.S. multinationals, and the U.S. standard of living was higher as a result of their activities. Foreign operations of U.S. multinationals—especially those in the Third World—were highly profitable, far more so than comparable domestic operations. The profits derived from these operations helped fuel domestic investment and output and contributed to the great boom of the 1960s and the early 1970s. Opening up vast new supplies of raw materials, the multinationals depressed prices U.S. consumers paid for sugar, coffee, and aluminum foil. For a time they also helped to perpetuate U.S. industrial hegemony and supported the balance of payments.

In the 1960s and the 1970s, overseas investment by U.S.–based multinationals boosted U.S. exports of capital goods and other industrial materials. Generally these exports, which often took the form of intrafirm transactions, dwarfed U.S. capital goods imports. This surplus in capital goods helped to offset growing imports of televisions, radios, and other consumer goods, thus contributing positively to the U.S. trade balance. While overseas production by foreign subsidiaries of U.S. multinationals usually exceeded U.S. exports three- or fourfold, the growth of these subsidiaries fueled demand for capital goods exports, machine tools, and the like. Economists were quick to point out these "benefits" to the U.S. standard of living, particularly when they argued with graduate students about whether multinationals represented a new form of economic imperialism. The mistake some writers made was to argue, in effect, that everyone loses as a result of the spread of multinationals. In those days, the United States clearly was benefiting.

But that era is over. The multinationalization of production is a result of the fact that capital is mobile and labor, by and large, is not. With the growth of worldwide sourcing, telecommunications, and money transfers, there is no pecuniary reason for U.S. firms to pay Americans to do what Mexicans or Koreans will do at a fraction of the cost. This is why "elite" U.S. working-class jobs are being sent abroad and "outsourcing" is the current rage in manufacturing. As a result, American multinationals remain highly competitive and their profits are booming, while the United States itself is becoming less and less competitive. In the 1980s, U.S. capital goods exports have collapsed, while imports of both consumer and producer goods have surged, no doubt in part because U.S. firms are now importing these products from foreign lands. In other words, we once exported the capital goods used to manufacture our consumer imports; now we are also importing the capital goods to run what remains of our domestic industry. Even a growing percentage of output in "sunrise" industries like computers and telecommunications is moving offshore. At home, the result is downward pressure on wages and chronic job insecurity for remaining manufacturing jobholders, who are more docile as a result. Meanwhile, the castoffs from manufacturing and mining plus new labor-market participants flock to low-productivity jobs serving coffee, making hamburgers, and running copying machines. Barring protectionism or a decline in U.S.

wages to Korean or Mexican levels, this situation will persist and, in fact, will probably get much worse.

The forces tending toward multinationalization of production have been building for decades and would have blossomed eventually even if Ronald Reagan had never been born. But the destruction of domestic manufacturing capability surely got an assist from the Reagan administration's exchange rate policies and its aversion to industrial policy. Since the decline of U.S. economic power is such an unpleasant notion to most Americans, Reagan's message was sugar-coated with simple-minded rhetoric about the magic of the marketplace. While austerity was painful, we were told, it was necessary, and in the long run it would make things better for everyone. Increased productivity and open markets would raise real living standards at home. It is now obvious that this was a Big Lie, whether or not Reagan himself recognized it as such. After all the sacrifice and suffering meted out to the work force over the past few years, U.S.–based industry is not "lean and mean" enough— as evidenced by the ongoing trade deficit—so things are not going to get better.

In fact, someone should tell the American worker that domestic austerity is not over, it's just beginning. Now the captains of industry and government want Americans to work for Korean and Mexican wages. While politicians of both parties babble about restoring "fair trade" and "competitiveness," for a real guide to the future listen to Walter Joelson, chief economist at General Electric: "Let's talk about the difference in living standards rather than wages. What in the Bible says we should have a better standard of living than others? We have to give back a bit of it." How much is "a bit"? If Stanley J. Mihelick, executive vice president for production at Goodyear, is correct, then "we" may have to give back a lot more than "a bit." According to Mihelick, "Until we get real wage levels down much closer to those of the Brazils and Koreas, we cannot pass along productivity gains to wages and still be competitive." With factory wages in Mexico and Korea averaging about $3 an hour, compared with U.S. wages of $14 or so, it looks as if we have a long way to go before U.S. wages will even be in the ball park with the competition.

That the decline of U.S. industry is the natural and logical outcome of the evolution of the multinational corporate economy over the past twenty-five years has been a bitter pill to swallow and it will become increasingly distasteful as time goes on. One consequence will be a nasty decline in the standard of living in the United States. While being an industrial factory worker has its disadvantages, it is clearly preferable to a life of enforced idleness or shining shoes. To be sure, women's entry into the work force was long overdue. But it is questionable whether women and their children are better off because mothers have exchanged housework for $175-a-week jobs at Kmart. Yet, given the destruction of our traditional manufacturing economy and job base, what choices do they have?

In the nineteenth century, an angry German philosopher coined an expression to describe the reduction in living standards in the name of profits. He called it "raising the rate of surplus value" — in other words, making people work longer and harder to maintain their previous standard of living while the fruits of their labors are pocketed by others. For fifty years a social contract between American capital, labor, and the government did mitigate the worst effects of the free-trade mechanism and technological change. Now the social contract itself is being undermined by the active mobility of capital and the growing obsolescence of American labor. We are told we can no longer afford the social contract, but, of course, we can still afford to pay Mike Milken $30 million or $40 million a year in salary and bonuses to carve up the remnants of our industrial economy. Greed is clearly in the driver's seat, but the irony is that all the greed in the world cannot solve the problems of the U.S. economy. As Robert Lekachman said, powerfully and prophetically, as Reagan entered office, "Greed is not enough."

How does this decline in American living standards square with the rise in consumption that so worries conservatives[12] and that has taxed the balance of payments in recent years? The key lies in the explosion of debt, both public and private. Total debt in the U.S. economy (government, corporate, farm, and consumer) rose from $1.6 trillion in 1970 to $4.6 trillion in 1980 and reached $7 trillion at the end of 1986. The rate of growth of debt, which was supposed to slow down when inflation collapsed, has actually risen from 11 percent in the 1970s to 12 percent in the 1980s. Debt has grown much faster than GNP. This explosion of debt has provided pure demand-side stimulus to prop up consumption, investment, and thus domestic economic growth. While a lot of ink has been spilled over the growth of government debt, which has doubled since Ronald Reagan came into office, consumer debt and corporate debt have also grown enormously. Politicians and economists of both parties tend to blame our problems on debt, yet clearly debt increases demand and, along with second jobs, helps Americans maintain their standard of living.

Far from being a drag on the economy, debt, like unemployment insurance, serves as a quasi-automatic stabilizer for the domestic macroeconomy. Take consumer debt, for instance. Several years ago, critics of Reaganomics predicted that falling real wages and the resulting "shrinkage of the middle class" would depress aggregate demand and reduce GNP growth. While this may be true in the long run—and in the short run in some troubled regions of the country—in general the decline in real wages and worsening income distribution have been offset by the explosion in consumer credit. From the end of 1980 until 1986, total outstanding consumer debt doubled, from $371 billion to over $740 billion. Home mortgage debt grew by another $760 billion, or 65 percent, during the same period. Despite record levels of loan delinquencies and historically high ratios of debt to income, banks and finance companies have been flooding households with credit card and home equity loan applications and adjustable-rate mortgages. As a result, demand for housing, autos, appliances, electronic gadgetry, and a growing array of services has held up quite nicely. In fact, final sales have held up a lot better than GNP growth.

It is true, of course, that our patterns of consumption in recent years have resulted in a surge in imports. This fact has given rise to the bizarre notion that our economic woes stem from "consuming more than we are producing." Arithmetically we may be consuming more than we are producing, but the implication that these are functionally related, or that if we consumed less we would be producing more, is false. Rising domestic consumption did not cause U.S. output or exports to lag. Nor did rising consumption by itself cause the surge in imports, which is characteristic of a business cycle expansion in the United States.

There is no question that one of the villains responsible for our trade woes was the strong dollar. In one of his few great blunders,

Paul Volcker, spooked in 1983 by monetarist gibberish that the domestic economy was "overheating," suddenly tightened credit. Interest rates stopped dropping and rose until mid-1984. The dollar, which had stabilized, started to rise again. It was the stage in the business cycle when the dollar would normally be expected to fall, as the United States tries to stimulate a world recovery by lowering rates. This time, however, even as the trade problem worsened, the Fed was driving the dollar up.

But while the Fed's policies and their effects on exchange rates are important, they explain less about the rise in imports and sagging exports than is generally believed. Other factors are at play. As foreign brands have become more entrenched in the U.S. market, Americans have continued to buy what they believe are products of superior quality or status, even at the higher price resulting from a lower dollar. Also, foreign producers who gained a more secure foothold in the U.S. market during the "strong dollar" period were willing to accept lower profit margins in order to maintain market share after the dollar started to fall. And, as we will see later, the U.S. economy continues to grow faster than the austerity-ridden economies of Europe, Japan, and the Third World.

Yet, while these are all factors contributing to America's persistent trade deficit, an equally if not more important reason why we are "consuming more than we are producing" has to do with the globalization of production, not with some alleged excess in consumption. When Americans buy bicycles manufactured in Taiwan by U.S. firms, the U.S. trade deficit grows. *Not* buying the bicycles would *not* encourage Huffy to make the bicycles in Ohio or Alabama. All it would do would be to lower our trade deficit by shrinking exports from Taiwan by U.S. firms operating there. How many bicycles Americans buy (and whether they pay cash or charge them) has no bearing on where the companies choose to manufacture them. These are totally unrelated phenomena. Of course, manufacturers might be induced to relocate to the United States if wages here fell to Taiwanese levels, but then fewer people would be able to afford bicycles at all.

Rising consumer debt may, of course, cause problems further down the road if an interest rate shock and rising unemployment cause widespread loan delinquency. Having hocked their houses to maintain their life styles, many Americans may find themselves in the streets or moving back in with their parents once the next recession hits. In the short run, lower consumption might indeed solve some of the problems that Americans have with their hearts, lungs, and psyches, but it is hard to imagine how lower consumption in the United States would be a boon for output or investment, either at home or abroad.

The impact of government debt in recent years has been similar to that of consumer debt: it has propped up demand and GNP. Under Reagan, the growth of federal deficits and therefore of long-term government debt has been a function of the tax cuts, the military buildup, rising interest payments on the debt, and the slow pace of the recovery itself, which resulted in part from the trade deficit.[13] Critics of the military buildup may rightly disagree with the composition of government spending, but there can be no question that output and employment are higher as a result of it.[14]

While it is obvious how the tax cuts and military spending contributed to the economic expansion, the effects of a loose fiscal policy do not stop there. The flip side of rising U.S. government debt and interest payments is growing income receipts by domestic and foreign bondholders. Net interest payments by the federal government tripled from $42 billion in 1979 to $136 billion in 1986 and amounted to 13.73 percent of the federal budget, up from 8.8 percent in 1980. Like stock dividends or interest payments on municipal or corporate bonds, the money does not disappear but is plowed back into additional investment, consumption, or both. In the long term, the fact that the United States depends on foreign capital inflows and the fact that interest payments are flowing increasingly to foreign-based institutional investors may be an important political and economic issue, but in terms of the present recovery it is quite obvious that these funds have by and large been reinvested in the U.S. stock and bond markets.

One of the more sophisticated critiques of rising government debt is given by Salomon Brothers' Henry Kaufman. Kaufman argues that cutting the budget deficit early in the economic recovery would have led to only a "brief slowing in the pace of economic activity" but, in the long run, to a radical fall in interest rates and thus higher growth.[15] Because Kaufman does not say why the adverse effects would have been short-lived, his argument amounts to little more than a dressed-up version of the conventional bond market wisdom. In fact, given that business investment fell in 1983, the first year of the recovery—when interest rates dropped—it is quite conceivable that the recovery would have died altogether without the boost provided by the deficit. Rather than blame the government's deficits and debts for the slow pace of the recovery, it is more appropriate to ask how weak the recovery would have been without the deficits. Surely Kaufman knows that the government deficit has stimulated demand and therefore investment, particularly in the leading technology-intensive areas where there are widespread military applications. If government deficits were crowding out private investment, as he must also know, interest rates would have gone up, not down, over the past five years.

Rising corporate debt is another matter entirely. A reading of the trends in corporate finance over the past several years reveals more about the health and future course of the U.S. economy than a dozen economics courses at Harvard or Princeton. The myth is that, unlike consumer or government debt, corporate debt is good because it reflects increasing investment, jobs, and growth. No doubt this is partly true. But despite the slavishly probusiness policies of the Reagan administration, business investment has been relatively flat in the United States and, on average, not much higher as a percentage of GNP than it was under Carter. From 1977 to 1980, nonresidential investment as a percentage of GNP averaged 11.6 percent; from 1981 to 1986 it averaged 12.01 percent. When supply-side guru Alan Reynolds proclaims that "from 1980 to 1986 U.S. business fixed investment rose from 11.9 percent to 12.4 percent of GNP,"[16] he conveniently ignores several things. First, investment was 12.2 percent of GNP in 1981, which could not possibly have been the result of Reagan's tax cutting, since the cuts were still being debated in Congress throughout most of 1981. Reynolds would no doubt reply that rising investment in 1981 was the result of business *expectations* of lower taxes. But then why did investment fall to 11.6 percent of GNP in 1982 and fall again in 1983, the first full year of the Reagan recovery, as profits were headed up?

The reason domestic investment has been so lackluster is that, despite the growth of debt, demand has been insufficient. With the economy growing more slowly, with more and more manufacturing being done abroad, with worldwide gluts in raw materials and excess capacity, why should business accelerate investment? Business, burned repeatedly in the 1970s by overeager investment and excess inventory accumulation, has been extremely cautious about the recovery since the beginning. In addition, computerized control of inventories—a relatively new phenomenon—and the ability to increase work shifts to meet sudden demand not only give business much greater flexibility than it used to have, but mean that business has been able to keep inventories trim in the event that the Reagan recovery dies. For all these reasons, business investment in recent years has been a big disappointment.

If business investment has been relatively quiescent during the Reagan years, then why the big jump in corporate debt? Between 1984 and 1986, domestic borrowing by all nonfinancial corporations rose by more than $500 billion, while investment was going nowhere fast. As a percentage of net worth, corporate debt went from less than 95 percent in 1980 to over 115 percent in 1985. This large rise in corporate debt in recent years has served mainly to fuel the restructuring boom that is altering the landscape of American business. Increasingly, corporations are taking on more debt not to invest in bricks and mortar but to finance acquisitions, to go private, or to fend off unwanted suitors through stock repurchases or greenmail. Others are buying back their own stock to shrink its supply and raise its price, thus keeping large institutional investors happy with management. Corporate funds have been flowing into the stock market, as companies buy their own and other companies' stock. The standard defense of the takeover and restructuring mania is aptly spelled out by Beryl Sprinkel, chairman of the Council of Economic Advisers. Writing in the *Wall Street Journal*, he argues that "mergers and acquisitions increase national wealth. These transactions improve efficiency, transfer scarce resources to higher valued uses, and stimulate effective corporate management. They also help recapitalize firms so that their financial structures are more in line with prevailing market conditions." Despite Sprinkel's apologetics, it is becoming obvious that about the only groups that the takeover mania enriches are investment bankers and lawyers.[17] Meanwhile, it worsens the performance of the U.S. economy—in the short run and in the long run.

To understand why, it is necessary to review how the mergers and acquisition game works. As attractive productive investment opportunities dried up in recent years, it became cheaper and less risky to buy capacity than to build it, so virtually all publicly traded companies became legitimate takeover targets. As company after company was either acquired or forced to pay greenmail to raiders, the practice of making quick and enormous profits from takeovers became an accepted way of doing business. Soon the mergers-and-acquisitions boom was feeding upon itself. Nowadays, before the raiders have even deposited the greenmail or buyout checks, their investment bankers are already busy lining up the next targets. Using the profits from the last deal, they take positions in new and vulnerable companies. Then they start leaning on management to agree to a takeover or to pay some greenmail. A statement widely attributed to one of the most powerful men on Wall Street is indicative of who calls the shots these days. According to legend, this particular mergers executive phoned the head of one of America's largest companies and informed him, "I just put you in play." Soon America's top corporate executives were spending their days, nights, and weekends trying to stay independent or to find white knights to avoid being taken over and broken up by hostile corporate suitors or by raiders such as T. Boone Pickens and Carl Icahn. Not an insignificant amount of time has been expended fashioning golden parachutes to make hostile takeovers more palatable to top managers.

Whatever the outcome of most takeover battles, all roads lead to higher levels of debt, though not necessarily to a more efficient and competitive corporate America. If raider A buys company B, A finances the takeover by selling bonds to investors. If company B buys back enough stock or swallows a poison pill to stay independent, B borrows the funds to do so or reduces working capital, necessitating some future borrowing. If company B is acquired by a white knight or goes private through a leveraged buyout, the transaction is normally financed by debt.

The merger boom of recent years has resulted in a profound change in the financial makeup of U.S. business. Basically, debt is being substituted for equity. In the last year and a half the equity base of U.S. business has shrunk by over $130 billion while debt has soared. The substitution of debt for equity is likely to have lasting effects on the U.S. economy—few of them positive. Sprinkel's claim that this ridiculous game "increases national wealth" is true only in an accounting sense and perhaps not even then. Companies that take on enormous loads of debt as a result of successful or unsuccessful takeover battles are normally so beleaguered that they adopt draconian cost-cutting measures in order to generate the cash flow to service the debt. In fact, one of the lures investment bankers use to sell these deals to reluctant boards is that they allow the combined companies to eliminate redundant facilities and employees — that is, to cut, cut, cut. While most economists worship at the altar of so-called microeconomic efficiency, such streamlining does not necessarily result in increased market share or international competitiveness, let alone better macroperformance. Projects that could yield revolutionary breakthroughs in science and technology, for instance, may be sacrificed to make a company a better financial performer. Whether the acquisition is hostile or friendly, the pressure to reduce costs means deeper cuts to service debt than would have been necessary to maintain stock dividends.

The whole process of restructuring corporate America might be worthwhile if it resulted in increasing exports and world market share for U.S. companies and expanding domestic manufacturing, investment, and employment. The U.S. trade deficit is a sad reminder that this is not happening. Instead, financial entrepreneurs and investment bankers are fighting over the pieces of the corpse rather than trying to bring the organism back to life. As they were at the end of the last century, the financiers, raiders, and latter-day robber barons are now in charge of the U.S. economy. Now, as then, they are interested more in short-term profits for themselves than the health and well-being of the American economy.

While America's current economic woes can in large part be traced to the decline of American economic power and the globalization of production, they are also the product of severe imbalances in the world economy wrought by the deflationist medicine of Volcker and Reagan. The long and deep recession of 1982 created profound financial and trade imbalances in the world economy that the current cyclical recovery has not ameliorated in any fundamental way. While economists and policy makers at home and abroad generally supported the great war on inflation — rescuing the dollar and breaking commodity price inflation — they saw the process as just another cyclical adjustment rather than the profound historical event that it was. It is true that Paul Volcker's credit squeeze succeeded in halting the worst inflation spiral since World War II, and that by crushing inflation, he reestablished the U.S. dollar as a store of value for domestic and foreign investors, earning him the sobriquet "Monsieur Dollar." But just as important, Volcker also led the world's central bankers down a path of deflationism that has hindered the current recovery and carries great long-term risks for the world economy.

After three years of squeezing, Volcker finally eased monetary policy in the summer of 1982 in response to the Mexican default. At about the same time, the cash flow generated by Reagan's 1981 and 1982 tax cuts began to leak into the economy via higher incomes and government deficits. U.S. consumption began to rise as a result. Following the U.S. lead, foreign central banks also eased credit. But, fearful that inflation would be rekindled, the Fed's and the Treasury's monetarists lectured our allies against too swift an economic expansion and pressed for continued austerity in the Third World.

The practical outcome of this series of events was to solidify the traditional U.S. role of guiding the international business cycle. But by trying to single-handedly lead the world recovery without the productive base the U.S. economy once possessed, we became, in Lester Thurow's words, the "buyer of last resort." The result was a lopsided recovery characterized by a large rise in consumption in the United States fueled mainly by imports, without a corresponding jump in U.S. output and exports. In previous business cycle expansions, it was not uncommon for U.S. imports to surge in the *early* stages of a cyclical recovery. In fact, this is normal, because by growing more rapidly the United States is able to lead the world out of recession. But in past cycles, after a time, corrective mechanisms have taken hold. The dollar has dropped and foreign growth has risen. Then, as U.S. exports have snapped back and imports have leveled off, the U.S. trade deficit has declined to more manageable proportions.

But not this time. Imports have continued to surge while exports have remained virtually stagnant. This imbalance has persisted not only because our productive base has declined—U.S. demand is being met by U.S. and foreign production abroad, not by production in the United States—but also because the rest of the world has been growing more slowly than we have. Still the world's largest market, the United States, with its increasing appetite for imports, has basically kept the world recovery afloat.

Lester Thurow has estimated that 50 percent of the European Community's growth in 1984 and 25 percent of its growth in 1985 resulted from higher exports to the United States. Most of Japan's export growth in those years was absorbed by the United States as well. And as the big banks and the International Monetary Fund kept deflationist pressure on the Third World, domestic demand in those countries collapsed and their economies became more export-oriented and thus more dependent on the U.S. market. From 1981 to 1984, the United States absorbed 85 percent of Latin America's exports. Between 1982 and 1984, the United States absorbed virtually all of the increase in Third World manufactured exports to the industrialized world. U.S. imports of manufactured products from developing countries doubled between 1980 and 1984, while Europe's declined and Japan's rose by a negligible amount. By 1985, the United States was buying nearly two-thirds of the Third World's manufactured exports. One suspects that behind this large rise in U.S. imports is the long arm of the multinationals selling their foreign products back to the U.S. market. Being less "multinational" than their U.S. counterparts, European and Japanese firms were under less pressure to load up on Third World imports.

While U.S. imports have risen markedly during the current recovery, the U.S. export performance, as suggested above, has essentially been flat. Indeed, looking at U.S. exports, you would hardly know that a recovery has taken place at all. The nominal value of U.S. exports in 1986 was still below the previous peak levels of the 1980 and 1981 period. And although exports in 1987 were up somewhat over 1986, imports, alas, were up even more. Even the large decline in the dollar since early 1985 has not improved the U.S. export performance substantially. Unlike foreign firms selling in the U.S. market, U.S. firms have been quick to raise prices as the dollar falls, rather than holding down price increases to build market shares. (Perhaps this is another attempt to increase short-term profits and keep the raiders at bay.) U.S. exports have remained pretty much unchanged since earlier in the decade, so there is clearly no long-term recovery of competitiveness going on. Western Europe took about the same percentage of U.S. exports in 1986 as it did in 1980. Japan took about 12 percent of U.S. exports in 1986, up from 9.3 percent in 1980, but the rise was gradual and not entirely correlated with currency fluctuations. Latin America, by way of contrast, took 18 percent of U.S. exports in 1981 but only 13.9 percent in 1986. The collapse of demand in Latin America has cost the United States an estimated $12 billion in exports in the 1980s. In addition, if exports to Latin America had held constant as a percentage of total U.S. exports, they would have been another $26 billion higher.[18]

While the decline of the dollar since early 1985 has not done much to reverse the growing trade deficit, it should be clear by now that slower growth abroad has made the deficit worse. Ex-chairman Volcker's soul brothers in London, Tokyo, and especially Bonn have repeatedly refused to "risk" some additional domestic growth and perhaps inflation to help stimulate world growth and, it has been hoped, U.S. exports. Similarly, the IMF and the banks have shown little willingness to ease their draconian grip on the Third World, even though doing so would probably do more for U.S. exports than all the Group of Five (G-5) conferences have done. Slow growth abroad has thus clearly accelerated the general shift of the U.S. economy away from production toward services, distribution, and finance—a development that makes it even less likely that U.S. exports will respond heartily to an upturn in economic growth abroad, should there be one.

Until late 1984, U.S. policy makers had no real gripe with austerity abroad and the rise in U.S. imports, because these conditions pressured domestic producers to get costs and wages down. It was only when James Baker switched jobs with Donald Regan after the 1984 election that U.S. policy changed from benign neglect of the trade situation to outright concern. Since America's trade position was not improving, Treasury Secretary Baker put on his Mike Blumenthal costume and began talking down the dollar.

By early 1985, the dollar had started sliding in the markets— a belated reaction to the shrinkage of international interest rate differentials and a more accommodating Fed policy. In September, Baker received the official blessing of the G-5 at the famous Plaza meeting to talk the dollar down some more. Now we would get the long-awaited "soft landing" of the world economy. The outlook was apparently bright for a fall in the dollar and the U.S. trade deficit and thus a slower buildup in U.S. financial obligations to foreigners. Progress on the dollar and deficit would zap protectionism in Congress. In a gesture to West Germany and to Volcker at the Plaza, Baker pledged that the administration would reduce the budget deficit, thus allowing U.S. interest rates to fall further. This in turn would allow West Germany and other countries to reduce their interest rates, spurring economic growth abroad. The other "Baker Plan"—this one for Third World debt—was announced one month later at the October 1985 IMF meetings. It was to provide multilateral support for increased bank lending to Latin America. Once countries had their credentials stamped by the IMF, the money would begin to flow and austerity would ease. Together, reflation in Europe and Japan and less austerity in the Third World would constitute the next "leg" of the world recovery. All of this was just the sort of multilateral currency and interest rate accord that the markets had been expecting. Stocks and bonds soared.

The honeymoon lasted little more than a year. In early 1987, with the U.S. trade deficit still running high and the J-curve gang running out of excuses, protectionist talk began to bubble over in Congress. To the foreign exchange markets, this meant one thing—the dollar had to head south. In a lesson he could have learned by telephoning Blumenthal, Baker discovered the hard way that long before a drop in the dollar corrects a trade imbalance, it causes a financial crisis. The February Louvre agreement to stabilize the dollar had virtually no impact. In April and May the markets drove the dollar below 140 yen and rumor was that it would take a dollar at 120 yen to make a substantial dent in the U.S. trade deficit. If that was true, would the Japanese unload more Treasuries, since the 7 percent interest coupons they were buying were being swamped by exchange losses? Domestic interest rates soared amid the huge losses in the U.S. bond market, somewhat higher inflation, Fed tightening, and fears of recession. As West Germany and Japan fretted publicly about the effects of a sharp rise in their currencies, Baker suddenly got strong-dollar religion.

Two years after the Plaza agreement, the U.S. trade deficit was still running at an annual rate of around $150 billion. The release of the disappointing second-quarter trade figures in August 1987 ignited another near panic in the foreign exchange markets. The dollar tumbled anew against the mark and yen, pushing long-term interest rates in the United States over 9.5 percent—the highest levels in nearly two years. Despite a nagging trade deficit, continued dependence on foreign capital inflows makes it virtually impossible to pursue a solution to our trade problems through a lower dollar, even assuming this would work. By now it is likely that nothing but a recession—if that—will bring the U.S. trade deficit down to politically and economically acceptable levels. Some tradeoff! Viewed from this perspective, the G-5 effort was really a sideshow. As Michael H. Sherman, the chief investment strategist of Shearson Lehman Brothers, Inc., puts it, G-5 "has not worked in the arena that really counts—the real world as opposed to the financial world." The dollar is way down from its peak, and so are U.S. interest rates. But the real economic benefits that were supposed to flow from these monetary adjustments have been few and far between. Growth in the major countries is still below par. Unemployment and underemployment remain high. Trade imbalances are as large as ever. The buildup of U.S. obligations to foreign-based institutional investors continues to accumulate.

Thus, we have the outlines of a true vicious circle: the world economy is dependent on growth in the U.S. economy, but the U.S. domestic economy is skewed more toward consumption than production and investment, and this consumption is in turn sustained by borrowing—at home and abroad. An economy sustained by debt, especially foreign debt, is always vulnerable to an interest rate shock, whether it is administered by the Fed or by the markets. Given foreign dependence on the U.S. market, a rate shock that is great enough to send the U.S. economy into a new recession thus virtually guarantees a worldwide economic collapse, with all that that implies for bankruptcies, defaults, and the widespread liquidation of debt.

History would suggest that a period of economic decline such as the United States has entered is basically irreversible. Different policies may accelerate or retard the decline, of course, depending on timing and implementation. Following a period of perceived Democratic weakness, predictably, Reagan was elected on a platform of "get tough" policies designed to restore American power and prestige. The program stressed vigilant anti-inflationism, assaults on the welfare state, and more after-tax income for the rich. A massive military buildup was combined with a new aggressiveness in foreign policy.

Even accepting the administration's stated values and goals, it was obvious early on that its policies were laced with conflicts and contradictions waiting to erupt. An ironic legacy of the Reagan years is that these policies have actually accelerated the decline of American power. The tax cuts and military spending were inconsistent with budget balancing and notions of fiscal responsibility. Forcing up the dollar to suppress inflation and wages was wholly incompatible with any semblance of recovery for domestic manufacturing, agriculture, and other basic industries. The strong dollar encouraged more U.S. firms to go abroad and buy cheap assets, and in this way accelerated multinationalization. On paper, the only way to resolve the morass of conflicts was to assume rates of growth (and therefore of tax revenues) that were fraudulently optimistic. When the administration's growth projections did not materialize, the government was left holding a big deficit, increasingly financed by foreign borrowing. If monetized, the deficit would probably result in a resurgence of inflation. Pressures to reduce the deficit, on the other hand, risk weakening the economy quickly, and that weakness could overpower efforts at countercyclical monetary stimulus. In short, Reagan has painted himself (and his successor) into a corner from which there are no obvious escape hatches.

The United States is first of all boxed in with respect to its trade options. With the deficit still running at an annual rate of $150 billion, it is obvious that pushing down the dollar has not worked. The J-curve is really an L-curve. Yet it remains very difficult to justify this situation politically—in the Republican South as well as the Democratic rustbelt—especially when relief has been promised over and over again. Talking the dollar down and jawboning the allies are the traditional responses to protectionist noises from Congress and the public. Yet talking the dollar down is dangerous, given growing U.S. dependence on capital inflows to prop up the stock and bond markets. The more the dollar drops, the higher domestic interest rates have to go to compensate foreign bondholders for currency losses.

That brings us to the second major difficulty confronting policy makers: balancing domestic monetary policy with our dependence on foreign capital inflows. The United States has been able to run a trade deficit for so long because, unlike most countries, it is capable of handling a tremendous backflow of funds resulting from its trade imbalances, as it did with Arab petrodollars in the 1970s and the Japanese in the 1980s.[19] The deal with surplus countries essentially has been as follows: you can run a big trade surplus with us provided that you put the money back into our capital markets. (Some countries like Taiwan do not permit the recycling of funds in this fashion and thus are double-dipping in the U.S. market.) This arrangement also allows the United States to buy time to deal with such problems, but it buys time only; it is not an open-ended commitment. To continue to attract foreign capital, the United States must maintain its currency as a store of value. That means keeping inflation down and money growth slow enough so that dollars remain reasonably scarce. But being a key currency country also means that there are limits to how much domestic monetary policy can be used to goose economic upturns and to counter downturns. Monetary stimulus cannot be too great, lest the dollar collapse and foreign confidence evaporate, leading to a dramatic rise in interest rates and the potential collapse of the stock and bond markets.

The question is not whether the Japanese money will leave the U.S. market and go elsewhere. There are no other money markets large enough to absorb it. They know it and we know it. The real issue is how they allocate their assets and what effects changes in their asset allocation have on the financial markets and the domestic economy. If they were to run from financial assets to real assets (gold, commodities, and real estate), as U.S. and foreign investors did under Carter, interest rates would soar and the stock market as a whole would dive. The basic dilemma, then, comes down to this: how high do interest rates have to be to keep the Japanese participating in the bond markets? Essentially, the Japanese must continue to buy enough Treasury and corporate bonds to keep interest rates low enough so that the United States does not enter a recession. While the Japanese stopped being net buyers of Treasuries late in 1986, this change in asset allocation has thus far provided a happy outcome: the Japanese have taken their money out of the bond market and put it in the stock market, providing much of the fuel behind the 35 percent plus move in the market thus far this year.

But the same enormous money flows that move markets in one direction can also move them in the opposite direction. Even the rumored boycott of the Treasuries market in the spring of 1987 and again recently was enough to send long-term Treasury rates soaring. Maintaining this delicate balance between domestic monetary policy and foreign capital inflows, then, becomes increasingly difficult; in the end we may have to let the trade deficit find its own level—regardless of the domestic costs. A dollar low enough to put a real dent in the U.S. trade problem would drive U.S. interest rates dramatically higher. Given that substantially higher rates would probably cause a recession, playing chicken with the dollar and the yen is self-defeating. The United States, having become a net debtor nation, has thus relinquished a good deal of domestic economic policy autonomy.

The third major obstacle policy makers face is the fiscal policy deadlock, but this problem is more self-imposed than the others. From a non-ideological standpoint, the budget deficit is, as noted above, not the boogie man it is usually made out to be. It has been blamed for the strong dollar and loss of competitiveness; now it is being blamed for the sagging dollar and loss of foreign confidence. Since the rash of tax cutting did not do much to boost business investment, raising taxes to reduce the deficit probably would not harm investment very much either. But a general move to reduce the deficit—either by increasing taxes (the predominant Democratic approach) or by cutting social spending (the predominant Republican approach)—could harm consumption, which so far has sustained the current recovery. With both Democrats and Republicans stressing their resolve to reduce the deficit, the real danger is that budget-balancing hysteria may break out at a time when the economy is already weak, sending the economy toppling into recession. A related and equally serious problem stems from the fact that if present trends continue, the U.S. economy will be headed into the next recession with a deficit that is already high by historical standards. As a result, there will be great political reluctance to use fiscal policy to help rescue the domestic economy. Failure to let the deficit grow could be the difference between a normal recession and an old-fashioned depression.

Finally, the United States—in part because of the policies of the Reagan administration—has considerably less leverage than it once did to apply unilateral solutions to international economic disequilibrium. The decline of U.S. power, which began in the late 1960s, has been accelerated by the twin deficits, the resulting growth of U.S. foreign debt, and, in turn, the increasing vulnerability of our financial markets. It is no wonder that the leading lights of business and politics are bemoaning the fact that the United States is now a debtor nation. Debt and hegemony do not mix—at least not for very long.

With both its monetary and its fiscal policy constrained by current imbalances, the United States is now dependent on the expansion of other countries' economies to keep the current recovery going. For without greater world growth, the United States will not be able to reduce its trade deficit and its accumulation of foreign obligations—indeed, they will only grow larger. Yet the United States finds it no longer has the ability to impose its will on the rest of the world, and even if it did, it is not clear that countries like West Germany and Japan could (or would) quickly take up the role of economic locomotive.

The Reagan administration's failure to get West Germany and Japan to reflate their economies illustrates this twofold problem. West German conservatives, ever fearful of inflation, seem wedded to fiscal and monetary austerity and slow growth. And while Japan does respond, in limited fashion, to U.S. pressure on its trade surplus and growth, it is more in word than in deed. To be sure, Japan has recently unveiled a $30 billion stimulation package aimed at speeding up GNP growth—and presumably imports of U.S. products—but no one seriously believes that this alone can do much to remedy the fundamental economic imbalances between the United States and the rest of the world.

Even if it were willing to do more, Japan, the largest surplus nation, is just too small to become the world's market. Moreover, it is not a little presumptuous to expect Japan, traditionally a society of low spenders, to alter its consumption patterns overnight—if at all. Yet, as the J-curvers—both inside and outside the administration—have become increasingly frustrated at their inability to reverse the trade deficit and sagging U.S. economic performance, they increasingly take to calling for what amounts to a reconstitution of Japanese society to solve U.S. trade problems. Indeed, economist C. Fred Bergsten, a dyed-in-the-wool J-curver, who is never short on solutions to the world's problems when he is *out* of office, is now touting U.S.–Japanese "bigemony" to steer the world economy into the twenty-first century. Consulting the fine print, however, one notes that this new marriage would require Japan to remake itself in America's image and likeness. One of the ways Professor Bergsten proposes to go about increasing Japanese consumption is to revolutionize Japan's architectural style and zoning laws to permit the construction of high-rise buildings. At present, zoning restrictions prohibit building above a certain height so that the sun may shine on either side of the street. This, Professor Bergsten reasons, inhibits Japan from becoming a true consumer society. With fewer rays available, the Japanese would presumably be encouraged to save less and spend more of their income at Crazy Eddie's and Kmart.

Japanese sun lovers needn't worry, however. Professor Bergsten's latest "bigemony" scheme has about as much chance of becoming reality as his proposal of more than a decade ago, when he suggested a similar arrangement between the United States and Germany. Only after Germany balked did he start courting Japan. Once Japan notices the price it will have to pay, it is also likely to pass.

The failure of such arrangements and of international economic cooperation in general points to a more basic problem of today's international system: the absence of a hegemonic power. International economic equilibrium—if there is such a thing—historically has occurred when there has been a sole hegemonic power; Britain from 1815 to World War I and the United States from 1945 to around 1970 are the clearest examples. With a sole hegemonic power, the rules of the game can be established and enforced. Lesser countries have little choice but to go along. Without a hegemonic power, conflict is the order of the day. "Shared" power arrangements usually fail because governments respond mainly to domestic, not international, pressures. As a result, the normal international trade and monetary conferences and summits seldom find real solutions to real problems. More often than not, they degenerate into photo opportunities. The system drifts along, and the major countries hope no big storm comes along to topple the ship.

Today there is no real hegemonic power in the capitalist world, and none on the horizon, for that matter. The United States still predominates in the military area—by a very comfortable margin—but it is faltering economically. The United States has played its hand very badly. We have attempted to reestablish hegemony by flaunting our military advantages and devoting a disproportionate amount of our natural and technological resources to war preparation. But while military spending may raise GNP growth in the short run, there is little evidence that perfecting the mechanisms of pulverizing the Soviet Union in space translates into practical commercial advantage here on earth.

Japan and the Pacific Rim (perhaps including even China and India) are clearly on the rise in terms of basic economic strength. Japan already has enormous financial and investment clout. As a result, if present trends persist, U.S. power in the economic and technological spheres will probably continue to deteriorate relative to the countries of the Japanese-led Pacific Rim. But given their relatively modest military power, it is not likely that the mantle of global hegemony is about to pass to Japan or any of the other Pacific Rim countries. Nor is Japan's newfound economic strength as overpowering as it might seem. That strength depends on an open world trading system and the willingness of Americans to tolerate Japan's large trade surplus with the United States. To some extent Japan's accumulation of U.S. paper has made it the Saudi Arabia of the 1980s—powerful yet vulnerable. In the future, a nationalistic administration of the United States could inflict on the Japanese a penalty akin to what it imposed on the Europeans in 1971, when we suspended the gold convertibility of the dollar pending trade concessions. Or, out of desperation, the United States might do to the Japanese what it did to the Iranians—confiscate their assets, rendering them worthless. Fred Bergsten and the other J-curvers want to keep these weapons handy, yet they fear that such actions will upset the apple cart of world commerce. True, the United States, with its vast natural resources, economic strengths, and greater capacity for economic self-sufficiency, would be in a much stronger position than the Japanese to weather such a confrontation. But as long as the United States abides by the rules of the game as currently defined—that the market knows best and will tend toward equilibrium—U.S. power will become increasingly irrelevant to economic events here and abroad.

Dropping our illusions about the market and unfettered competition, both domestic and international, would be a sounder approach than either going on indefinitely as we are or letting our frustration build to the point where it precipitates a major U.S.–Japanese confrontation. Yet I am highly pessimistic that what needs to be done by way of world reflation and a more managed economy will be done. While the Republicans are an easy target, much of my own pessimism results from realizing what a wasteland the Democratic party has become. The Democrats have conceded the major policy and ideological questions on the economy to the Republicans. After all, in 1984, the Democrats built their platform around the standard Republican refrain: reduce the government budget deficit. Have they learned anything from fighting the Republicans on their turf? Probably not, since most of the declared candidates, once again, are criticizing the twin deficits but refuse to get to the roots of what caused them.

They all favor a lower budget deficit but neglect to say how they would maintain economic growth without high deficit spending. They all emphasize improving U.S. competitiveness but, with the possible exceptions of Michael Dukakis and Jesse Jackson, fail to tell us how they would try to get U.S. corporations to invest in real production in America. They all are against the arms race, but decline to outline how they would end it or even to discuss the economic benefits of doing so. And despite all the tough talk on trade, the great majority of them are terrified of the trade issue, afraid of alienating the AFL-CIO on the one hand and the liberal BMW set on the other. In general, they practice what the *Wall Street Journal* calls "the politics of timidity." Even Republican real-estate mogul and undeclared candidate Donald Trump recently upstaged all of them (excepting, perhaps, Pat Schroeder) by showing how our economic decline vis-à-vis Japan and Europe is related to our excessive military spending on their behalf.[20]

But the Democrats need more than a willingness to fight; they need something to fight for. Politics begins with an understanding of the world, the sources of its problems and possibilities. But, sadly, the Democrats seem to be moving in the opposite direction. Not only are they timid, but they have all but abandoned the Keynesian view of how the world economy functions and how it might be fixed. They grasp for solutions to the present logjam because they have forgotten, overlooked, or underestimated the basic analytical insight of the Keynesian revolution: that a mature, free-market economy does not automatically tend toward full employment and price stability, either domestically or internationally. Contrary to orthodox theory, a market economy may function even less well in a world economy with relatively open markets. Activist policy is therefore needed, and choices must be made either to fight inflation *or* to encourage growth. Policy can steer the economy in one direction or another, but not both directions at the same time—at least not with great precision. In the 1980s, a political choice has been made to emphasize price stability, not growth. This has created major downside risks for the economy. Since most Democrats talk more about the budget deficit and continuing vigilance against inflation than they do about generating full employment, they either do not care about growth or mistakenly believe that a more balanced budget and lower inflation will produce higher growth.

Today's Democrats are the personification of what the late Joan Robinson used to call "bastard Keynesianism." Bastard Keynesians believe that grafting a small state apparatus on top of a reasonably well-functioning free-market economy will create economic bliss. American Keynesians like Paul Samuelson, Walter Heller, and Charles Schultz never shared the master's views regarding public enterprise, protectionism, and the euthanasia of the rentier as logical extensions of Keynes's *General Theory*. Blinded by what raw American power could achieve after World War II, they advocated a more limited role for government than he did. Specifically, they argued that once a countercyclical deficit and monetary policy give recovery a push, government can step back and the private economy will surge ahead to full employment and high output. This viewpoint had a good deal of validity from the end of World War II until about 1970, when America's industrial hegemony generated high levels of employment and output in the United States. But it became painfully clear during the 1970s and 1980s that the world economy no longer works this way.

As their brand of Keynesianism worked less and less well, particularly during the Carter years, bastard Keynesians confronted a basic dilemma: Should there be more Keynesianism or less? The option most chose was less. Making government spending the villain was popular politically, since it jibed with popular antagonism toward the welfare state and high taxes. Still, to justify selling out, bastard Keynesians had to abandon a crucial derivative of Keynes's basic insight: that mature capitalism suffers from a chronic shortfall of effective demand and that, as a result, a capitalist economy cannot function without regular and catastrophic recessions to correct the imbalances between excess supply and insufficient demand. The historic mission of Keynesianism was to mitigate the severity of capitalism's downward corrections so that society could avoid the mass economic, social, and political devastation of the 1930s. It is a fair conclusion that, were he alive today, Keynes would argue that the ever greater imbalances require more activism, not less. While the safeguards against economic collapse that exist today are better than nothing, they are less and less adequate as time goes on.

The underlying problem of today's world economy is not the U.S. budget deficit or excess demand but insufficient worldwide demand. With gluts in raw materials all over the world and tons of excess capacity, these are the principal problems to be addressed—not inflation and excess consumption. At any rate, a little more inflation is vastly preferable to deflation. Reducing the deficit while the economy is fundamentally weak is a prescription for recession, not recovery. And the smart money is saying that a new recession, in the context of all the debt and related abuses of the Reagan years, might be just enough to cause a big depression. It may not be politically popular to say so, but we need Keynesianism now more than any other time in the postwar period, save perhaps the critical years between 1946 and 1950. Vigorous public investment is needed to rebuild the nation's bridges, roads, and infrastructure and to boost domestic demand and production. A much more activist trade policy could force the big-surplus countries to boost their production here substantially—if they want to retain access to the U.S. market. More comprehensive regulation of the financial system is necessary to manage our dependence on foreign capital and to prevent a serious mishap that could ignite a real downturn.

But in today's integrated world economy, domestic measures are not enough. We need stabilizers at the global level as well. An international central bank with the power to create money and steer exchange rates could at least distribute the pain of adjusting to excess world capacity more equitably than it is being distributed today. A less deflationist IMF and World Bank could do more to alleviate the Third World debt burden and to inject investment into those areas of the world economy that now act as a drag on economic growth. Real détente with the Soviet Union could not only free up domestic resources for alternative uses, but also open up vast new frontiers for consumption and investment. It would also be the best way for us to "level the playing field" with Japan and West Germany.

Unlike some well-meaning progressives, I seriously doubt that the country is ready to vote for such principles in 1988 or be governed by them in 1989. I am optimistic about the prospects for real change, but only over the longer term. Today, American society is dominated by attitudes and values that are mean and selfish. For the time being, politicians of both major parties have chosen to cater to and thereby encourage what Christopher Lasch has appropriately termed the culture of narcissism. But will Americans always dance to this tune? Not, in my opinion, if each successive downturn in the U.S. economy affects larger and larger numbers of people adversely, as is the trend.

In his brilliant book *The Great Depression*, historian Robert S. McElvaine offers a solid rebuttal to the prophets of the politics of selfishness. He argues that the New Deal became morally and politically acceptable because the wreckage of the Great Depression changed American attitudes. Suffering was so widespread that cooperation and compassion replaced egoism and selfishness as the dominant values of American politics. As McElvaine explains:

> Americans have always been basically pragmatic. They were willing to accept an unfettered marketplace economy so long as it seemed to be working—so long, that is, as it appeared to be living up to Adam Smith's original moral belief that it eventuated the common good. . . . It took the Great Depression to convince them that the marketplace was not benign in its workings. During the Depression, America moved toward community-oriented values simply because so many were in need.[21]

If I am wrong in my presumption that, sooner or later, the excesses of the Reagan era will lead to a depression that devastates the lives of millions of Americans, then conservatives of both parties have nothing to worry about. They should dismiss McElvaine's and my views about the American people as wishful thinking. But the history of unrestrained capitalism is the history of violent business cycle fluctuations, of seven fat years and seven lean. Both the rulers and the ruled, but especially the rulers, ignore this history at their own peril.

Notes

1. *Economic Report of the President, 1985* (Washington, D.C.: Government Printing Office), p. 5.

2. *Economic Report of the President, 1987* (Washington, D.C.: Government Printing Office), p. 368.

3. Testimony before the Joint Economic Committee, June 30, 1987.

4. Michael Drury, "Dollar Demographics: Is the Middle Class Disappearing?" *Prospects,* August 1987.

5. *Economic Report of the President, 1987,* p. 293, n. 2.

6. On the left, Jeff Faux makes this mistake in "The Democrats and the Post-Reagan Economy," in Archibald Gillies et al., *Post-Reagan America* (New York: World Policy Institute, 1987), p. 15. On the other side of the spectrum, so does Alfred L. Malabre, *Beyond Our Means* (New York: Random House, 1987), pp. 47–48.

7. Andrew Bartels, "U.S. Productivity: Where It's Strong, Where It's Weak," *Prospects,* May 1987.

8. "Economic Decline, Reagan-Style: Dollars, Debt, and Deflation," *World Policy Journal,* vol. 2, no. 3 (Summer 1985).

9. *New York Times,* August 27, 1987.

10. This phenomenon was described with clarity and insight a decade ago by Richard J. Barnet and Ronald E. Muller in *Global Reach: The Power of the Multinational Corporations* (New York: Simon and Schuster, 1975).

11. *Wall Street Journal,* April 1, 1987.

12. Writes Alfred L. Malabre, a respected *Wall Street Journal* reporter, "The profusion of goods and services that most Americans enjoy in this century's closing years reflects a very different sort of tendency: to live beyond our means." *Beyond Our Means,* p. 3.

13. The latest supply-side whopper is that the deficit resulted from the "unexpected" collapse of inflation and thus overbudgeting in nominal dollars. What did the supply-siders think higher real interest rates and radically lower money growth would do, raise inflation? And incidentally, I don't recall Jack Kemp et al. leaning on Cap Weinberger to spend less in 1982 because inflation had collapsed.

14. But not necessarily higher than an equivalent amount of civilian spending. See Gordon Adams and David Gold, *Defense Spending and the Economy* (Washington, D.C.: Center on Budget and Policy Priorities, 1987).

15. Henry Kaufman, *Interest Rates, the Markets, and the New Financial World* (New York: Times Books, 1986), p. 31.

16. *Wall Street Journal*, July 27, 1987.

17. For a different viewpoint, see Benjamin J. Stein, "Investment Bankers: Not Worthy of the Name," *Barrons*, July 13, 1987.

18. *Trade Deficits, Foreign Debt and Sagging Growth*, Domestic Staff of the Joint Economic Committee (Washington, D.C.: Government Printing Office, September 1986), p. 34.

19. It is true that in the 1970s, most Eurodollars were recycled through London, not New York, but the Eurodollar market was largely a creature of U.S. banks and in those days was controlled by foreign branches of U.S. banks.

20. In a full-page ad in the *New York Times* of September 2, Trump observed, "Over the years, the Japanese, unimpeded by the huge costs of defending themselves, have built a strong and vibrant economy with unprecedented surpluses. They have brilliantly managed to maintain a weak yen against a strong dollar. This, coupled with our monumental spending for their, and others', defense, has moved Japan to the forefront of world economies. It is time for us to end *our* vast deficits by making Japan and others, who can afford it, pay."

21. Robert S. McElvaine, *The Great Depression* (New York: Times Books, 1985), pp. 337–38.

Index

453